KEITH D

The Letters

edited by Desmond Graham

CARCANET

First published in Great Britain in 2000 by
Carcanet Press Limited
4th Floor, Conavon Court
12–16 Blackfriars Street
Manchester M3 5BQ

A CIP catalogue record for this book
is available from the British Library.

ISBN 1 85754 477 3

The publisher acknowledges financial assistance
from the Arts Council of England.

Set in 11/12pt Monotype Bembo by XL Publishing Services, Tiverton
Printed and bound in England by SRP Ltd, Exeter

Contents

Introduction   vii
Acknowledgements   xiv
Recipients of letters   xvi
Chronology   xx
Sources   xxiii
Abbreviations   xxv

The Letters

1925–1931   I
1931–1938   35
1938–1939   59
1939–1940   77
1940–1941   147
1941–1942   181
1942–1943   249
1944   311

Appendix A
    Two autobiographical fragments   345
Appendix B
    An essay: 'Poets in This War'   350
Appendix C
    Three short stories:
    'Death of a Horse'   354
    'Giuseppe'   356
    'The Little Red Mouth'   359

Index   363

Introduction

Keith Douglas was almost sure he would be killed in the war. By the time he was in the second wave of tanks landing on Gold Beach in Normandy, he had completed a collection of poems for publication, a narrative of his experience of the desert fighting, *Alamein to Zem Zem*, and illustrations for both the prose work and his poems. He was killed on 9 June 1944, at the age of twenty-four.

Never one to stand by and watch time be wasted, Douglas packed into what he believed would be a short life as much living as possible. Acutely lonely, with what he saw as an oversized chip on his shoulder – through lack of a father from the age of eight, lack of a parental home from the age of six and, on leaving school, lack of any money at all while moving in a relatively upper-class world – Douglas fashioned for himself a truly romantic and astonishingly creative life.

From the age of fourteen he had been writing exceptionally accomplished poems, an early start which allowed him to get in a full ten years. From a meeting at a New Year's Eve dance in 1937, he embarked on the first of six eventful romances. Reckless, self-regarding, full of life, he had started early looking for an ideal woman, and three times at least, he thought he had found her. In March 1944, adding a last poem or two to the collection he would leave behind when embarking for Normandy, he completed a farewell poem to four women:

> *To Kristin, Yingcheng, Olga, Milena*
>
> Women of four countries,
> the four phials full of essences
> of green England, legendary China,
> cold Europe, Arabic Spain, a finer
> four poisons for the subtle senses
> than any in medieval inventories.
>
> Here I give back perforce
> the sweet wine to the grape

give the dark plant its juices
what every creature uses
by natural law will seep
back to the natural source.

The choice is not surprising: Kristin (Christine), Yingcheng (Betty) and Milena were the three most important relationships in his love life up to that point. Art, however, can mislead: Olga was a great and important friend, as these letters show, rather than a lover. On the other hand, Antoinette (Toni) with whom a lot of his second year at Oxford was consumed, makes no appearance in the poem: perhaps because Douglas looked back on that romance as a mistake; perhaps one representative of 'green England' was enough for the poem? For in fact, at the time of writing the poem Douglas was already attempting to add another woman from 'green England' to his list, Betty Jesse: though far from feeling like bidding her farewell.

Art and life do not quite coincide although they do overlap continually, as these letters show. A larger gap remains between a collection of letters and the full story of a life. Only those letters which survive can be collected. To Kristin, there are only two letters surviving, both from early in their friendship. To Milena there is just one, written after they had split up. To Yingcheng there is one wonderful love letter, with Douglas, unusually, presenting himself as the great poet, and four other letters, after she had given him up. To Olga there are nine fascinating letters, among the best he wrote, and perhaps these were all the letters he wrote to her. Letters obviously get destroyed or lost over time. Mrs Douglas kept all Keith's letters from his first months as a boarder at prep school: yet what survives from the further five years he spent there is, mercifully perhaps, a small fraction of what must have been a weekly letter home. Over fifty letters survive from Douglas to Antoinette during his second Oxford year. As these letters reveal, Douglas was using the writing of letters to work out something about himself: he didn't keep a diary, but in these letters to Antoinette we can hear him, virtually day by day, attempting to convince Antoinette and himself that he really could be relied upon to love her.

Loneliness, the desire to receive a letter, or simply having some spare time may often be the occasion for letters, meaning that they can be unreliable as a guide to the full character of their writer. On the other hand, writing of the hour and the week and the day, letters are most revealing of their own times. The pains and self-inflicted wounds of Douglas's correspondence with Antoinette at the end of 1939 and the start of 1940 may show him at a particularly vulnerable time, attempting to put himself together after being jilted by Yingcheng, but they also give a measure of the feelings of desperation and bewilderment which hit many undergraduates at the star of the war. They knew about the Great War. They had read Owen, Sassoon and Blunden. They knew they were the next in line but they did not know from term to term how long they had at university and, in a more sinister sense, they did not know how long they had at all.

Once Douglas experienced the distance of being abroad, he not only had more obvious reason to write, he often had more interesting things to report: the voyage and its sights; a trip with his troop to Syria; impressions of Egypt and Palestine; a delighted encounter with Tunisia; and, of course, his experience of the desert war and its aftermath. It is distance, too, which prompts Douglas to a truly literary correspondence – to editors, publishers and friends, sending poems and discussing their presentation. For Douglas, by choice, was not a literary person at all. At school he filled the school magazines with his poems – yet his school friends remembered him from riding, rugby, and the Cadet Corps, and for his sense of humour. Similarly, at Oxford, writing a great deal and publishing widely, he did not choose literary friends. Consistently, however, in his letters he does write (just as he talked) about his art work. He writes of the pictures he paints; what he puts on his walls at Christ's Hospital; painting a portrait in Oxford; scraping decorations on the walls of his hut in the Middle East; preparing illustrations for his prose and his poems in 1944. Numerous sketches and little cartoon-like drawings fill spaces in the letters. Often the most lively moments in letters come from his eye, his seeing: sharp, neatly or wickedly observed features. His world is vivid and full of characters, designations of people which can move towards the stereotypical, whether as caricature or frank racism. David Roberts, the History master who greatly admired him, wrote after Douglas's death of his 'splendid prejudice'. It is easy to see how Douglas's skill in being rude or blunt could be most companionable and amusing. In a letter, it occasionally takes an effort of placing remarks in period to come to terms with his momentary outbursts of racism. Their saving grace may be that they are too absurdly inconsistent to be serious at all – one minute the Arabs are abused, at another, praised; one minute the Jews are abused, at another, their intellectuals are sought after, and at another, he is identifying himself with them.

From the Middle East the letters start to tell us more about his writing. First John Hall proposes a three-man selection of poems and Douglas has to make suggestions. Then we have poems sent back occasionally to Hall and to Blunden. Gradually the poems start to come into the letters. It is around this point, in mid-1942, that the reader who is unfamiliar with Douglas's work might choose to start. For here we can directly see the development of the writer: the relationship between what goes on in his life and what he is doing in his poems. Poems become letters as he sends them and letters tell us about the poems. A story which had been intermittent in the letters now becomes explicit. Douglas, like most writers, but to an acute degree, wrote directly out of encouragement. From early on there is a coincidence between his reporting some bit of good news about his work and his writing of a new poem. Now he puts the two together directly: 'Dear Tambimuttu, Thank you for your letter, and for publishing my poems – I had given up all idea of writing in the Army until your efforts and John Hall's nerved me to try again. I'll go on sending poems as they come – I send you one – "Aristocrats", with this' (Letter 281). Douglas had also gained encouragement from being published in journals. In the Middle East, meeting up with David Hicks who edited *Citadel* had led to poems; then, through the poet Bernard Spencer, *Personal Landscape* (edited by Lawrence Durrell and Robin Fedden) welcomed his work and it was in the coterie around that magazine that Douglas, despite very few appearances, left his strongest mark. So much so, in fact, that Durrell brought his version of Douglas into the *Alexandria Quartet* as the character Johnny Keats.

If Douglas needed encouragement to write or at least to write more, he seems to have needed misunderstanding to write about his own work. The wonderful and often quoted letter of 10 August 1943 which defines his work so accurately at the same time as it defines his outlook on things, came as an answer to criticisms from Hall: 'Incidentally you say I fail as a poet, when you mean I fail as a lyricist. Only someone who is out of touch, by which I mean first hand touch, with what has happened outside England... could make that criticism. I am surprised you should still expect me to produce musical verse...' (Letter 285). Two other letters to Hall around the same time make valuable observations about his own writings.

Douglas could write with seemingly effortless insight about his own work, yet, surprisingly, he rarely bothered to do so. A critical essay on why there was as yet no war poetry from his war, written about this time, May 1943, is included in the Appendix. Douglas, with a publisher, with plenty to write about and, at last, some measure of free time, did not hesitate. Along with his war poems, in these months of 1943 he wrote most of *Alamein to Zem Zem*, as well as short stories of the war, two of which are included in the Appendix.

Douglas returned to Britain at the end of 1943 and the letters of early 1944 are full of exciting ideas about the publication of his work by Editions Poetry (London): a selection of poems with prose and photographs and drawings; selections of his letters with his own pictures and poems and parts of his prose narrative, in various combinations. Douglas completed work on his collection of poems and completed *Alamein to Zem Zem* by mid-April 1944. By then, however, he had also stolen enough time to embark on a final romance. His meetings with Tambimuttu's assistant, Betty Jesse, to discuss publication plans for his work, rapidly developed in a more personal direction. Under pressure from the preparations for the Normandy landings, the strict censorship and security relating to the invasion plans, and his own ignorance as to his immediate future, Douglas sought to find one special fitting moment from this relationship, to set against powerlessness and the war's assault on his identity. The letters of those last weeks pursue the story. He was not looking for a future, simply something to carry him forward. The last of the poems he sent to Betty for his collection, 'On a Return from Egypt', was an epitaph:

> And all my endeavours are unlucky explorers
> come back, abandoning the expedition;
> the specimens, the lilies of ambition
> still spring in their climate, still unpicked:
> but time, time is all I lacked
> to find them, as the great collectors before me.

Douglas knew he had the talent of the greatest collectors, greatest writers, and reading his poems and prose narrative, we know it too. The letters show, however, how determinedly he made use of what time he did have and how he achieved the one form of fame available to him: to be the true successor to the best poets of the Great War, taking their concerns and their language into a new, more modern world. That Douglas's work was greatly appreciated and supported by many who came across it is abundantly clear from these letters. A combination of chance and bad luck with the posthumous publishing of it, however, meant that it was only in the mid-1960s, through Ted Hughes's active championing of it, that his work started to gain a wider audience. Douglas himself had known that his achievement did not fit readily into a specifically English context. As he urged Hall to understand in that letter of August 1943, what he felt and what he was doing fitted thinking elsewhere in Europe. To find early echoes of his words we must look in places he did not know but which would not have surprised him: in the writings of the survivor poets of post-war Eastern Europe. They, too, had done with lyricism. They, too, called for poetry which was reportage. In the 1960s British poets caught up with where Douglas had been: at least, that decade found an audience for Douglas which, forty years on, shows no sign of diminishing.

The correspondence is divided into the main biographical segments of Douglas's life: prep school; Christ's Hospital; first Oxford year; second Oxford year; Army training in England; service in the Middle East before action; El Alamein through to departure from the Middle East; final months in Britain before departure for Normandy. Such a structure will occasionally split letters from a single year, and the section '1944' actually starts with a letter on arrival in Britain, in December 1943. Each letter is numbered and those letters not by Douglas are given the number of the preceding letter with 'a' or 'b' or 'c' added.

Two new letters came to light in the Harry Ransom Center at the University of Texas while this collection was in proof. They have been incorporated in the text without altering the numbering of the letters, and are indicated by an asterisk.

I have included all the poems Douglas sent or enclosed in letters as long as they are reasonably current with the letter. Thus I have omitted the Oxford poems he sent to Alec Hardie in 1941 as well as the earlier poems he sent Olga when he first met her. I have included as Appendices two autobiographical pieces, Douglas's essay on poetry of the war and three surviving short stories.

In the case of the letters to Toni Beckett (sometimes two written in an evening) it has been very difficult to find an accurate order. The ordering in this section (1939–40) is therefore somewhat provisional. Douglas rarely dated his letters and although it is often possible to date a letter from circumstantial evidence – reference to a film performance, the type of paper used and so on – many dates are conjectural. All conjectures are in square brackets.

One reason for the timing of this edition is the move of private stories into history as the years pass. On only a few occasions have I still felt it necessary to omit names for privacy. In the army Douglas occasionally mentions the 'censor' and censorship in his letters. As he was the first censor of his own letters, often signing the envelope as censored, there are few problems. He is aware, however, that the letters may be opened: this self-censoring is almost exclusively towards the naming of places.

Douglas's hand is always elegant and pleasing, and once one is familiar with it, there are few problems of legibility. It is sometimes difficult, however, to tell what is a capital letter and what not, what is comma and what a full stop. Punctuation and spelling are left unaltered in letters up to 1931 (though Douglas's use of spacing as an occasional kind of punctuation is not followed). After 1931 punctuation and spelling have been silently corrected, except where there is some ambiguity or expressive effect which would be lost by correction. The forms for dates, addresses, names and titles of books etc, have been regularised. I have followed the text of the poem as in the letter and have indicated where this has variants from the text in *The Complete Poems*.

Acknowledgements

First I would formally like to thank copyright holders of work I have used: John Hall, for the Douglas material; Claire Blunden, Mrs Valerie Eliot and Carcanet Press for material reprinted from *Keith Douglas A Prose Miscellany*. I would also like to thank libraries which have allowed me to use and quote from their archives: The British Library, The Brotherton Collection at the Brotherton Library, Leeds University and the Harry Ransom Research Center at the University of Texas. I would also like to record my thanks to the staff of these libraries for their help in finding and making things available for me (sometimes at the eleventh hour), particularly Chris Fletcher of the British Library, Steve Lawson of the Harry Ransom Center, and Scott Krafft of Northwestern University Library. I would like to thank Brenda Flatman, Jean Guest and Betty Relle for their help in dating and annotating material and lending it to me. Sadly, many of those who gave me material and discussed it with me over the years, have since died: I would specially like to record my thanks to the late Milena Gattegno, Betty O'Neill and Toni Haysom. I am most grateful for help from Toni's sister, Elizabeth; Noel Burdett, Prof. Jack Morpurgo, and Tony Hogarth-Smith. I would like to thank the BBC, Christ's Hospital, Lady Margaret Hall, Merton College and Cheltenham Ladies' College for most helpful answers to queries. I am most grateful to John Hall, for his unfailing and gracious help with regard to Douglas's work.

I would like to thank the AHRB for a year's funded leave which gave me precious time to complete this project; the British Academy, whose personal research grant enabled me to obtain various kinds of assistance; and the Research Committee of the University of Newcastle for travel funds. I would like to thank Dr Sarah Ferris for all she did as my research assistant and for her lively sharing of the world of archives and very much more. I am happy to thank my colleagues and students at Newcastle for all their help, especially Prof. Linda Anderson, Bruce Babington, Rowena Bryson and Dr Michael Rossington and my former colleague, Prof. Bob

White. At Carcanet, I would like to thank Robyn Marsack for helping me with Keith Douglas once more. The compiler of the index, Tom Norton, deserves special thanks for working with grace under pressure. Finally, I must thank Milena and Trude, 'women of two countries', but in a different sense, who keep teaching me about poetry, and who made the completion of this book possible.

Recipients of letters

Baber, Jocelyn Engaged in work with refugees in London, from December 1942 she employed Douglas's mother as housekeeper at her family's house in East Grinstead. Douglas stayed there with the Babers and his mother on leave in 1944. See *KD* pp.229–30.

Beckett, Toni At Lady Margaret Hall in Douglas's second year at Oxford. 'Stars' (*CP* p.29) was dedicated to her, as 'Antoinette'. See *KD* pp.81 and 83 (photograph). She died in 1999. During the war she did important work on codes: see obituary, *Daily Telegraph* 23 February 1999.

Blunden, Edmund An Old Blue who very much identified with Christ's Hospital and often returned there, he was Douglas's Tutor at Merton College, Oxford. A poet and prolific writer on poets and poetry, his prose narrative *Undertones of War* (1929) is one of the finest works on the First World War. He left his Fellowship at Merton in 1944: see Barry Webb, *Edmund Blunden: A Biography* (1990).

Castellain, Charles Douglas's maternal grandfather; grandson of a French aristocrat, he was educated at Harrow and Balliol, retired from cotton-broking in Egypt to Kent. He died in 1927 (See *KD* pp.3–5).

Castellain, Mrs Charles Douglas's maternal grandmother; the daughter of John Towse, she was the second wife of Charles Castellain. She died in 1932 (See *KD* pp.4–5).

Douglas, Captain Keith Sholto Douglas's father, born in 1882 and educated at Tonbridge and Dunstable. At twenty-two he set out to see his mother, who had returned to live in Canada, getting only as far as New York where he worked for the Vandalia Railway Co. He trained for two years as a civil engineer and in 1914 was commissioned into the Royal Engineers. He embarked for Gallipoli in July 1915, landed at Basra and won the MC bridging the Diala under fire. Leaving the army in 1919 he saw little of his son Keith until summer 1922 when, back in Cranleigh, he started a chicken farm in 1923. It had failed by 1927 and he took a job in Wales. In November 1928 he asked his wife for a divorce and set up house with Phoebe, who had helped with the farm. When Keith left school, Capt. Douglas wrote to Keith suggesting they should meet: Keith did not take up the suggestion. (See *KD* pp.2–5, 10, 16–17.)

Douglas, Marie J. (known as Josephine, or, more commonly, Jo) Douglas's mother, Jo Castellain was born in 1887 and brought up outside Cranbrook. After six months in Switzerland at sixteen, at eighteen she left home to work as a housekeeper. Married to Keith Sholto Douglas in 1915 she had one son, Keith. Before and during his infancy she worked for the artist Lawson Wood. *Encephalitis lethargica* in 1924 led her to experience years of ill-health. Her husband left her in 1928 and she supported herself largely through housekeeping and lady's companion posts. She died in 1981 (See *KD* pp.2 and 9–10).

[Douglas], Phoebe A family friend of Keith's mother in Cranleigh, she joined the Douglas household to help with running house and chicken farm in 1923. In 1925 she returned home. She was to join Keith's father in Wales and become his second wife.

Douglas, Dr William Douglas's paternal grandfather. A Scot educated at Belfast and Edinburgh, he was a physician in private practice, specialising in mental illness. Around the time of Keith's birth he retired to Staines. In his eighties, in November 1928, having bought an annuity with most of his money, he died. He had for fifty years been active in the BMA: see obituary, *British Medical Journal* 3 August 1929; and *KD* p.10.

Eliot, T.S. The writer; editor at Faber and Faber, to whom Blunden sent Douglas's poems at Douglas's request. See *KD* pp.117–18 and 138–9.

Gutierrez-Pegna, Milena Her father was a native of Gibraltar, her mother an Italian; she worked for Saccone and Speed in Alexandria. Both 'The Knife' (*CP* p.95) and 'I listen to the desert wind' (*CP* p.96) were dedicated to her and she appears in 'To Kristin, Yingcheng, Olga, Milena' (*CP* p.131). See *KD* pp.150–4 and 151 (photograph). She died in Australia in 1999.

Hall, J.C. An Oxford acquaintance of Douglas's, he was Oxford editor of the Oxford/Cambridge poetry magazine *Fords and Bridges*. A poet himself, Hall edited and appeared with Douglas in the *Selected Poems* they shared with Norman Nicholson in 1943. Hall was the first writer really to discover Douglas's importance and for the rest of his life, as Trustee of the Douglas Estate, as editor and promoter of his works, he has been central to the growth of Douglas's reputation.

Hardie, Alec An Oxford friend at Merton, with whom Douglas edited *Augury: An Oxford Miscellany* (1940). An academic, Hardie went on to write, among other subjects, on Edmund Blunden.

Hicks, David An Oxford acquaintance of Douglas's, Hicks shared with Bernard Spencer the Cairo flat which was Douglas's base on his numerous visits in 1942. Hicks edited the largely literary monthly *Citadel*, from the Anglo-Egyptian Institute, Cairo, where he lectured. See *KD* pp.147–8.

Jesse, Betty Assistant to Tambimuttu at *Poetry (London)*, she was an important helper of poets and artists in the literary world around Tambimuttu in London during and after the war. See *KD* p.232 and p.233 (photograph).

Jones, Brenda A younger friend from a farm near Christ's Hospital where Douglas and his friends used to ride. See *KD* pp.49 and 50 (photograph: Jones' farm, not Brodie's).

Meiersons, Olga From a Latvian-Jewish family, she worked at the Kedem bookshop in Tel Aviv where Douglas met her in 1942. She appears in 'To Kristin, Yingcheng, Olga, Milena' (*CP* p.131). She returned his letters to Douglas's mother and remained in touch for several years. See *KD* pp.145–6.

Spence, Sir Reginald An Old Blue who remained devotedly attached to Christ's Hospital, he regularly invited pupils from the school to stay and took a guardianly interest in their careers, Douglas's among them. He was retired from his wine merchant's business and lived at Blackboys, Sussex.

Stanley-Wrench, Margaret In her fourth year at Somerville when Douglas came up to Oxford in October 1938, she had already won the Newdigate Prize (*The Man in the Moon*, 1937) and had a collection of poems published, *News Reel* (1938). See Obituary, *The Times* 15 January 1974.

Sze, Betty Educated at Cheltenham Ladies' College, she was at Lady Margaret Hall when Douglas arrived in Oxford. Her father was sometime Chinese ambassador to Washington. Douglas addresses her by her Chinese name, [Ying]cheng, in the poem 'The Prisoner' (*CP* p.67) and 'Stranger' (*CP* p.25) was dedicated to her. She remained behind many of his poems, and appears in 'To Kristin, Yingcheng, Olga, Milena' (*CP* p.131). She died in America in 1999. See *KD* pp.71 and 77 (photographs).

Tambimuttu, M.J. Arriving in London from Ceylon in 1938, he founded and edited the bi-monthly *Poetry (London)*, the main poetry magazine of the war. No.10 of the magazine, a book-sized issue of December 1944, included his memoir of Douglas and poems by him. Tambimuttu had sought Douglas's poems having seen one in Hall's *Fords and Bridges*. He was himself a poet and, also editor of Nicholson and Watson's 'Editions Poetry (London)'. He published Douglas's *Alamein to Zem Zem* with Douglas's illustrations and an appendix of poems, in 1946. He left London in the later 1940s, before bringing out a collection of Douglas's poems: the *Collected Poems* 1951 were edited by John Waller and G.S. Fraser. Tambimuttu died in 1983.

Turner, Jean At St. Hilda's when Douglas came up to Oxford, after a year out in 1939–40, she returned to gain her degree. She then served in the WRNS. See *KD* pp.76 and p.70 (photograph).

Waller, Sir John (Bt) An Oxford acquaintance of Douglas's, he edited first *Bolero*, then *Kingdom Come* to which Douglas contributed. In the Middle East as a military journalist, Waller was involved in various publications including *Salamander*. He published a first collection of poems in 1941, *Fortunate Hamlet*.

Woodcock, Christine Douglas met her at a New Year's Eve dance in 1937. She is the 'Kristin' of the poem of that name (*CP* p.17) and appears again in the late poem 'To Kristin, Yingcheng, Olga, Milena' (*CP* p.131). She gave Mrs Douglas the letters Douglas wrote her, printed here. See *KD* p.70.

Keith Douglas 1920–1944

A Chronology

1920	24 Jan.	Keith Castellain Douglas born at Tunbridge Wells
1920–6		At Cranleigh, Surrey
1926–31		Boarder at Edgeborough School, Guildford
1928		KD's father, Capt. Keith Sholto Douglas, leaves family; KD does not see him again.
1931–8		At school at Christ's Hospital, Horsham
1935		Holiday at Gorizia in northern Italy
1936		Makes first collection of poems
1938	March	Published in *New Verse*
1938–40		At Merton College, Oxford, reading English with Edmund Blunden as tutor
1939	September	War declared. KD enlists at once; call-up deferred, returns to Oxford
1940	April	Editor of *The Cherwell*, publishing many poems there and in other Oxford periodicals. Makes his second collection of poems
	May	Co-editor of *Augury*, a literary miscellany
	July	Joins up as cavalry trooper, Redford Barracks. Leaves collection with Blunden in hope of publication
	Sept. Oct.	Training at Army Equitation School, Weedon
	Nov.–Jan. 1941	Officer Cadet at Sandhurst
1941	February	Commissioned into Second

		Derbyshire Yeomanry at Ripon. T.S. Eliot praises collection passed to him by Blunden, but does not offer publication
	March–June	With regiment at Wickwar, Glos.
	May	Gunnery Course at Linney Head. Sends four more poems to Eliot
	June	Sails for Middle East. Leaves collection with mother
	August	Arrives in Egypt
	October	At Nathanya, Palestine, convalescing after ear infection. J.C. Hall proposes publication of KD's poems in a shared selection
	28 Oct.	Joins cavalry regiment, the Sherwood Rangers
	November	Visits Syria
1942	February	Posted to Division H.Q. in Palestine as Camouflage Staff Officer
	May–June	In Cairo; spends time with David Hicks, editor of *Citadel*, and meets Bernard Spencer
	July–Sept.	In Alexandria
	October	At Wadi Natrun, to be with HQ in forthcoming offensive. First poems in *Poetry (London)*
	23 Oct.	Battle of El Alamein begins
	27 Oct.	KD defies orders and leaves HQ to report to his regiment at El Alamein; in battle next day
	9 Nov.	At Mersa
	23 Nov.	Leaves Mersa and rejoins advance towards Tripoli
1943	15 Jan.	Wounded in action at Wadi Zem Zem
	25 Jan.	Arrives at No. 1 General Hospital, El Ballah, Palestine. In six weeks there writes first group of war poems and probably begins his narrative of the desert fighting (*Alamein to Zem Zem*)

	February	*Selected Poems*, by KD, J.C. Hall, and Norman Nicholson, published
	April	On leave in Tel Aviv and Alexandria
	6 May	Rejoins regiment outside Enfidaville; no further part in fighting; campaign ends eight days later
	May, June	In Tunisia, regiment resting; made captain. Writes second group of war poems
	11 July	At Homs, Tripolitania, agrees to prepare a selection of poems for Editions Poetry London
	Sept.–Nov.	In Cairo; meets contributors to *Personal Landscape*
	17 Nov.	Embarks for England and training for new campaign
	mid Dec.	Begins three weeks leave in England. Preparing selection and by January 1944 has 73 poems to give publisher
1944	Jan.–April	Training at Chippenham, Cambs, for European campaign
	February	Receives contract for poems; prepares illustrations for war narrative and for poems. Eleven days leave
	March	Chooses title *Bête Noire* for the selection; receives contract for war narrative
	4 April	Sends last poems to publisher
	6 April	Moves to top-security camp at Sway for final training in sea-borne invasion
	6 June	Commands a tank troop in main assault on Normandy beaches
	9 June	Killed near St Pierre

Sources

BL
Most of the letters are in the British Library (BL). All except the most recently acquired have an Add Ms number and are foliated. The largest single volume of letters from Douglas is Add Ms 56355 but many letters are dispersed through various volumes. In the text, BL is followed by the Add Ms number and folio number.

Texas
The Harry Ransom Humanities Research Center at the University of Texas at Austin has an Edmund Blunden archive which includes all the surviving letters from Douglas to Blunden.

Brotherton
The Anna Gordon Keown Collection in the Brotherton Library at Leeds University holds Douglas's surviving books, copies of magazines, photographs, memorabilia and poems. It also holds one letter from Douglas to Thomas Moult in its Thomas Moult Collection.

Graham
Surviving letters owned by Betty Sze were given by her to Desmond Graham. Mrs Douglas also gave Graham various books together with a few photographs and items of memorabilia. The Waller Letters, one letter to Milena and one letter to Baber are taken from photocopies given to Graham by Sir John Waller.

Hall
Surviving letters owned by J.C. Hall: other letters to and from him are in the British Library.

Private Hands
Originals lent to Graham, except the letters to Toni Beckett whcih are from photocopies given to Graham.

Sources for the Appendices
'An Untitled Autobiographical Story': Brotherton
'From An Unfinished Autobiographical Fragment': BL 56359L
'Poets in This War': *TLS* 23 April 1971 (original MS in BL)
'Death of a Horse': *Lilliput* July 1944, pp.51–2
'Giuseppe': BL 56357
'The Little Red Mouth': *Stand* vol. XI no. 2, 1970 (original MS in
    BL)

Abbreviations

Alamein
Keith Douglas, *Alamein to Zem Zem* (1946; Faber and Faber, 1992)

CP
Keith Douglas, *The Complete Poems* (Faber and Faber, 3rd edition 2000)

KD
Desmond Graham, *Keith Douglas 1920–1944: a biography* (Oxford University Press, 1974)

Miscellany
Keith Douglas, *A Prose Miscellany*, comp. Desmond Graham (Carcanet Press, 1985)

PM
Post mark or franking

One

1925–1931

1. *To Charles Castellain*   BL 59833 f.1

6 July [1925][1]   Dalkeith

Dear grandpapa
thank you for your card. I hope you are enjoying your self.
love to all.
From your grandson
K.C. Douglas

2. *To Mrs Charles Castellain*   BL 59833 f.2

n.d.   .   6 Albert Rd/Bexhill

Dear Granny,
I am sending you the photos Nurse took.
    We are enjoying the Marmalade you made and I think it is very
much nicer than bought.
    I have cut a new double tooth and some more are coming.
    With best love to Grandpapa and yourself
from your loving grandson
K.C. Douglas

3. *To Mrs Charles Castellain*   BL 56355 f.1

14 April 1926   Dalkeith

Dear Grandmam,
thank you for the book that you sent me. Also the nice Easter egg.
    I have got an Awfully nice camp and I am going to roast potatos
in the camp fire with David and Robin.
Very best love to you and Grandpapa
From Billy[1]

---

1 Dated by Mrs Douglas. Original spelling and punctuation is followed for letters
   up to No. 46.

---

1 He was affectionately called 'Billy' at home, after the cartoon character 'Billy
   the Bean'.

4. *To Charles Castellain*   BL 56355 f.2

26 June [1926]   Dalkeith/Cranleigh/Surrey

Dear Grandpapa,
Mummy thanks you for your letter and please thank Grany for her's.
Also No.9 Lands and Pooples. I went to a Fate yesterday and a
Consert too. I bought a gun for 4d. wich was marked 6d. at the toy
storl there.
Love to you both
from
K.C. Douglas

5. *To Charles Castellain*   BL 59833 f.3

25 August 1926   Dalkeith/Cranleigh/Surrey

My dear Grandpapa,
thank you very much for the tricks I think they are very fasinating.
I went to a fair on saturday last, and had a ride in the swingboats
and also on the merrygorounds. I had throws at the cocoanuts and
hit one.
    we have had a lot of Wood-peckers in the garden close to the
house. hoping you and granny are quite well. With lots of love from
K.C. Douglas

6. *To Charles Castellain*   BL 56355 f.3

22 September 1926   Dalkeith/Cranleigh/Surrey

Dear Grandpapa,
thank you for your nice present of the little purse to half crowns
that you sent me. Aunty Elyon came over yesterday and we went
out in a boat and when we came back we landed on the opessit side
of the river to the one we got on dord on.
I am always your loving
Grandson
K C Douglas

4

7. *To Mrs Charles Castellain*   BL 56355 f.5

22 September 1926   Dalkeith/Cranleigh/Surrey

Dear Granney,
thank you for your present of the nice Lakeland pencil set I like it
very much I am using one of the pencils now to write this letter it
marks very well. Today I am going to tea with Miss Tomsen with
Mummy and as you know tomorw to school
I am always your loving
Grandson
K C Douglas

8. *To Marie J. Douglas*   BL 56355 f.7

25 September [1926]   Edgeborough/Guildford[1]

Dear Mother,
thank you for sending the cases and shorts. I hope both you and
dadda are quite well and thank you for your letter as well. I am very
much engoying myself. the little boy I sleep whith is somtimes nice
and somtimes rather boring. I played rounders the other day but I
did not make a rounder althow my side won I thingh. I do not have
very much to much lessons and half an houres brake, plenty of play
besides that.
love to you both
K.C. Douglas

9. *To Capt. Keith Sholto Douglas*   BL 59833 f.5

25 Sept. [1926]   Edgeborough/Guildford

Dear Dadda,
I hope you are quit well. I am engoying myself very much. It is
saturday you write if you can not spell very well but if you want to
you can write on sunday as well. There are 6 boys in our form
counting me.
    At first they thought I could not read but when they tryed to find
out they found I could.
love to you both
K.C. Douglas

1   Douglas started as a boarder at this prep. school on 23 September 1926.

10. *To Mrs Charles Castellain*   BL 56355 f.8

29 September 1926   Edgeborough/Guildford

My dear Granny,
I hope you are quite well. I am engoying myself very much I play
games of football and have my colours stocings jersy ect. At present
I am in the 1st form but I have three friends and engoy myself just
as much as I would if I was in the 2nd form and more I thingk
lots of love from
K C Douglas

11. *To Charles Castellain*   BL 59833 f.6

29 September 1926   Edgeborough/Guildford

My dear Grandpapa,
thank you for your letter. I am engoying myself very much. I play
smal games of football and have my colours (stocings and gersey ect)
I hav got three friends here and one of them I am sharing a garden
whith, his name is weekly and he is a day boy and is 8 years old and
has to be seen acros the road to go home at present I am in the first
form but am engoying myself just as much as if i was a 2nd form
boy in fact a little bit more I thingk I am going to get a torch.
lots of love from
K.C. Douglas

12. *To Marie J. Douglas*   BL 59833 f.9

8 October 1926   Edgeborough/Guildford

Dear Mother,
I have got the torch and will let you see it when you come to see
me, I will draw it for you on a sheet of this paper [a sketch is on
verso]. Thank you for your letter which I was very glad to have. I
have not had a boxing lesson yet but I would like to very much. I
have a good manny games of football at the field and enjoy them
very much. I have not had another game of rounders yet, I hope I
shall soon.
Give my love to dadda and tell that he will find his letter in the
same envelope as this one with his name on it.

Lots of love from your loving son,
K.C. Douglas

13. *To Phoebe*[1]   BL 56355 f.21

n.d.   Edgeborough/Guildford

My dear peobe,
thank you for your letter. I do want the childrens newspaper every
week. I am engoying myself very much, I did play a game of
rounders the other day. I am engoying myself very much and have
a lot of friends. I have half an hours break in the morning lesson, I
come highter than a boy of 7 in form order, I am starting to do latin
now and french I am going to get a torch with a red and green and
plane light in it and and then that will complete the engoyment of
school. I play football every afternoon except sundays. I am glad
you had such a nice holyday and such fine weather for it
lots of love to all of you
K.C. Douglas

14. *To Capt. Keith Sholto Douglas*   BL 56355 f.9

8 October 1926   Edgeborough/Guildford

My dear Dadda,
if Mother comes over on the 16th of October will you come to.
I have a good lot of games of football at the field. I lost my jersy the
other day but found it again so it was quite all wright.
Lots of love from
K.C. Douglas
[on verso] To Dadda
with best love
from
K.C. Douglas
Sorry it is such a short one but I realy could not think of what to
say.

1 'Olwen' in *KD*; her full name at this time is not known.

15. *To Mrs Charles Castellain*   BL 56355 f.12

10 October 1926   Edgeborough/Guildford

My dear Granney,
I am above a boy of 7 and a half in form order. Phoebe is sending
the Children's Newspaper evry week, and Mother and my
Godmother are coming over on Oct 16th to see me. and are brining
the blok that Grandpapa sent with her. I have got a torch with
coloured lights and play about whith it a lot and that is why I am
so happy also the biger boys make me model gliders like doctor Scot
used to make, they are very fasenatine toys.
Lots of love from
K.C. Douglas

16. *To Grandfather Douglas*   BL 56355 f.14

17 October 1926   Edgeborough/Guildford

My dear Pater,
I hope you are quite well. I am enjoying myself very much at school.
I play football every afternoon except sundays, I enjoy that very
much. I sometimes play in the 3rd game and sometimes in the 4th
but mostly in the 4th but both games are just as exiting as each other
I thingk. before I played football their for the first time I played
rounders but did not make rounder. at night I play with soldiers
with one other boy.
Lots of love from your loveing Grandson
K.C. Douglas

17. *To Marie J. Douglas*   BL 56355 f.15

30 October 1926   Edgeborough/Guildford

My dear Mother,
I wrote to you on Sunday but was not able to send the letter I wrote
because we have a sort of prep before chapel. Matron says that if
you would like to you could come to chapel which if you came to
chapel you would have to be here shortly before half past eleven.
do you want to come to chapel on Sunday that you come to see
me? (if so you can.)

8

Thank you for the gloves which were very useful in fact I wore them this morning they have not varyed a bit since I first had them but with soldiers I was not fortunate. all of the 3rd Madras were boken except one but none of them bercken.
Lots of love from
K C Douglas

18. *To Capt. Keith Sholto Douglas*   BL 59833 ff.10–11

6 November 1926   Edgeborough/Guildford

My dear Dadda,
thank you for your letter. I hope both you and Phoebe are quite well and that Mother will be able to come over to-day or to-morrow.

on Sunday I will write to you again. is Granny quite well and Grandpapa as well? Have you seen little Gorddon yet or has Phoebe, I hope we will be able to go over together and see him in the holydays. How is Jean Kenet? and how is Joan Cooper geting on at School at Miss Paps, I expect She likes being the same School as Robin at least I hope she does at any rate.

Have you seen Granny and Grandpapa lately? Do you think that they would sell you some fireworks for the day after tomorrow.

Miss Streeter told me she saw me on the way out of the School drive when I went to Paters.

I am glad the British won in the mach you told me about in your letter.

Mr Fitzgerald said that I was geting very good at Boxing yesterday, I can not tell you who I boxed because I have forgoten.

Tell Phoebe I would like to see her as soon as she can come over.

We are playing two matchs against Sunnydown at our Football field and one at theirs.

I hope Mother will come over tomorrow instead of today because we have not been out on Sunday yet and I would rather go to see the Huths in Bromley than go to the playing field in Guildford because I often watch matchs here and I do not often go to the Huths do I?

I am geting on quite well in Latin and in frenche as well.

I am going to write to Granny and Grandpapa tomorrow, and to you again on Saturday next.

Have you been to any realy exciting films yet.

I am longing for the holydays and Cristmas say. I got a letter from Granny the same day as I got two letters from you and Mother. Reid is not quite so cheeky now but gets in awful bates when he is pushed when he is playing marbles.

I am shure you would laugh at Moffet Potts when the pudding comes in at dinner he abserlutly Stares at it.

Lots of love from

K C Douglas

19. *To Marie J. Douglas*   BL 59833 f.13

13 November 1926   Edgeborough/Guildford

My dear Mother,

thank you for your nice letters. I hope you are quite well. I did have an Armistice service and we sung 'Valiant Hearts'.

I have not writen to Grandpapa or Granny lately or aunty Eliane.

Please give me Ted's Address because I want to write to him. I am going to write to Grandpapa today if I can that is to say if Reid will lend me an Envelope because I have only got one left and I am using that to write to you. I do not go to Chapel on Saturdays you see so I have a little time to rite two letters. I will writ you a long letter like Dadda's next Saturday to-day I will have to make up for it with drawings[1]

lots of love to you all from

K C Douglas

20. *To Marie J. Douglas*   BL 56355 f.17

14 [November] 1926   Edgeborough/Guildford

Dear Mother,

I wrote to Granny and Grandpapa. I hope you got your letter because I wrote to you yesterday as well.

I am sorry I do not rite to Dadda as often as I do to other people but I shall soon I expect, I long for the holidays because Cristmas comes in them.

---

1 Possibly the picture of an aerodrome, 59833 f.12.

How is the White Wiffle-stick and Katterpertuse and Jib and the other Children of the Katterpertusis family?[1] I long to see little Gordon and Margeritea Chagy Espeshily.[2]
Give my love to Phoebe and Dadda.
Lots of love to you all from your affectionate son.
K.C. Douglas

21. *To Marie J. Douglas*   BL 59833 f.14

20 November 1926   Edgeborough/Guildford

My dear Mother,
thank you for the Envelopes and Children's Newspaper it had a very nice thing one of those Cinirmas I get top mrks for Arithmetic and the other day I had a page of nothing but ticks and Rs by the side of sums and in the middle 10 out of 10 which was full marks I am on Ex. 17 in Latin Exercise and a boy called Creigh is on Ex. 10 and Donald is on Ex.7 and Reid is on Exercise 3 Creigh is 10 years old and Donald is 8 years old and Reid is 7 years old. Miss Streeter says she hopes I shall go up in to the Second form next term when I am 7. Reid does not know Amavi yet and I know what Victoria and Belgae mean and what Cotta means.
    Tell Dadda I got on quite well at boxing.
Lots of love from your Affectionate son
K.C. Douglas

22. *To Marie J. Douglas*   BL 59833 f.15

27 November 1926   Edgeborough/Guildford

My dear Mother.
Thank you for your letter. I pulled my tooth out myself so I did not have any thing to make a fuss about. I just pushed it forward and I heard it snap and then pulled and it came out. Donald is lending me a sheet or two to write my letters on. The weeds in my garden are not weeds, they are some Flowers that Peter Innes gave me. I am sending some Cricketers in my letter so that I do not get tempted

1   Presumably names taken from a children's story (not found).
2   The reference is not known.

to swap them becaue I am colecting and have not got a swap. give
my love to Phoebe and Dadda.
We are playing Sunny down again to-day and I hope you will be
able to come over.
Lots of love from
K.C. Douglas

23. *To Marie J. Douglas and Capt. Keith Sholto Douglas* BL 56355 f.19

11 December 1926   Edgeborough/Guildford/Surrey

my dear Mother and father
I am getting very excited about the end of the term being so near,
I hope you are both quite well. Will you be able to come next
Saturday to the party if Mrs James[1] says you can, I hope she will say
you can, she probably will. I have thought of some lovely Christmas
presents for you. Send me a list I will find out which one I think
you would like best and if I have got enough money to I shall chose
cheap one if I think you would like it I expect it will be one you
would like.
lots of love from K.C. Douglas
[on verso: map of 'Smugler's cave']

24. *To Marie J. Douglas*   BL 56355 f.50

n.d. [January 1927]   Edgeborough

Dear Mother,
I have been enjoying myself very much this term. Moffet Potts came
to-day, he says he had a very nice Christmas these Hols, he did not
say any about his father though I know it was his, and so does every
one at Edgeborough. How is Dadda getting on with his Business
since I went, is he still doing Builders now?[1] Do you know of anyone
who wants the house yet? Mr Fitz Gerald read to us this Morning
in form I liked it very much, I think every one else did too.
Lots of love from Billy

1   Mrs James: wife of the Headteacher at Edgeborough, and school matron.

---

1   Could read 'Butchers', referring to the sales of chickens. In 1927 the chicken
farm was given up.

n.d. [PM 30 January 1927]   Edgeborough

Dear Mother

Thank you for the sweets and the pen, and please thank father for the half-crown which I liked very much and Aunt Elease sent me an other. please give me her address, I have forgotten what comes after Blackwater Road.

Marks

Weeks Order

Form II

Lusey ma 100

Learmouth 94 just a few. I am 3rd to Bottom, I have beaten Moffet Potts who is 11 and a half now and Donald and Wheatly and I am just 7 every Body looked at me this morning when the Marks were put on the Black Board.

Lots of Love to you all

Keith

[on verso of envelope (f.23) PM 30 January 1927] and pleas give me Jock's address as well. I am in my 3rd dorm now.

26. *To Marie J. Douglas*   BL 56355 ff.24-5

20 February [1927]   Edgborough/Guildford/Surrey

Dear mother

I hope you have not got another cold just yet and that you will be able to come and watch the match on Wednesday and Granny to come with you – can Dadda come as well. Have you heard from Phoebe or Jock or Mummy yet.

Sometime I hope Granny will be able to come where we went yesterday or Dadda and Phoebe or the whole lot of us together perhaps these coming hols we might be able to do it. I am longing for the time when we shall take Mason out it will be nice will not it. I do hope we beat Cranleigh though I think they will take some beating. Donald Taylor is top and Pat Meek is bottom and I am 2nd to bottom then comes Learmouth and then Lucey ma. and then Johnston Ma and then Taylor. I hope if we beat Cranleigh that it will be an exciting match something like 18 points to 16 so that we have sort of only just won it is miles more exciting I mean if we only just win. Quite a lot of the Cranleigh boys are bigger than us. How are Robin and Jean Kennet getting on. I must write to Margarete next Sunday I hope to be top of the weeks order somwhere round next week or the week after that at anrate. Dunbar Magor was very pleased when I gave him two of my sweets and every one else in the Dometry had two which was Dunbar ma Jack ma Street and Myself they all thought that they were very good, and I can tell you I did I had 5 of them last night and I enjoyed every one. I want next time we go out to bye some Chocolate Cream for Dadda and some of the Pepermint Bull's eye for Granny some for Phoebe and you and please bye some Chocolate Cream for Mason and Me I am pretty sure he will like it Whitfield was also bying flowers for Mrs James so she will have quite a lot will not she?

I hope Edgeborough will be as victorious in Rugger matches as it was in soccer last term.

I do not get very many sweets on Sunday but to day I shall be able to take some more out of the Bull's eye Bottle because I did not give it up.
Love from Billy

27. *To Marie J. Douglas*   BL 56355 f.27

n.d. [?envelope PM 15 May 1927]   Edgeborough/Guildford

Dear Mother
it is only New boys who have to wait a month before so can you come next Sat. or Sun.. I am above Taylor who has got 53 and I have got 56 please come one Saturday and watch me play Cricket I generaly start by hiting Boundrys. please send my bat and ball if you can not find the ball at first go on looking and send the bat strait of as I shall want it very badly and shall be glad when it comes. How are you all I [hope] noone is or has been ill or having bad headaches[1] since I left sometime could Granny come with you when you watch me play cricket.
Love from Billy
[on verso] thanks for my stumps

1 A reference perhaps to his mother still suffering the symptoms of *encephalitis lethargica*, which had struck her down in 1924; see *KD* pp.9–10.

n.d. [June 1927[1]]   Edgeborough/Guildford

I was wacked on wednesday thank goodness not by Mr James[2] this time But by Mr west in the Changing room. I have got 41 Marks and Taylor got 37 I am getting above him every week and hope to beat him at the end of the term. I want to take the following Boys out this term

[IN A FRAME]:   Taylor
Street
Wells-cole
Dunlop
Sworder

cut the list out and tick the ones that I can take out off and send it back to me in your letter Read the letter first and then it will be easier to cut it out as you will be able to cut out part of the letter.

    I am sending a letter to Phoebe inclosed for you to adress to her as I do not know the address.[3]

Love
from Billy

29. *To Marie J. Douglas*   BL 56355 ff.64-5

n.d. [June 1927]   Edgeborough/Guildford

Dear Mother
Thank you for the sweets which I Recieved safely Last night they are Very Good how is Granny Getting on I hope she is very well Can you come on the nineth Did you say I can't Remember The Ball was just what I wanted But I am afraid that I shall Lose it soon. I soon Finished the Chocolate Cream But still have some of the Edinburgh Rock left as there was much more of it I took Quite a lot up to the Dorm and Gave it out. And am Taking the Rest To-night That will Finish The Lot And Then I shall wan't Some more soon After That at Least shall not I? Don't you Think So eh! Can you Come over Some Time with the whole family and Miss

---

1   Dated by Mrs Douglas.
2   Headmaster at Edgeborough.
3   She was to join Keith's father in Wales.

Thomson as well and take me out to Newland's Corner and Have a Picnik as one of us Could Go By Bus and that would make it alwright you Could Go into Guildford and then Drop Somebody to Go By Bus.. I am Afraid I shall not see The Eclipse from where I am. Can Miss Smith Come and see me Once or twice or Mr I [for 'it'?] Does Not matter which as long as one of them Comes. how is Pater I must write to Him that Reminds me. and How is Dadda I am expecting To Get a Letter from Phoebe soon, when Did you Send the Letter on to her eh? I am trying to make this Letter Longer than the Last I wonder wether I Shall Sucseed. The Term seems to have Gone very Quickly It seems that I have only Been Here about a month and The a [are] only about five weeks Left not that now But not four yet, Still they won't take Long Will They at Least one thing is they won't seem Long.

I am The Sencond in the following II Form Order.

II
Jack mi 46
Douglas 35
Meek 33
Lees-Smith 30
Creigh 27
Taylor
Clarkson-Webb } 26
M. Potts 24
Sworder 23
Moore 14

[Down the side] Mr Fitzgerald says that I am getting Better Taylor Just Beat me Last week By 1 mark and I Have Absent Part of time at last Beaten Him more and worse Than he Beat Me. In the 3nd Form Mayne who was Bottom of the Form Last Term is Getting top every week now. Soon I must Say Goodbye.
Give my love to Miss Smith
Love from Billy

1[5] June Sunday [1927]   Edgeborough/Guildford

Dear Mother,

I hope you will be able to come on Monday or the Day after. Thank
you for your letter. In what way are you not feeling well? How are
Granny and Dadda? I can not get you a fixture card now as I did
not get one given me at the time and it is probably too late Now
But I will find out the Date of the Next Match so that you can come
over or probably the one after that, or after Next Sunday and will
tell you in my letter if you do not come over and if you Do I will
tell you then and then you may be able to see it. Can I have a Rubber
ball light Green please if you can because I want one very badly they
are a lot of use to poeple in the Diferent Gangs, each have Diferent
Coloured Balls. the Gang against which we are fighting has a Purple
one and another Gang I know has a Dark Green one and all the
Gangs use them for signaling if somebody belonging to the Gang
with a light Green ball sees a light Green ball thrown up twice and
caught twice they know they are wanted. they are Different Signals
according to the number of times thrown up and not one is the
same. How are the Animals? and Have the Kittens Gone Yet. I have
not looked at the order yet but will tell you how many marks I have
got. I Just am going to look

Now I have looked and I am Third above Taylor having 117
marks got in one week. I am writing this on the stage. I am Longing
for when I go out next. the Names of the New boys this term are
as follows in order of Form

Clarksonwell 2nd Form
Sworder 2nd Form
Mallock 1st Form
Gibson 1st Form

Clarksonwell is quite Decent Gibson's Mother after being Badgered
for a long Time has Invited me to tea Gibson is seven but does not
come to my shoulder quite He is also Decent. Mallock is not at all
bad But is Very Cheeky. Reid I must tell you is not half so Cheeky
as he was though still very Cheeky. And Sworder who is in my
Dormetry and is also very Decent. I am having cold Baths now but
Do not like them Too Much when will you be taking street out I
think there will be room to take him out one time and Donald out
another I would like to take Street out first I think so write and tell

me when you will come and fetch him and please come as soon as you can for as I said further back in the letter I am longing to come out again and when he does come can you get some pancakes ready for pudding and some sweets as well. do not forget to send the sweets that you forgot to Give me here. By the way the Empire toffee was very good I am sending the letter I got with it in my next Letter as I forgot to Bring it Down today, it is rather Comical Give Granny and Dadda my love will not you eh and be sure to remember. I am trying to make a Letter of at Least five Pages this time so Here is the 5th. could you bring Dash when we go for the Picnic to Newlands Corner as I shall be very pleased to see her and I am sure she will be pleased to see me because she was very last time. and can Granny come too I hope she can I expect so. Sworder has lent me an envelope this time but can I have some more please as he can not share anymore for he has only a little that I could see and also he told me. I am getting on fine now But will soon be wanting some more sweets for they go very quickly here as I should think you know but not quite as fast as they do at home I should not think would you? I am writing in Pencil as I have not got a pen but I Don't think you will mind will you? at least I know you won't. I have now beaten my Record Number of pages 3 Poeple Left our Dormetry which were as follows Such Mi. Such Ma. and Dobson in whose place I have come in to the Dormetry. Street is in Walker Ma.'s Dormetry Just Next to me and we often have pillow Fights. First I was in Sedgewicks Dorm then I was in Dunbar Ma's Again only He has not got the same Dormetry as lst term that is now my old Dormetry which as I have just told you is now Sedgewick's He has got Maxwell Dobson Mallock Clarksonwell Johnston Mi. and Taylor and Himself. Taylor is longing to go out so is Street.
No I must end up so
Goodbye. Lots of love to you all From
Billy

31. *To Marie J. Douglas*   BL 59833 f.7

2 October [1927]   Edgeborough/Guildford/Surrey

Dear Mother
I enjoyed myself yesterday very much in spite of the rain so we diddled the rain after all, did not we?

You forgot to give me those butter-balls so do you think you could send me a box of sweets in place of them, and them have for home Granny likes butter balls herself. I have remembered not to talk about food too. don't forget to get Cheasars too. (Chesnuts.) there might be some left when I come back for the Hols, do you think there would eh?!

Mr James has just said do not stick your letters up and he was talking about School Lists

I will send them too for dadda or phoebe or granny or Mummy Lawson-Wood[1] in fact for the whole house in General. This is a short letter but is trying to be more newsy
Love from
Billy
[sketch of ships at sea] a mile away from Douglas harbour (lecture on the Isle of man last night Saturday night)

32. *To Marie J. Douglas*   BL 59833 ff. 17–18

n.d. [?1928]   Edgeborough/Guildford

Dear Mother,
I forgot to tell you yesterday, that the tank went fut last Sunday. I was very glad to see you yesterday it was quite a surprise.

I am second in the Scripture Exam with 26/40 Taylor is top with 36/40.

We had the Sir Roger de covely Last night it was lovely. We marched round the room in a long single file at the end. then we inwards wheeled as it is called and came up in fours and so on until we came up in two ranks then we left turned and Bowed.

I boxed Reid on Friday he kept on butting me and not using his fists at all.

I am 4th in the week's order. with 124 marks.

it seems to be getting more every time does not it?

How did Phoebe get on with the Net ball? who won the old girls or the new.

It was rather funny that Mr James did not ask who was going out just that Sunday that I went home. he asked who was to-day. I want

---

1 Mrs Douglas had worked for the artist Lawson Wood during the First World War.

to know whether I can walk home on the last day of School across over the downs to Newlands Corner.

I know the way and I could go with Chalks (Chaldecotte) as far as his house and then go on up that little road past the 'Titing Estate' and across the downs.

and from Newlands Corner down the Road past the Silent pool and down and then through down vicarage lane and up to the house and in.

Now you see I know the way properly remember the pad
Love to you all from
Billy

33. *To Marie J. Douglas*   BL 56355 f. 67

Sunday 4 March [1928]   Edgeborough/Guildford

Dear Mother
I seem to be in good luck. I have found the Envelopes and–: the EIGHT BOB!!!!! (in the purse)

(at least another boy found it and gave it to Matron and she will give it up to Mrs James.) so you see I have found it all Eight bob, tangerine (=foot-ball.) and Envelopes.

I expect you will be pleased when you read this letter.

I am very pleased too because I counted the Eight bob directly I saw it.

Please remember that I collect foreign money and if you can get me any new pieces it will be a part of the treat.

I am really mostly pleased about the money because now I am no longer overdrawn and there will be no extra money down on the bill for you either. How is this writing.

Will you give my note to Mrs Jack please?

Now if I am going to Mrs Jack too I must End up, so lots of love to you all from –:
Billy

34. *To Marie J. Douglas*   BL 56355 ff. 52–6

n.d. [?1928]   Edgeborough/Guildford

Dear Mother
Can you come Next Sunday or Saturday some time in the summer

hols could you make some Bannana ice or perhaps sometime when you take me home as I have not had them for such a long time and like them so much and have Aunty Ellyane over the same Day if it is in the Summer hols. Do you think my letters are Getting better or not. Did you get my last letter I forgot to ask you when you came over. I am longing for the hols to come and the time to go to Dimchurch, I am sure I should enjoy myself there. Saturday nights are about the best nights in the week shall I be able to come home this term on any Sunday or not, I hope I shall Don't you. Now Dadda has has [*sic*] got the Motor Bike there is more Chance of it than there was before Don't you think. how is granny and how are you I hope Miss Thomson will come and watch some of the matchs this term she said she would so she probably will. Have you heard from Phoebe and will she be able to come over and watch a few Matches, I hope she will, and can Granny come a few times as well I sopose she will won't she. How is Dash? and how are the Kittens have you still got them or have you heard about them from Mrs West? has Dash killed any more Rats over the road or not eh? I am having a fine time here so can you unearth a tennis ratchet for me as I can only play tennis for about 10 minutes at a time because Mrs James keeps on wanting her Rachets back so they are not much use and plracticley everyone esles has got one only Donald me and Reid have not got one. and the bigger boys always get the Rachets whether they ask first or last because they are above you. I am longing to get a few more rails encluding points and New Engine then also a four arm gantry signal I have bought a Cricket scoring book yesterday after tea. I have managed to get a new block from Mrs James on which I am writing and am trying to make a longish leter out if it
Love to you all
from Billy

35. *To Edward Sharp & Sons Ltd/Makers of the*   BL 56355 f.79
    celebrated Super-Kreem Toffee

Draft letter n.d. [23 August 1928]

Dear Sirs,
I wish to tell you that many of my friends and I have decided that no other Toffee-makers can hold a candle to your firm for quantity,

quality and Flavour.

I enclose a drawing which I hope you can m[ake]use o[f]. I have entirely decided that Sharp's is the Toffee that is worth spending money on.

Sharp's have hit the mark entirely. I suggest a Toffee Club. And I am willing to make any Designs for it.

Hoping that I may, in future years be of some use to you.
Yours affectionately [crossed out]
Yours faithfully
K.C.D

35b. *From Sharps to KD*   BL 56355 f.81

24 August 1928

Dear Sir,
We thank you for your favour of the 23 instant and appreciate the drawing which you have sent us.

We are very pleased to hear that you like our Toffee so much and we trsut [*sic*] that you will always buy and enjoy this. Possible [*sic*] you have not tried the new lines which we are just bringing out and as we are sending you a sample we shall look forward to a big increase in sales from the Cranleigh district for our new Toffy-choc as a result of your interest in our toffee.
Yours faithfully
Sales Manager, Edward Sharp & Sons, Ltd.

35c. *From Sharps to KD*   BL 56355 f.80

7 September 1928

Dear Sir,
We thank you for your letter of September 2nd and much appreciate your kind remarks in regard to our Super Kreem Toffee.

We also appreciate your suggestion in regard to a Toffee Club, but regret that we do not see our way clear to put this into operation at the present time.

Thanking you again, we beg to remain,
Yours faithfully
Sales Manager, Edward Sharp and Sons, Ltd.

n.d. [1929]   Edgeborough/Guildford

Dear Mother

Thank you very much for this pad. I will send you a piece of Translation we had to do in French yesterday. How do you like this writing?

I will now tell you all the names of stops I know in French. (I do not know how to spell any of them but I think you will be able to make them out. Small writing seems to me to make it easier for you to write a lot. Here are the stops –: ? = point d'interragasion [*sic*] .= point. and when he reads them out in french Dictation (Dictèe Francaise). I am sorry I have put the accent wrong in dictée Francaise but I did not change it when I found it because if I changed it it would make the letter look untidy. I like this writing and I hope you do too.

Here is the French translation –:

<u>En Chine</u>. (in French 1st).

Peice 12.

<u>Lectures Faciles</u>.

Un voyageur vit un jour, assis au bord du chemin, un grand et fort Chinois, de quarante à quarante-cinq ans, qui pleurait à chaudes larmes.

– 'Mon ami, lui demanda le voyageur commpatissant, pourquoi pleurez-vous? ainsi, comme un infant?

Oh Monsieur, repondit l'autre, mon père m'a battu.

L'êtes vous pas honteux? Comment pouvez-vous, à votre age, pleurer pour si peu de chose?

Ce n'est pas pour les coups que j'ai reçus que le pleure, répondit le Chinois, mais j'ai senti que mon pauvre père n'a pas longtemps à vivre – son bras devient plus faible de jour en jour.

English.

A traveller saw one day sitting on the side of the road, a big and strong Chinese, of forty to forty-five years old, who was weeping bitterly.

'My freind asked the traveller compassionately, why do you cry so, like a child?

'Oh sir' replied the other 'my father has beaten me'

Are you not ashamed? How could you tell me, at your age, to cry for so little a thing?

It is not for the blows that I have received that I cry, replied the Chinese, but I have felt that my poor father has not a long time to live

His arm is becoming weaker day by day.

———

please send a few corrections to that if you find mistakes, but that is my version of it.

I did an awfully silly thing. and that is the reason that my Sunday letter came late.

I put as the address when I sent it off on Sunday
Mrs K.S. Douglas
Edgeborough
Guildford
Surrey.
so it was posted and came back to me then I delayed a day in sending it on and then made a boss[?] and so as not to waste my last envelope sent it to granny and asked her to forward it or rather I knew she <u>would</u> so I did not but hoped for the best. I hope you will like this letter it is quite Long.

I hope you will be able to take me out next Sunday and I wonder if Pater is better and would let me bring someone else as well.

Thanks very much for bringing my things over.

This letter is realy not very newsy but it is long

I am sending back to you the envelope which came back to me.
Always your loving son
Billy
P.S. Hope I will see you soon
P.P.S. Here's a drawing.[1]

37. *To Marie J. Douglas* (fragment)   BL 56355 f.39

n.d. [?1929]

This is the week's order
DOUGLAS 187
Milligan 173
Taylor 151
Mallock 144

———

1   No longer with the letter.

Goddard 118
Mobbs 115
Jordan 98
Lloyd 95
Bond 91
Milsom 68

I am getting on much better at rugger now. I am reading a 'sapper' short story book, called 'The dinner club', have you read it? It has some very exciting stories in it.

It is about a club in which they take it by turns to give all the others a good dinner and tell them a story, if it does not keep the others awake, the teller has to pay £10 to a charity.

They are men from each proffession.

Soldier, barrister, ordinary man, writer, doctor and actor.

Your affectionate son, Billy [crossed out] Keith.

38. *To Marie J. Douglas*   BL 56355 ff.31–3

Tuesday 29 [May] 1929   Edgeborough/Guildford

Dear Mother,

It is a lovely day to-day. We have bathed three times and I was not aloud to bathe the first time, I had not tried any strokes except dog-stroke, and I <u>can</u> do that alright. Thanks for the golfer cutting and letter, I got the stamps cutting and paper that you sent. I am keeping the papers for Jock.

I am in the 3rd game at present but the last one I played in the 2nd I took one wicket, a catch which was quite easy when I went down on my knees to get it.

I'm getting on fairly alright in work. We are having Geography off.

I have 700 and something stamps, 721, I think it is though two of them are not put in yet. In English hour to-day and to-morrow we have to write out 'The Rime of the ancient mariner', not in verse, but cut down as much as we can, we are aloud to use the book which has like this:

> 'Her beams bemock'd the sultry main
> Like april hoar frost spread
> But where the ship's huge shadow lay

The charméd water burnt alway
A still and awfull red'

'Beyond the shadow of the ship
I watched the water-snakes
They moved in tracks of shining white
And when they rear'd the elfish light
Fell off in hoary flakes'

[in margin beside 2nd stanza] By the light of the moon he beholdeth
God's creatures of the great calm.
In History we were read Boadicea:
1st verse

When the British Warrior queen
Bleeding from the Roman rods
sought with an indignant mien
counsil of her country's gods.

Having been read it, we had it read again leaving out words which
we had to put in.
    Then he read us some of 'Puck of Pook's hill'.
    Thanks aobut the Irish Commem: stamps.
    Sorry about Sunday but I had a lot of business to do with S.D.P.
& Coy.[1]
Goodbye
Always your loving son, and do try hard to get some persian stamps
Billy the Bean
[and with his signature] Keith C Douglas

39. *To Marie J. Douglas*   BL 56355 ff.35–6

n.d. [Envelope PM 8 December 1929][1]   Edgeborough/Guildford

Dear Mother
I played in the 3rd and shot 2 goals and tipped in one that might
have gone in, in the scrum, one was from half-way!

1   His friends; perhaps Street, Dunlop and Potts.

1   Around this time Mrs Douglas found she could not afford the fees and would
    have to remove Keith from Edgeborough. On 12 ?December 1929 Mr James,
    the Headmaster, wrote and assured her that Keith could stay on at school free
    (Brotherton).

26

The one from half-way, I was told by about 5 people was one of the best shots in the game, which is saying rather a lot, because the match in 3rd we won 18–0! In the second they won 2–1, scoring the 2nd goal in the last 4 minutes. All the forwards in the 3rd, with exception of one, scored goals. Luckily, I was not that one! They seemed to slip past me and get out of my way as hard as they could and then as you got through to shoot they slobbered up behind you and you had to pass and that is why I only got three goals, because I took it up about 10 times but had to pass so much. When I say I took it up I mean I and the wing passing like running along the road with a ball while they banged and slid about us.

I've practically never had such a good tea as we had then and I stuffed hard and pressed the person next to me to eat too much. He was one of their boys and at the end he stuck his fingers in the crumbs and licked them! He kept on looking round too [*sic*] make sure no one was watching him. We had a Sir Rojer de Coveryley last night and a sing-song after it. I've about 4/- left so I shan't spend any more. There is collection to-day – Gosh! I do feel <u>sleepy</u>! – And I have given 1/- (a nice new one.), to it.

Could you get me a Gamages catalogue? The films and things I want to see are 'Wings', 'The Ghost Train', 'Speedy'. 'Shoulder arms', 'The Gold rush' 'Treasure Island' and Olympia and any 'Scarlet Pimp' films. The one I should like most is Olympia.
Goodbye.
Billy
The Dance is on Tuesday (after next.)

40. *To Marie J. Douglas*   BL 56355 f.38

2 March 1930   Edgeborough/Guildford/Surrey

Dear Mother
I clean forgot to ask you what happened to my drawing, did you forget to send it up?; or did you forget to send me the drawing lesson?

Also could I have a Wright's Coal Tar soap wrapper again, please? In fact all the wrappers, because I cannot remember whether it was the outer or the inner wrapper, and it does not much matter, if I might win two guineas, does it? I am 4th in the week's order, with 341, it was awfully close this week, and the top only got 358, but the bottom got 147.

There will be a match on Saturday next, the 8th against Highfield.

I shall have to write to Miss Smith, after this, she sent me a box of Cocoanut Ice.

Now I shall have to try and think of some more news.

Cranleigh beat us easily both at home and away.

I hope you will take me out soon.

Goodbye,

Your loving son,

Keith C. Douglas

41. *To Marie J. Douglas*   BL 56355 ff.71–4

n.d. [PM 5 March 1930]   Edgeborough/Guildford/Surrey

Dear Mother,

I was second in the Algebra paper and second in the work we did today in Algebra. In English we had to write a poem on any subject in History.

This was mine:
'Waterloo'

1.

'Napoleon is charging our squares,
with his cavalry he is attacking;
let the enemy do what he dares,
our soldiers in braveness aren't lacking.'

I forgot bravery for the moment, so I used Poet's license and put 'braveness'.

This is the second verse:

2.

But naught does his charging avail,
he cannot do anything more;
for not one heart does fail
e'en when tis at death's door.'

And this is the third

3.

'I have you!' Napoleon cries!
but he has a great mistake made;

for every French soldier flies,
and is caught by a fierce cannonade.'
And this is the last

4.
Napoleon is charging our squares,
but only in memory now;
we remember his charging mares;
and we always will, I trow.'

Thank you very much for your letter, and the large consignement of sweets. our dorm: is over the extra work room, and last night we heard mysterious bangings on the floor and when the captain Lloyd went up, he found they were breaking of the candy, which had gone up early, though of course he said nothing!

I picked up 'The Flight of the Heron,'[1] – that book I found in the flat in London, – in the library, and am reading it now. I think I told you there is a match next Saturday.

I wish I could have either 'The Autocar', or 'The Children's Newspaper.

Now I had better say goodbye, and [a few words missing]. I have given up grumbling for lent – if that is possible, – and have not 'broken Lent' yet.

Now, good bye,
Your loving son,
Billy
P.S. I had some lovely pancakes yesterday, and by the way, please put on the missing piece.

42. *To Marie J. Douglas*   BL 59833 ff.19–20

n.d. [?1930]   Edgeborough/Guildford/Surrey

Dear Mummie,
Thank you very much for your letter. I'm glad the old grannie liked the letter I wrote her. I tried not to abbreviate things to much, in fact I don't think I abbreviated anything. I took care not to say 'hols'', because I thought she might not understand; she did not

---

1   By D.K. Broster (1925). It tells of a Capt. Keith Windham in the Royal Scots
– one of Douglas's preferred regiments on enlistment a decade later.

seem to, when I was staying there with you, did she?

They are just going to put up the 5th form order now, so I'll tell you where I am.

Oh! I'm third, well anyhow, I have not gone down, because my place is 3rd in form

I got Full for English the other day 15 out of 15, and for Dictation 19 out of 20.

Then again for Geography I got 36 out of 36, at the end of the term, Geography counts as English, for one latin Ex, I got 48 out of 50. But all the same I'm afraid I shall stay in the 5th.

Because I am miles down in Maths. It is not at all a nice day but it is only in the morning so far, and yesterday and the day before it was nice in the afternoon and nasty in the morning.

I have had a head ache all yesterday and it has continued all this morning so far.

I hope it will be all right to-morrow, because matron says, if the weather continues fine in the afternoon, which is the time we bathe, we shall start bathing.

One of the Mc Halls has made a little cricket set, and the boy who made the little aeroplane made him a box, wth a little partition for balls. The Box is about this long. [sketch follows] and the bat is this long. [notes on the sketch:] (the handle painted black) painted splice./Black cotton binding/ imitation writing.[sketch of ball] ball, this size, painted red, made of squeezed up bread, they are two in number.

the lid is hinged by sticking plaster! don't you think that's rather neat?

Now as there is nothing else to say except good bye, I will say it, Goodbye.

your loving son,
Keith

43. To Marie J. Douglas   BL 56355 ff.40–2

11 May [19]30   Edgeborough/Guildford/Surrey

Dear Mother

I am 4th in the order but I have been in bed for two days with a cold, it seems silly, but they never make you work in bed.

Do you think you could send me an Empty bottle and a small 6d tin of Ice foam instead of a 6d saw and sandpaper please? Do them up with packing to hide the shape, too, please.

Please put this in an address book on the last page, that I want, when I have a Gramaphone again a 1/3d record called 'U.S.A. Patrol', on the other side of which is 'The Warbler's Serenade'.

It is a 'Broadcast' record, the same kind as the one I got with 'the lost policeman' on it.

We have all had to don grey jerseys. Have you looked at any houses?

It's not a nice day to-day.

Dunlop minor comes back to-day.

Griffiths came back yesterday.

They were the two who first got whooping cough last hols.

Jordan has a loveley gramaphone, the 5 guinea one that his aunt gave him.

He also has some lovely records among them 'Bunkidoodle-ido', (H.M.V.3s) The 'Piccaninnies picnic' (Columbia 3s). U.S.A. Patrol, and on the other side 'The Wabler's Serenade', (Broadcast, 1/3d).

Fisher has a nice one called 'Merry Little Goblins,' I'm not sure whether it is H.M.V. or Columbia, but it cost 3s.

Jordan has a full size, 12 in, his Gramaphone takes 10 in, but will take this, too, It is called, 'Selections from "Silver Wings" and has selections on both sides, it cost 4/6. And is, I think, Columbia.

Now I will say 'good bye'

Your loving son,

Keith

44. *To Marie J. Douglas*   BL 56355 ff.69–70

n.d. [?1930)]   Edgeborough/Guildford/Surrey

Dear Mother,

You would have found something comic to tell me if you had waited and looked at yesterday's Sketch; but as you did not I can tell <u>you</u> now. When Capt. Campbell was coming home on the boat he was on deck when he saw a man fall overboard, he immediately threw a lifeboat at him! Dunbar is going to send it up to 'punch'. Mr Stokoe[1] says he will get 5/- I don't quite see why, because Punch

---

1   His English master and the first person to see Douglas's literary promise.

ought to be able to see it for themselves.

I enclose instead of a sketch, apologies [a second 'l' crossed out], (spelt wrong I know, but I can't remember how to spell it and that is the nearest I can get.), and a ship, it came from China. We played 'Pinewood' yesterday at Rugger, we had never played them before and, as they play Rugger in the Xmas term, so I heard, they beat us hollow. I was one of the Edgeborough forwards. It does seem grand, (as Grannie would say, to be in the First XV! we did not have much of a tea – 'by their teas ye shall know them!' but we ragged about in their gym after and that was jolly good sport, they are the nicest lot of chaps I've ever played against. well, goodbye, your loving Old Bean

P.S. The matron at Pinewood was awfully nice, and she said that when she says to the boys at night that she'll be round in a minute, they say she's always round!

45. *To Marie J. Douglas*   BL 56355 ff.43–7

n.d. (?envelope PM 11 February 1931)   Edgeborough/Guildford

Dear Mother,

Thank you very much for your letters, the lovely stamps – wherever did you get them?

I enclose a few drawings. I am second in the order this week with 126 marks: the top boy, Goddard got 135.

But I beat him hollow last week.

I enclose a few drawings. The Autocar was a fine one, it had an awfully interesting thing in it called 'The Open Road',[1] I don't know if you read it before you sent it on to me.

It is about an ordinary English road first it tells how, deep down under it the Romans, first captured the Britons, and made them make roads, then about the Cavaliers who rode years later on the same road.

Then last about the Highwayman, who stopped m'lady's carriage on the bridge.

Street, I, and some others, including Taylor, are going to Act a play, which Strasse, pronounced Straaza, (Street), and I, wrote.

1   'The English Road in History', H. Langford Lewis, *Autocar,* 2 January 1931.

It is about 3 German spies who murder Professor W. Cooper, who has discovered some poison gas, and they are all killed by the poison gas. And then the police come, and first of all, when lot the animals screams, constable 'arris hears it rushes in, and then after some fruitless efforts, he at last makes the telephone work, but can only stutter out that there is a murder at 77, Park Lane, before he, too becomes a victim to the gas.

There are only 43 more days!

I'm longing for next hols. It was 5 foot in deep end when the bath got shallow. and now they have filled it up it is 6ft.

This is the play caste.

Street	Johann Beck (murderer)
me	Fritz von Schwartstein (another spie)
Taylor	Superintendent Bliss
Milsom	Inspector Mander
Dunlop ma	James, (a butler)
Bond	A. Cooper, (son of murdered)
Mobbs	*W. Cooper (murdered)
Milligan	P.C. 'arris
Benton	= another spie, Hans Kopff.

Always, I remain
your loving son,
Keith
*Proffesor

46. *To Marie J. Douglas*   BL 56355 ff.68 and 83

n.d. [1931]   Edgeborough/Guildford

Dear Mother,

Thanks very much for the Lovely stamps, there were some lovely battle scenes, one Turkish one of Turkish soldiers in the trenches, and another of a Portuguese knight in a battle.

Wherever <u>do</u> you get them? I enclose an official caste of the players. I am looking for ward to seeing you again.

The name of that road was <u>Hillier</u>.

I had a letter from Granny thanking me for mine.

She said they had as awfull storm and the dog was terrified of it! She seemed quite pleased with my letter, although I did not have time for much.

Could you manage to get the Ice foam before the picnic please.

Do you think I could have that 10/- from the old granny next hols for either train things or a camera? I <u>think</u> a camera would be nice, don't you? I am going to get a few play things such as a moustache, next hols with my other money. Now I will say goodbye
Always your loving son
Keith

[At top of sheet:] KCD
CASTE

Johann Beck	= J. Street.
Fritz von Schwartzein	= K. Douglas.
Hans Kopf	= A Benton

Professor W Cooper	= G. Mobbs
Arthur Cooper	= J. Bond.
James (butler)	= C. Dunlop.

Superintendent Bliss	= D. Taylor.
Inspector Mander	= D. Milsom.
P.C. Harris	= J. Whitty.

A Police Sergeant

Two

1931–1938

47. To Marie J. Douglas   BL 56355 f.89

Saturday 19 [September] 1931   Lamb A/Christ's Hospital

Dear Ma,

I have not nearly settled down yet. I wonder how soon you will come and see me.

I have not even found out what form I am in yet, but I think it is IIIb.

The only lesson I have had is in Carpentering, where I started to learn to draw for making things.

I almost wish I had chosen your pen; this nib is so thin.

There is no more work to-day.

I have just been to the tuck-shop and bought some NU-CHU, some 'Cydlo'[?], like 'Cydeax'[?].

I will write again to-morrow, so you will get two letters.

Your loving son,

Keith

P.S. Soon I shall be weighed in my 'Housie' clothes (5.0 to-day).[1]

48. To Marie J. Douglas   BL 56355 f.90

Sunday (PM 20 September 31)   Lamb A/Christ's Hospital

Dear Mother

I am not in 3B but L.E.E. I went nutting with the other new boys this afternoon but most of the nuts were bad. Out of about 30 only 6 were good! I will write and tell you more about the school when I know it.

I can't do my bands yet,[1] but I am slowly realising the way, I think.

I hope you returned safely home, and I think Doris and Violet will be with you now, won't they.

The term seems to go terribly slowly. We only have the school band for going in to dinner, and apparently not always then. We did not to-day, but there may be a rule about not having it on Sundays or something like that: anyhow I have not yet heard about it. I do get rather teased, and have made no friends yet, but still, I

---

1   Keith had started that day at Christ's Hospital in Horsham, Surrey.

---

1   Tied at the neck: see Letter 49.

can't hope to on the second day! I see quite a lot of the boys in other houses; they seem much nicer than the boys in Lamb A. And Blake who, by the way is a bit of a friend of mine, (but I can't call anyone actually a friend after two days, if you know what I mean) and several others, (new boys), from other houses, all say they don't get teased a bit.

I wonder if you will be able to come down to the dedication of the new organ which is either on the 10th, 11th, or 12th of October, I don't quite know which, but I will find out later.

Please excuse the awful writing, but this pen does not suit me all.

I have seen quite a lot of Miles for two days, (mostly round the tuckshop).

I am not allowed into the School Library until I get my 'Broadie' buckle, which I get when I get into the middle school. It is like this O 'Broadie' (white), and ☐ ordinary, (silver), buckles.

I get awfully bewildered about forms still, and where to go at such and such a time etc but I expect I shall find out about that soon.
Your loving son
Keith

49. *To Marie J. Douglas*   BL 56355 f.105

n.d. [September 1931]   Lamb A/Christ's Hospital

Dear Mother,
Thank you very much for your three letters. My 'options', or what I study, are Latin and Greek. The latter I have never done before. I have got quite settled down now, and can do my 'bands', these things [sketch] (the white things which go round my neck.)

The lights have fused to-night, so I have to write by the window.

Everyone seems jolly decent now, and I don't get teased any more now.

I must stop now as it's Prep time.

Yours,
Keith

Sunday n.d. (PM 27 September 31)   Lamb A/Christ's Hospital

Dear Mother,

I wrote a P.C. yesterday as well as this letter, so I think you will get them both by the same post. Everybody here makes an awful fuss about my drawing. The art master say[s] I draw well, and everyone else says I shall be an art Grec![1]

I have managed not to swank about it yet, I think, except, I suppose, in this letter.

There are some jolly good books in the house library, also there is a house gramophone.

We had a rugger match against another house (Thornton B), who are the foulest team I've ever played against.

One of them, their hooker, a chap called Moore went about hammering the wind out of people with his fists. He winded me and another boy, and hit several other people extremely hard catching hold of one boy round the neck and hammering hard and repeatedly on his back when he had not got the ball.

For some reason this was not given as a foul: I don't think the ref: saw it.

The opening of the new chapel organ is a fortnight to-day.

There are two slide lectures next week, on Saturday and Sunday. I do not know what the first is on, but the 2nd is on Dr Barnardo's homes.

My 'options', that is, my special subjects are Latin and Greek.

I am getting on quite well at everything (including German, which I have never done before) except Greek. I enclose a drawing.[2] Please fix it and press it.

Please send me some jam, or jelly, preferably home-made, for tuck; you are not allowed to send tinned stuff, as I can buy it at the shop.

There were a great many parents here today.

Your loving son

Keith

PS Give my love to Granny.

---

1   'Grec': 'Grecian', Christ's Hospital term for a sixth former.
2   No longer with the letter.

n.d. (PM 4 October 1931)   Lamb A/Christ's Hospital

Dear Mother,

Thank you very much for all your letters. I did write, but went and forgot to send the letter off!

You would have to get here pretty early, about a quarter to 11, I think, to come to the morning service. You don't have to be invited. The service is at 11.15 and the opening of the organ is in the evening at 5.15, also an organ recital.

There is not a single person in the house who is not jolly nice now, although I don't have much to do with a good many of them in the Upper school. Did I tell you we were read to on Sunday nights in bed by the monitors?

I am getting on just a little better at Greek, and quite well at everything else.

I am quite used to the clothes. In the dormitory we have to blow our noses solidly for about a minute, night and morning.

Matron inspects us at night, except when we have baths, to see that we are clean.

When you send the drawing I will do you some drawings of various parts of 'Housie'.

You join the O.T.C. when you are 14 and the scouts when you have been at 'Housie' a year.

I have not written to Mr James yet because I can't think of much to tell him that would interest him about 'Housie'.

I will write something this week, though.

I wrote to Whitty ma. (a letter), and a P.C. to Whitty mi. They have not yet written back.

I am looking forward to seeing you next Sunday, but am afraid you will not be able to arrive for morning Service, but the Dedication is in the evening, also an organ recital by the organist of St Paul's Cathedral, Dr Stanley Marchant.

Your loving
son
Keith

n.d. (PM 15 November 1931)   [Christ's Hospital letterhead]

Dear Mother,

That Turkish Delight was simply fine. Did you make it to the Rahat
Lacoum recipe?

Anyway, thank you very much for it, and the toffees, and the
jam, none of the pots of which was broken.

Yesterday we played a rugger match against Coleridge B.[1] I had
to stay in to do some German, so arrived late, but I did manage to
get a try, and nearly get a free kick over the bar; it was something
like this (P.T.O.). [sketch follows indicating:] place I kicked from

I think it is about the highest place kick I have ever done.

It was a match II ball, like mine.

I scored the try on the goal-line, (at least half over,) in the corner
marked so O, making a run like this [sketch follows].

I don't know whether you will understand my rather confused
drawings.

They had a sort of exhibition, organized by the Natural History
Society, on all sorts of subjects.

I saw photographs, several nature film, and two slide lectures; also
some electric stuff, making blue crackles in the air, and a lot of germs
and things through microscopes.

Then I was going to go into another Nature films, but I found it
was time for letter-writing, so came back.

I saw a film on an otter, trout (in which they were filmed hatching
out of their eggs, and growing up) a pine-marten, and a comedy
film to finish up with.

Also a lantern lecture on 1931 excavations, and on Beetles.

Yesterday evening, there was a lecture on flying, but it was all
mucked up, and half the film got spoilt.

What there was of it was quite good.

I have still got my fountain pen.

I have lost count of how many weeks we've been here, but I
think it is eight weeks last Friday, is it not?

Your loving son

Keith

---

1   Another of the Houses at Christ's Hospital.

n.d. (PM 20 January 1932)   Lamb A/Christ's Hospital

Dear Mother,

Thank you for your note and the photographs. I have arrived quite safely and unpacked my trunk. The other shoe got packed in another boy's trunk, but I have it now, and could I keep the others here and bring them back at the end of the term? Because it costs so much for postage.

I may not have time to post this letter, but you will get it by Friday, anyway.

Barnard was very pleased with the boat. I have not drawn anything yet but will send any good ones I do.

I have the Scotchman quite safe and have worn my plate all the morning, and then I took it out for dinner, and have not been able to put it back except once, and then I forgot!

We had a practice this afternoon. The journey back was long and uninteresting.

I will send you copies of the hunt photographs, if I get any to come out decently.

Please write as often as you can, even if it is only a note like I got to-day.

I hope you will be able to come and take me out soon.

I have not found out about my trade or trades as yet, nor if I am allowed to play cards, though I gather from the boys that I am not.

I have got everything, but next time we must put my shoes in the suitcase as I don't get my trunk till next morning. Please send the tube of glue, or better still a new tube of seccotine. We must remember to put me in a pen next time, as this time I had to buy one.

How is Granny? Give her my love please. Have you been in to Barbara[1] again yet or has she come in?

Have you heard any more about the person who wanted to make an apppointment yet? Matron has not said anything about the plate yet.

Don't forget to send my drawing pads. The Black one you gave me, and the other one with the address in it.

Please do not send any more food <u>yet</u>?

Did Aunt Elise's lot arrive?

1 An aunt.

I must end now. I hope this letter is 'newsey' enough.
I am afraid the chocolate milk needs a spoon, so could you send
one?
Your loving son
Keith

n.d. (PM 16 October 1932)   Lamb A/Christ's Hospital

Dear Mother,
Please do as you said with the 2/6. I am doing some painting in my
sketch work and am going to try my hand at embroidery in art.

My picture that I have designed is this:

[sketch follows of Robin Hood type archer in front of trees,
aiming at stag]

I hope you can come down soon and get my models that I have
made. Please send some coarse and fine sandpaper, some dead
matches, and – if possible – some white paint. I wrote to Mr James
at the beginning of term. I have played in two matches, scoring three
tries in one and one in the other.

We had one v Lamb B, and were 40–0 by half time, when they
gave up, and asked to make it more even. I had a bathe to-day, my
third this term. We had a lecture last night about two British officers
who tried to escape from Turkey by pretending to be mad. Their
idea was that the Turks would get tired of them and send them
home. But in the end they were exchanged. Will I have to write to
Auntie B. and Aunt Elise? I shan't have much time as I am a swab[1]
now. I will write to Tony as soon as possible. I have left your letter
in the changing-room and the mon. won't let me get it, so I must
answer it properly another time. I will write on Wednesday if I
remember – please remind me if you've time.
Your loving son
Keith
PS My swabmaster gave me a pot of black-currant jam, because the
other mons. did not like it. It's much nicer this term, with all the
snobs gone up into the senior dorm and only one beastly monitor
instead of about 4.

---

1   A kind of 'fag', doing odd jobs for a senior pupil, a swabmaster.

55. *To Marie J. Douglas*   BL 56355 f.106

n.d. [1932–3]   Lamb A/Christ's Hospital

Dear Mother,

I was unexpectedly taken out to tea so could not write till late, and this will have to be a short letter. I have not done many drawings yet, only a knight and a design for a menu which I thought we might send to Mrs Lynch-Staunton. Something like this. [sketch of design for menu: two Tudor waiters and horse and rider.] I must make some fishing boats. I have now two and a cutter, also a destroyer, and an aeroplane, and two racing yachts. [sketches of them with inscriptions including:] small ones which you said would be useless/ stuck on paper with jelly and other just on paper. [sketch of plane] Aeroplane – view from back [another sketch of plane, with words 'even has a dashboard']. Well I must say goodbye and post this. Your loving son Keith

THANKS VERY MUCH FOR LOVELY PARCEL.

[on verso] NEXT PLANE will look like this. [sketch of seaplane]

56. *To Marie J. Douglas*   BL 56355 f.107

n.d. [1932–3]   Lamb A/Christ's Hospital

Dear Mother,

Thanks very much for your letters and parcel.

I have gone and lost your letter again though – but I will try to answer a few of the questions.

I am not under Mr Edwards[1] again, but am under another nice master, Mr Tidmarsh. I have seen quite a lot of Wilkinson, Barnes and Pascoe. I have started a model-making firm with some of the other boys, so please if there is any Durofix or Seccotine in the house, send it.

The models we have made are these. [Sketches with titles under them:] '(Dutch Yacht)' '(Cutter)' '(tiny fishing boat on paper with wooden jetty)' '(tinier still fishing boat on paper)' 'Lyons cake box with racing Yacht on sea of crumpled paper painted green flecked with white' 'decorative drawings on paper stuck round sides', a

---

1 Housemaster of 'Lamb A' (see *KD* pp.33–4), a very popular master with whom Douglas was to fall out.

sketch of the 'top view' of this and three more sketches together with sketch and comment 'length of yacht is about' [and another sketch.] I made Dutch Yacht, first tiny fishing boat; and yacht on box.

I am getting on quite well in Greek (3 week order – 5th). I came bottom (19) in Maths because I lost a paper. Other orders. Latin 2nd German 2nd Form 2nd. No other orders given. I do not do Geography this term.

I am not doing embroidery in art this term but a design for a class-room frieze. Something like this [sketch with castle, trees and knights jousting].

I must stop now, as my swabmaster will be wanting me any moment – yesterday I had to go over to Mother Hubbard's[2] for him to get a pint of milk, and carry it back in a jamjar without a top on it!

By the way, Mother Hubbard does not as far as I know, sell home-made jam.

Now I have forgotten what I had to say, but I don't think it was important so
Goodbye till next letter,
Your loving son
Keith
(Swabaster wants me)[3]

57. *To Headmaster of Christ's Hospital*   BL 56355 ff.108–9
    (fragment)[1]

n.d. [December 1935]

hunger first made Preece trades-monitor, and then broke open the cupboard. Someone told Mr Edwards[2] that I had kept the key in order to have the biscuits to myself. He believed it joyfully.

He then had me in, and, with tears in his eyes (this is no sarcasm, but truth) told me how rottenly I had treated him ever since I had

---

2   The tuck shop.
3   The handwriting of the last three lines shows his hurry.

---

1   Autograph copy of a letter, three surviving pages of a seven-page letter; Douglas had 'borrowed' a rifle from the school armoury and was threatened with explusion (see *KD* pp.34–5)
2   His Housemaster (see Letter 56).

been in the house, adding that he would accept no apology, as he knew I should not mean it. I did apologise, whereupon he growled that he preferred deeds to words.

So I am a thief – driven out of all self-control by what I fancied to be injustice: a liar – to a man who could believe anything untrue against me. But you have behaved squarely to me in all things save one, and I have told you no lies. I have nothing against Major Hodgson,[3] who sets spies and expects lies. But to Mr Edwards who expects loyalty and gives none, I cannot be loyal. If I were a monitor I would be loyal to the house – and tell him fewer lies than any other monitor – bar Nash.

But that would not be hard.

Now (if you have read thus far) you have my own point of view. Everything I have set down is true.

I shall expect punishment. But you cannot give anything worse than insults you heaped on me before Major Hodgson. If you could have refrained from laughing, when you were discussing whether to make or break a boy's career, I would not mind so much – As it is you cannot punish me more. This letter is for you and I ask you not to show it to anyone but Mr Edwards. He shall see that it is the truth, though scilicet he will say he knew nothing of some of it.

Perhaps he could have guessed, had he not been so ready to believe things against me. If you remember that in addition to these things I have had boils, work, extra work, games and extra Certificate A parades to think of perhaps you will think less hardly of me.

Yours sincerely

Keith Douglas

P.S. If I have been rude, I must apologise. It is hard to write coolly of something about which I feel so strongly.

58. *To Marie J. Douglas*   BL 56355 f.110

n.d. [December 1936]

[on top, above start:] I would actually rather have the money than books from all those people. The more we collect the more likely it is that we can get you a fur coat.

---

3   In charge of the School's Cadet Corps.

Dear Mother,

Thank you for your letter. I don't know exactly when I get in but I expect it is 10.30. Is Mrs Rudd[1] with you now, and/or will she be there for Christmas? Have you seen Mrs Phelps lately or managed to call on Mrs Rochford? The poem has not been printed in the December number of *Sussex County Mag*: so I shall have to wait till January.[2]

6/- sounds very little for a nightgown. Or is the stuff paid for? As to books I have found several already from which you can choose. No catalogue yet, so I may find something I particularly want. I was talking to Rance last Sunday about Sandhurst and he says that you can get in there quite free and pay nothing there. Bishop left from Ba: 'B'[3] last term and passed in 90th, and he has nothing to pay. When you go into the army you get £50 for uniform from the army and apparently Housey also help if you do well.

I am very much inclined to mistrust the Headmaster in this after the way he behaves otherwise. He put Sir Reginald[4] off when he asked about my returning to Lamb A by saying that he wanted me to make good in Mid: B.[5]

I now find that he has taken careful precaution that I shall not be house-captain and probably not get a study. He never told me as I suppose he imagines I will go on behaving myself better if I think I may be house-captain.

Whereas the only reason I shall behave myself is that I have no doubt he would get rid of me at the slightest excuse rather than admit a mistake. He himself is not fit to be a house-monitor with such a sense of justice, let alone a head-master. His whole character is shown in his behaviour to people under him. He treats the masters very obviously as inferiors, and when he was taking us in the library

1   Mrs Douglas had shared a house at Boarshead, Sussex, with Mrs Rudd. Her nephew, Tony, who lived with her and was four years younger than Keith (see *KD* p.16) wrote a memoir of his service in the RAF, *One Boy's War* (1990) which includes comments on the news of Douglas's death (pp.102–3). Mrs Douglas and Keith continued their visits when the Rudds moved to Painswick in 1932 (see *KD* p.25).
2   'Pan in Sussex', *Sussex County Magazine*, January 1937.
3   'Barnabus B' a House at Christ's Hospital.
4   Sir Reginald Spence, a retired wine merchant, acted as a kind of guardian to a series of boys from his old school, Christ's Hospital (see *KD* p.25).
5   See above: Douglas had been allowed to return to school on condition he changed Houses to Middleton B (see *KD* p.35).

and a small boy was sent in by another master, to get a chair our polite head master bit his head off and kept up a solid fire of abuse until he was out of the room, as if it was the boy's fault. It's disgusting that such a man should earn money. However I still smile politely at him and laugh at his jokes.

Your loving son.

Keith

59. *To Edmund Blunden*   Texas

28 January 1938   Middleton B/Christ's Hospital

Dear Mr Blunden,

Thank you very much for your letter. I have shewn it to Mr Roberts,[1] who asked me to write to you originally, and to Mr Macklin,[2] who has taken over most of my English work from Mr Roberts, now that I have dropped History.[3] Mr Roberts agreed with you more or less entirely, I believe, but he will write to you himself.

Mr Macklin however, since most of the Old Blue[4] authors are by no means fresh ground to me (and he thinks I should tackle something on which my mind is more or less a blank) suggests that I should study the one least known to me and least noticed by the school English curriculum, Leigh Hunt. He had already started me off, (before your letter arrived), upon a course of drama, to specialise in the Elizabethans, but including some work on mimes and miracle plays from classical times.[5]

I have an Oxford Edition of Chaucer's Works which I read for my own amusement but I am afraid I have not read any comment on them, except G. K. Chesterton's book.

If this compromise between your plan and Mr Macklin's original

---

1 The Hon. David Roberts was an extremely popular master who taught Douglas History and befriended him; see *KD* p.48. A letter he wrote about Douglas survives: BL 56356 ff 81–5.

2 Douglas's English teacher, who became a Yeats scholar.

3 As there were no 'English Grecians' at Christ's Hospital, Douglas gained his scholarship in History on the understanding he would read English.

4 Former pupils of Christ's Hospital: these include Coleridge, Lamb, Leigh Hunt, Peele and Blunden.

5 Douglas's Housemaster at Middleton B rescued Douglas's exercise books from the wastepaper basket. They are now in the British Library (Add Mss 59834, 61938–9; some items are reproduced in *Miscellany*).

one of general reading and Elizabethan poetry and drama will do I will start on it as soon as possible. I have already begun the drama, which is keeping me very busy. I hope this does not seem to you an impatient and impertinent rejection of your advice: if you still think it would be better for me to take all the O.B. authors I can start work on them as soon as your letter arrives to say so.
Yours sincerely
Keith Douglas

60. To Christine Woodcock   BL 56355 ff.163–7

n.d. [?January 1938]   Middleton B/Christ's Hospital

[At the top] I have got a poem taken by *New Verse*[1] and 'The Mummers' poem mother sent you for the comp: is one I sent to Edmund Blunden which he liked best of all.
THIS IS A HELLUVA LETTER. TAKE YOUR TIME.
Dear Chris,
M.H.R. for your birthday and really thank you for your letter – it was lovely to find it waiting for me when I arrived in the evening and the rain. I shall love writing to you because we never had to make friends, we just were more or less immediately, and I know there's nothing I need leave out of letters to you. There are millions of things I can't tell mother and long to tell someone, so I shall never lack any material for letters. You are in for an interesting time.

I am writing during prep: in my study – a dirty little room which I will describe. It is wooden mostly – partitioned off from the dayroom in which most of the house work. It has a half glass door, and windows looking into the dayroom as well as outside. All these are curtained with white stuff which has a green repeating pattern woven into it. The wooden and plaster walls are green (dark) up to about waist high and then yellow plaster, or window. These walls are covered with initials and burnt lettering of various kinds (particularly the lower part of the door, which is brown). Indelible fingermarks of past owners are profusely distributed. I have a little table, a lot of books, an armchair, a deckchair and a settle. The wall is decorated with a large curtain (same stuff as the others) hiding where I wrenched away a hideous fixture school bookcase, and

---

1 'Dejection', *New Verse* March 1938.

49

elsewhere with various small coloured reproductions of Van Gogh and 1 by Pollitzer, and a large tempera picture by me of soldiers at bayonet practice. This picture dominates the study and catches anyone coming in full in the eye. It was painted with the idea of taking people's attention off the dirt. The composition, colouring and technique are mainly modern, but the soldiers' attitudes and faces are intentionally reminiscent of old French paintings, religious canvases and early stained glass.[2] The colours used are 2 greens, 2 greys, red, red-brown, purple, mauve, very dark blue-grey, black, white, and yellow. Predominant colours are green and red. This picture is the most important thing in the decorative scheme, such as it is.

Also in the study are a card table, covered with a rug of the Douglas tartan, (mainly green), and a dirty fireplace, with a fairly cheerful fire in it. Boys from other houses come periodically down the asphalt path outside in the dark to tap on my window and talk through it when I open it. Outside in the dayroom I can hear forms and benches creaking under people doing prep. On my mantelpiece is a model of a Greek Brigantine with all her sails but two sets and some rigging missing. I hope you can see the study now.

I myself am in a long coat of blue kersey, white linen bands at my throat, fourteen silver buttons down the front of me, black knee-breeches and yellow stockings. I have black velvet cuffs turned back, with more silver buttons. Now can you see me inside the study?

I am contemplating turning our fez into a lamp-shade, but can't bring myself to make a hole through the top of it.

[sketch: sailing ship]

My hand got tired of writing so I let it draw you the brigantine. I made her from a photo and she is called ΑΠοΛΛΩ (Apollo). There was a figurehead of Loxias Apollo on the front but it got knocked off. The villainous crew of three, the captain [sketch], the mate [sketch], and the cabin boy [sketch], all made of cotton wool, were lost overboard. The two lifeboats are adrift, you can see them beside her. The stern is carved (chalk) gold scroll-work, with the name cut, and painted in black on a pale blue ground. In the single cabin are a plain table and two bunks, but no lantern.

Chris, in spite of all your Pat Rats (or is it Wratts?) and Glessings,

---

2 This anticipates his use in 1944 of a postcard (see Letter 312) as source for an illustration to *Alamein* ('Pietà').

are you rather lonely? I wonder, because you and I may have a lot of things in common. The other thing I wanted to say was, to tell you about the sort of clothes I would design you, if I did design any. You could look (to use your favourite word), marvellous, if you would only wear the right clothes for your figure and colouring. I would hesitate to tell you in a way because you would be surrounded with boys in no time and forget all about me.

First, never wear dresses when you needn't. Your figure is either willowy or skinny. If you wear a roughish, but well-cut tweed coat and skirt, brown or dark green, plain or check (small check), you are willowy and lovely open-air lady immediately – lipstick and nail-polish to match would help. In your thin dress you are skinny and unhappy-looking. Go in for checks and autumn sort of woven scarves and you would be the best of yourself, and attractive. You may despise sporty people, but they dress well.

Here's a try at your coat and skirt.
[sketch: woman in sporty clothes and 'darkish stockings', 'wear tough "golfy" sort of shoes']
I've put you in a wind because you look best windswept. I apologise for the fact that the wind blows two different ways at once.

You wear a pale blue polo sweater, but you would look yards better in dark brown or green. Your colours are the colours of woods and fields in summer and autumn – open air colours – the best colours in the world. Chris don't be offended by all this, but I would love you to look as nice as I know you could. The reds and yellows you wear now aren't the good clean eternal colours that the medieval people and the Greeks – the best dressed the world has ever seen – wore. They weren't thought of until mass-production and state-run brothels were invented.

Will you do this thing for me and dress like this, (if your mother will let you).

If I can do anything to look better for you, tell me when you write. Who knows, even I might look presentable with someone else's advice!

I have had to write a new last page to this letter because I read through this morning what I wrote during prep last night and felt sure you would think it as silly as I do this morning, unless you read it at night. I don't know, but I seem to have an infinite capacity for dreaming stupid dreams at nights and evenings, and they get into the letters I write then.

One dream that must come true is that we are going to be having a damn good time together next hols and afterwards. Write as soon as you can and answer all this.
Yours
Keith

61. *To Edmund Blunden*[1]   Texas

13 May 1938   Middleton B/Christ's Hospital

Dear Mr Blunden,

I am writing to tell you how I have been spending my time during last term and the Easter holidays. I don't know whether Mr Macklin, or Mr Roberts has written to you, but in any case you may be interested to have my own account of it.

I began by reading some miracle plays and various early comedies, *Ralph Roister Doyster* and *Gammer Gurton* among them. Simultaneously with these I studied Leigh Hunt's life and works and wrote an essay on him and another on his poetry.[2] I also read Allardyce Nicholl on *Masks, Mimes and Miracles*, and on *The Development of the Theatre*. I took notes on this but did not write anything actually about it although I used it with reference to other essays.

I read two plays each of Lyly, Peele, and Greene, and wrote on all three of them together. Then I read Nashe's *Lenten Stuff* and reread *Tamburlaine* taking notes on the verse. After that I wrote a very hasty essay on the verse of *Tamburlaine*, the matter of which pleased Messrs. Macklin and Roberts more than any of my other efforts, although the expression, being hurried, was bad.

---

1 For Blunden's reply see *Miscellany* p.36. The correspondence between Blunden and A.H. Buck published in *More Than a Brother* (1996), ed. Carol Z. Rothcopf and Barry Webb, includes a letter to Blunden from Buck, Douglas's former Latin master, (3 May 1938): '[David Roberts] would welcome a chance to talk to you about Douglas, that highly promising but difficult young man you're taking at Merton in October. The things to say about him are not easy to put on paper and would proceed more comfortably by questions and answers. Chances of an action for libel would be reduced, and so forth.'

2 This proved useful in filling *The Cherwell* when Douglas edited it; the 1 June 1940 issue included 'The Poetry of James Henry Leigh Hunt' (reprinted in *Miscellany* pp.63–5).

In the holidays I read a long essay on Lyly by Bond, and all his plays, and wrote notes on them, from which I am now writing an essay. I managed to read Heywood's *Woman Killed with Kindness* – and *Sense and Sensibility* and *Amaryllis at the Fair*[3] as a change.

Another book I read was James Hilton's *And Now Goodbye*. I wonder what you think of his writing? I have only read four of his books; and taking them as short stories – which, except for *Lost Horizon*, they seemed to be – I admire them.

I have been attempting some short stories myself, and have sent two in for a Short Story Competition run by the Cambridge Literary Agency.[4]

This term I shall go on working at Elizabethan drama, which really interests me.

I hope this letter will not bother you, and that you wanted to know what I have told you.
Yours sincerely
Keith Douglas
PS I am sending 2 pictures to the Sussex Art Exhibition if I can finish them in time.

62. *To Marie J. Douglas*   BL 56355 f.111

Monday evening [n.d. July 1938]   Middleton B/Christ's Hospital

Dear Mother,
I did manage to write you a short line on Monday, but my swab didn't post it. I couldn't possibly write today, until now, having 2 exams and a Corps competition, and having arranged to jump Nabob this evening. We had to remove a loose hind shoe first, and after much wrenching, got it off. Burdett[1] also jumped, for the first time, and got on very well, although he hasn't quite got the rhythm yet.

Pam and Pearl and Chris duly came down on Saturday, and I think enjoyed themselves – they spent the afternoon wandering round the school and had tea in the study. We hope they are coming

3   A novel, by Richard Jefferies (1887).
4   No record survives; a story by Douglas about entering a poetry competition, however, does survive: 'Drunk', reprinted in *Miscellany* pp.50–2.

1   A school friend at Christ's Hospital (see *KD*, esp. p.49).

down again in about a fortnight, and will stay a bit later.

Cunningham[2] has returned from Henley, where Kent school won almost everything they went in for, and says they will be on the broads from 6th to 13th August. I said I thought I could go, but would possibly have to go for only 4 days and come back early. The people are allowing me £1 for fares, 5/- a day for entertainment and 16/- a day for food. I doubt if I'll eat all that so I ought to make a bit on it. They don't seem to expect any change. So I can come back after camp and take the boy for the 4th and 5th and go up on the 6th stay the week and come back. He will get as much of me as he would have before. Anything more than £1 spent on fares I can take out of the immense food money allowance. I told Christine he is coming on the third. She wants to go to the Pony Club camp, but I haven't found out when it is yet.

I will write to her again this evening, also to ask about p.g.[3] or not. I hope I have earned about £3 in prizes today – it remains to be seen. I get a 25/- Exhibitioner's prize anyway, and possibly a George Moore Divinity prize, though I doubt it.[4]

I must stop now and write to Chris before I go to bed. Sorry this is so late.

Love
Keith

63. *To Christine Woodcock*   BL 56355 ff.170–2

Monday [n.d.]   Stakers/Southwater Sx.

[ink sketch: cat with half its body shaded] There is a semi-detached cat here
Dear Chris,
Since writing the card which will arrive with this I have had a telegram from Mrs Rochfort to say that she can't have me until the 29th, that is, Thursday. So I am staying on here until then but it

2 George Cunningham, an American boy at Christ's Hospital: Douglas was looking after him to gain some pocket money. After Douglas's death, in December 1945 he wrote telling Mrs Douglas that he was naming his son 'Keith Douglas Cunningham' (Brotherton).
3 Paying guests, perhaps?
4 Douglas's surviving prizes are among his books, collected at the Brotherton Library. They are listed in 'Keith Douglas' Books', *Book Collector*, Summer 1981.

doesn't matter, we'll have a week. In that case I will come on Thursday evening – would you have the time and inclination to meet me and come out to a film and/or supper? If you would like that reply, by returnish, and say what film. It is poss: I shan't have the money, in which case you'll have to take me and I'll pay you back. Did you get the frames? No need to ask if you got the camera. I am rather hard up at the moment, because Mother promised to send some money and forgot to enclose it. So I have only about my fare. But perhaps the belated cheque will turn up, or I'll get my p.o. savings book back in time to get that £4.15s out. It took me hours to pack and now I'll have to undo it all again.

In spite of the busy farm life etc, I don't seem to have nearly as little time for letters as you do. I think little of you.

I went to supper with Daddy Roberts, ex history master, and wife, where we ate mushrooms and told ghost stories. The crisis, for once, was not mentioned.[1]

Lizzy has gone to be governed this morning, in a furious temper. I gave her a ticking off the other day for behaving so queenly and Rünt, one of the Dutch girls came and congratulated me afterwards and said she did not know that anyone dare to say such things.

We went to South Riding[2] again and the Lancia broke down about halfway. We had to push it about ¾ mile in very wet darkness to a garage. But Mrs Brodie made six journeys in her little Morris and got us all in and out again in time to see the Big Film. We were going to Worthing to see *Time and the Conways* – it's a good thing we didn't.

We had a party of Housey people here yesterday and played an absurd but amusing game and ate mushrooms. I went to gym the other day, taken by a master who has just come back from learning the real dirt in Denmark. We sweated blood for an hour and a quarter. First [pencil sketch: man running] running with knees up, then [pencil sketch: man leaping] leaping, then various jumps [pencil sketch: man jumping] and toe touchings [pencil sketch: man toe touching] and head, [pencil sketch: prostrate man], chest [pencil sketch: prostrate man] and legs [pencil sketch: man with raised legs] lifting, more [pencil sketch: man running] running. Parallel bars

1 The 'Munich Crisis', following Hitler's occupation of Czechoslovakia, led to the Munich agreement, signed on 29 September 1938.
2 The farm belonging to Captain and Mrs Brodie, who entertained Christ's Hospital boys there. They had a fifteen-year-old daughter, Liz.

[pencil sketches: man exercising] and horse and mat [pencil sketches of man using them]. Well well. I must stop.

Darling I am sorry I can't come today, I'm longing to see you again you sweet person. Rite me a nice luving letter, you're on my mind and in my heart.

All my love
Keith
[pencil sketches: horse, 'I am riding Gonaway', lady in riding outfit, 'genial Moss Bros Hacking Coat', rearing horse, 'Sheila is well']
I knew about the Kris[?], didn't I tell you? Has Pam been to see Tim yet? Hurry and write.
[8 pencil sketches of horses at Brenda Jones's farm with captions]

64. *To Edmund Blunden*   Texas

13 September 1938   The Rectory, Withyham[1]

Dear Mr Blunden,
This is a letterful of questions, which I hope will not bother you too much.
1. I have received a notice requiring me to come into residence on October 7th. Is this an earlier date than the day on which the whole College comes up? I have heard that freshmen are required to come up earlier, and was not certain whether October 7th was the earlier date or not.
2. Would it be unusual for me to have luggage, etc., sent to Merton 2 or 3 days before I am required to come into residence?
3. I have not been able to get a list of College rules – to whom should I apply for these?
4. Some months ago I had sent me from Merton College a statement that the amount of my Exhibition was £30 p.a., and that a further grant was to be made, of £50, subject to adjustment if 'further emolument' was obtained. Well, further emolument has been obtained, but I still need the £50 p.a. Would it be possible for you to find out what adjustment, if any, has taken place; and can you tell me how this money would be paid, or allowed me?

I am sorry to buzz at you with so many queries, some of which must seem to you pointless – but I shall be bewildered enough even

1 Where Mrs Douglas and Keith stayed with the Miles family; see *KD* p.25

when all these are answered. When I see you I shall still be loaded with a charge of more particular enquiries.

My address will be the one at the top of this letter until the 19th, from which date until the 27th September I shall be at Stakers, Southwater, Horsham. After the 27th until I go up to Merton I shall be at St Hugh's Cottage, Oakleigh Rd., Little Common, Bexhill. Not the least of my difficulties is this continual migration while I am making arrangements.

Yours sincerely
Keith Douglas

Three

1938–1939

65. *To Margaret Stanley-Wrench*   BL 57977 f.1

Saturday   [Letterhead] Merton College, Oxford
[n.d. October 1938]

Dear Miss Stanley-Wrench,
Mr Blunden, referring to you as the Senior Poetess in statu pu.,[1] a
rather forbidding title, suggests that I, being about the most junior
incipient poet, introduce myself to you. I said you would be too
busy and know too many people already; and if you are and do, I
shan't be particularly put out if you don't answer this.

But if you have time to come, perhaps you will invite yourself
to tea with me on any day next week, except Tuesday, at about four
o'clock?
Yours sincerely
Keith Douglas
P.S. You won't have to read my poems.

66. *To Margaret Stanley-Wrench*   BL 57977 f.2

n.d. [October/November   [Letterhead] Merton College, Oxford
1938] (card)

Dear Margaret,
Thanks awfully. I'd love to come on Sunday, although I shall be
terrified of venturing within a women's college: won't I be stopped
and interrogated at the frontier? If I get through unhurt, expect me
at 4.0 o'clock.

Thanks for giving me directions. I hate asking. I ought to have
done the same for you really.
Yours
Keith D.
[ink sketches: horseback riders, 'mine aren't as confidently drawn as
yours I'm afraid']
[At top] A friend of mine, Marjorie Walters, in Somerville says she
knows you. Don't you think she's awfully nice? I hope so because
she wants to know you better.

---

1   *In statu pupillari*, in a condition of pupillage, i.e. an undergraduate.

67. *To Margaret Stanley-Wrench*   BL 57977 f.8

Friday [n.d. [?] November   [Letterhead] Merton College, Oxford
1938]

Dear Margaret,
What about sherry? You didn't finish explaining and I was, as you
saw, snatched away by that rather forcible Canadian without even
being able to say goodbye politely (sorry) at the end. What time to
where am I to go for sherry? If you don't manage to let me know,
I will be at the Moorish at 7.45, or earlier, outside unless I find
someone within.
Yours
Keith

68. *To Margaret Stanley-Wrench*   BL 57977 f.5

n.d.   [Letterhead] Merton College, Oxford

Dear Margaret,
Thank you for your letter and invitation (accepted, thanks very
much). I am a lousy dancer so I hope the rest of you aren't too good.
I expect Mary [one word illegible] will come if she possibly can,
being very keen on dancing and pretty good, I believe.
    I shall turn up and Sassoon[1] at the English Club tonight.
Tomorrow I've got to go to see an eye man in London. I keep trying
to think what [it] is I'm doing on Thursday – I know it's something
important, but blow me if I know what. I think I shall stop, it's a
bit of a strain writing with this pen, although as you see I am
gradually evolving a handwriting to fit it. You will be glad to hear
I have tidied up my room.
Yours
Keith

1 Hamo Sassoon, at Merton College with Douglas: nephew of the poet Siegfried
   Sassoon.

69. *To John Waller*   Graham

n.d.   [Letterhead] Merton College, Oxford

Dear Mr Waller,
I have been unable to sell any copies of *Bolero* owing to the fact that
you omitted to say the price of it, and no one either knew this or
was willing to buy any without knowing it.[1] Sorry I've been too
busy to tell you before.
Yours sincerely
Keith Douglas

70. *To John Waller*   Graham

n.d. (card)   [Letterhead] Merton College, Oxford

Dear Mr Waller,
Here are what poems I can muster. I hope one or other of them
will be some use to you.[4]
Yours sincerely
Keith Douglas
Sorry they're v. carelessly typed.

71. *To Margaret Stanley-Wrench*   BL 57977 f.3

n.d. [December 1938[1]]   Crossways/ Little Common/ Bexhill

Dear Margaret,
Thanks awfully for your card – the comp. is much better. I'm
terribly sorry to have failed to send you a card but I never thought
you would send me one and didn't want to put you in the position
in which you have now put me. Excuse pencil because I have no
writing materials, being stranded at a Tea-Room with nowhere to
go, until we can find a house or flat.[2] I exercise horses every
morning: there is a skewbald pony (mare), a 17–hands hunter mare

---

1 Waller, himself an undergraduate, edited the Oxford magazine *Bolero*.

---

1 'Kristin' and 'Forgotten the red leaves' were published in *Bolero* Winter 1938.

---

1 Dated by Margaret Stanley-Wrench.
2 Mrs Douglas had had to let the bungalow she had then (see *KD* p.69).

with 8 inch ears, a chestnut thoroughbred mare, a black pony, a grey gelding and a gloomy little bay mare. They are respectively Peggy, Jill, Gail, Gipsy, Abbot and Molly. All but Molly are very fresh and provide some excitement. I have bought a red navvy's dinner handkerchief and a check cap, also a lovat weskit with brass buttons and so look very horsey indeed.

I have done nothing with the snow except sweep it away, and now its going, damn. I must stop and answer two other unexpected cards. Luckily I had no presents except five given me by hand so I've no letters to write.

Yours

Keith

I really haven't said enough about how I liked your card because I liked it very much.

72. *To Jean Turner*   Private Hands

n.d.(card)   [Letterhead] Merton College, Oxford

Dear Jean,

Would you like to come to tea some time before the end of term or did you have enough of me at the dance? Tell me at the English Club, if you're turning up to it. If not, scrawl a reply. You can easily say you're occupied for the rest of the term – I expect you are anyway.

Yours

Keith Douglas

If you can do lunch and not tea, say so.

73. *To Jean Turner*   Private Hands

n.d. (card)   [Letterhead] Merton College, Oxford

Dear Jean,

I have got to RSVP about Eng. Club C. Secs tea at St Hildas, to you. I can come, but where in St Hildas?

Keith D

74. *To Jean Turner*   Private Hands

n.d. (card)   [Letterhead] Merton College, Oxford

Dear Jean,
Take as much sympathy as you want. And Thursday or Friday will
be OK, let me know which. How do you know it doesn't irritate
me to have esq. left off my envelopes? Actually, I prefer it to be left
off.
Keith

75. *To Jean Turner*   Private Hands

n.d. (card)   [Letterhead] Merton College, Oxford

Dear Jean,
Can you come to the Exhibition in the morning on Friday? Because
I have just realised I am painting someone's portrait at 2.30, and
taking her out to tea afterwards. Would you like to include yourself
in the tea?
    If you can't come in the morning when can you come? Saturday
p.m. is no good: otherwise I think most any time.
Keith

76. *To Jean Turner*   Private Hands

n.d. [March 1939] (card)   [Letterhead] Merton College, Oxford

Dear Jean,
I knew there would be something – but there are other evenings, so
I'll wait until you say with awful clarity that you have no, not one
evening this week, before I go to flicks by myself. So if you can raise
an evening this week say which and I'll wait going till I hear.
    Next week I have no exam from Monday afternoon till Saturday
morning so I hope you'll find at least one thing to do with me during
that time. I am quite keen on the idea of wandering in the
countryside on one afternoon, but I fear you won't be.
    It's a good thing you didn't come to flicks today as I am utterly
cast down, in spite of selling 5 books for 11/-, so I can pay for you
when you say you can come! Hurry up and say.
Keith

26 March 1939   Preston Cottage, Sidley, Sussex

Dear Mr Blunden,

I don't know whether this will catch you in time, but I hoped to
see you at the end of term, and this letter will have to say what I
meant to say then. The week of no exams during P. Mods was more
taken up than I expected, because I had to do some of Hamo's share
of preparing for Anglo Saxon, since he was busy about his other
subjects. Most of the time here since I came down has been taken
up doctoring a sick horse with a constantly renewed rash which
takes half the day to wash and the other half to anoint. My essay is
only half done, and will therefore probably arrive written in pencil
on a notebook during intervals of cycling in France.[2]

Meanwhile I have not obtained two certificates from you which
I meant to get at the end of term. One is for the Mitchell City of
London people[3] and they want it at the end of this month – this, if
you can conscientiously sign it, is to be a tutor's certificate of
residence and satisfactory progress.

It is rather important that I should have this one, because if I don't
get the Mitchell money I shall be about £12 short at the beginning
of next term for paying my battels. The other is a certificate of
residence to be sent up immediately at the beginning of next term,
and as they are very late with the money as a rule, I should like to
send it the moment I arrive. The Mitchell one is to say I have been
in residence, the other to say I am in residence. If you could send
me the Mitchell certificate, to this address as soon as you have time,
I should be very glad.

All that remains to do to my essay is to write it. That is to say I

---

1 For Blunden's reply, see *Miscellany* p.39. Another mysterious reference to
Douglas occurs in the Buck–Blunden correspondence, *More than a Brother*:
'Sorry about [Keith] Douglas. H[ead] M[aster] says if kindly talk is required,
Hornsby (his late housemaster) is the man: but if a 'rond turn', then he himself
will act. Anyway, I think H.M. would welcome further detail' (from Buck to
Blunden, 16 March 1939). The subject could be Douglas's work as this letter
shows him to be well behind in it. (Blunden writes to Buck with his recollections
of Douglas, 5 October, 1944.)
2 Douglas and Hamo Sassoon went on a cycling tour (see following letters) and
KD pp. 74-5
3 Trustees of a fund from which Douglas received a grant while at Oxford.

have got all the notes and the general outline, and references and quotations, so I will send it as soon as possible.
Yours sincerely
Keith Douglas
PS If the certificate comes to this address I will see it is sent to the Mitchell people at once, even if I am in France. I have brought home Chaucer, Gower, Saintsbury.[4] KCD

78. *To Marie J. Douglas*   BL 56355 f.113

(Post Card, Quay at Dieppe) n.d. [April 1939]   Dieppe

Arrived 2.0 a m this morning and slept on boat till 8.0, then came ashore. We are off to Amiens now. The crossing was fairly calm and warm. It's quite hot here.
Love
Keith

79. *To Marie J. Douglas*   BL 56355 f.112

(Post Card, Amiens Cathedral) n.d., [April 1939]

Got here in the dark it was about 100k. (80 miles?) Hamo and I got separated and only just rejoined last night as we were both in a crowd listening to M Daladier's broadcast.[1]
Love
K

80. *To Jean Turner*   Private Hands

n.d. (card)   [Letterhead] Merton College, Oxford

[At top] I told the ghastly Merton toughs and they will likely be waiting on you in a body and a rage.
Dear Jean,

---

4 Saintsbury's, *A Short History of English Literature*, annotated by Douglas, is in the *Brotherton* Library.

---

1 The French premier announced that Germany had broken the Munich Agreement.

No I haven't dropped you. On Tuesday evening I had been having a shot at not eating much and whether owing to that or summat else, I more or less passed out on the floor, and was not feeling so much like Helen Simpson as just plain Hell ha ha. Anyway thank you very much I would like to come to the dance. I don't know when it is, so if you can bring yourself to give any relevant information and keep off errant 'buses, please let me know more; excuse pencil and the envelope, a souvenir from Soissons which has got to be used up.

Keith

81. *To Margaret Stanley-Wrench*   BL 57977 f.4

n.d. ['Spring 1939'[1]] (card)   [Letterhead] Merton College, Oxford

Dear Margaret,

Will you come on Friday next week then? Thank you for your letter. I will try and turn up to the English Club this evening. I haven't seen *Bolero* – I shall borrow one, probably yours – may I? If so bring it with you next Friday. I don't even know which poems he has put in it of mine.[2]

I'm not going to Mr Waller's party next Saturday, unless one just walks in. Anyway I couldn't, I'm having 2 people to dinner.

I haven't met Herbert Howarth,[3] although I've often written to him or had letters from him.

Well I'll see you on Friday, minus cold I hope. I don't think I've caught it, touch wood.

Yours

Keith

P.S. I have actually written another poem. Great stuff. I've only shown it to Hamo Sassoon who said 'Ugh! Strange and awkward', and a Canadian who read it without asking and said nothing.[4]

1 Dated by Margaret Stanley-Wrench.
2 'Point of View' and 'Sonnet: Curtaining this country' appeared in *Bolero* Spring 1939.
3 A leading light at Cambridge, he was the Cambridge editor of *Fords and Bridges*.
4 It is not possible to say which poem; it could be 'Poor Mary' (*CP* p.24).

[15 May 1939[2]]

So death the adept subtle amorist[3]
has cheated from you what I might have kept
fast in the queer casket of my heart.
You were beguiled to grant away that part
that was the whole of you. Then death crept
like a secret jeweller; the amethyst, the

treasure that I toil for, he took
O rich man, death, you sent your creature
from your country, disguised with life, to steal
a gem you never wanted. You cannot feel
its worth. She yielded with the first gesture
of her awakened hand. My darling – look –

it was death's emissary who took your love
to hoard it in the quiet land, nowhere.
He followed death's instructions from the start,
and when you said goodbye, he stepped apart
delivering the stone to death, the rare
bright plunder. Death retains the precious stuff

Still I, the loving fool and last courtier
attend you. And my service is still yours
for little profit you enjoy of it,
use my emotion and occasional wit
to colour each opaque hour, the course,
despoiled lady, of time you must spend here

[On verso of envelope] With apologies for the unavoidable use of
pencil, K

---

1 Douglas had started going out with her in February: see biographies of
   recipients.
2 Dated by Betty Sze on the envelope: 'Written Monday 15th and mislaid/Given
   me Wednesday 17th May'.
3 'So death the adept subtle amorist' first published in *Cherwell*, 27 April 1940
   with the title 'To a Lady on the Death of Her First Love'.

n.d.   [Letterhead] Merton College, Oxford

[on envelope sketch of a crest of crowned heart with wings over flame and the motto:] toujours en avant

Dear Betty

These lines, written by the famous poet in his youth, just before he went to the dogs over a woman, are more sincere than they sound.[1] The trouble with him was that he always fell in love with the wrong girls, and wrote no novels about it. After his affair with a Chinese girl, who treated him shockingly, the poor poet cracked up completely, and was sent down from Oxford, where (of course) he had just commenced a promising career.

I wonder, perhaps you will be able to sell this one day, but meanwhile I expect you'll forget to keep it. I'm afraid it will get into one of those trunks at Guildford and that will be that.

I have said enough silly things for there to be no need to write you a love letter, besides, if this gets shown to Peter[2] – darling I'm so sorry, you can't even answer back, and I should hate you to tear the letter up. I'd better send you a photograph and then you can spit on it or throw darts at it when you come to the infuriating bits in this letter.

If I paint you a picture, it will be Hamlet saying to Ophelia 'I did love you once', although in this case it is more likely to be Hamlet found floating.[3]

Perhaps you would like Ophelia for your name? Ophelia Sze; perhaps not. Personally although I admit Margaret isn't good, Marguerite Sze sounds well enough. The trouble with Margaret is that it is Marguerite faded, all the scent gone and a poor dusty blossom altogether.

Do you remember which piece of wall we sat on, where for 10 seconds you became one of the world's great heroines? I shan't bother to go and sit there but my shadow will be on duty for me. When you have given me up and spoilt the [sketch of heart with blots on it] few good bits there are left in my heart, you will see that shadow every time you come past late at night. Maybe it will come

---

1 The accompanying poem, 'What in the pattern of your face'.
2 Presumably her current boyfriend?
3 Douglas painted two portraits of her (one in Hall's possession, one in Graham's).

and block the way of whatever man is with you, like the angel standing in the the donkey's path.[4]

I suppose you have read A.E.Housman. If you will take as from me the saddest and most moving love poem he ever wrote, and read it well, you will have much better what I want to say than I could tell you.[5]

I will forget you sometimes, and since I must be sad sometimes, I may as well be sad about you, and who knows what gracious experiences await me when one is complete. There are so many for everyone

> Stars, I have seen them fall
> But when they drop and die,
> No star is lost at all
> From all the star sown sky.[6]

Good old sky! I shall keep my eye on it.
Yours etc.
The old flame
[sketch of flame]
P.S. buy me a telescope

[Accompanying poem]
To his lady, who must not be too critical, these verses of a bewildered poet.[7]

> What in the pattern of your face
> was writing to my eye, which came at once
> like a pioneer in your beauty's land
> to find that venerable secret stand
> somehow carved there; and ever since
> has rested still, enchanted by the place?

---

4 When, next year, Douglas's wrote 'Canoe' the returning spirit was more benevolent, 'kiss[ing] your mouth lightly'.
5 Douglas could be referring to 'From Far, from Eve and Morning'.
6 The first half of 'Stars, I have seen them fall'.
7 'What in the pattern of your face' first published in *Cherwell*, 9 March 1940 with the title 'Stranger' and dedication 'For Y.C.S.'.

Cast up along your eyes' dark shore
or in the carved red cave of lips
my heart would spend a solitary spell
delighted hermit in his royal cell.
For your eyes and your precious mouth perhaps
are blessed isles once found and found no more.

You are the whole continent of love
for me, the windy sailor on this ocean
who'd lose his ragged vessel to the waves
and call on you, the strange land, to save.
Here I set up my altar and devotion;
and let no storm blot out the place I have.

84. *To Edmund Blunden*   Texas

[14 June 1939]   Fellows 2.2.[1]

Dear Mr Blunden,
Please may I have your recommendation of the renewal of a grant
of £50 from the Mitchell City of London Charity and Educational
Foundation? I am a little late applying so I have dated my letter of
application from tomorrow (15th), Thursday, and hope I may have
your chit by then. The essay notes are going well, but getting
complicated.
Yours sincerely
Keith Douglas

85. *To Betty Sze*   Graham

15 July [PM 16 July 1939]   Hadlow House/Hadlow Down/
                                          Nr Uckfield/ Sussex

Addressed on Envelope: c/o P.S.N.C.: Passenger S. S. Orbita to
Bermuda: (Sailed July 13th Liverpool Docks)
Darling Betty,
This is with a quill, so I don't know how far I'll get. Thank you for

---

1 Douglas's room at Merton College in Fellows' Quad.

your beautiful letter sweet, I was very glad to get it, and I hope we shall be able to make things go when you come back.

I did little work at Housey but got all the books I wanted and found little Blunden in the library so I made him tell me which books.

The London Symph. Orch., which was down the day you sailed, were good but there was too much Bach. *Eine Kleine Nachtmusik* was good, and so was some Elgar.

The school is practically in revolt – the Lady Superintendent was hissed out of Hall and pelted with bread, fishcakes, insults etc., and she has very foolishly destroyed her only line of defence by feeding dirt to the masters too.

I hope you are having a lazy time getting rid of your tiredness. I felt just as bad without you and still do, more so now I am stuck out in the country. I got no riding at Housey as Nabob has been sent up North to show-jump. There are 2 horses of Peter Duncanson's here but I know he won't let me ride them.

I am still seeing about a car, which I shall buy for use in vacs, if poss. The chauffeur here has a Riley, same date as ours, bought for £25 with a new hood; and he has tuned it up to do 33 to the gallon and 75 m.p.h. It just shews. He is only licensing it for 2 quarters and says it comes to about 3/6 per quarter more than licensing the whole lot at once. So I think Mother might manage tax and insurance if I do the actual buying. With Noris [*sic*] here to do tuning up and instruct me in the innards, I expect something good, *IF* I manage to get it.

I am walking into T.W. to see about Munich money as I have £25 to spend on it.[1] I think Ilett may come with me.[2]

Anyway I shall have [to] stop this and acknowledge the £25. Write to me again soon darling – I doubt if this will reach you so let's here [*sic*] if it does.

It is sunny and rainy in bits and the first thing I get when I arrive is [a] tennis invite which I refuse because no racquet. But I hope to borrow one from somewhere before I go.

Well I really must cease and finish letters and get into T.W. Mrs Dunc[anson] lets me drive the car when she doesn't want it but she

1 T[unbridge] W[ells]. The unused travellers cheques were still in Mrs Douglas's hands in the 1970s, when she gave them to Desmond Graham.
2 Norman Ilett, Douglas's best friend, who had stayed on at Christ's Hospital. He was to come up to Brasenose College, Oxford, in the autumn.

does today so I must either bus or walk. I elect to walk as 15 miles in a mac should reduce me quite a lot.

Well goodbye for now sweet and write soon. Still lots and lots of love and your kisses returned, with 3 original ones.

Keith

PRINCIPAL   INTEREST
XXX   ⊗⊗⊗

I think 100% is a good rate of interest.

[on verso, first sheet] I forgot this page so must do a drawing. What of?

[ink sketch 1: Housey boy at writing desk] Ilett sending you his love.

[ink sketch 2: man with arms raised, wearing 'red' (scarf), 'the check one' (jacket), 'the green ones' (trousers) 'the shoes'] 'me jealous in background'

86. *To Edmund Blunden*[1]   Texas

11 [September 1939][2]   The Rectory, Withyham, Sx

Dear Mr Blunden,

I shan't be coming up next term being a Calvary Trooper at the moment and getting a commission in about 6/7 months.[3] If I am about when the war ends – or 'above ground', as the O.T.C. Colonel puts it so neatly and unoriginally – I hope I'll be back. If you'd like to set me some long-distance essays 'Shakespeare's Historical Plays and their bearing on C[avalry].T[raining]. Vol III', or 'The Language of Chaucer's Knight as compared with that of an English Cavalry Officer', (which has been done by Bairnsfather anyway), please set them and I'll try to get one or two done. I wonder what is happening to you? I hope you'll stay on at Merton. I saw C.T. Hatten[4] late of C.H. who is to be a Gunner Officer, (also Lawrance, who preceded him as Senior Grecian). Hamo had not been called up when I last heard of him, but he will be, perhaps into the same lot as I go to.

Thank heavens I can't see what is going to happen to us all as

1 For Blunden's reply see *Miscellany* p.41.
2 War had been declared on 3 September 1939; see KD pp.78–9.
3 Douglas had enlisted on 7 September, in Oxford.
4 'Senior Grecian', head boy at C[hrist's] H[ospital] in Douglas's time. For the meeting with Hatten see *KD* p.79.

clearly as you must be able to. Perhaps there'll be a German Revolution before I get through my training.

I have managed to read a lot of Saintsbury Literary History, some Dekker, Utopia, T. Tusser, *Defense of Poesie*, John Heywood, and other early drama filling in where I got to at Housey. Malory has also taken up my time. Just lately I have been too occupied for anything in the way of reading, but now I know what's being done with me I have nothing to occupy me until I'm called up.

Tomorrow I'm hiring a car for the tremendous sum of £3.5s to collect stuff from Merton. I'm not allowed to pay 17/6 and drive it myself because I'm under 21. At 19 however I'm quite old enough to be allowed to be used in keeping the country safe for other road-users.

I hoped to see you while I was up being enlisted, but didn't have time to go out to Woodstock and you apparently didn't come to college while I was there as your letters in the lodge remained untouched and continued to accumulate during my three days up.
Yours sincerely
Keith Douglas
PS I never got to München.

Four

1939—1940

87. *To Margaret Stanley-Wrench*   BL 57977 f.6

n.d. [October 1939][1]   Univ.[2]

Dear Margaret,[3]

I am at present parked at Univ. and sharing a room with someone
who does nothing but play bridge with a lot of noisy friends and I
don't like him much. I have written to you once in answer to your
letter, for which, thank you very much. I had however lost your
address and have now lost the letter. So I'm writing you another
and sending it to Somerville. I hope they know where to send it. I
meant to ask you to come and see me when you were up on the
19th, but I didn't realise it would be upon us so soon, and so I hope
you wouldn't have had time anyway. Just now I am sneezing
violently and very miserable. Shortly I shall go out and buy some
rum, in the hope that it will do me good.

I'm sorry I neglected you a bit at the end of last term. As a matter
of fact I neglected everyone except, of course, the Chinese girl Betty
Sze, with whom I fell very violently in love. We became unofficially
engaged and went to Paris on a still more unofficial honeymoon,
after which Betty went on to Bermuda and became properly
engaged to a rather rich American inhabitant of the island. I suppose
I am well rid of her, but it takes a bit of getting over.

I must stop. I'm supposed to be meeting someone in Merton a
quarter of an hour ago.

Yours

Keith

88. *To Jean Turner*   Private Hands

Friday [n.d.]   [Letterhead; beside it Douglas writes:]
                                 'At' University College Oxford

My dear Jean,

I'm sorry you're not coming up – very much. And about your
trinket – as my evening dress suit has been recently cleaned, I'm

1 Dated by Margaret Stanley-Wrench.
2 Merton was taken over by the Ministry of Agriculture and Fisheries, so Douglas
   moved into University College.
3 She had not come up for the new term.

afraid it's probably gone beyond recall.[1] However, I'll institute a search, and ask Mother what she did with it when she cleared out the pockets.

I'm up for at least a term although I am now a Trooper in Reserve Horsed Cavalry of the line. They don't want me till I'm 20, which isn't till January 24th. There is to be some sort of intermediate exam at the end of this term for a War Degree, apparently. Why don't you scrape up for a term and take it? Financially I am for the moment in jam, and if £20 is any use to you to help you come up for the term you are welcome to it, and I don't want it back. I'm afraid you will be silly enough to refuse it, but I hope not – I mean to offer it – and its straight from the limitless coffers of the Sussex Education Committee. I suppose you haven't taken yourself off the college books? I've got to pay about £53 for this term, and I get £16 from Christ's Hospital, £23 from Merton, £20 from Mitchell C[it]y of London, and £30 from Sussex, and some odd shillings. The idea is that I use the surplus to pay for my vac, as I have no home to go to, but I can easily arrange next vac, practically free, so if you want the £20, don't 'old back.

Anyway do come up for the week-end some time, or if you're in town when I have to go up to my eye man, come and have lunch somewhere.

Betty Sze has given me the air. We went for a sort of unofficial honeymoon in Paris for a fortnight, after which she went off to Bermuda, and I returned to England for some months of brokeness and boredom. For eight weeks or so I scarcely spoke to anyone under forty. Betty hardly wrote, and when she did, it was only to say what a good time she was having and how many handsome young men there are in Bermuda. Her last letter complained of me insulting her, said she had only been kind to me because she thought I needed encouragement as an artist, and now I could go to hell.

Now she is back in Oxford trying to get off with a fresher whom I introduced to her at Christ's Hospital last term.[2] So I'm in the market again in a very battered condition. Kristin would relish the situation if I told her, so I haven't.[3]

If you had been up I should probably have come up to St Hilda's

1 An enamel pendant on a silver chain, it broke loose at a College dance and Jean put it in Douglas's top pocket.
2 The fresher was perhaps Norman Ilett, now up at Oxford.
3 Christine Woodcock.

and cried on your practically non-existent bosom.

Well I must stop and do something or other. I hope you'll manage to come up somehow after all. And if you accept my £20, don't think I shall come after you with a poached-egg look in my eye and say 'Naturally, my dear, I expect some little return'. I shan't.

Cheer up, anyway, you sound very fed up. Think how miserable I am and laugh merrily. I'll write you sometimes.
Keith

88a *From Betty Sze to Toni Beckett*[1]   Private Hands

Monday [n.d. October 1939]

Dear Toni,
Have you seen *Carnet du bal* yet? If not and you would like to go, I wonder if you would allow a very charming friend of mine to take you? His name is Keith Douglas, he's second year, reading English, a poet and artist and quite respectable (should I have said that?) anyway he's longing to meet you and I said I'd introduce you to him. Let me know; will you?
Betty

89. *To Toni Beckett*   Private Hands

n.d. [October 1939]   [Letterhead] University College, Oxford

Dear Toni Beckett,
Apparently it's Betty Sze's idea that you should come and see *Carnet du bal* with me, because she's decided she doesn't want to see it again. An entirely undated letter from Betty which arrived sometime yesterday says 'Toni Beckett can come tomorrow but that's the only day she can manage;' and I'm to say when I can meet you at L.M.H. Well, if today's the day you can come, I'll meet you outside L.M.H. at 4.0 and take you out to tea first, or if you are having tea outside L.M.H. it would be more sensible to meet at the Scala about 4.30, shortly after which *Carnet du bal* begins. In any case will you come out to some kind of supper afterwards, if you'd like to. Will you

---

1   Both were from Cheltenham Ladies' College: Toni had just come up to L[ady] M[argaret] H[all]; see biographies of recipients above.

send a note to say which time, or ring up if you can't get a note here in time.

I hope you'll like the film, even if you find me unpleasant.

Yours

Keith Douglas

I think my tutor is beginning to have some kind of influence over me, as I am beginning to write like him. See that incredibly neat signature – I shall be putting E. Blunden without thinking soon. How awful.

90. *To Toni Beckett*   Private Hands

Wed. night [n.d. 25 October 1939]   [Letterhead]
                                        University College, Oxford

Dear Toni,

As soon as I got back I wrote you a letter. I don't know if I'll send it you: I'll decide in the morning, when I feel more sensible. But this is just to say write and arrange about *Earnest* soon and if you could forgo work so far as to come and see me about 3–30 and then have tea and mess about, you wouldn't really be wasting your time.

Mess about sounds bad, but I didn't mean quite that.

Yours

Keith

91. *To Toni Beckett*   Private Hands

10.45 Wednesday night   [Letterhead]
[n.d. ?25 October 1939]   University College, Oxford

Dear Toni,

Do you realise what you've done? In the morning perhaps you'll feel more sober, and regret having committed yourself so far. If you do, for God's sake tell me immediately. Because, if you are going to come and see me often, you must realise first that I need someone like you so badly that if you *are* kind to me, I shall study to repay you the only way I can, with complete devotion; so that once I've let it happen, only you can stop me loving you for the rest of my life. I'm quite willing to risk you getting sick of me, and if you do, you can remind me that I said this, though I'll remember well

82

enough. And if you do it nastily enough, you can stop me loving you quite easily.

Whatever you decide, this evening will remain by itself, as something I shall go on thinking of. When you said you would see me again, and listened to my not unusual hardluck story, you gave me something I've never had from any girl before, a sense of your sympathy. (This sounds awfully like a married man being unfaithful to his wife, but I can't help it.) I've only been in love with two people so far: the first I forced myself to be in love with because she seemed to be in love with me and I hadn't anyone else. Afterwards it turned out we were both dutifully behaving, each as we thought the other one wanted. The next was Betty, and she held me because she was strange and really summed up in herself the satisfaction of my desire to go and see places like Bali and Hawaii and bathe in tropical moonlight etc. etc. à la Rupert Brooke. I knew she never sympathised with me or really understood me.

There isn't anything strange about you – nor am I carried away by any excessive beauty, nor do I think you need me. I just have an idea that you're someone I've had in mind for years (I'm trying not to call you my Ideal) and I've tried to persuade myself the others were you: and managed pretty well until it turned out they weren't.

All I know is that after tonight, until you do something to damp me down, I don't care about anything else much – the war doesn't worry me, even if I do get killed – and in intervals of thinking of you I'll be able to do a lot of work quite cheerfully.

Don't analyse this moonlight drivel, but see what sort of impression the whole of it gives you, and I believe that'll be what I'm trying to convey.

I would have kissed you tonight if those people hadn't been there, as I think you must have realised, for I never meant a kiss more in my life, and I think you were pleased to have it. Now to the whisky. Goodnight, Toni.
Keith

92. *To Toni Beckett*   Private Hands

n.d. [October 1939]   [Letterhead] University College, Oxford

Dear Toni,
I hear you turned up today, and I'm very sick I wasn't in. I had

hoped I'd see you at coffee this morning, but I expect you had a lecture or felt foul still, or just didn't get my note(s) in time. Anyway when I was considering what I'd do this p.m., I thought its no use trying to work, I shall keep rushing out to see if there's a note from Toni (you). So I thought to myself ah, I'll go for a walk to see about the riding at Elsfield,[1] and then when I come back there'll be a note waiting for me. So here I come, very tired of walking and ready to find your note. But no note. I'm awfully sorry – I would have put off anything including a tut[orial]: if I'd known – and yet it would have been much more pleasant not knowing, if only you'd found me in.

Well anyway, you admit the L.M.H. food is foul. So at 1.0 tomorrow I'll be outside L.M.H. to take you out to lunch. I'll wait till 1.15 and then if you're not there I'll go for a walk and spit in the river or something. I've got to play rugger at 2.30, in the first league match, so I *can't* keep you long. And remember if you aren't there I'll just go and walk and not have lunch: which will be good for my figure no doubt.

I hope you got through my long letter without beginning to fear I may turn out too intense – I won't. But I hope you kept it till 10.30 p.m.

Goodnight.

Keith

I've thought of another thing. I want to see *Algiers* again, next week. Will you come with me? I wish you had been with me this afternoon – it was a pleasant walk, or would have been with you – I got a bit sick of my erudite companion. If you want to see a poem of mine there's one in this week's *Oxford Mag.*[2] and one in the Jon Cape selection of this year's pansiest verse,[3] when it appears. I might bring one tomorrow. I'll see. K

1 Just outside Oxford.
2 'Invaders' appeared 26 October 1939; 'Pas de Trois' 9 November 1939; 'Stars' which Douglas was to dedicate to Antoinette, appeared there as 'Addison and I' 30 November 1939.
3 *The Best Poems of 1938*

93. *To Toni Beckett*   Private Hands

12.45 p.m. [n.d. October 1939]   [Letterhead]
                                                University College, Oxford

Darling Antoinette,
I have been scribbling on the envelope of the note I wrote you so
in case you never get it, this is to say
    you   10.0 at Univ.
            or if you're not
    us   11.0 at Fullers
            or if you're not
    me   1.0 at Milk Bar
            or if you're not
    me   2.0 at L.M.H.
What about seeing about *Jamaica Inn* or *Earnest* tomorrow.
Love for ever
Keith

94. *To Thomas Moult*   Brotherton

28 October [19]39   University College

Dear Mr. Moult,
Thank you for your letter. I should be very glad to get a guinea from
anywhere, and I think I can justly claim it.[1] But decide for yourself
– I have £250 a year in scholarships as long as I am up here. This
has to pay all college and university bills, club subscriptions, buy my
clothes and keep me in the vacations. Rhodes scholars get £400 for
the same thing. The only difference is that they get more invitations
than I do and save more money.
Yours faithfully,
Keith Douglas
PS By next term I shall be getting 2/– a day and no scholarships.[2]

1   Douglas received the guinea (see Letter 120) for his poem 'Forgotten the red
    leaves' (in *CP* p.19 as 'Pleasures' in Moult's annual, *The Best Poems of 1938*
    (London: Jonathan Cape).
2   When he would be, as he expected, in the army.

n.d. [Sunday 29 October 1939]

Dear Toni,

Excuse this, I haven't any other paper and I still haven't any other ink. I've thought about nothing else than you ever since I saw you yesterday, and I'm still just as sure I'll go on wanting you. I've got a whole lot to say to you which I'm not going to write: in fact I'm only writing because I hoped I'd find a note from you and I'm very disappointed, so this is to work off the disappointment, so that I can get some work done. I'm going to stay up all night, I expect. Perhaps I'll write you another note early in the morning.

You've never told me if you enjoy getting notes from me and you don't know how much I want one from you.

Betty Sze was round seeing Norman Ilett today: you and I are a great joke to her and the Shattock, those two delightfully cynical women of the world. I am beginning really to hate Betty, and as for that Shattock bitch, she could do with being turned inside out. By chance, I suppose it is *you and I* who are the joke, and not just you-all laughing like hell at me? Its a horrid thought.

I am longing to see you tomorrow evening, and just in case we don't manage it, will you come to coffee on Tuesday at 10.0, Fullers. I'm afraid *The Importance of Being Earnest* is going to be impossible, but come to *Jamaica Inn* and *Algiers*. If we just want to meet and talk without eating sometimes, and get tired of using Pennock's room or having Frank Brenchley's silent bad manners to endure here, we could go to the Ashmolean and sit among the statues.

My head is whirling with dreams and plans for us – and if any of them comes off and we are even half as happy as I expect, then Betty and M. Shattock and any other witty prostitutes who feel like laughing can laugh their guts out and it won't hurt us.

I wish you were here, as I've wished you with me all day. Dear Toni.
Goodnight.
Keith

n.d.   [Letterhead] University College, Oxford

Dear Toni,

Yet another note in this foul green ink. I hope you'll let me take
you out again without someone else – I was afraid it would be
somewhat like it was – not that you weren't both very nice, in fact
we were all very nice, just like we were very nice listening to the
gramophone. But you said 'please' so nicely, I let myself in for it. I
don't know you well enough yet to want to be with you without
finding out more about you; and I hated sitting by you, and just
sitting and sitting and refusing cigarettes, and being a polite little
man, and you probably said to each other afterwards, wasn't he damn
silly, rushing about buying chocolates and thinking himself so very
dashing and polite. Well, I didn't.

Excuse the way my hand is trembling all over the place – I've
just performed the very delicate operation of climbing into Univ.
through Logic Lane – with disaster very near all the time. I just
escaped it. Remind me and I'll shew you the site of my heroism.
Its like this

[ink sketch, gate draped with barbed wire]

I think we'll get on very slowly if you don't write some notes to
me occasionally and say something. Perhaps its not a good thing,
but you do know more or less what I am thinking of you, and how
I am enjoying (or not) going out with you. You know it from what
I write, not what I say. But if you don't even write and won't say
either, any more than I do, how'll I know? I'll probably do
something wrong or tactless because of ignorance of what you're
thinking about us. You see it's fairly easy to put down on paper
when I'm not there one or two things you mightn't think of when
I am.

Any successful relation between a man and a woman is most due
to each realising what the other one wants, and when. The more
hints we can give each other the better time we can have. And I
can't help thinking that I haven't got an awful long time before I
leave this lazy life, possibly for good. And I shall leave you with it,
to my successor, unless we're changed somewhat by then. I feel
rather one of many with you at the moment, and I don't quite know
why. In fact I feel very at-a-loose-end, and I don't want to. If I ever
get near a firing line, I want something to fight for. Not a country,

not my family, not even a girl entirely – just the chance of a life worth living afterwards. I'm one of many in too many ways, and yet I'm desolate and isolated. [in the margin:] Very *Daily Mirror*, but try and take it seriously.

And Christ, am I sentimental?

Goodnight

See you over coffee – more to eat and drink. After that, Monday evening.

Keith

And let's walk next Sunday (after Guardian Sunday)[1]

97. *To Toni Beckett*   Private Hands

n.d.   [Letterhead] University College, Oxford

Dear Toni,

I'm afraid once more I've made myself very objectionable for no apparent reason. I'm sorry, particularly when you'd tried so hard to be nice most of the evening. If there really is no reason for my doing this sort of thing it proves I am a foul person. But since I'm sure I'm quite nice really, and I never have had rows with Kristin or anyone else except Betty and you, I feel I ought to find some reasons.

Well firstly I'm very much more emotional than most people seem to think, and the fact that when everyone else is quite calm and indulging in ordinary silly converse, I am often in a tolerably seething state, may explain one or two things. It's easy enough for people who don't get like that to censure or make fun of those who do. They also assume that emotional people have no sense of humour because they resent being ticked off without being understood.

To this you may retort that you are equally emotional yourself – if so heaven help us. It was because Betty was as strung up as I was that we were continually biting each other's heads off. But I don't think that's so between us. Often you are perfectly calm and good tempered, innocent of any particular emotion yourself and quite oblivious of my condition until my bad temper persuades you that I have what you nebulously call a 'mood'. Now when anyone is in

---

1 Probably, the Cheltenham Ladies' College mid-term event when the guardians of new pupils are invited to lunch.

a bad temper, from whatever cause, they are usually more incensed still, if everyone round them says and does exactly what they were expected to. Of course it's the fault of the person in a bad temper (me) but the others could perhaps avoid making it worse. This doesn't always apply, and certainly didn't last night.

But you do other things too. You complacently accuse me of being very young, behaving in a silly way, etc. at what anyone listening to the two of us would immediately recognise to be the exact psychological moment for making me quite livid. You also amuse yourself by taking my arm for a minute or two and then pushing me away as if I were dirty or smelt. Finally you are continually telling me how I am tired of you, and one of these days I shall probably snap back that I am tired of you, and I shan't mean it in the least. But it's going on and going on at people which often results in their admitting crimes they never did.

And this party business. I have lived for all the time since I was about eleven without the chance of going to any parties at all. We never had any money to give them and mother never had any time to call on people: so no one noticed us, and I had no one of my own age to go about with until I was fifteen and then only one person from Housey, whom I wasn't particularly in line with. I don't expect you to understand the state of mind that sort of thing produces. You can't be expected to imagine what it's like to live on the charity of one or two rich and condescending old people and never to see anyone young except people I don't know going about together and enjoying themselves. This, to people like you and Betty, must seem a strange state of things. And, during term-time at last, it's over for me now. But it leaves me with an aversion to parties and the people who go to them which I had carefully built up for some years in order to spare myself a good deal of fruitless longing.

Now to a person in that state (and there are one or two other things I haven't told you yet which contribute to it) it may be quite true to say 'You're just acting silly', but it doesn't have a very good effect. You blame me for being intolerant and expect me to behave as easily and have the polished manners of your rich or comfortably-off young friends who have always had plenty of friends of both sexes and a home to go to, or anyway somewhere they belong at. At those times you are in danger of identifying yourself with a class of people I *hate*.

I can see your point of view and I realise how foul I'm being, but neither you nor Hardie do anything to help. Pennock[1] and Ilett are probably more my friends than most people, because they understand me and my state of mind and attitude to other people more than you do. It's not fair to expect you to understand without being told (and it's because Pennock did realise without being told that I think he's more perception than the super-intelligent Alec,[2] who's so sure he quite understands me). Well I *have* told you now darling, anyway some of it, and any more you want to know just ask me. I hoped you would have seen there was more in the party business than met the eye, but anyway now you know. I'm still very sorry indeed for the way I behave, and don't consider I've justified it in the least, but I do hope you'll understand more and it'll hurt you less.

I'd like to meet you this evening and do something, unless you still don't want to see me, so I shall be *outside* L.M.H. at 6.0. this is once I *should* like you to be on time, and to come out with me by myself.

Love, and many apologies

Keith

97a *From Betty Sze to Keith Douglas*   Private Hands

Sunday 5 November   [Letterhead] Lady Margaret Hall, Oxford

Dear Keith,

If the picture is ready by Friday would you care to come to tea with me here that afternoon? I'm frightfully busy with two essays till then or I'd ask you some other day.

You can have a Ramsey and Muspratt then if you still want one.[1]

Did you see a scrap of paper I left on your window ledge yesterday? There were some sweet horses going frightfully cheap and I wanted you to see them. I bought such a lot of things!

1 Raymond Pennock, a fellow undergraduate at Merton.
2 Alec Hardie, a Merton friend with whom Douglas was preparing the Oxford miscellany published as *Augury*.

---

1 Presumably the portrait photograph of her, reproduced *KD* p.77.

I had a charming letter from your mother yesterday.

4.15 Friday outside L.M.H. then? – bring someone else along if you like and I'll ask Toni to make a four.

Betty

98. *To Toni Beckett* (fragment)   Private Hands

n.d.

for you didn't want to do that, did you? The more I think of it the more it seems all to have been my fault, and the worse I feel about it. Try and remember what I was like at the Welsh Pony the first night, and when you were ill. And for god's sake help me, and don't think I'm pleased with myself: that's the one thing Betty realised, that I'm trying to have confidence in myself in the face of a conviction that I'm no use. I would have brought this to you today, but I think I should lose all control if I found you had brought Jock, with or without friend, up to your room. If we're never nearer than this to cracking up again we'll be safe. This moment's over, if only you can do your part in crushing the effect of it. I'm very sorry for what I did to make it, but I was too tired out to care. I tried to concentrate on the unseen, but you laughed at me, and that was that. I hope to god you don't think this letter is funny, or that will be that again.

My being happy and all my destiny depends on how you answer this. Come at one tomorrow and eat in my room – pork pie etc. and *destroy this letter.*

Keith

Betty has asked me to tea on Friday and you too if you want to go. Shall we or shall I or shall neither of us?

99. *To Toni Beckett*   Private Hands

n.d.   [Letterhead] University College, Oxford

My dear Toni,

As I can only find a mapping pen I had better give you an example of my skill. This is bad paper and a bad nib, or I could manage something smaller and more legible. There's one thing – if I wrote like this no one could read any of my letters except by design, could they? I bet Misses Sze and Shattock would like to see what I write to you.

We are a couple of moonstruck idiots – I walked away with all your books in my pocket and never arranged about a meeting tomorrow. So I'll see you at Fullers at 11.0 o'clock unless you get this note in time to come to Univ. by 10.0. If you don't even get it in time for 11, I'll be at the Milk Bar at 1, and outside L.M.H. at 2.0, if one o'clock is fruitless.

I hope you'll go on feeling as you do about me. There are some things which thrill, surprise or excite you now, which will stop thrilling you when you get used to them. But for compensation, you'll find some other things about me that you never knew, every day if you know me for years. And other things you'll go on loving and become so used to loving that you will find I am indeed a part of you and when I go, part of you goes too, and part of me stays behind.

What we have begun to experience is the most exalted and many sided pleasure yet invented by Gods or men and so long as you come to know, like I do, what pleasure and magic and power we have in our hands, we shall be lovers as happy as any in the oldest and most fantastic of romances. And when we are unhappy, even then we shall be elated to find what comfort there will be in our complete sympathy. We shall become so that no one and nothing in the world can hurt us – perhaps not even Death. I will not sleep tonight unless I can dream of you.

[Sketch with dialogue: mother counselling daughter, 'My dear, this is almost the first letter your father wrote me. Let me show you his latest. You see, they're just the same.']

Goodnight, Toni. I hope you can bear the weight of love there is on you tonight: and I hope you'll be sure soon.

Ever affuring you, dearest mistreff, of my continuing humble adoration, your slave to serve you

and love you.

Keith

[Sketch with dialogue: lovers moon gazing, 'Look here, who the devil's this you're going about with? It's certainly not me; not tall enough. You'd better not have any more to do with him, see?']

n.d. (card) [Letterhead] University College, Oxford

Darling,

I've been trying to read *Othello* but Brian Bevan (another ex C.H. (medical) person) came in and found me asleep over it. I'm going to bed, quite tired out and I'll write you tomorrow if I don't hear from you. Dear Toni, I'll honestly try to be worth your love, for I love you very much indeed, and most when you are in trouble or pain. I must get a job soon, but God knows it'll be hard to get and hard to keep.

Love for ever – I'll think of you all night – awake or asleep.

Keith

101. *To Toni Beckett* Private Hands

Sunday morning [n.d.] [Letterhead] University College, Oxford

Dear Toni,

I've just been auditing my accounts. I've got just £10 for the whole vac: and the rest of this term. So we shall either have to start making money or spending yours (which is no more than mine, is it?) or just not spending.

I think we'd better cut out morning coffee and never meet till afternoons. On the agreement that we both work during mornings, and don't go out to coffee with other people. I know if I'm asked out to coffee I'll succumb, so I'm going to ask Pennock and Hardie & Co not to ask me.

Please do your best to get me a job, through your guardian or someone. My qualifications are – I can coach in French, German, History, Latin, English, Art, Greek (if necessary but not very advanced) teach riding, swimming, P.T., drive a car and teach anyone else to drive. I can also do housework, and might make quite a good 2nd footman.

Also can you sell, through your influence (?) in arty circles – an original watercolour on celluloid from the film *Snow White* at any price over 6 guineas?[1] The more over, the better.

Could you possibly spend Christmas either in London, at Bexhill,

---

1 No record of this survives.

or at Tunbridge Wells? Or get to any of those places, preferably Bexhill or T.W. any time next vac? Or Horsham?

I think I shall try and sell some books, if nec. but I don't want to.

I do hope you aren't feeling too foul my sweet. Tomorrow at 2.0, unless there's another phone message to say you're in bed, I shall wait on the spot marked x, for a quarter of an hour. I shan't wait outside L.M.H. because I can't face the stare from all those windows and the faces behind them: and I shan't come up to your room in case something has prevented you ringing up and you're still in bed surrounded by nurses. I assume as nothing is in your phone message today about it, that you can't be seen by me, so I am going to tea with Robert and Daphne Levens (Editor of *Oxford Magazine* and wife) in N. Oxford and spending rest of day working.

Nevertheless I'll be thinking and worrying about you all day and until I see you. I am amazed and shocked, that I have so far departed from my selfish habit, as to love someone else better than myself. And so much more. Rest you well, my heart.
Keith
[Ink sketch: 'As you were: there's no room here. P.T.O.'; on new sheet a map of roads by L.M.H., at top, 'Me, waiting 2.0–2.15' and at foot 'So there – See?']

102. *To Toni Beckett*   Private Hands

n.d.

Toni my poor sweet, you didn't miss much of a day, did you? And tonight there is a high wind rushing amongst the stars to make a clear and glorious day for us (I hope), as soon as we can enjoy it together. I have had a horrid feeling all day that perhaps if I had turned up I would have been allowed to see you: but at any rate I haven't wasted my time: in the morning I wrote to you and a long letter to mother, answering hers as completely as I could. She is in a nursing home at Brighton at the moment getting over her blood poisoning. Then I went round to Ilett's room, fetched my book, and did some work till about three, going without lunch. Sometime during that time I went out to try and find Hardie, to see if he had a special book on *Othello* or if he could tell me the way to the Levens in North Oxford. Then I walked out there, not having found Hardie, and discovered the place, and had tea with the Levens etc, surrounded by infants clutching at me and sucking my fingers, shoelaces etc., but nevertheless managing to discuss the Merton Floats play and scenery[1] with a very superior young pimply squirt of a fresher called Roberts, and Daphne Levens, who had some difficulty in dealing with tea and two infants at the same time as she drew plans of the stage. A very domestic scene: Roberts, still looking like a don, but like a don a little touched, dangled things in front of the infants and made cluckings at them. Luckily they realised how silly he looked and laughed merrily. Eventually we decided to go and see the stage tomorrow, and I said that I hadn't time to act but would paint and design them a backcloth or so, and Daphne persisted in calling me Mr Douglas and I got quite fed up and ran home in the rain. Then I had dinner and being still hungry went out with David Beaty who talked about death, and we decided he will get shot down in no time, in flames and I will be blown up, horse and all.[2] Then I came back and wrote a short and brilliant essay on *Othello*, with no quotations at all in it and no facts at all. Now I am writing to you, it being about a quarter before one in the morning. After that I shall commence to look up and type out some facts and quotations from *Othello*. Then I shall go to bed and I hope I shall be too tired to worry about you, but will just think tranquilly of you and sink into a contented stupor and oblivion. You have made me an awful coward about the war, darling. Or rather I've made myself by loving you. I wasn't going to care a damn one way or the other, but now I'm in the boo hoo I don't want to die class. I have thought of a new and most excellently polite method of making love. Lets read the balcony scene in *Romeo and Juliet* to each other.

Well, Juliet, I will lie with thee tonight
in my almost too powerful imagination. Goodnight darling, be well when this reaches you.
Keith

---

1 *The Secular Masque* by John Dryden was performed 5 and 7 December 1939: Douglas prepared masks and painted scenery (see *KD* pp.86–7).
2 Beaty survived and wrote novels about the Air Force and post-war flying.

103. *To Toni Beckett*   Private Hands

n.d.   Univ.

Toni darling,

Maybe if I type this it'll keep me sober – not that I did get drunk
after I left you, but I felt fairly drunk after you said it was settled you
love me. I kept poor Daphne Aye Moung[1] waiting half an hour in
Pennock's room, so I said I had been getting engaged, which was
the only excuse calculated to allay her wrath. This effected, we had
supper and turned up to the committee meeting very late. Needless
to say, I didn't make the same excuse there.

This typewriter keeps going wrong on red so I'll turn black now.

Darling I don't think you are quite sure I'm not just taking the
first I get, are you? Straight away though, you can be quite certain
of this – even if I only keep you until I no longer need your
sympathy, it'll be for the rest of my life, if you want it to be, because
it's not over the Betty Sze question I need help, it's over everything.
And I'll make you sure I love you for good soon. You'll see I've
only implied a proposal. I'm not going to ask you to marry me till
I've seen you again a few times, because I want you to be sure, and
you must hear a bit more about me too. But in case you think I
only want a university affair, I really do want to marry you.

And as to whether anyone would have done as well – I knew my
only chance of getting over this affair properly was to get someone
quickly. Also I was determined not to fall flat for any one person.
So I arranged all sorts of meetings, some through Betty and some
on my own. But unfortunately they rather fell through when I had
that evening with you on Wednesday; and ever since I first heard
of this bust up with Betty I've been trying to make myself fall for
several girls – four in fact. I tried very hard because I was terrified
of having no one, but it didn't work. As soon as I got away from
each of them I knew it was no use. But I never tried to fall in love
with you. I only came to have a pleasant outing, thinking that after
Betty I wasn't running after any more ex debs. And as far as I
remember even when we were trying to get into Merton that night
I still had no idea of falling in love with you. And then it just
happened, and I know I'll never want anyone else while I've got

1 An undergraduate, on the committee for *Augury*.

96

you. I wish you were here.

I wrote to Betty earlier today and said she could now feel quit of any obligation to me. She replied: 'Thank God! But don't be lured into putting all your eggs in one basket. But then again perhaps that's your way.' Well I'm afraid it is my way.

Why did you turn your lips away from me when I kissed you? Was I scratching you with whiskers or don't you like me to kiss you even now?

Dear Toni, heaven bless you. I pray we'll be happy. Goodnight, I do really love you and no one else will do instead, ever.
Keith

Dear sweet, please write to me – why is it so hard for you? We are going to have a celebration soon, eating again, and drinking.

104. *To Marie J. Douglas*   BL 59833 ff.21–4

n.d. [PM 14 November 1939]   [Letterhead]
                                        University College, Oxford

Dear Mother,
Thank you for your letter. I think Toni and I have thought of everything you put down – and since we look like having to be engaged for at least three years, we ought to be quite sure of our minds at the end of that time. Either of us can terminate the engagement at any time during the three years, so I haven't tied her down particularly. What with the things Dadda did that were mistakes, and the mistakes of other people which Toni has heard about, and the mistakes I made with Betty, we have had plenty of things to think of that we will not do. Toni, I'm afraid still thinks I am going to get tired of her. So do most of my friends, so does her guardian, and so (I think) do you. All this is bound to make me very nervous of getting tired of her, because she is such a very nice girl, and she is so much in love with me she can't help it any more. But it also makes me quite determined to do my best not to. It is possible I could meet someone who was both very intelligent and very original and very beautiful, and in love with me; and that such a person would suit me better. But it is very unlikely indeed that I should meet a person like that, and not certain they'd suit me better if I did. Toni is not by any means unintelligent or bad looking. She dresses very well, has been an art student and done ballet. The chief

difficulties of marriage for us seem to be three – one of which you mentioned. The one you mentioned is the difficulty of getting a job – particularly as Toni wants to have children as soon as possible. The second is the danger of her finding it a strain to keep up with me intellectually, and the third, I am quite sure after seeing some photographs of the lady, is her Mother, who luckily is in India at the moment with her Father, a judge in the Punjab.

Of these the chief one is the intellectual question, which I think I can circumvent. As to the job – Blunden has said he thinks he can get me on the *Times Literary Supplement* when I go down, and anyway I should manage to get something of the sort. This will not be much, but although we want money, we could live on very little and enjoy ourselves. If I have to go out to the Front, we shan't hastily get married – though I wish Toni could go and live with you. She's trying to get me a job in town, for the vac., or somewhere, through her incredibly rich guardian, who is also 'someone' in art circles and *might* do me good there. I'll try and do something with an Agency – such as Oxford Employment Bureau. But I'm so very very busy – with work and Toni and editing an anthology and doing scenery for a play and masks for a masque, also possibly acting in the play and dancing in the masque. So if I sent you a couple of pounds, could you do something for me – about Gabbitas and Thring, who are advertising most days in *Times* and *Telegraph*, or put an ad. in one of those papers for me? The answers can come to me here and I'll deal with them.

I should like a pullover like the one without ribs down the front: but not *very* urgently. I suppose you couldn't get up to Oxford to meet Toni? Or meet us both in town for lunch some day. As soon as I have a photo of her I'll send it you – or a portrait. I only have a very big one taken when she was presented at court and it's not in the least flattering.

I don't know what I'm doing for Christmas, but I hope to arrange jobs so that I can spend all my money on having a good Christmas, wherever we can both go. It would be nice to collect some other people – I suppose Withyham[1] would be as cheerful as most places, if only they'd let you cook the Christmas dinner. Or to spend it with Aunt Elise: or I'll think, and you think, of anywhere else. A London Christmas would be nice, even a blackout. I want to be

1 See Letter 64.

where there is (a) Toni, and (b) dancing, but it's hard to find anywhere we could both go. I shall try though.

Toni would have started seeing about a job today but she's ill and staying in bed for a day. She came and watched a rugger match the other day when she shouldn't have, with disastrous results.

I must stop and get some work done. We went to the *Importance of Being Earnest*, *Design for Living*, and *Jamaica Inn*. The first two were excellent. *Earnest* had John Gielgood [*sic*], Edith Evans, and Gwen Françon Davies in it and we sat in the 2nd row stalls and saw from about 10 yards away. *Design for Living* had Diana Wynyard, Rex Harrison, and Anton Wallbrook, and was very slick. We saw that in 1/- seats after cuing [*sic*] for hours. The Charles Laughton Film *Jamaica Inn* is very disappointing. *Algiers* has also been here so I saw it for about the 5th Time, and *Carnet du Bal* about a week ago. *Four Feathers* is here next week – I suppose you couldn't get here for it?
Love
Keith

105. *To Jean Turner*   Private Hands

n.d. [?November 1939]   [Letterhead]
                                          University College, Oxford

Dear Jean,
Thank you, you must be pretty sick to write me one that length. I am well, but I don't think I shall be for long as I have Groups in a month, and also I am (and don't you tell anyone *at all*) engaged all over again. She is probably going to chuck me quite soon, but at the moment parental and guardian opposition are stimulating her to stay engaged. Once again I have ensnared a member of the upper ten, a last year's deb. with the imposing Christian names of Antoinette Gabrielle. She is very determined at the moment that my brokeness shall make no difference, but let her once meet again the vastly rich young gentleman whom I have cut out, and off I go again in quest of further beauty. That is as it should be, for I feel much less left out in the cold being engaged, and at the same time there is no prospect of getting married for at least 3 years, by which time the thing will obviously have gone up in smoke, so I am not really so very tied down, or up.

I don't think I shall ever get married, because the person I want would have to be a cross between Kristin and Betty, which is obviously impossible.

Jean if you are going to be a schoolmarm, suppose you stop putting things like s'pose and p'raps in your letters, or you'll be the most typical schoolmarm that ever stepped. I do wish you'd get married though, because I know you'd like it really, and surely you could procure some bright young gentleman – they aren't all as oversexed as I am, and lots of very nice people indeed would marry you and enjoy life without making love to you all day. That is I am afraid what my wretched wife is in for, and why my fiancées always become my mistresses, and then chuck me.

Be a mistress [a line connects this word with the previous use of 'mistresses] (there is no relation between these 2 words) in a school where there are some masters, and marry one of them. *Some* schoolmasters are very pleasant chaps indeed. I hate to think of you just becoming an unsatisfied maiden lady of uncertain age.

Talking of Denise, I had a very pleasant ride yesterday on a most energetic horse which consented to jump gorse-bushes and cleared about 5ft very nicely.

And talking of horses, do you happen to know, I wonder, whether Margaret S.W. ever got my letter in reply to hers? i.e. has she written to you saying she has heard from me?

I hope you and any other Oxford friends of yours who ought to be up this term, (whom you can inform of their duty) will send some sort of prose or verse (not short stories or politics) for Oxford Miscellany, which is what I am mixed up in, to me, or more officially to Alec Hardie, 16 Long Wall St. Oxford. If you're writing to Margaret you might tell her, in case Daphne Aye Moung has forgotten to.

I must stop, having written you a much longer letter than I should have, though not so long as I could have.
Love
Keith

106. *To Toni Beckett*   Private Hands
n.d.

My darling fiancée,
I think this may turn out to be the longest letter you've ever received

from me, and one of the longest I've ever written. On the way back I thought of four or five things to say to you but they have all flown out of my whirling mind again and I must write on until they come back. One of them has come back immediately and that is, we must never try each to do different work in the same place – but if we each help the other, we shall get more done than if we did it, one in L.M.H. and one in Univ. There is one thing I hesitate to say to you – it sounds so like a story made up to comfort you – but it came into my mind on the way home and it's true. I've already told it you in a different way, but it's worth repeating. I said the most miserable time and the time I was most in love with Betty was when she was away; do you see what was the reason? It was my ideal I loved, and my longing for her was only my passionate desire for that ideal person. As long as she was away, I could make her fit the vacant place. While I was with her, it was not the same. In Paris, at times, it was a wonderful adventure, and I enjoyed it. But what I enjoyed was being in Montparnasse, the haunt of Romance, among artists and Bohemians to be as Bohemian as any of them, and Betty was a piece (a big piece, but only a piece) of the Bohemian atmosphere: it was the same, on a larger scale, as when I took her to Christ's Hospital.[1] When I was sleeping with her, she said, at a moment when I *should* have been almost mad with emotion: 'my God, how I love you'. And I thought: 'my God, how affected and insincere that sounds'. All the time I was detached and watching us, thinking how I would tell Ilett of it and we'd be cynical about it when we got home. So you see, with all those thoughts, it is no wonder I had to lie to Betty. When the bust-up came, it was the disappearance of my dream which filled me with misery. I think you must realise I love you too much to make all this up simply for the sake of allaying your fears. And it is true that I have never till now been so utterly carried away with love, and yet able to consider difficulties and disadvantages quite coldly. I've never wished so much to give myself entirely in every possible way. If I could truly believe you didn't want it, I'd go without kissing you, even without seeing you, though I might crack up in a day or two and beg you to give in. It's true I've kissed girls before, but never with the whole of my body and mind in the one contact. Did you feel my tears, or did you wonder why I put your hand to my eyes? I've only twice in the last four

1 In a red sports car, to some effect.

years been moved to tears by intense emotion: once was at the end of the film *South Riding*,[2] and once was tonight. No girl has ever made me like that, or to feel so utterly humble as I do always before you, and as I did more than ever when you cried. I felt utterly unworthy, because at that moment there was nothing I could do to shew you that my love for you was my real love, that no-one has had before or can have again. We are promised to each other and I hope to God we're sure – I am in a maze of happiness – but it's not all happiness – some is just an indefinable emotion which is so powerful I am afraid of it, and which I suppose must be love, undiluted with pleasure or companionship or hope or physical desire. Physically I want you so much I can sometimes hardly bear it – and yet I know that there is something else there which will always give me the whip hand over that. Don't believe we're too young – the fact that we feel so intensely is because we are both young, and innocent. For I am innocent, my heart hasn't hardened in the least towards my original dream, which you fulfil. When you smile at me after we've turned suddenly to look at each other, I am struck almost with fear and wholly with adoration by the beauty of your expression.

From today and this enchanted evening we are promised to each other, and we shall be able to walk at will in our own fantastic paradise. On either side of us our friends will go, even touching us and talking to us, and we shall not be with them. On Sunday we'll celebrate – at supper we'll just drink wine, but afterwards we'll drink to our love, outside, from our own glasses; and when the toast is drunk we'll smash the glasses, over our shoulder against the wall. And some prosaic passing people who hear the tinkle, will wonder what it was.

I think I shall go to bed soon because I am gradually becoming quieter inside and very exhausted. Not only spent but depressed to think of tomorrow morning. What use will your lectures be to you I wonder. I almost wish I had some control over my emotion towards you. But not quite. I know I am content to be lost in love, and passionately anxious to continue so lost for ever. It's like being picked up by a huge hand or a wind out of heaven and moved helplessly. It's an enchantment, and yet I know everything in this fairyland is quite, quite real. I don't think you can ever make me

2 From the novel by Winifred Holtby, made in 1938 and starring Ralph Richardson.

feel conceited over having you: for when I consider your love for me, this person I know so well, I am utterly abased. We are two very emotional sentimental people – and because of that we're like gods.[3] Goodnight my darling Toni, there are no words or combinations of words to tell you how very very entirely I am filled with love for you. Bless you and thank God, or whatever made you exist, for your existence and your love. Keith

[on an added sheet] I think you'll be able to see I've never been carried away enough to write a letter like this before.

It's now about 1.30, over an hour since I wrote to you, and said I was going to bed. So now that I am setting off on the long cold journey up to my room, this is to say that although the fury of emotion has passed, I'm still utterly consumed with loving you. It shakes me a bit, somehow.
Keith

107. *To Toni Beckett*   Private Hands

n.d.   [Letterhead] University College, Oxford

Toni my heart,
I'm too full of thoughts to write to you. I wrote four pages and tore them up. They wouldn't do after a day like this. I'm tired and desolate now without you: and I must try to work. I still want you to be my mistress, if only you can feel right about it. Because the relation of lovers is something quite as good as marriage and quite different, and I want more than I can say, for us to have both.

It may seem horrid to be furtive: but it's not horrid to be sharing each other in secret, independent of everyone in the world: and that's something we'll never have if we wait till we're married.

When we are married, you'll have some safeguard: you won't be giving yourself quite entirely and perfectly, because you are guarded from disgrace and the world. And I am afraid when we are married you may suddenly understand what we missed, and I shall have known all the time.

I can imagine you saying quite firmly 'You know that's rot Keith'. But I don't know it's rot, at all. I know it isn't, because just enough

3 'I think a thousand hours are gone/ that so, like gods, we'd occupy', the lines are from 'The Prisoner', dedicated to 'Yingcheng' and written around a year later.

103

(and it was very little) went right between Betty and me in Paris, for me to see how things could have been if she had loved me, and if I had completely loved her, instead of making cynical remarks about her to Ilett, and writing to Kristin, quite sincerely and long before things came to a head, to say that it was an affair and wouldn't last. If it had been you, and our love, in those circumstances, in England or France, a fortnight together would be a complete thing, perfect in itself and subject to no regrets. I don't want less than a week, now I've thought of it. And in a way I'd rather it wasn't when I had to be busy all day seeing about uniform, and when I knew you were forced by circumstances almost as much as by love to give yourself. I'm afraid it's true what I said today: I want so very much, painfully, that you should love me so entirely as to be proud to give yourself and to put yourself for me, in a position in which you could lose everything. To get as high as the summit of life, you, and I too, must give everything: I want, as much as I want you, to put myself in that position for you, to risk disgrace, imprisonment or death, or simply in your defence to be battered into insensibility by a professional thug.

Yet as long as you feel unhappy about giving yourself to me, as it may seem to you, casually, we could be naked together in the one bed and embrace and kiss till our tongues lay together, and you could not force me to take you, though you lost all control. Nor can you prevent me from sleeping with you tonight, and I shall. Yet I must try and work first. Heaven keep you unhurt. G'night Toni.
Keith

108. *To Toni Beckett*   Private Hands

Thursday morning [n.d.]   [Letterhead] University College, Oxford

I finally sent you the letter I wrote late last night. Don't take too much notice of it, at the moment. I don't want to spoil everything by a kind of hysterical outburst to start with. Let's simply take things as they come. I'm going to Fullers for coffee today at 11. Will you spend Sunday afternoon with me? It would be nice to walk, but if you want to work, bring some, and meet me in Univ. about 2.0? Sorry to inflict you with 3 letters.
Keith
[at top] It's funny how much better I like everyone since yesterday.

n.d   [Letterhead] University College, Oxford

Dear Toni,

I think you ought to have stuck to the idea last night if you didn't want to see me today. Do you remember you said: 'Of course I'll see you tomorrow, darling'. I don't think you should have – and for once perhaps I've a right to be hurt. Today is quite wasted for me; but I'm not going to sit and mope, so don't worry, my sweet.

I hope you'll reconsider Wednesday evening – what saddens me considerably is that you seem to be trying not to let yourself go. I don't mind if you can't but surely if I have, you ought to try and let yourself go (badly put, sorry). After last night you ought to trust me not to take advantage of you.

Also we haven't (perhaps) very much time, I might even be called up next term. I suppose it would be safer for you to get out of it now and leave me to go off and fight by myself. But you won't, will you darling?

I spent two hours this morning doing your unseen, and I then went to find you for coffee and give it you. Instead I found Betty, and after running there too. Poor little boy.

I wish you hadn't spilt that scent: I love you too much, dear Toni, you must realise – it's perhaps partly why I look at your hair and not your eyes. Our ordinary converse in a Milk Bar hangs on a slender thread, in a way. We both know what there is in the background of our thoughts.

It was really unfair of me to tell you you've made me miserable today: for I'm sure you are too. But don't take Wednesday evening from us too. Or do you want to go out with Rosemary or Jock? This is where this letter would degenerate into hysterical declarations of love, and O my darling I want you so much I'll be quite, quite paralysed and useless today. I can't stop thinking of you. I can't even stop talking about you. I shall make the wretched Pennock sick of you.

Till 10.30 tomorrow in Fullers, so there.

My darling Toni.

Keith

Antoinette Beckett. Latin Unseen. 211. Simple diplomatists.
And when they had already brought their siege works up there,

delegates came from the town; whose discourse had an ancient simplicity, as of men who would make no mere pretence of fighting, if they had the strength. But they asked that they might be allowed to go [to] the camp of the Celtiberi, to get help. If they did not obtain their request, in that case (tum), they would go away from the Romans and take their own counsel. With Gracchus' permission they went away and in a few days came back bringing another ten delegates with them. It was in the heat of the day. They asked the officer nothing but that he should order drink to be given them. When they had drunk their first cups, they asked for more; much to the amusement of the bystanders, that they should be such boorish souls, and ignorant of all politeness. Then the eldest of them said: 'We have been sent by our people to ascertain, whateffer, for what reason you are making incursions upon us, relying upon arms, lookyou'. To this peroration Gracchus replied that he had come with confidence in his splendid army. If they wished to see it for themselves so as to take a more definite report back to their friends, he would demonstrate his strength to them. And he ordered the sergeant major to parade all ranks, horse and foot, adding that they were to come on parade in battle order.

110. *To Toni Beckett*   Private Hands

n.d.   University

Toni darling,

I am quite lethargic this evening and although I have tried, I haven't managed to do much work. I am now so sleepy I don't know whether I shall stay awake to finish this letter. I think in spite of rugger the Oxford atmosphere must be getting me down. Or is it just that I've undertaken too much at once and can't do any of it? Perhaps I shall feel better after a ride on Monday, and our walk on Sunday.

Your photograph is on the table looking at me in a quizzical kind of way, and beside it I've put Betty's. How utterly different they are. You certainly put some love in your eyes when you looked at the camera and Betty I think in a way has shewn her state of mind for she is looking rather pensively sideways as much as to say, now look what I've landed myself with. And when I think of that ham she's engaged to, I must say I think she'll be sufficiently punished before she's finished with her happy married state. It seems impossible to credit, that I should have loved Betty so much, and now care nothing at all for her, and love you. But it is actually fairly easy to explain. I seem to be made up of two very different parts: I'm almost two people. One wants exoticism, travel, adventure. That's why I loved Betty, and why I still love the person I pictured her to be in my imagination, when she was away. It's why I want you to do something very well, to be original and outstanding, and to be looked at, and why I have a terror of perishing into an ordinary existence without having tasted a hundred strange pleasures and experiences; that's why I am afraid of us getting fat: because fat is not romantic, or adventurous, it's either a nuisance, or ludicrous, or disgusting, according to how much there is of it. There is always in my mind an ideal companion in these adventures, and I love my ideal with one part of my love, very intensely. Betty is too cheap to fit that ideal, but you aren't; for you're sincere, and you don't want to be ordinary any more than I do. The other part of me is tired of fighting, wants to be settled, to have a real aim for the rest of my life, above all wants a companion, someone to sympathise with me and to love me, and to whom I can give all my love without fear of being hurt, and who will need my protection and consideration. This you seem to me to fulfil already more than I thought possible. As long as you love me and want me as you do now, I can't grow tired of you. I feel you are under my protection, and that I must do all I can to prevent you from being hurt and to make you happy. And you don't know how I love to do things for you, and to do things with you. That is a real love and companionship which I only had with Betty for one day during the whole time I knew her. And I wonder if it was really true then. It's there all the time between you and me. You feel it too, don't you?

Added to these kinds of love is physical desire, and you satisfy that in me more than anyone ever has: certainly Betty never did. And I like to have someone presentable to take about, which may sound cheap, but really I shouldn't love you if you didn't dress well and walk well and look full of breeding and confidence. So altogether we have as much chance as most people, and more, to make a success of living together. And we have thought out the drawbacks, and stand more or less prepared. We must just go on consolidating, and things like Sunday walks and above all seeing each other in places away from Oxford: most important of all, living in the same house and spending whole days together doing things, will make us sure because it will make us need each other.

It's now midnight and I'm going to bed.

I hope I haven't said anything very obscure.

Goodnight my poor tired sweet.

Dearest Antoinette.

Keith

111. *To Toni Beckett*   Private Hands

n.d.   [Letterhead] University College Oxford

My sweet,

I've sent your photo to Mother – in it you are looking so sweet and innocent she is sure to approve of you. I have also written to scholastic agents and the Editor of *Riding* about a job in the vac. Failing everything I shall go to Somerset where little Stawey's father is Employment Officer in Taunton, and there work as a navvy or a Christmas postman.

You must be having a good effect on me because this is the first time I've ever really sweated to get a job. I must go out on Sunday and do that picture for Hardie, so as to get thirty shillings.

See you *heute morgen* my darling.

Love Keith

What a hurry I am always in over doing nothing.

112. *To Toni Beckett*   Private Hands

n.d.

Toni dear,

You are wrong to have thought I was being beastly today: it was your imaginings which hurt you, almost all the time my darling. And yet I was teasing you. But Toni I truly didn't know it was hurting you, and it hurt me much more to know I had hurt you afterwards. I am glad we got it straight before we had to say goodnight because I know what a foul night we should have had. I know it seems silly that we should be hurt so easily, but it is a proof we're in love. Another proof I'm in love is how much slower and worse my typing has got.

Love

When I put love how are you to know what I mean unless you stop and think? So stop and think, and then

Goodnight and goodmorning Toni.

Keith

113. *To Toni Beckett*   Private Hands

n.d.

Toni dearest,

Of course I succumbed and went to eat at the Kemp Hall, and then feeling very weak willed I went back to Merton and listened to some music. One of the good things about Pennock going about with Joan Isaacs is that there are now a lot of most expensive records in his room, such as Haydn's military symphony[1] and a Brahms concerto. I thought I was fairly calmed down after today but I must still be pretty tired, because I had put a record with a chip out of it by itself until the chip could be stuck back, and when I found someone had taken it down I flung the whole thing in the corner and smashed it into most satisfying fragments. Then Beaty[2] and I went out and consumed soup at the Milk bar.

   I think I am going to bed now, I'm too tired to think or I'd get on with some work or with my novel.[3] I think you were sweet today – I want our day out to be soon. Please let me off a London wedding.

Keith

114. *To Toni Beckett*   Private Hands

n.d.

Toni darling,

I'm quite quite drunk – much too drunk to write with a pen. In

---

1   Douglas's poem 'Haydn Military Symphony' was first published in *Augury: An Oxford Miscellany* (Oxford, 1940).

2   David Beaty (see Letter 102).

3   One of several references to writing novels. No trace of them remains.

fact I doubt whether I shall get through this letter before I slump into a tipsy sleep over the typewriter. I can just manage to write but damn me if I can read what I'm writing so I don't really know what I'm putting. In fact the only thing I know is that drunk or sober I still love you just as very very nearly to distraction asxever [*sic*]. Sorry about that x. But take it as a kiss.

During a kind of sober moment I have – I feel rather low about what happened this afternoon – and yet glad. If I had taken you there and then I couldn't have felt more bound for ever to you. You've given me all of you and all of me is yours. In the mists of my drink sodden brain I still remember, too, your letter to me today. Thank you always my sweet. If we went to pieces tonight you'd have had more of me than any other girl ever had. And if I wasn't tight with hock in large quantities, sherry in large quantities, and a certain amount of beer, I should be intoxicated still, as I am every minute of the day, with the thought that you are mine.

I hope you don't have any pains – and if you did, I wish I could have them for you. Now I'm going to bed and when I am in bed I shall read your letter and then lie and think of you until I go to sleep – indeed until I see you for coffee tomorrow at Fullers at eleven, when I shall probably have a hangover and be like a bear with a sore head or one of those,
Goodnight my special person,
my beloved Toni
Keith (too tight to sign)

115. *To Toni Beckett*   Private Hands

n.d.   [Letterhead] University College, Oxford

Toni my sweet,
I'll be round the corner from L.M.H. (where I was before) at 9.30 on Sunday (tomorrow). Don't tell anyone (because *anyone* might mention it by accident) that you're going out the whole day with me, because I've written to Rachel and Betty to say I've a Miscellany meeting at 12, so I couldn't *possibly* be going out with you.

Tear this up and DON'T LEAVE it about!
Love
Keith

n.d.   [Letterhead] University College, Oxford

Dearest Antoinette,

I'm sorry I'm not going to see you today, but glad you had the self control to put me off. I shall endeavour, between intervals of seeing Hamo and painting Roger's portrait,[1] to do some work, and be worthy of you. If it's fine, I shall go out into the meadows and try to earn 30/-. My writing is getting more and more Blundenesque the only thing being that it still isn't spaced like specially designed type on very expensive hand-made paper.

Tomorrow I daresay Hamo will still be here, as it's difficult to come from Sussex and only stay one day in Oxford, particularly as trains are missing at the moment. So I shall try and arrange for him to meet you tomorrow. I expect you'll like him better than either Pennock or Hardie, though he is a woman hater.

I think I had better stop and get something done. I must write to mother soon though.

Very much love.

Keith

n.d.   [Letterhead] University College, Oxford

Toni dear,

This is all I've got to write with. I've been doing notices about the book all the evening and god I'm tired. Sweet, I hope you'll soon be able to tell me about everything without hesitating. It's going to be lovely doing things with you, and I know things will go right. You can make me completely happy, and even now, you do, for moments.

Ilett has been asking me whether I honestly think you are beautiful enough to keep me from running after other beauties for the rest of my life. And thank god I was sure, you are: as long as we don't let any kind of thin end of the wedge force us apart. We mustn't lose touch over anything: as long as we're sure of each other

---

1 Probably Roger Lancelyn Green, who was with him on the editorial committee of *Augury*; later a writer of children's books.

we'll be safe against anything. We must share everything too, all our friends and our thoughts and occupations. There mustn't be any secret corners in either of us, not even a little bit that the other doesn't know and understand, because secrets are what make the trouble. That's why I've introduced you to my friends and why I shewed you mother's letter and my poems. We must become so that we can change minds and think just as easily from each other's point of view. Loving each other as we do, there'll always be some easily found reason if things go wrong. And we must have enough perception of each other's thoughts to feel it.

These notes I write you during these first days, and those you write me, are very valuable. To reread them, if we ever come to a crisis, might pull us back when we were almost too far gone.

But we won't have a crisis darling. Surely we'll always understand. It doesn't matter what kind of people we are, loving each other makes us change.

I'm too tired to think enough to express all this. Soon after eleven, I'll see you at Fullers.

Dear Toni, goodnight, bless you.

Keith

118. *To Toni Beckett*   Private Hands

n.d. [?November 1939]

Darling,

I have stayed up till 2.30, not working, but writing a poem for you about the stars, that will help you to remember tonight.[1] I hope you like it. I have also written one about Haydn's military symphony,[2] which remind me to shew you. I think I may do one about the clock symphony too.[3]

I am too tired to write any more now. I hope the poem will do by itself, as it's definitely for you and when it's published I shall put that at the top.

1 MS missing, text taken from *CP*. 'Stars' was first published in the *Oxford Magazine* with title 'Addison and I'; in *Augury* (1940) with dedication 'To Antoinette'.
2 See letter 113 n.1.
3 He did: 'Haydn Clock Symphony', first published in *Kingdom Come* (December 1939–January 1940).

With all my love
Your adoring constructive poet,
Keith

> The stars still marching in extended order
> move out of nowhere into nowhere. Look, they are halted
> on a vast field tonight, true no man's land.
> Far down the sky with sword and belt must stand
> Orion. For commissariat of this exalted
> war-company, the Wain. No fabulous border
>
> could swallow all this bravery, no band
> will ever face them: nothing but discipline
> has mobilized and still maintains them. So
> Time and his ancestors have seen them. So
> always to fight disorder is their business,
> and victory continues in their hand.
>
> From under the old hills to overhead,
> and down there marching on the hills again
> their camp extends. There go the messengers,
> Comets, with greetings of ethereal officers
> from tent to tent. Yes, we look up with pain
> at distant comrades and plains we cannot tread.

119. *To Toni Beckett*   Private Hands

n.d.

Well I've been out getting drunk again but I'm fairly sober now. I felt so miserable I consumed some port in the J.C.R., went to the East Gate, met Ilett, Abu,[1] Pennock. There I put away a quart of beer and some port and lemon, and went back to Pennock's room. Here we went mad. The table and chairs were put back, Abu strummed negroid rhythms on the piano, and we all danced and tap-danced. Pennock took over the piano sometimes, and at other times we had the radiogram. We've broke a lot of Pennock's

---

1 Aleba Albert Taylor, a Nigerian undergraduate reading law at Merton 1938–41 (see *KD* pp.87–8).

crockery, and I painted pictures of lewd dancers on the lampshade, with the wrong end of a pen and Pennock's ink. After that we all reeled out again, said goodnight to Ilett, and went off down the High and along the Corn singing and crashing into policemen and soldiers. We ended in the milk bar, where we sobered up, and where a pathetic old man sold us obsolete communist propaganda, and I gave a shilling to him. He asked my name, and promised that although he was 71 he would come to Pennock's room, and Pennock should play on the piano, and he would sing 'Gordon Douglas', or 'Douglas Gordon' or something, in my honour. I wonder if he'll come. So you see what miscellaneous results a chance remark of yours about me feeling pleased with myself can have.

I still feel depressed, and wish to God I had you here – to try and explain why I wrote you that maudlin and ridiculous letter. Pennock tells me that what's wrong with me is frustration – and it goes for both of us. We shall have to have each other soon.

Goodnight Toni dear. Try and understand what an odd person you've got hold of, before he has to go away and be blown unrecognisable.

I love you as painfully as ever in all our long acquaintance, dear sweet.

Keith.

I'm so glad there aren't any blue veins – I was afraid you'd be covered in them after what you said. I think you're very beautiful – I'll shew you when you pose for me. O god how can I wait till tomorrow – you may be furious or disillusioned.

[ink sketch: four carousing figures round a piano: Abu, Pennock, Ilett and ?]

120. *To Toni Beckett*   Private Hands

n.d. [December 1939[1]]

Toni darling,

Thanks for your note and telegram. I will duly turn up in town on the appointed date. Till then I shall sleep in little Hardie's garret in

---

1   Dated by Toni Beckett.

the Broad. I didn't have lunch with Betty App[2] as her ridiculous father had decided to address 7000 letters and she stayed to help him. So I took out a very ugly C.H. school candidate to the Chinese restaurant, where I presented the lady with a 5/- box of black magic, from all of us. She sends you her thanks and I shall probably demand some of the 5/- from you and Hardy [sic]. I had supper with Michael and Evelyn last night and Meric Dobson came with Jon Mayne, whom I accused of having been at school with me. He was. I met him again taking exams this morning, and we indulged in some polite converse.

The exam has gone pretty well so far, and I have only one more paper to take. I'll write and inform mother of arrangements as at present. Will you find her a room or flat near? You needn't take it as long as when she appears you can say there's a room at so and so. I must stop and grab some lunch before my last paper.

I'll answer your note when I have time or by word of mouth.
Lots of love
Keith
PS I've got Jon Cape's guinea.[3]

121. *To Jean Turner*   Private Hands

n.d. (New Year Card)

[Linocut of centaur blowing trumpet on front; inside, linocut, '1939/good wishes/1940']
Keith

122. *To Toni Beckett*   Private Hands

n.d. [PM 30 December 1939]   Hadlow House,
                                              Hadlow Down, W. Uckfield

Darling Antoinette,
I don't enjoy not being with you a bit; but I suppose I'll get used to it in time. I wish you could be staying here – it's foul now, but

2 Betty Appleton, with her sisters Joan and Bridget, became friends with Douglas through *The Secular Masque*. They lived in Masefield's old house at Boars Hill (see below and *KD* pp.90–1).
3 For publication in *The Best Poems of 1938* (see Letter 94).

you would make all the difference and we could have such a marvellous time because the house and garden and country round are lovely. Sir Reginald (corsets) Spence[1] has so far forgotten himself and us, as not to send either a letter or a present – in fact I, having counted upon receiving some £5 in Christmas emoluments, find a measly 10/- waiting for me, which I ought to give to mother anyway.

An anxious telegram from Alec[2] came last night saying do we expect you Thursday? I shall have to wire him today – I bet I forget. Anyway I get the push from here tomorrow. Dear Mrs Duncanson has not yet even opened the letter I wrote her in the hope of getting mother off for Christmas. Blast her soul.

You never gave me Rosemary's[3] address, sweet, so this letter will take some time to arrive. I believe you told it me but I haven't it written down; so this will have to be forwarded. I think this looks rather like the Aye Moung's[4] writing somehow. [Paragraph cancelled.]

Have a good time at Rosemary's and I'll endeavour not to get too exasperated with Alec: if you go up to Oxford early I'll endeavour to get there too. [Two lines cancelled.]

I am going to write to the War Office now and to Albert Rutherston about going to the Ruskin next term. I think I shall also write to Walter Douglas[5] and ask what the result of my exam. When I get to Alec's I'll write to you whenever I have time. Mother keeps talking at me now while I'm writing, and pottering about the room and so I can't think straight.

Darling I do love you now, I'm sure of it: but you still must find something to do of your own. I do wish you'd do something about drawing because honestly you could be good. You'd only have to be taught a little about composition and colour, which I could teach you – then you'd be quite as good as I am and could go on from there. I think it's not having any real family life that makes us both a bit aimless and undecided. If only I could get more confidence in

1 See Letter 58 n. 4.
2 Alec Hardie.
3 A friend of Antonette's.
4 Daphne Aye Moung (see Letter 103).
5 At the Ruskin School of Drawing, he contributed to *Cherwell* under Douglas's editorship later that academic year.

myself I'd have more confidence in you and in my love for you lasting. I feel such a thoroughly weak and degenerate person just at the moment. And it's no good saying I'm not because there's no doubt of it. The only question is can I pull myself together, and that remains to be seen. At the moment I'm rather doubtful – I seem to have no self-control at all, and being with Alec or anyone like him is not going to help me much: I think really you need something of the sort too – no one makes it very easy for us though, do they? I wish I could have got a job this vac:- it might well have pulled me up a bit. But it would have done me out of staying with you, and I certainly don't regret that – it was lovely, and I really enjoyed the whole time I was with you. It keeps striking me, when I see you or hear you at odd moments that I haven't really appreciated what I've got yet. I wish you could come for some long walks with me in country like this: perhaps in the summer we could manage it. We spend far too much time indoors, don't we? I suppose it's partly the feeling that we aren't ignoring our work quite so much if we stay near it, but a good bit is the influence of Alec, and Roger, so far as he can manage it. I found one of his guest cards waiting here for me when I arrived.

I have thought of a lot of things to write – I hope I'll have time to do them – one is a novel – and several poems.

Please try and write to me often – but never for the sake of writing – only when you have something to say. This *is* a funny pen – it inspires me to write in the most peculiar hand – all the time I'm holding it back so now I'll let it go and see what it wants to write like. For see it is getting away with me – I think I'd better pull up again.

For some reason my razor has shaved me properly today. Almost as good as with an ordinary razor. It's jolly cold here: I ought to go out though. But at the moment I've far too many letters to write and I must finish this one. Goodbye my darling little person.
Keith.
It's now snowing very thick and fast and lying very thick and fast. Mother apologises for her manner but the Butler told her she was wanted on the phone by a Miss Betty, and so she was very puzzled and trying to think why Betty wanted to ring her up and didn't realise who you were, being rather tired and muddled anyway. She says she'll write to you when she has time.

n.d. [January1940]   [Letterhead] Rookwood, Allbrook, Hants[1]

Toni my sweetest girl, I may go on with this tomorrow because I am very sleepy indeed, but I must write a bit in bed tonight. Thank you for a marvellous letter – and enclosures. You misjudge me, as you may have discovered – I wrote you at once, but had to send it to L.M.H. c/o Rosemary, as I couldn't even after much brain cudgelling remember the address.

My impulse at the moment is to write you a letter full of impassioned promises to love you for ever and to marry you and never to speak to anyone else. But I'm not going to risk breaking them, so I won't make them: that doesn't alter the fact that I'm brimming over with love for you, and I do miss you very badly. If I manage to see Kristin this vac, I'll tell you all about it.

I'm feeling just now as though nothing on earth could change how I love you – and I don't think it can. You see, what held me to Kristin before was that she understood me and kept pace with me, and you didn't. But that seems to have changed since my visit to town. I was longing to see you when I got out of the train, and when I did see you you looked even sweeter than I'd expected. Of course you contrived to do the worst thing possible by chasing me away from my luggage but I was so pleased to see you I didn't much care. And I went on enjoying myself more and more: I *shall* be *glad* to see you when we get up for next term – though it begins to look as if I may be called up before term ends. I'm glad our relationship has changed as it has, because although it makes you in a way dependent on me, it makes me very much more bound to you. And you were so wonderful in town in every way, never losing your temper with me or quarrelling, that I began to love you more and more. Any ways your mother told you of catching men you seem to be employing most skilfully, my darling.

I am driving the Hardie car, a massive wagon capable of 90 m.p.h. up to town on Wednesday, for the day, so I hope to get my Greek lunch. We had a most Scottish and cheerful new year lasting till 5.30 a.m. and today Alec and I walked to Winchester. The family are incredibly Scottish, and almost unintelligible. Alec's name is in fact Ollick as they say it, and although no-one has yet said 'Hoots mon'

---

1 Alec Hardie's family address.

they habitually employ 'canna and didna' and say things like 'ye're no' fou the noo onyhoo'. Last night cousin Davie appeared and sang such things as

> The fouk wis ta'en, the bisem wis ga'en
> The barry widna row its lin
> An' siccan a sos ye niver had seen
> As the muckin o'Geordie's byre

And Pop sang, quite truthfully 'I'm fou the noo, I'm absolutely fou'. I must stop and go to sleep soon.

I thought your parents' letters eminently sensible. I'll compose a letter to them and enclose some suitable verses.[2]

Lots of love and write soon. I keep discovering how much I love you.

Your very loving sleepy Keith

124. *To Toni Beckett*   Private Hands

n.d. [PM 5 January 1940]   [Letterhead] Rookwood,
                                                                    Allbrook, Hants

Toni darling,

I'd like another letter from you. Alec and I can't believe its the 12th we have to go up, but that's what you said isn't it? I shall barely have time to do anything: I'm trying to get to Bexhill and Horsham for 2 days each. I'm afraid I've settled the Kristin question just how I didn't want to, because I wrote and explained about you and she never replied, which probably means she is very hurt and is going to shut up like a clam. It may be best in the end though.

I haven't got any riding here because of ice on the roads – but ice or no ice I took the Hardie car out to the New Forest to look for riding schools and in spite of skids touched 76 m.p.h. Going to London tomorrow I want to reach 85 if I can, which is about its maximum – but it'll need a very long straight with no ice. We are hoping to get to ὁ λευκός [illegible] at last and sample Retsina. I must say I think it's most trusting of Mrs Hardie to let me drive the car on icy roads without Mr Hardie knowing. He was down for Hogmanay, a very large heavy Scot – and got drunk and kept trying

2 See Letter 126.

to kick me – much to the shame of Alec and Mrs, who tried in vain to prevent him.

I met Alec's pursuing female yesterday; she looks quite nice but seems very dumb and her voice is a cross between Gracie Allen and Jean Arthur.

There are some lovely horses at the place in the New Forest but I don't think we'll get to them this time.

I got a most horrible and traditional card from Lise, with a letter written all over it. I'm sorry you don't like mine to Rosemary – what don't you like? However if she does it's o.k.

I'm trying to become a little less of a mental, moral and physical wreck before we meet again. I have been for some long walks and sawed wood and today Alec and I ran four miles before breakfast (which was only 1 cup of coffee). I still have several chins, but I think they'll begin to give in soon.

I must stop. Lots of love, sweet, [two lines cancelled]
Keith
[ink sketch: Keith 'Before and ... after treatment']

125. *To Betty Sze*   Graham

n.d. [PM 8 January 1940]   [Letterhead]
                                    Rookwood/ Allbrook/ Hants

Betty dear,
Thank you for your letter – I may have been feeling benevolent and reminiscent, isolated etc., when I wrote it, but when I decided to write it I was staying with Toni, and really having rather a good time in a mild way.[1] Nor have I regretted writing it, even once, because whatever I was feeling like I wasn't letting my feelings dictate much – see the piece about being comfortably in love. I wrote it at Hadlow House which is where I spent the most unpleasant weeks of the summer vac, in fact I think the most miserable of my life so far, and naturally 'it all came back to me', and my impulse was to be very emotional indeed and explain how you had only to call and I'd come running etc. But I sit on myself with some competence and write what I had originally conceived, though not in such academic language perhaps. Thank you for

1 No letter has been located.

understanding and in return for your understanding, here's another sweetmeat for your pride. I more or less lost all self-control last term, did no work of any kind, ate and drank far too much, and hardly took any exercise. I topped this up with an uninvited appearance at Jon Mayne's party where I made violent love, being quite, quite drunk, to (i) a fat person called Kay Fiske, who appeared to be about 30, (ii) Rosemary Brown, who was unfortunately sober, and (iii) Claude Furneaux, who was if possible, drunker than I was, and kept screaming, quite truthfully 'I won't be raped, I won't be raped'. Possibly some echo of this episode may have reached you. Afterwards I climbed to the top of the Logic Lane railings and after swaying backwards and forwards some 7ft above the cobbles, was violently sick and fell back into University College, somewhat gored by barbed wire. The funny thing is that this term of debauchery was not something I set out upon intentionally, and was *really* due to you, not just an absurd gesture to be blamed on you afterwards. I don't *blame* it on you anyway, but possibly knowing that may explain some more, if there's more to explain. Perhaps there's not.

I drove the huge Hardie Humber to London yesterday and we were held up at 5 miles an hour for some miles behind what appeared to be an entire battleship on a 32–wheel lorry. When we eventually scraped past I prepared to make up for lost time but we ran into a lot of antiskid sand, at about 76 m.p.h., and it had contrived to make a sort of paste with the wetness of the road, so we braked rather erratically. Coming back was very like our drive from Horsham,[2] and culminated in my being directed up a wrong road. As I was a good way up it before anyone realised, I tried to turn, only to find that this vast car was as wide as the road, and that we were dead opposite a lamp-post. My efforts to batter this down having failed and reduced Mrs Hardie to hysterics, we were pushed gradually round by various bystanders, and set off once more. In town we had lunch at a Greek restaurant, where we drank a wine called retsina. It tastes exactly like rubber. We had a dish called Shashlik which turned out, as I hoped, to be our old friend Schacklyk though it wasn't brought in in flames.
[ink sketch: burning kebab]

New Year here was extremely Scottish and included reels, sword dancing (on the sword-cane) and the singing of such things as

2 When he took her to Christ's Hospital.

the grape wis ta'en
the besim wis ga'en
the barry widna row its lin
An' siccan a sos ye niver ha' seen
As the muckin' o' Geordie's byre

and a Scottish version of 'Phil the Fluter's Ball'. I shall come up speaking very broad Scots next term as the whole family (bar little educated Alec from Oxford) speaks the broadest I ever heard outside a music hall. The song above is not far from their everyday talk.

I have been going for 4 mile runs in 6 sweaters before breakfast, and exercising Airedailes (Airdailes Airedails?) dogs to get thinner. Also splitting logs with wedges.

I'm sorry I shan't be up early next term – but when I appear I'd like to take you out if you'd like to come out. Only I think you must let me kiss you once or twice, because the horrible atmosphere of bright politeness when you came to tea and borrowed the umbrella was mainly owing to a kind of barrier between us that can only be done away with by that. I hope you'll trust me not to overdo it – I shan't.

I think I have a fair chance of as much happiness as I can get now with Toni. But you, however cheaply you behave, and whatever other people think of you, will always be the only person I love completely – you'll become almost a goddess or a mania if you go away. Whatever you do I don't think you'll ever lose my respect, or make me believe that you don't love me. And so if you ever can decide that things could be all right (you must have discovered a little more about me by now) please have the courage and confidence in me to come back. I imagine your good looks aren't going to last you very long, but I've thought well and good about it and I don't think it'll matter. So if it's a matter of months or years, you can get me any time, *unless* I've taken so much from someone else that I owe it to her not to leave her. I shall try not to get married for some time. I pray constantly, as far as such a completely faithless person can pray, that you will come back, though I can't believe you will. I'll never mention any of this again or ask you to come back. But remember it, and remember I'm quite sure. Wanting you has become like wanting the moon, though, and I'm long over the worst pain of not having you. And yet the pain is there, and if you ever step down I'll be almost overcome with joy. Well there we are. I'll never mention it any more, and I trust you never to allude to it, to anyone, unless to say the impossible has come about. If now after consideration you *know* you'll be happy with Ewing, please tell me honestly, because I really (much to my own surprise) want your happiness more than my own, and I'd gladly do without you then.

Burn this, please, and write or say when you've done it. If you let anyone else hear of it, I'll never forgive you.
Keith
P.S. Mother would like to accept your invitation sometime – but doubts if you meant her to. I said yes you did.

126. *To Mr and Mrs Beckett*   Private Hands

n.d.[early 1940[1]]   [Letterhead] University College, Oxford

Dear Mr and Mrs Beckett,
Toni has asked me to write to you, and to send you some poems, which I am now essaying. By now I expect you'll have heard a variety of assessments of my character, to which may I add my own? I spent a fairly stormy career at school and most of my holidays were alone with the result that I came up here a very defiant and rude person with vulnerable but concealed feelings and the wrong attitude towards most people. I shall never get over the idea of the world in general as a powerful force working for my hurt: nor would I wish to, for this conception of things saves me many disappoint-ments. I am over critical of everyone – luckily of myself too, though I do my self-criticism in private. I work rather in spurts and am often plunged into helpless despair. I hope knowing Toni will help to cure this: in return for my cure I should like to give her some more definite object in life than she seems to have at present; to help her concentrate her talents, which are there in widest readiness, on some certain achievement.[2] She isn't helped much by her tutors, who seem to demand only hard work without inquiring whether there is much point in the work they set. My tutor, (as most men's tutors), takes a personal interest in me and I spend a good deal of time with him apart from tutorials. But to her tutors, Toni is always Miss

1   Dated by Toni Beckett.
2   During the war Toni was to become a successful code breaker: see biographies of recipients.

Beckett and the tutorials appear to go on in an atmosphere of cold and ridiculous politeness and mutual boredom.

We have broken off our 'engagement' as such, because we prefer, after thinking it over, that there should be nothing whatsoever to bind us but our own liking and sympathy. This does not mean there is less conviction, but rather more, in our minds. We still have a good deal to learn about each other, but we are learning it. I am likely not to be called up at least until the summer, because there is not going to be any room in horsed cavalry for some time.

Reading this through, I must say I think it sounds rather a conceited letter: I wonder if you'll think so – I believe if so Toni and a lot of other people will agree that I am conceited. Myself, I believe I alternate between extreme conceit, and an extreme inferiority complex. During intermediate periods I am however normal and tolerable. I hope you'll meet me at one of those times, and that you'll like the poems I enclose.

Yours sincerely

Keith Douglas

[Poems enclosed: 'Sanctuary', 'Exotic', 'The Creator', 'A Symphony of Haydn', 'Stars', 'Pas de trois', 'Do not look up']³

127. *To Toni Beckett*   Private Hands

n.d.   [Letterhead] University College, Oxford

Toni sweet,

Don't start not working *again* darling – we must be good this term and impress a few people in the right way. I went to Saunders passage today and Evelyn was pleasantly surprised at the change in my looks. I'm going to the Ruskin on Monday, and will you come to the ballet on Monday evening? I think that's a legitimate entertainment: Alec has booked some seats – 4. Ilett may come, or if you like bring Rosemary (if she likes).

[X—] went up and took possession of his girl-friend [Y—] for a day or two, or rather a night or two, during the vac. I asked him what he'd do if she had a baby and he seems certain that if she knew

3 'Sanctuary' *CP* p.34, 'Exotic' *CP* p.19 (as 'Pleasures'); 'The Creator' *CP* p.34; 'A Symphony of Haydn' *CP* p.31 (as 'Haydn Clock Symphony'); 'Stars' *CP* p.29; 'Pas de Trois' *CP* p.27; 'Do not look up' *CP* p.28. Except for the last of the poems, the texts vary slightly from *CP*.

in time she could either take pills or go to a doctor who would remove it in a few minutes.

Darling when you're sure you're well started on your work, let me know and come and spend a day with me. I'm longing to hear if Mother liked you – I'll let you know as soon as she writes. I think she was rather prejudiced to like you beforehand. You seemed to get on alright together anyway.

I wonder if you could come and see me all day on Wednesday – or for a good time? Or shall we make it every Sunday and leave it at that? I've bought a red weskit – I hope you'll like it. It was a 22/6 one marked down to 10/6. Alec has some jodhpurs, a new riding stick, and a new tie. He has given me a velvet tie and I bought another silk one. Most extravagant. We walked miles today, and saw about horses at Rhodes School in Walton St.

I feel it *would* perhaps be a good thing if I saw a little less Alec – but I don't see how it's to be arranged – yet.

I have a feeling I'm going to do some work this term. I've written a poem which I'm sending to *The New Statesman*, and which I enclose.[1] Not the sort you'd like dedicated to you I fear.

Are you going to have to take the one subject you failed in again? You'll pass them all this time anyway my dear.

Goodnight, and am I sleepy.

Your

Keith

128. *To Toni Beckett*   Private Hands

n.d. [16 January 1940][1]

Dear Toni,

Burning the midnight electricity again darling and try and forgive me for my apparent boorishness and stupidity – though I'm probably not as much under strain as you are, I am affected. Dearest things *will* be allright – I'm only sorry that it's left to you to do things now and I just have to wait. Excessive exercise *may* do the trick unaided. Will you come and see me a whole lot of Sunday?

1   No poem survives with the letter.

_____

1   Dated by Toni Beckett.

I am perhaps reviewing a film for the *Cherwell* next week – will you?

I beg Quentin's pardon, Robert Levens appears to have been trying to pretend I was under contract to him or something. If the *Cherwell* doesn't turn out to be exactly as it was last term, (which I fear it will) I shall write for it, and if Robert doesn't want my stuff on that condition, he needn't have it.[2] He always makes an advertisement sandwich of it anyway. I read 47 pages of Milton today (triumph) and gave a lecture on poetry to an earnest young man from Magdalen. And I've been to see the *Cherwell* printer, more ballet, Edmund, and Robert: and written another poem which I don't suppose you'll like. It would be fun if the *New Statesman* took one.[3]

Love and Goodnight sweet.

Keith

I love this pen it can swish and swosh.

129. *To Toni Beckett*   Private Hands

n.d.[17 Jan. 1940][1]

Dear Toni,

Excuse the picture on the other side[2] but I need a real good large piece of paper. Of course I've thought all the way home, and I think I have my present feelings clear enough. Sunday is an awful long time so here are some remarks now. Firstly – so far from being near our tether's end I think we really shew some sign of beginning to get acquainted. I think you understand quite a lot about me and I'm beginning to get some inkling of the way your mind works too. One thing about me is this. I lived alone during the most fluid and formative years of my life, and during that time I lived on my imagination, which was so powerful as to persuade me that the things I imagined would come true. So I have been looking for them

2 Robert Levens edited the *Oxford Magazine*, to which Douglas had contributed the previous year.
3 No record remains.

---

1 Dated by Toni Beckett.
2 A Disneyish vamp, holding a playing card.

to come true exactly according to the way I had imagined. I am beginning to find that things don't happen like that. If they *never* happened in the least like I imagined it would be easy to take a new line – but sometimes they do, for a little, so I have to keep my eyes skinned. Your statement that I am self-centred is a triumph of underestimation – I am hopelessly, and by now quite involuntarily and even unwillingly submerged in myself, swamped by myself, tied to myself. If we break up now the little way that I have got away from this curse will be quickly retraced. If we go on, I really think that we may get my own psychology straightened out, and in turn put yours about lovemaking and everything else straight. Not only do I not want to be self-centred, but I want very much to submerge myself in someone else, and there's every reason why it should be you. But you must understand me and I you, and you must be just as submerged in me. This doesn't apply to our intellectual or active pursuits, it doesn't mean we have to go about with each other all the time. It means that there must be an attachment between us which will be the thing which always shows up the difference between our relations with each other and our relations, however intimate, with someone else. The very fact that (evidently without finding it out) you have already shaken my conviction on several points of which I was before quite sure argues that there are greater things to come. You have, you say, noticed some very bad bits in the Clock Symphony poem:[3] well, I know for a fact that it's a bad poem, and doesn't compare even with the last I sent you, which does really express what I set out to express.[4] If you have understood this, it will give me more respect for you. When I seem supremely misunderstanding you, reflect that I may be attributing to you motives, thoughts, emotions, which I imagined for you some time ago, I may be subconsciously 'fitting you in'. Then you must shew me what you really are thinking, and we are a lot better off. I don't mean that this is an excuse for my behaviour but it is a reason, and if you understand it you may forgive it or anyway not be so hurt or estranged by it. Then you say, quite truthfully, that we often put each other's backs up. I can easily tell you how you annoy me, and

---

3 First published in the Oxford magazine *Kingdom Come*. edited by John Waller, December 1939–January 1940.
4 It could be 'Pleasures' which, under the title 'Exotic', is with the letters to Toni Beckett.

I think if I did, you probably wouldn't do the things again, and even if you did, they wouldn't infuriate me any more. So could you tell me.

If we are to get on perfectly, we must eventually be able to enjoy sleeping together – for the fact of that means to me a way of expressing and feeling complete union, which I believe you will understand. I still think this will come and I don't feel inclined to hurry it. If only you will never try to tell me things which aren't true to spare my feelings. I think I can tell you the truth too and I think things will be allright. I may be arguing rather desperately because I feel that I shall crack up and go backward again if we break – but there's some chance we both will. You say that I have an inferiority complex. In fact, you are right, but it is only the feeling that you love me and have some respect for me that wards it off. You may think you know me well enough to see that this is not true, but just think for a moment of the possibility and the probability. I am never likely to have an inferiority complex towards men. But I am very much in danger of having one towards women, of feeling that I am too unpleasant for them to want anything but an intellectual relationship with me, that women would have me with them like an amiable dog, but never allow me or dream of allowing me more liberty with their persons than they would a dog. That may sound silly, but that's the feeling I've had before, and I'm very liable to have again. It very soon becomes a general inferiority complex, and acts even towards men in a way, for though I may feel their intellectual superior, I know that compared with them I am abnormal – not capable of the ordinary behaviour of life of which they are capable and I have felt and may again feel a monstrosity. If you still love me enough to think it worth while to try and straighten out the mess I am at the moment, use this letter and anything I may tell you on Sunday to help you do it. If there's anything here you don't understand, or which infuriates you, make sure to tell me.
Goodnight and I do love you
Keith

130. *To Toni Beckett*   Private Hands

n.d. [18 January1940][1]   [Letterhead] University College, Oxford

Dont make as heavy weather reading my last night's letter as I did
writing it: but it contains *some* sense. If I've done any work by 6.0
today I'll come up to L.M.H. to pick you up. Otherwise see you at
the theatre, 7.10. Don't forsake me yet.
K

131. *To Toni Beckett*   Private Hands

n.d.   [Letterhead] University College, Oxford

Toni darling,
I'm afraid the promised letter will arrive late. I've been having a
bilious attack all day, feeling so lethargic I could hardly crawl about.
I went out to try and wake up but came back and slumped to the
floor. Then after lying there about an hour and a half I went to have
a bath and passed into a kind of stupor in which I remember feeling
indefinitely sorry for whoever was going to find my body. Then I
came to a little more, dressed and came back to my room and slept
for 1½ hours. I wish I could go on sleeping but bloody Alec and Mrs
Blunden are coming to collect me and go to *Midsummer Night's
Dream*. At any rate I can sleep all through that. I hope you've enjoyed
your day more. Perhaps I'll see you tomorrow, if I'm not dead.
Love
Keith

132. *To Toni Beckett*   Private Hands

n.d. [early February 1940][1]   [Letterhead]
                                          University College, Oxford

Dear Miss Beckett,
You don't really deserve a letter at all so I shall confirm it by writing
to you an illegible one – I know you won't write one to me for you

---

1 Dated by Toni Beckett.

---

1 Dated by Toni Beckett.

consider yourself too busy, as if in addition to your work, *you* were being an editor, giving riding lessons, and attending an art school, instead of enjoying yourself with a *very large* collection of young men. I however have simply loads of time – so much that I *may* even draw and write you a Valentine, though I doubt it. Stanley will send you a six and sixpenny one anyway.

I have been writing round for jobs this morning. I may get one from the Cambridge man, and have offered myself as secretary to Sir Reginald Spence (who wears corsets). That would give me another large car to play with. I wonder where you will be?

I simply must stop writing with this foul pen before it gets too large for the page.

Love
Keith

133. *To Toni Beckett*   Private Hands

Friday [16 February 1940]   Univ.

Toni darling,

I'm sorry I wasn't at your tea party – John Waller[1] who isn't nearly as bad as he looks or as Alec made out, and Keith Elliot, came to tea. Then I went and saw 39 *Steps* which I think is passable but not good.

Also I'm sorry if I seemed a bit dumb when you and Alec came to see me yesterday – I was feeling pretty ill and it was rather an effort to speak at all, and anyway I couldn't fathom why you should come and see me for 2 minutes just at 7.15. I hoped perhaps you'd stay and be there when I came out of hall, but you weren't there in spite of my eating in a great hurry.

I fear I shan't see you today either, unless I turn up at about 2.30 or so and wait to go to Ray Cooper's sherry party with you. I don't know if I can manage the sherry party. Anyway I'll try and see you sometime this afternoon.

Pennock apologises, for missing your party, but says he couldn't face going by himself. I hope the model wasn't too boring. Perhaps you asked Alec?

I went to the Art School this morning and saw various people.

1   He edited *Bolero* and *Kingdom Come* at Oxford.

Stanley has 'flu and hopes you'll go and see him. I told him you probably would and that I might go too (as Evelyn suggested) so as to catch a glimpse of you.
Love
Keith
I'm sorry you didn't even like my last note enough to thank me. I hoped it would please you.

134. *To Toni Beckett*   Private Hands

n.d.   Univ.

Darling.
I'm afraid I hurt your feelings by being sarcastic at you this afternoon, and I'm very sorry. The boy was just born malicious. There's no good in him at all, and he'll come to No Good in the end.
Really I am sorry, sweet. Remind me to show you a new letter from Mother, most favourable.
Love in loads
Keith

135. *To Toni Beckett*   Private Hands

n.d.

That was a bloody silly letter to write. I ought to have said it to you or just kept quiet, because things will be all right. I'm sorry. I hope you won't think it such a ridiculous letter as anyone else picking it up and reading it would have. Love to you. Come at one tomorrow. Please don't be late and please be kind to me.

136. *To Toni Beckett*   Private Hands

n.d.

Darling Toni,
Work being nullified for tonight let me write and say what a swine I am and how much that swine loves you for being an angel tonight and yet perfectly sober and enduring my terrible and really drunken behaviour. I am even drunker now. It just shews what determination

to get tight will do even on one sherry, 2½ glasses of Vin rosé, a vodka and a gin and lime. Goodnight my sweet, and how sweet. Keith

137. *To Toni Beckett*   Private Hands

n.d.

I came to take all my stuff back – reckoning that you'd be out so it needn't worry you again. I feel all this, though it was the third time, was for no reason but just flared up. It was all so unnecessary, when you had come to see me feeling so happy, and brought me a plum. Then I was horrid and didn't take the plum and went on at you, and now I feel like death. I've just wandered round Oxford ever since – I can't believe it, or couldn't at first, but now it's coming into my mind and I'm done. I've tried and tried harder than I've ever done anything, to make a go of this, and I'd go on trying for ever. I love you so much I feel knocked out. You asked me to write you a real love letter and you seem to be getting it. I must see you again darling – I can't bear it – this very usual stuff is enough to make anyone sick of me but I can't. I'm utterly dependent on you. I've tried while I was walking around to decide it was all for the best and I went in to see Pennock and he said he'd just begun to think everything was going all right and was very surprised. For god's sake be kind and even if you hate me, patch it up for this term, bear with me till I go away and let me get over it while you're not there. Come back if it's only to get me through my exam. I can't humble myself any more. It can be all right – you only made me say horrid things because you teased me. I must have you – I can't get on without you saying nasty things to me, and that you don't like my tie and you wish I'd get a shoelace and you like my hair and you hate the *Cherwell* cover. I want you to say it, the nasty things as much as the nice ones. I can't let you go away now. This is no solution at all – it's made things far far worse. If you'll come back, by all means stay away for a bit but come back. I know you want to like hell. I'd go on my knees to you in the High if you want me to, or hold my hand in the fire – anything to shew you.

I had a long letter from your father, of course I had to get it when I went into Merton. I also met Basil Mitchell and Natalia who both asked after you. I shall stay in all this afternoon and wait for you.

You must come and see me, you can't take away everything I've built up.

Please give me to the end of term to try and make up for my horridness. You don't realise how utterly dependent on you I am. You'll wreck me for the next few months, just when I was beginning to get going with the *Cherwell*[1] and the anthology and Appletons. It's no good saying it's all rot and I must pull myself together. I must stop thinking before I could go on with the magazine and I shan't stop thinking of this for months. And Mother's coming up hoping to have a good time. I shall be foul to her too.

It's no use darling you've absolutely got me wrecked. If you think it's worth it stay away. I swear I see your point of view and I know what you think – but you do love me and I won.

138. *To Margaret Stanley-Wrench*   BL 57977 f.7

n.d. [March 1940][1]   University College

Dear Margaret,
The number of times I've written to you is rapidly mounting, but the number of epistles posted remains almost nil. I've very sleepy at the moment so I must confine myself to thanking you for a Christmas card, hoping you got mine, promising to write a real letter only in reply to one from you, and

> requesting you urgently
> to send as many as four
> poems to me for an Oxford
> Anthology which goes to press
> in a week or two and is almost
> destitute of really good contributions
> except of course for those of

Yours with love
Keith
Please send something quickly.

---

1   At first co-editor with David Beaty, Douglas became sole editor of the Oxford weekly in Trinity Term 1940.

---

1   Dated by Margaret Stanley-Wrench.

139. *To Toni Beckett* Private Hands

n.d.

Toni darling,

As the anthology is in the throes of going to press, I'm afraid the long letter won't come yet. I have also to arrange somewhere for Mother to go as Betty's ill, and hasn't found anywhere. And there is still the *Cherwell* and my exam. There are lots of other things when I have time. The stars poem is going into the Anthology dedicated to you. Also this poem and another translation are to be included without my name under them.[1]

I hope you'll be well enough to take P. Mods and pass. It would be so foul to have next term mucked up with them.

Mother arrives tomorrow. I may have to send her to the Apps.,[2] who have also asked me to stay, for the whole vac. if I like, and possibly edit a children's mag. which App wants to run.

If I don't see you for a bit, it will only be excessive business.

Get well soon.

Love Keith

Pennock sends his best wishes for your speedy recovery.

K.

140. *To Toni Beckett* Private Hands

n.d. [PM Oxford 21 March 1940]

Toni darling,

I have now recovered from my cold and yesterday went to the Cheltenham races with Miss Sze, where we picked the winner of the gold cup, unfortunately the favourite, also of another race at 6 – 1. But as we only bet in bobs and 2 bobs it didn't help much. I tried to see Gigi,[1] but (a) she was apparently working and (b) she

---

1 Douglas's translation of 'Horace Odes I:V' is typed on verso of the letter; the other translation included in *Augury* was of Rimbaud's 'Head of Faun'.
2 The Appletons (see Letter 120).

---

1 Toni Beckett's sister.

was out at Cowley, so I couldn't. This was probably a good thing as your father would have found out I went there and told everyone I was trying to seduce Gigi behind his back, by making secret visits to her at C.L.C. [Cheltenham Ladies' College]

I have spent the morning electric sweeping and have done every room in the house except the bathroom, 2 lavatories, (whose seats must get pretty regularly dusted anyway) and the attic – no mean feat. I have also drawn the requisite ruddy angels and the rider on the white horse out of Revelation for old App., but there is no talk of paying me. However I found £1 I didn't know I had, so I'm not so badly off. In spite of your being kept away from the house Bridget[2] got bilious with excitement, so the little toad *was* in bed for her birthday.

I hope you are now enjoying yourself and feeling well, surrounded no doubt by Brians and Sallys or their substitutes. I am trying to borrow a bike and go down to Horsham for a bit, and so on via Withyham, Tunbridge Wells and Uckfield and back here.

I met a peculiar tough egg called Miss Wilson at C.L.C., also the matron of the San and a female skeleton, (unidentified). On one occasion I got ushered into a roomful of multi-sized girls, causing instant confusion. I visited the Prefects room, which smelt like a Prefects room, St Margaret's, St Austin's, and various corridors: and I was privileged to catch a glimpse of Miss Barham or Barret or Something, forging along on a bicycle.

So now you know how they all are at the dear old school: judging from Miss Wilson's conversation, you and Betty are the only 2 old girls not married.

I must stop: I would send you an Easter egg, did I not know how embarrassed you would be at receiving it, not having sent one to me: actually I hadn't found anything worth sending, but you can buy yourself a chocolate one from me if you like and I'll pay you next term. If I find anything later I'll send it.

Love

Keith. Write when you've time.

2   Bridget Appleton, younger sister of Betty and Joan.

Monday [n.d. ?25 March 1940]   Hill Crest[1]

Toni darling,

Thank you like anything for that marvellous book. The letterpress I haven't yet begun to decipher, but the illustrations are marvellous, particularly the cat, is it Siamese? I will send your results as soon as I see them. I'm sorry Margaret is taking part in the general parental idiocy, but not much surprised. I see there was some native unpleasantness and three people killed in Lahore – did I say that before. I have been collecting my poems together and almost have enough to publish now.[2] The proofs of the Blackwell book have come, and it all looks very nice but VERY thin.[3] There are some nice misprints such as Joan Waller and no one having a more insensitive appreciation of Oxford poetry than Basil Blackwell. I have done a new cover design for it and some illustrations which you saw before.[4] One of the poems (Stars) looks very chaste with For Antoinette written above it.

I will enclose some prints of the linocuts if I can find some or the paper to do some more on, if there aren't any left.[5] I went to try and ride the App. uncle's horses yesterday, but had to come away after trying to catch the sods for four hours, with an immense expenditure of carrots and temper.

I heard a story alleged to be true, and which sounds authentic, about the Salvation army. One of their bands had been playing and all the brothers and sisters singing for some time to no one at all. When they had finished Holy, Holy, Holy, for the second time to an audience of 2 cats and whoever happened to be passing hurriedly by, the band master with a look of angelic resignation says. 'Come on, brethren. Let's give 'em Oly Oly Oly once more, and then we'll bugger off ome.' Which they done.

Tomorrow I go to see Marx bros at the Circus, yoohoo. You can have no idea how many angels and riders on white horses I've

1 The Appletons' house.
2 Typed in red, they were sent to Blunden who returned them on 21 May (see below): part of the collection survives in BL 56357.
3 The proofs of *Augury* are now in the Brotherton Library.
4 Drawings and linocuts survive among the Douglas papers at the BL.
5 Sent to Graham by Toni Beckett and in his possession.

drawn: but apparently I've got it right at last. I think only because I told him I wouldn't draw any more however wrong they were.

Betty's asthmatic curate is coming down on Thursday. As a matter of fact from photos he seems to be rather handsome. But so he should be if all the rest is true.

There must be some redeeming feature.

Old App. turns out to have a bee in his bonnet about Roman Catholics similar to your grand mother's in re jews. He says the whole country is seamed with R.C. secret societies, hand in glove with the Nazis, working our destruction. They should all be put up against the wall etc. Even Saunders passage[6] he regards with some suspicion. He attributes [Z—'s] evil odour to the fact that she is an R.C.

[new sheet, something missing] talking of your grandmother, did you tick her off and if so what did she say?

I must stop now: I'll send your results as soon as I find them. Now I'll look for some linoprints.

Much love and kisses, in spite of the fact that you forgot, I hope it was forgot, to stamp your letter. XXXXXXX 7X is the strongest they make here.

Keith

142. *To Marie J. Douglas*   BL 56355 f.114

Monday [n.d. ?25 March 1940]   Hill Crest

Dear Mother,

The parcel with the second pair of trousers has just arrived. I don't know what you mean they'll only do to sit round in. It's a masterpiece, and Mrs App. and in fact the whole family are overcome with admiration. Thank you very much: it may be my short sight, but I don't think the darn shews at all.

I went to try and ride yesterday on Mrs App.'s brother's horses, but after four hours still hadn't caught them and had to come home. On Bridget's birthday I organized a highly successful treasure hunt in the garden and wrote all the clues in verse.

The proofs of the anthology have come and it looks quite good but very thin. One of the misprints states that no one is more

6 Where artist friends lived in Oxford; see *KD* p.84.

insensitive to Oxford poetry than Basil Blackwell.

Alec is coming up next Saturday so I expect we'll get it finally straightened out then.

I am getting an awful lot of car-driving as I do all the chauffering for the whole family. I have also nearly completed a collection of my poems for publication.[1] The novel has got no further yet.[2] But as I have at last drawn the angels, white horses etc., to old App.'s satisfaction, I may get started on it soon. He has said no more about paying me but I shall see he does as soon as the drawings are printed.

I seem to have an awful lot of clean clothes for once, and manage to look quite presentable most of the time. I have been to the baths once and hope to go again soon, and next time I won't let them send the garage boy to help me and then I will catch those horses. Then I am supposed to be going to teach Betty to ride. I am also teaching her to dive, and Joan. In return for this they speak of teaching me to dance, but after a sample lesson yesterday I don't think I should ever have time to become good enough to make it worth while.

I think I had better stop now as it's about lunch time and anyway there doesn't seem to be much left to say. My typing is getting much faster but however fast or slow I type I can't avoid about one mistake every two lines.

I hope soon either I'll get to see you or you'll get to see me.

Love,

Keith

PS Enclosed are illustrations and cover design for the anthology. They'll look better printed from a press.

143. *To Toni Beckett*   Private Hands

n.d. [PM 11 April 1940]   [Merton College letterhead, deleted]
                                                Hill Crest

Toni darling,

Thanks awfully for writing to Mother – she was very glad to get your letter and I expect has written to you. Anyway she wrote to

---

1 See Letter 141.
2 No record remains.

me this morning and said it was a very pleasant surprise. So you may consider your good turn done.

I have gone on drawing things for old App. and am now doing designs for backcloths, there being some idea of doing a show entirely composed of masques, including the Dryden one done properly. He hasn't paid me any more but I can't very well ask to be paid as I am eating everything within reach and using up petrol. I even pinch his stamps.

I can't tell you anything more about Betty Sze's digs than you probably know – namely that they're 3, Banbury Road, and I've never been inside them. They are apparently pinched by Balliol men as a rule, but there may be some free next term and anyway there are in the vac.

I wish you'd come up early and relieve my boredom a bit. I don't do much now except go swimming, and am I fat. I must stop this and then I can post it when I take Bridget into town in a minute. Nothing ever seems to get collected from the box. If you're not coming, write. Your last letter didn't say much about you.
Love
[ink smudge 'K'] Keith Douglas 's mark.

144. *To Toni Beckett*   Private Hands

n.d. [April 1940]   'Beth-el', Boars Hill.
                            [Merton College letterhead, deleted]

Dearest Antoinette,
I could not let slip the opportunity of letting you participate in our great joy: we have found the Master through prayer, and through dear Mr Appleton's very deep and *searching* articles in the *Sunday Companion*![1]
How happy we are! And look forward to a Blessed time of prayer, only stopping to eat our dispepsia tablet every four hours.
Yours in His service.
Cedric Umbrage

1 A series of weekly devotional articles, 'The Silent Fellowship', by E.R. Appleton.

n.d. [May 1940]

Toni darling,
Here is a belated easter egg for you, if you would like it. If you think
it's very bad send it back and I'll do you something else which you
probably won't like any better.

I hope you got the telegram announcing you had passed in three
subjects – you took four, didn't you. As far as I remember what you
passed in were Latin, French, and Constitutional law and History.
Does that sound right? I failed to get a distinction in Milton, though
of course I passed – as though that were any use. I don't think I shall
take it again because I think I deserved a distinction for that paper,
and as that didn't get one I doubt if I would after another term's
work unless of course Blunden is correcting papers again next term.
We shall see.

The Betty App. curate has come to stay: he is rather like Jock
Neilson only six feet two, and seems quite sane. God knows why
he should be a curate. He hasn't been asthmatic yet this time. I think
the new Marx bros picture is damn good almost all through, and
managed to enjoy it in spite of the shade of you sitting beside me
patiently saying do you really think this is funny. I've also been to
see *Gulliver* which seems pretty feeble and very obviously copies
Snow White.

I heard a funny story about Sally the other day which arrived in
a letter to the Apps. I expect he will have told you about it if he has
seen you since. We had a most awful woman staying here. She was
so foul I don't think I could have lived in the house with her while
she was here if I'd worn my glasses all the time. She is very fat and
has a face like a close up of one of the three little pigs, only mottled
and kind of poxy. She has a shrill voice and a hideous loud laugh
and I have never heard anyone gush so much even on the stage. She
is called Margaret Scott and getting on for fifty. Were we glad when
she went. However apparently she got in a train with Sally – 'A very
nice young man who said he knew Keith. We got into conversation'
– this is one thing Scotty does really well – 'and he said he had met
Betty over the telephone. He is very interested in acting and has
been in a lot of shows in college. His name is Walter Salmon. When
we arrived his people met him in a car and he *insisted* on giving me
a lift, and was *very* anxious that we should meet again.' I knew Sally

was pretty depraved but I didn't know he'd got to the stage of running after mottled old women. She works in a cake shop, as far as I could make out. She is similar to Kay Fiske (whom of course Sally knows) only a lot worse.

Mother has been ill again and had more or less what Blunden had, including the pleurisy, and I expect would be most touched and gratified by a letter from you, if you're interested in touching and gratifying her, which I doubt. The address is Hadlow House, ditto Down, nr Uckfield, Sx.

I have painted two more watercolours in addition to the one I am probably going to forget to enclose. I have also done a big one on calico of these horses, which I don't like much at the moment though no doubt I shall like it better later.[1]

I suppose you are going about having what my grandmother would have described as a high old time. Let me know about it some time. You would be surprised how much I miss you, if you could believe it, but I don't suppose you could. Walter Douglas is back painting in a very very high studio a little further along the Broad towards George Street than Saunders passage. Meric has a girl friend staying with him, and Evelyn is still there. Everyone else seems to have departed, though I have no doubt that careful search would discover Vilassily, or however she spells herself, and other members of the Slade.

I think I shall stop now and write to bloody Alec, who has been writing letters full of puerile wit.

Love and write soon

Keith

146. *To Toni Beckett*   Private Hands

n.d.   [Letterhead] University College, Oxford

Toni darling,

Thank you very very much my sweet: you did behave marvellously and I was very grateful. You make an awful lot of efforts for me now, and although I'm sometimes sorry they have to be efforts, I'm very appreciative, though I mayn't appear so. I was also very

---

1 These don't appear to have survived; a self-portrait, however, was with the letters to Toni Beckett.

impressed with you for not losing your temper with me in the Indian restaurant, and altogether you're very sweet. This isn't very well expressed because I'm almost asleep. Goodnight my darling.
Keith

146a From *Edmund Blunden to Keith Douglas*   BL 56356 f.8

21 May 1940   Merton College

My dear Keith,

I restore your MSS., no, TSS. with the assurance that you have here produced a most attractive series of poems, interesting alike in the way you think about things, the painter's quality in the treatment, and the originality with which you vary normal metres. You will find a very few pencil markings on the pages; so far as I can judge there is scarcely any item which it would be best to exclude, the vitality of eager feeling and shaping seems to me to be present in nearly all.

But now, what is to be done? Will you send the MS. up to a publisher? it is a ghoulish moment for such matters, but possibly publishers are less afflicted with MSS. than in normal times. I would suggest (1) J. Cape or (2) Faber. With Mr Hart-Davis of Cape I have an ancient friendship, and can speak to him of you and your work, – but I have no real contact with Faber, and indeed my name *there* might only cause Mr Eliot (who perhaps 'reads' for the firm) to suspect you were in some sort of my poetical platoon, and do nothing.

Let me thank you on my own account as a reader for the pleasure and quickening your verse gives me, and this is naturally all the better to reflect upon in view of our old C.H. We have had some pretty good poets, Peele, Coleridge, Lamb, Hunt, but the line must be extended! and I think you can do it.

Yours ever, *EB*

147. *To Edmund Blunden*   Texas

[June 1940]   [Letterhead] Hadlow House, Nr Uckfield, Sussex

Dear E.B.

I'm not to report for a week or 2, so I shall have time to clear things

up a bit. My poems are packed up and in transit here by goods, with the rest of my stuff – but when they come I think I shall send them to you for safe keeping, and if at any time you think it worth while handing the[m] over to J. Cape please do so and I will write them a letter from wherever I am at the moment. Meanwhile I am going down to Housey to get as much riding as possible before I actually get to the cavalry, and to learn up Cavalry training and Horsemastership.
Love to Sylva
In haste
Keith
Do you know Hamo Sassoon's address?

148. *To Toni Beckett*   Private Hands

n.d.   Marlhurst, Southwater, Nr Horsham

Dearest Miss Gabrielle,[1]
I put that on the address for various subtle reasons. I had to send it to L.M.H., not remembering Rosemary's address. But had I sent it to Miss Beckett they would almost certainly have forwarded it to your address without looking at the c/o Mrs Rosemary Brown. On the other hand I didn't want to address it to Rosemary because it would be such a disappointment to open it if she happened to be wanting a letter. So I sent it thus addressed.
   I shall be catching the 4.45 from Paddington to Oxford on Friday. Could you meet me at Victoria at 1.0 when I come up from here – I'll meet you outside the buffet
                    [sketch: Paddington station platforms]
Excuse this being so short and untidy it's written on my knee just before going out and I can't concentrate with everyone else in the room. If you can't manage 1.0 I'll see you on the 4:45?
Lots of love, sweet,
I'm longing to see you.
Keith

1   In May Toni had told Keith she was unable to put up with his jealousy any longer, and they had finally split up: see *KD* p.97.

149. *To Betty Sze*   Graham

n.d. [?July1940]   Marlhurst, Southwater, Nr Horsham

Dear Betty,
Please excuse this appalling paper. I borrowed it. I am staying near
Housey, and went to see the Roberts the other day for the first time
since I took you. It isn't a year yet since the girl at the Cowley Road
garage casually announced you were getting married; but it *is* very
nearly a year, and anyone so youthful and susceptible as I am should
have completely recovered by now. I think I *am* as near recovered
as I shall ever be, but I shan't ever fall for anyone else so hard. I keep
thinking all is well and then I get the very feeling, just as badly, that
I had when I first realised you had finished with me. So I suppose
I shall love you hopelessly till I die, at the expense of whomever I
meet afterwards. Which of course is just what all authentic poets
should do. I still fall tremendously in love with people while the
circumstances are right and romantic, but you're the only one who
survived the cold light of reason. When I quarrel with other girls I
really feel furious or annoyed with them – but when I quarrelled
with you I always felt as miserable as hell until it came right, in fact
the very sensation which has lasted so well now that it has gone
permanently wrong. That was why I could never exercise much
charm over you any more than any but the most incredibly self-
controlled person could look his best walking a ricketty bridge across
900 feet of space. I knew what I was in for if I fell and that made
me too nervous to behave ordinarily.

Well as far as I can see Oxford is over for me now and I go to
Edinburgh, to the Scots Greys, on the 18th of this month. I'll write
you from there, but I think more than likely we shan't meet again,
so this signs me off except as a literally distant acquaintance. I begin
off with some months as a trooper, during which I shall be too busy
grooming, cleaning saddlery etc., to think much.

All I meant to say in this really was, I'm afraid I still love you just
as much, and I hope you'll write sometimes, and probably goodbye
Keith
PS I believe a volume of my poems may come out some time, if J.
Cape have any paper. If so it will be partly dedicated to you, if you
don't mind – perhaps only under your Chinese 2nd name.[1]

1   Yingcheng - the name Douglas used when dedicating poems to Betty.

150. *To Edmund Blunden*   Texas

[June/July 1940]   Marlhurst, Southwater, Sussex

Dear E.B.,

Thank you for your card – I am as you guessed more or less at Housey by now. I got out at C.H. station yesterday evening and walked up through the serried ranks of the corps to the shop, where I took an innocent drink before walking on out to Southwater. I met Mr Buck[1] who seems very well, and asked after you.

I am likely to have at least one ride per day while I'm here, and shall spend most of the rest of my time hanging about the school, unless the Head chases me off.

Thank you for accepting the protection of my poems – I'll send them you as soon as I get back to Hadlow Down. I doubt if I shall write any more for some time – I am now trying to learn Cavalry Training and the Manual of Hosemastership by heart. Already I know that the horse has a very small stomach, which I never suspected, and that he requires from 5 – 15 gallons of water a day. I never met one that took anywhere near the 15. I suppose he would be regarded with awe by his companions as a 7 bucket-man.

I must stop now, as I want to catch Mr Roberts before he comes out of school and makes for Horsham.

Best wishes to you and Sylva.

Keith

151. *To Edmund Blunden*   Texas

[July 1940]

Dear Edmund,

I'm afraid I have to cancel the dinner engagement for tomorrow night, as I've been called up and have to go to Edinburgh (I think) immediately. I'll let you know further developments. I'm so sorry.

In haste

Keith

---

1 Hector Buck, a master at Christ's Hospital and a great friend of Blunden's; see Letter 61 n. 1.

Five

1940–1941

152. *To Marie J. Douglas*   BL 56355 f.115

n.d. [PM Edinburgh 19 July 1940]   327210 Mr Douglas KC
                                                         D SQDN Room 23
                                3rd Cav. Tr. Regt./Redford Barracks/Edinburgh[1]

Dear Mother,

The old hag in the carriage wasn't bad; but very talkative. I slept about 4½ hours, and arrived on time in pouring rain. I hung about the station after having a bath and a shave and breakfast and eventually met another Oxford man who came in on a later train and borrowed a mac from his cousins who live here. I had lunch with him and tea with the cousins and we reported about 5.30. We are issued with uniform tomorrow, and I believe begin to ride at once.

Work will obviously be very hard and I shouldn't like to have it indefinitely but I ought to stick 4 months. These are huge barracks and take some finding your way. There are several jockeys here and we have a dummy horse in our bedroom like a full size rocking horse, to do exercises on.

I have been watching people cleaning saddlery and looked at the horses – there are no more than 2 greys in the lot thank God.

I have a very shifty-looking jockey next bed to me, who looks as though he'd pinch anything he could, so thank goodness I've got a padlock.

We have a beer room, restaurant, smoking room, and bedroom with 24 beds, about the size of a housey dormitory with a wireless going all day all over the barracks, and a locker over each bed.

There are large numbers of OUOTC [Oxford University Officers' Training Corps] people. Dances and shows and canteens for troops in Edinburgh when we've time off. The uniform is most handsome.

The ordinary troopers are very decent about shewing us everything and telling us what to expect. There is a theatre in the barracks for concerts and that's about all I know.

Love
Keith

---

1   Douglas trained for over three months in the cavalry before going to the 'Mechanized Wing' at Sandhurst.

153. *To Marie J. Douglas*   BL 56355 ff.117–9

Friday [PM 4 November 1940]   [Letterhead] Royal Military
                                      College, Camberley, Surrey[1]

Dear Mother,

Thank you very much for this pen and the other enclosures. I thought your article very impressive (you can write journalese though, as well as any editor).[2] I hope you have done the other article you were asked to do – you don't say.

There isn't much news that I haven't told you. This week we have been doing the theoretical part of a petrol engine. Next week we spend taking engines to bits and the week after, driving. After that we have an exam. Not passing it is our first opportunity of getting sent back to the ranks. Then we go to Lulworth and are finally judged on our Gunnery marks there. When we come back (we go about the end of Dec.) our course is virtually over, for better or worse.

Hamo Sassoon goes today, with a commission to the Inns of Court Regt Armoured Car (Fighting) Unit, which is forming at Farnborough. Julian Pitt-Rivers has arrived here with all my stuff. He didn't send it because he heard we were coming up to Edinburgh from Weedon, which we also heard. Then he heard Weedon had disintegrated and didn't know where we'd gone.[3]

Don't be surprised if you only get very short letters for the next 3 weeks because this is the main part of the course, and after that, Lulworth is almost as important. I may get home Christmas leave in between but I don't know where I can go. Oxford term ends tomorrow. I've heard no more of my poems.

Yes I want a strap on my map case to hang it by, please, from the top corners (i.e. corners at the end). If you are taking time about it, could you sew the celluloid into a stiffened canvas case, instead of putting it on a board with rubber bands? Like this [two sketches follow with comments 'map slipped in here' 'shoulder strap' 'celluloid' and 'back view' 'stiffened canvas back' 'pocket for extra map' 'pockets for chinagraph pencils'].

1 From 1 November 1940 Douglas was at Sandhurst.
2 Mrs Douglas had written in the *Sunday Express* about the condition of Prisoners of War in Germany and elicited a strong response (see correspondence in the Brotherton Library).
3 Douglas was in the last group to train at the 'Army Equitation School' at Weedon, which closed down on their departure.

The ideal case is one which opens out and holds 2 maps so that you can work on large and small scale maps simultaneously. [two sketches with comments: 'shoulder strap' 'map goes in' [left side] 'map goes in' [right side] 'view shut up']

I must stop this it's dinner time. Lots of love. Get an invitation for us both for Xmas out of your fan mail.

Keith

153a *From Blunden to Douglas* (postcard) [extract]   BL 56356 f.10

16 December 1940   Merton College

The Works have gone off to T.S.Eliot, including the latest pieces: I have sent all that were in my hands... *EB*[1]

154. *To Jean Turner*   Private Hands

n.d. [December 1940]   [Letterhead] Royal Military College, Camberley, Surrey

Dear Jean,[1]

I don't doubt that this will get lost or become illegible on the way, but I feel like writing to you and I don't feel like writing to anyone else so the letter will start out, anyway: unless I forget to post it.

Actually, I have been in the mill for 4 or 5 months – it might have been as many years, it seems so long since my previous existence ceased. I have all the disadvantages of army life, but at present, no advantages. At least if I had as much money as most officer cadets I could hire or seduce an obliging young lady to spend my leaves with me. But I haven't even got anywhere to go if and when I get leave. I had a touching but painfully moral romance with a girl in a hat-shop, when I was a trooper in the Scots Greys in Edinburgh.[2] She still writes to me devotedly and rather illiterately. Here I just work, though in very luxurious surroundings, and hitchhike to Oxford on Sundays. There I walk desolately about

1   For the full letter see *Miscellany* pp.71–2.

---

1   Now back for a second year at Somerville.
2   Actually, Third Horsed Cavalry Training Regiment, with NCOs from the Scots Greys.

trying to find people in, until it's time to come back.

I hope you get this letter because I should like one back from you. I suppose you will be leading a helpful existence coping efficiently with about 6 things at once. I'm afraid you were born to be so – if only I had fallen in love with you, it would have been lovely, because as it is I only fall in love with girls who are such idiots that I'm soon cured. But you are so ruthlessly 'sensible' as a rule that no one dares approach you – platonic written all over you. The only time you thawed was at the St Hilda's dance, which I suppose is about the last time I saw you. Perhaps since then you have married a shy, squinting pedagogue: I hope not.

As it is you're the only female friend I have, whom I like just because it's pleasant to be with you, and not for obvious masculine reasons. What a horrible letter this is, I think I'd better stop. Please reply though if only to tick me off. I shall pass out of here into a tank in a month or two, and that I think will eventually be a final exit. Meanwhile Blunden is sending my poems to T. S. Eliot and in fact the whole silly business continues. Betty Sze broke my heart for no reason at all, blast her, because she isn't going to marry her smooth Bermudan after all. So she'll be an old maid, in all but the technical details, I expect: or else a society wife. Poor silly girl.

I am just about at the end of my hopes. I can see nothing more attractive than active service and final oblivion, to which I quite look forward. I shall feel such a chap dashing about with stuff blowing up everywhere. I am trying to get East as soon as possible: and when I get there I shall make for the nearest harem and leave the rest to Allah. We lost our horses only a month ago and that seemed the last straw. Until then I had a handsome chromium plated sword to play with and felt comparatively happy.

I must stop I'm so sleepy.

My love to you, Jean.

Keith

155. *To Jean Turner*   Private Hands

n.d. [10 December 1940]   [Letterhead] Royal Military College,
                                        Camberley, Surrey

Look here, schoolmarm. Didn't I give you a proper address? [Arrow and at top of page: 'Sorry if I didn't.'] Your letter's been following

me round stamped insufficient address squadron/company
unknown etc. Well anyway I'm very glad you've appeared again,
only I'm sorry I didn't know in time for last Sunday. I *was* over and
only just managed to find someone in. I may be booked next Sunday
but anyway I think you'll have gone by then. You don't say where
you're going. I am leaving about next Sunday week either for a
gunnery course at Lulworth (Nr. Bournemouth) or else on a week's
leave. Anyway I shall be at Lulworth till after you return from
Oxford. But if you can get here from wherever you are, before the
Sunday after next, let me know. I can escape next Saturday
afternoon, and I shall probably be free on Sunday but don't know
yet. After that I'm free on Wednesday next week. If I get a week's
leave, would you come and spend it or some of it with me, if I could
find anywhere? This is not an improper proposal, particularly – but
I may well have to spend my leave alone otherwise. Anyway, let
me know where you'll be – perhaps it'll be somewhere near
Lulworth?

I think it's about the 10th now. Anyway this is written on Tuesday
night. I am very tired and sleepy so I'm going to post this and go to
bed. I'm so glad you're about again.
Love
Keith
Get this straight: 327210 Officer Cdt. Douglas K.C./33 TP. A
SQUADRON INNS OF COURT REGT/ROYAL ARM-
OURED WING OCTU/ROYAL MILITARY COLLEGE/
Camberley/Surrey.

156. * *To Edmund Blunden*   Texas

n.d. [December 1940]   [Letterhead] Royal Military College,
                                                  Camberley, Surrey

Dear Edmund,
Thank you very much for your letter, and for submitting my stuff
to T S E. I shall be anxiously waiting to get the great man's opinion,
(if he deigns one). I have just finished learning to ride a motorbike
in 2 lessons. The first was more or less in private, the second began
on a main road, and took us through a town, across a blasted heath,
up and down very steep wet sand tracks and through a pinewood,
going in and out among the treetrunks. I have driven a tank about

4 miles, but there's more of that to come.

I think I told you we miss Christmas Leave. But I may be in Oxford on Saturday next, till Sunday morning, on my way to Lulworth. There my address will be 327210 O/C Douglas K C/33 (Weedon) Tp. 101st OCTU/Gunnery Wing, AFV School/ Lulworth, Dorset.

I still don't know what Regiment I'm going to, should I pass various exams (I successfully lectured for 6 minutes on the differential the other day); but I suspect the East Riding Yeomanry. Anyway I hope it will entitle me to wear skintight patrols with a stripe down my leg and long dress spurs.

Merry Christmas (it's no use wishing me one back) to you and Sylva.
Keith

[Another sheet: ink drawing of angel, ears blocked, surrounded by engine parts, with words including: 'The angels keep their ancient places'; signed 'Keith 40':] This was to have been my Christmas card, if I'd had time to make one (this or the other design, in pencil). Perhaps it would do for *Kingdom Come*'s new cover.

[Another sheet: pencil drawing of angel, machinery, words; signed 'Keith 40'.]

156. *To Jean Turner*   Private Hands

n.d.   [Letterhead crossed out]
~~Royal Military College, Camberley, Surrey~~

Well, you horrid girl. Why didn't you write back – you're no better than the rest. I may be pretty grim but I did think there was someone who'd write and cheer me up, at least if they were asked. However I seem to be wrong. I really must raise some more (girls). The present list is a bit depleted – so –

~~Betty Sze~~	cancelled
~~Kristin~~	cancelled
~~Toni~~	cancelled
~~Jean~~ (you)	too lazy to write
Netty (Scots shop girl)	occasional illiterate scrawl
~~Natasha~~[1]	too lazy to write
~~Joan Appleton~~	too lazy to write

1 Natasha Litvin, who later married Stephen Spender.

This is the filthiest scruffy hole I've ever fallen in. It's a concentrated army nightmare. We're put on charge for having a bath. We have to scrub out lavatories. We have to sweep rooms, clean washbasins, make beds. We have to walk everywhere through at least a foot of mud. Everyone either swears at us or is very grim or morose. We have to walk 300 yards through a bloody blizzard and queue up for 20 minutes to get a plate of dirty grease and a few lumps of offal or gristle, as the case may be. We are kindly allowed to spend our miserable pay on doughnuts made without sugar and unrecognisable tea. Occasionally a cold ex-fried egg may be bought for an exorbitant price and anything up to ¾ hour waiting. We are pulled out of bed (if it can be called a bed, being 3 planks raised 6 inches off the floor) at 6.30 by a lance corporal. And so it goes on. This is because we are officer cadets. When we were troopers we had spring beds, got up on our own, had 4 good meals a day and got off every evening.

I don't know if this will reach you but if it does see you write back, you stuffy old pedant(e?). I'll be here from now till two weeks. I have already spent a delightful Christmas wandering round Bournemouth finding all the hotels and restaurants either full or shut.

In this way what might have been quite a good person is being reduced to a malevolent idiot. It's a subtle process worked out to minute detail.

Keith

157. *To Jean Turner*   Private Hands

n.d. [January 1940]

Thank God you didn't use all the paper.[1] I can't raise any anywhere – Thank you for a most pleasant letter Jean. I'll write more when I've paper: (and thanks for your offer to knit – how sweet.) I'll see

---

2 Deirdre Newstubb, a Slade student.

---

1 The postscript in the fragment of Jean's letter on verso, shows that their badinage could have limits: 'If you call me stodgy or sensible again I shall neither write to you or see you.'

you in Oxford – I go back to Camberley for 3 weeks next Saturday. Please do something for me: whether you know about my affairs or not you know I'm stuck for a girl at the moment. Well for God's sake don't let me try to make love to you. You're the only girl I like enough to hope it won't happen. It always ends in a muck-up. So don't let me start.

Love
Keith

158. *To Jean Turner*   Private Hands

n.d. [January 1940]   Royal Military College, Camberley, Surrey

Dear Jean,
I'm sorry I was prevented from coming today. I'll manage to get there on Sunday, definitely unless I'm in bed with flu. So Hilda's entrance hall, 4 o'clock? Excuse this, my last piece of paper.[1]

My goodness I feel dopy [*sic*]. It's the depressing effect of incipient flu and the fact that I've just spent £23 of a £30 grant and only got ½ my uniform. Also there are thousands of arrangements to make, and I am very tired and flabby.

Failing all other meetings will you come to a party on Sat 31st (I'll let you know place when we know it). It's a 21st party, and you are urged to bring a gift in liquid and alcoholic form, your hosts being broke, but determined to miss nothing for that. Bring Denise[2] if she's about, also anyone else charming enough. Do you know Simha Valero[3] or some such name and has she been interned or gone? If not bring her. Also Patsy Mulcahy Morgan[4] if she's up (you'd better invite her specially from me and say I hadn't time to write).

4.0 Sunday next.

Love
Keith
PS Also ask Madeleine Fisher and the Agawalas[5] please – David Lockie[6] pro Keith

1 'The Prisoner' on verso crossed out: stanzas two and three with revisions.
2 Denise Dudley, 2nd Scholar at St Hilda's.
3 At St Hilda's.
4 At St Hilda's.
5 He had met Bunny Agarwala at the Appletons'.
6 David Lockie was at Sandhurst with Douglas.

159. *To Jean Turner*   Private Hands

n.d.   [Letterhead] Royal Military College, Camberley, Surrey

My dear Jean,
I thought you were a goodish person but I must say I didn't think
you were as good as all that: you seem to have blossomed out. David
(Lockie) was most emphatic in your praise. And I was more content
just wandering about and being rude to you than I've been for
months. I hope you can stand me as easily as I can stand you.
However I don't do this sort of thing very well, having said it too
often when I don't mean it, so let's get on with what I've let you
in for –

Please invite.[1]

Jocelyn Jacoby	Slade Sch of Art
Aileen Sam	L.M.H
Rosemary Brown	..
Douglas (Harvey) and Anita	Univ.
Michael and Evelyn Young[2]	(enclose in Harvey's)
Natasha Litvin (and beautiful	
'cellist) (just like that)	The Shire/St Clements Oxford
Michael Meyer	Ch. Ch.
Ruth Victoria Grey (if you can find address O.H.S. anyway)	
Natalie Jiminez	1, Wellington *Place*
Madeleine Fisher if you haven't. Patsy etc.	
Meric Dobson	1, Newinhall St.
Lance Thirkell	Magdalen
Robin Chadburn	Exeter
Yvonne Martin	Slade
Nancy Hugill	..
Margaret Thomas	Ruskin Sch Art
Margaret Buchanan	Wychlea, Bardwell Road/ and Banbury Road
Abu Taylor[3] and Stella	Merton
(instruct Abu to ask Ch. Onyama)	

---

1 Blue ticks in the margin by Jean, indicate invitations made; beside 'Rosemary
   Brown' she has written '+ Bolder'
2 Friends from the Saunders Passage flat, where many of the students from Ruskin
   and the Slade gathered.
3 Aleba Albert Taylor from Merton, see Letter 119 n. 1.

Iris Murdoch[4]	Somerville
Kay Fiske	?, Beaumont Street
Claudia Furneaux	Somerville
Humphrey Sassoon[5]	Merton
John Boldero (enclose in Rosemary Brown's)	
John G Davies	Wadham

Form of Invitation

> Douglas and Anita No presents, only
> BOTTLES, please
> Please come to
> Keith Douglas' and David Lockie's
> 21st Birthday Party
> above
> The Noted Snack Bar, High St.
> 5.0 p. m. till?
> Saturday 1st Feb
> RSVP to Jean Turner St Hilda's

I know how foul this is for you and it *is* sweet of you, Jean. I hope you'll be able to ask me to do something horribly arduous for you soon.

Personally I think it'll be an awful flop – David and I aren't the sort to give parties. We still have to have glasses from somewhere and we may split the party in two and have half in Magdalen for a bit.

Do what you can about a radiogram. I hope to see you 4.0 in St Hilda's entrance Hall on Friday.

Love

Keith

Mind you bring a St Hilda's selection. Do you know anyone who plays a guitar. Get your trumpeter.

160. *To Jean Turner*   Private Hands

n.d.   [Letterhead] Royal Military College, Camberley, Surrey

[The following poem is among Douglas's letters to Jean Turner. It appears not to have accompanied any of those which survive. It is

---

4 When asked years later, she had no recollection of the party.
5 There was a Humphrey Sassoon at Merton, as well as Hamo Sassoon.

not collected.]¹

The Critic

This severe building and barrack square
with the guns of Waterloo exactly as they were

whence officers and gentlemen would go
to seek their fame a hundred years ago

should make me copy in the end
the lieutenant who cried Floreat Etona to his friend

and immediately tumbled bravely in the dust
happy to have finished how he must.

(On every wall portrayed
such deeds are hung and cannot fade.)

But I cannot produce that grand moustache
and was never issued with a sabretache.

and when I prepare to die behind my gun
I shall not glow with fervour like a sun.

Then, whatever will restrain
the coward reasoning closely in my brain?

I think it will be that I am mad to see
the whole performance and what the end will be.

161. *To Edmund Blunden*   Texas

[January 1941]   33 Tp.B Sqn Royal Armoured Wing, RMC

Dear Edmund,
Thank you for the card – I hope the Great man¹ doesn't lose the
poems – I've lost all other copies of some of them. The party is to

---

1   See Letter 179 and see *CP* (1978) p.vi, *KD* pp.117–18. Douglas made revisions
    to his text including possible alternatives in pencil: 'The Officer Cadet' for title;
    l.7 'at once' for 'immediately' and 'heroically' for 'bravely'; l.8 'Dying correctly'
    for 'happy to have finished'; l.10 'will not' for 'cannot'; l.13 'if I do prepare' for
    'when I prepare'.

---

1   T.S. Eliot; see Letter 153a.

be on January 21st (Saturday) from 5.0 onwards. Birthday presents *in the form of bottles* will be gratefully received. We are having some difficulty in finding anywhere to hold this gathering, but when we do I'll let you know. Will Silva and your daughter come too? And if your daughter can produce any goodlooking and brilliant conversationalists from Somerville they will be most welcome. Over to you ...
Keith

162. *To Jean Turner*   Private Hands

n.d.   33 (Weedon) Tp. B SQN/R.A.C.Wing R.M.C.
Camberley/Surrey

Dear Jean,
I may be in Oxford on Wednesday and in that case will meet you Hilda's at 4.0. If I don't telegraph and cancel it will you wait there ¼ hour at that time? If not I'll see you Saturday or Sunday.

I am to be commissioned to 2nd Derbyshire Yeomanry (Armoured Cars) stationed in Ripon, on Feb 8th after a week's leave.
Excuse haste
Love
Keith

163. *To Jean Turner* (telegram)   Private Hands

[PM 8 February 1941]   338 RP 5.0 TUNBRIDGEWELLS

PLEASE MEET ME PADDINGTON 3 PLATFORM ONE OCLOCK TUESDAY WITH RESPIRATOR AND HELMET LEFT MERTON LODGE OR PUT THEM ON TEN TWENTY CARE OF GUARD PLEASE COME ANYWAY EVEN MINUS THINGS REPLY PRIORITY HADLOW DOWN 239 WILL REPAY AND ENTERTAIN YOU URGENT URGENT = KEITH +

n.d.

Dear Miss Jean,
I hope I shall see you in London but if I don't then you have to
answer for wasting the 5/10 I spent on telegraphing you, (and of
course I shan't go to the ballet by myself). I had a beautiful orgy of
sentimentality in Oxford from which you will be glad to hear I have
emerged safely, though admittedly only with the loss of one
respirator and one tin hat. I have spent my time since, sending reply
paid Priority telegrams in all directions, and arguing with one of my
tailors who, though in appearance incalculably old, has apparently
forgotten how to make Victorian riding trousers. I ordered some
which appeared first as [sketch: wrinkled-trousered legs] then on a
note of compromise, as [sketch: baggy-trousered legs] and at last
after much pinning we have arrived at the final stage (I dare to hope)
[sketch: man in elegantly fitting riding clothes] in khaki corduroy,
to be worn with spurs!

Has Denise ever tried to get you out riding? I should think you
ought to be good at it once started: (you've never mentioned it so
I *suppose* you aren't already an expert?)

Please excuse the sudden appearance of this gryphon griffin
gryphen or legendary monster. Mother is presenting me with a
signet ring, to remind me that I really am a little aristo, and this is
one of the more unsuccessful attempts to draw something for the
maker of signets to copy. As this is all the writing paper that seems
to be left, the Gryphon [sketch with quote 'JAMAIS ARRIERE']
etc will have to stay put. Don't take his expression personally; griffins
etc always look like that, and it is this very characteristic which
makes them such suitable devices for the use of haughty noblemen
like myself. I am not quite clear what that is underneath the gryphen,
and the fact that it is called a chequry doesn't help. I very nearly
used the coat of arms instead which seems more suited to my general
habit of foolish sentimentality [sketch of crowned, winged heart
with 'wings not foliage']. Well now I haven't really got room to say
what I meant to begin with which is to write what I said and that I
didn't accept everything you and Denise did as casually as I seemed
to and I really am grateful.
Love
Keith

n.d.   C Sqn [Letterhead] 2nd Derbyshire Yeomanry,[1]
                                                      c/o GPO Ripon

Dear Jean,

I am so sorry that this letter is not enclosing a present for you – but I shan't buy just anything. Partly because it would be waste of an opportunity for spending an enjoyable time choosing, and partly because if I bought just anything it wouldn't [be] worth having or be likely to give you much pleasure. In the end it will probably be a ring of some kind, because I am more likely to manage in sending it safely to you. I wish I knew why it was 'impossible' for you to come to London. I always found that in Oxford nothing was impossible and even tutorial times could be changed – but perhaps you had some previous engagement too good to break.

I wish there was someone whom I could ask to meet me somewhere suddenly, and know they would. I had vaguely thought of a day in London with you ever since before Christmas: perhaps because you described in a letter how you enjoyed (with John Hyde wasn't it?) almost the same things as I wanted to do. Well I did them; with Mother. It was nice and anyway she certainly enjoyed it. But you know the difference. Perhaps you really were sorry because you couldn't come. I was.

And it let you in for taking an awful lot of trouble for no reward. I should have done the equivalent for you, and liked it because I like you, but still I'd have hated it really and I bet you did. So that's two kisses I owe you when the circumstances arise. (the other is for goodbye).

I believe we are coming South on March 2nd to relieve the 6th Armoured Division Nr Gloucester. So once again I may ask you to meet me in Gloucester, or in town, or perhaps in Oxford.

My love to you Jean dear and I hope you'll get your present soon.
Keith

---

1   A brief account of the regiment's activities in England when Douglas was with them is to be found in *The Second Derbyshire Yeomanry: An account of the Regiment during the World War 1939–45* by Capt. A.J. Jones (1949).

n.d.   C Sqn [Letterhead] 2nd Derbyshire Yeomanry
                                       c/o GPO Ripon

My dear Jean,
Thank you for your letter. I think, that though your principle is
excellent, that was just one time when you were wrong to refuse.
But that's probably conceit anyway; forget it.

As for Ripon – I've hardly seen it: we're quite busy and though
I've passed through it I've never been there longer than ¾ hour and
that in the dark. We are under some feet of snow here and there's
quite a lot to do with the cars, and guns. We have just finished firing
– rather a farce: after a whole afternoon and morning working on
the guns and driving 6 miles through a blinding snowstorm, we fired
for perhaps 10 minutes and returned, to spend another evening and
morning cleaning.

Today I jumped one of my biggest fences – I had my first row
with my troop sergeant. He was troop leader before I came, as there
was no officer available, and has got too used to being on his own.
Today I ordered a parade in one place and at the last moment he
found one of the guns needed cleaning again, as the barrel had
sweated. So he and the troop never turned up. This was, I realised,
the crucial point, etc. etc. If I had let him get away with it, I should
never have caught up again. So I had a good snap at him, which
required some courage, as he knows much more about a lot of things
than I do and so I'm dependent on him over car maintenance etc.
However I snapped my snap, and smoothed things over as soon as
I saw he'd got it straight, so I hope to God I won't need to do any
more snapping. I followed it up with an incredibly authoritative
tactical lecture, just to show I know more about some things than
he does, and I hope all is now well. Because he's an excellent chap
and the troop are all very cheerful and amiable, though 2 of them
think by numbers, and with a good pause between each thought.

I don't know what your communist acquaintances have to say
about the War Office. Communists usually have no sense of humour
and the wrong end of the stick. The War Office is an unholy mess
but more in the Pay and Admin. departments than in the fighting
side. The army is fairly efficient everywhere, very efficient wherever
it's fully trained (regulars and present fighting troops) and rapidly
growing more trained and more efficient. We have most of the cars

guns etc we should have and are getting more.

I must stop. You're the only person who writes to me reasonably often. Please go on.

Much love

Keith

166a. *From T.S. Eliot to Douglas*   BL 56356 f.12

15 February 1941   Faber and Faber

Dear Mr Douglas,

I have been somewhat delayed by illness in considering your poems which Mr Blunden sent me some time ago, but I have now read them several times with continued interest.

They seem to me extremely promising, and I should like to keep in touch with you. I should much like to know whether circumstances permit you to keep on writing at the present, or whether we must expect a silence of indefinite duration.

My impression so far is that you have completed one phase which begins with the very accomplished juvenilia and that you have started on another which you have not yet mastered. Of the first phase I feel that, as might be expected, there is a certain musical monotony in the rhythms. That does not matter in itself because it is a good thing to go on doing one thing until you are sure that its use is exhausted... I think you have definitely an ear.

What I should like to see is the second phase which you have begun developed to the point of formal mastery, and meanwhile I think it would be useful to get poems in periodicals outside Oxford. There are not, of course, many periodicals now in which to publish verse, but I shall be very glad to draw the attention of the editors of *Horizon* to your work. If you are still writing I should like to see something.

I am keeping the poems which Blunden gave me until I hear from you.

Yours very truly

T. S. Eliot

167. *To Jean Turner*   Private Hands

n.d.   C Sqn /[Letterhead] 2 Derby Yeo c/o GPO Ripon

Dear Jean,
Coo! I had a letter from T S Eliot today – quite nice on the whole
– promising young man – send some more when you've written it.
How much can I sell his autograph for? Will you come and meet
me in Gloucester or Cheltenham when we get South? There are
buses and trains there from Oxford and London. We move on
March 1st to a village near there.
That's all – I just wanted to tell you about TSE.
Lots of love
Keith

168. *To Jean Turner*   Private Hands

n.d.   C Sqn 2 Derby Yeo c/o GPO Ripon

Dear Jean,
Will you put up with being written to on a page of Army Notebook?
I am feeling most fed up, as usual. Why is it that I always want other
people's women? I hope it isn't just because they're other people's.
But I begin to wonder. I have written to Natasha Litvin and called
that off for good anyway. Stephen Spender can have her (sour
grapes). I went to a dance last night at a hotel in Harrogate and met
someone with whom I danced every dance but 3 for the rest of the
evening and those 3 we sat out. She looked marvellous, she talked
sense and she's the best dancer I've ever danced with. And so, of
course, she's married, and probably has been for years. I should think
she was about 30. She danced so well and we had such a lot to say
that I haven't the vaguest recollection of her name and I doubt if
she knows mine. Why do I always pick on those sort of people?
There must be an unmarried, unengaged edition, but where do they
hide?
    I think (did I tell you?) I am getting a car, which I am going to
share with the Weapon Training Officer of this regiment.[1] The
point of that is that as Weapon Training Officer he has to visit other
squadrons, and division, etc, and can ∴ get free petrol out of

---

1   A Bugatti.

ordnance. So you may see us chugging into Oxford sometime – we shall be 50 or 60 miles away by road, not more than 2 hours run. About 4 gallons there and back. I may even take over W. T. Officer myself. Anyway car or no car we can meet in London and do what we weren't able to before. Mother will be bucked I'm coming within range again.

We may be in England as late as July, so I hope I'll be able to come on the river now and then in the summer term. Perhaps we can engage Denise to punt us up and down at about 50 miles an hour (or knots, I suppose).

What a lot of letters I write you – that's all of this one anyway.
Much love
Keith

169. *To Jean Turner*   Private Hands

n.d.   C Sqn [Letterhead] 2 Derby Yeo Race Course, Ripon

My dear Jean,
What the hell do you mean love I suppose! I'm glad you like [   ][1]. So do I. I never knew him at school, but he was a beautiful little boy and grew up of that persuasion. He is changing over gradually, but when I was up he still lived on his elderly men friends. They never got any more for their money than his company, but it paid well, as he told me when he was drunk once. Incidentally he says such a lot about himself that I should think you needn't ask me much about him.

My flourishing correspondence with Denise was limited to one letter, which she didn't answer. So I don't think you need be hurt. As a matter of fact I had forgotten I'd written to her. This disproves the popular supposition that 'as a matter of fact' usually precedes a matter of no fact of all, but a lie; because I really had forgotten.

They told us we were moving 20 miles from Oxford. But now it's Gloucester, or did I say in my last? I must stop -I'm very busy.
Love (I'm sure, but not *in* love as yet)
Keith
If you hear of a good ancient car going cheap, let me know, or m'bike.

1   The name is withheld.

166

Sunday [n.d.]   C Sqn 2 Derby Yeo Race Course, Ripon

Dear Mother,

The mess room paper is used up so you'll have to put up with a piece of army notebook. I have been seeing about advantages and disadvantages of having a car this end. So far it's mostly advantages. Owen Bodycombe will share it with me, and we shall use it for regimental duties so as to get ordnance petrol. It should be O.K. if you insure it for any driver. Then if I apply for extra petrol or if you do, we say that you are lending it to me for my leave and can I have some extra petrol. Owen has had a car before insured in his father's name. Apparently there is no time limit for paying mess bills. But I think I shall put my money into Glyn Mills after all because if I have it in my own bank I shall get it almost a month later every time. The Army don't pay it into Glyn Mills for about 10 days, but people with accounts there may draw it as soon as it's due. And then it would take about another 10 days before Glyn Mills had paid it into my bank. So really it ought to be better in Glyn Mills. After all if they are going to deduct pay, they'll deduct it in the end anyway.

I have worked out I'll be about 50 miles from Oxford or between 50 and 60, so with a car that's no distance at all. Therefore if you came to stay with Mrs Lockie I could come and see you, and anyway there's always a good train to town from Cheltenham.

Yesterday I went over to Harrogate with Owen to see a film and ended by leaving the film and going to a dance at the Majestic hotel there, where I was provided with a partner by the dance hostess. She danced better than anyone I've ever danced with and we hardly missed a dance for the rest of the evening. She was also much better looking than anyone else in the room and since I don't suppose many people realised she was married, and not to me, I must have been most envied. Anyway it was a very good 5/– worth, and Owen and I found a drunk who would buy us any amount of drinks as long as we let him talk about his experiences in the last war. As some drinks were 3/– each this saved us quite a lot. We got a lift back to Ripon and walked out here. The dance ended at 12.0 and we were in bed by 1.30, and up by 8.30 this morning feeling quite fresh. I started dancing in the leather waistcoat so I must have taken some waist measurement down.

Today I'm going to Harrogate again to meet Pennock's girl friend

Lorna. I really must get one of my own. The last 5 I've taken out have been other people's. It's an outlay of money for nothing.

We move actually on Sunday, next Sunday, and should be there by Tuesday if we don't have too many breakdowns. These cars are awful – yesterday the gear lever of mine literally came in 2 in the driver's 'and. On the other hand a car in another troop drove through a narrow gate with its machine gun traversed round sideways and although the gun barrel is only 1½ inches in diameter at its thickest piece, and tapers, it knocked a brick wall down without damaging the gun at all.

The snow makes everything very difficult – I hope this is the last of it – perhaps it's gone in Gloucestershire. We are going to an area where no troops have been before – heaven knows why, we ought to have been in Dickie Dawson's place. Dickie has passed out of Sandhurst and is spending his leave hunting in Ireland. Then I think he'll be stationed in Oxford.

I must stop – I've got some work to do before I go out.
Love
Keith

171. *To Marie J. Douglas*   BL 56355 f.122

n.d.   [Letterhead] 2nd Derbyshire Yeomanry
                                                    C Sqn

Dear Mother,
I hope you got my last letter, saying it would be O.K. about the car. I've not had even a p.c. from the Oxford N.P. bank to acknowledge either of my letters. Perhaps you will have some letters to forward to me, which you're keeping till you hear my new address. Could you let me have a quid or so until I hear from the bank that I've got some money paid in? I've had so little notice from them of anything I've said, that for all I know there may be some already.

We shall have a terrible journey down. We are the last squadron of the Regiment and the whole Division is moving in a column nearly 18 miles long, even if they keep closed up. Since everyone here seems to know where we're going and how, we shall no doubt be dive-bombed. Thank heavens my 3 cars (touch wood) are running well and doing about 10 miles to the gallon. I'm afraid most of the journey will be in low gears though. We stop the night in

Lutterworth and move on to arrive on Monday.

Is my ring ready yet? By the way Fooks[?] sent a bill – I think it's about £3 12. I'll enclose it if I can find it. And if not, will you ask him to send it to you. I've heard no more from T.S.E. but don't suppose I will for a bit – I think I told him to write to Hadlow House again.

I'm very much looking forward to getting the car. Could you scrounge enough petrol to get it to Oxford? I'll collect it from there, but otherwise I suppose it would have to come by rail to Cheltenham or somewhere and probably get mucked on the way.

I'm getting very fat again due to eating and drinking such a lot to keep warm, and getting no exercise. We had been snowed up until today, and though I've done a lot of standing about in it, I haven't done much walking. We did a scheme (the Squadron) for the Commander in Chief Home Forces, Gen'l Brooke. The Great man did not actually speak to anyone himself, but the Divisional General, McCreary asked me a lot of questions, in fact I was the only person in the squadron who was spoken to at all. I answered them all satisfactorily and the Colonel (our Colonel) was tremendously pleased with me, as he had expected me to be frightened of all the Red hats. As I was able to bob down into my turret again the moment they asked anything I didn't know, and as I was disguised in thousands of scarves, overalls, glasses and earphones, I felt quite safe. [sketch of incident, the car named 'Cephos'].

I have bought for 11/3 some beautiful blue overalls so in battle order I now appear like this [sketch].

I must stop and get on with various other letters – I believe I forgot to post a reply to Lacey.

Love
Keith

172. *To Jean Turner*   Private Hands

n.d.   [Letterhead] 2nd Derbyshire Yeomanry

Dear Jean,
Would you like this unique picture of your soldier hero?[1] I am tempted to keep it and look at it whenever I feel wicked – I couldn't look it in the eye and then commit a caddish act, could I? Talk about

1   Perhaps similar to that reproduced in *KD* p.105.

the flower of Britain's youth (I had it done for my identity card).
Keith
New address – C SQN. 2 Derby Yeo/C/o P.O./Wickwar. Glos.

173. *To Jean Turner* Private Hands

n.d. [21 March 1941] White Horse Inn,[1]/ Wickwar, Glos/C Sqn
[Letterhead] 2nd Derbyshire Yeomanry

Dear Jean,
I think it's about time I heard from you and even if you've gone down I suppose you'll get this some time. I have sent you this address once and even if I hadn't, you had Mother's to send it to. So what have you been doing?

I'll tell you what I've been doing – what is known in the army and elsewhere as sweet F.A. for most of the time, and some dangerous driving thrown in. The other day we walked over to the remains of a German plane and the rather less amusing remains of its crew, which stank. One of them was hung in a tree some yards away from his own head.

Next week we go to Bristol for a week. Although we are only 16 miles away, and Bristol is blitzed about every other night with heavy casualties, and although all we have to do there ends at 4.30, we are ordered to stay there to save petrol. Possibly when half this squadron is blown to hell they'll let the next squadron off going there. I can't say I mind very much, or am very surprised. One expects that sort of imbecility from any authorities, army or otherwise. Anyway it'll do me good to come in contact with a bit of the war and all this British heroism.

We were at Cheltenham for the Gold Cup yesterday and in view of the company I was keeping, I had to stump up a quid and go in the members enclosure with a little ticket marked Officer and Gentleman or words to that effect. Every horse I backed to win came in second and every horse I backed for a place came in nowhere. Mrs Fulke Walwyn, the jockey's wife, was there with both arms in slings, one is broken and the other has 18 stitches in it, she having been in the Café de Paris when the bomb fell.[2] She

1 Used as the Officers' Mess.
2 8 March 1941.

kept her date for lunch next day apparently, and Séan Magee who was with her and carried her out, was riding yesterday. I must be getting quite a socialite, I actually met about 20 people I knew in the members' enclosure.

Needless to say Denise did not write but I suppose I should be properly grateful to her for meaning to. You seem to have started meaning to now. I still haven't got my car, so I can't meet you anywhere yet. If I thought you'd have sufficient energy or interest I'd say come and stay at Wickwar for a week. It wouldn't cost much. Keith

174. *To Jean Turner*   Private Hands

n.d. Officers Mess/C Sqn [Letterhead] 2nd Derbyshire Yeomanry
White Horse Inn/Wickwar/Glos.

Dear Jean,
Honestly you are a dope – you addressed your letter to C SQN, c/o GPO Ripon. You may see nothing wrong with that, but there is always more chance of a letter reaching someone in the army if you put his regiment in. I don't care *what* you do with the drawing – though I'll say what I think, when I see what you have done.

We are now cut off from the world, in a remote hamlet of Gloucestershire where everyone knows everyone else. Within 24 hours I cadged acquaintance with Squire, or rather Squire's wife, Lady Gunston[1] – and now we're going to sherry with them this evening. Sir Derek is like the Squire out of a *Thin man*[2] film would be, just a bit too typical, M.P. and all. His secretary would be nice if she had some more teeth.

Broken-hearted at the collapse of my relations with Natasha, I am solacing myself by driving armoured cars at top speed all over Glos. with one wheel in each ditch. Whatever happens, it won't be suicide because nothing I hit can make the least impression on a Guy[3] (touch wood).

Enclosed Eliot's letter if I remember[4]

1 Sir Derek and Lady Gunston: see *KD* p.114.
2 Adapted from Dashiell Hammett's last novel, *The Thin Man* (1934) and its sequels were sophisticated comedy-mysteries.
3 armoured car.
4 For Eliot's letter see 166a; no copy survives with the letters to Jean.

Love
Keith
[sketch: armoured cars at speed causing chaos]

175. *To Edmund Blunden*   Texas

[March 1941]   C Sqn [Letterhead] 2nd Derbyshire Yeomanry
                         White Horse Inn/Wickwar/Glos.

Dear Edmund,
Thank you for your letter and the poems: I shall look through them,
just to assure myself that I really used to write poetry once, and then
I think if you'll consent to sit on them for me again, I'll send them
back.[1]

Do you take Eliot's letter (as I take his to me) as an excessively
polite refusal to have anything to do with my efforts? I really think
I give up – I may try and write a novel but I doubt it. As a poet I
seem to lack the correctly exotic style and don't really get on very
well with the present rulers of poetic society. I am inclined not to
destroy my poems as yet, but another reason for returning them to
you is that on impulse I am quite likely to burn them.

I hear another *Augury* is to be produced[2] and wish it better success
than the last, of which Basil Blackwell finally said 'Thank God we
managed to get some burnt in the blitz on London.'

I am drinking much too much and gradually ceasing to think. I
don't think anything will get me out of it this time – anyway my
military efficiency is unimpaired, and I get on quite well with my
troop who don't mind a bloated out-of-condition appearance and
no epigrams.

Thank you for taking so much trouble over the poems.
Love to Silva
Keith

1   Blunden had returned the collection to Douglas, having got it back from Eliot
    (see *Miscellany* p.75).
2   See Letter 179 n. 2.

176. *To Marie J. Douglas* (telegram) BL 56355 f.123

[PM Brighton 27 March 41] 'PRIORITY'

PRIORITY DOUGLAS HADLOW DOWN
MANY HAPPY RETURNS OF YOUR BIRTHDAY MAY
GET 48 HOURS SOON LETTER FOLLOWS KEITH

177. *To Jean Turner* Private Hands

n.d. C Sqn [Letterhead] 2nd Derbyshire Yeomanry
White Horse Inn/Wickwar/Glos.

Dear Jean,
I don't suppose you'd believe me capable of being anxious about
anyone's existence but my own: but I *should* be quite glad to hear
from you since as far as I know you were in town for the last
concerted effort from Berlin.
Keith

178. *To Jean Turner* Private Hands

n.d. C Sqn [Letterhead] 2nd Derbyshire Yeomanry
White Horse Inn/Wickwar/Glos.

Dear Jean,
I have sent a note to St Hilda's and this is to town to know if you
have escaped or survived the latest bombings. Please reply as soon
as poss.
Keith

179. *To Alec Hardie* Hardie

n.d. Bristol/As from/C Sqn/[Letterhead] 2nd Derbyshire
Yeomanry/c/o Mrs Thayer[1]/High St/Wickwar

Dear Alec,
Herewith what poems I can find.[2] I am afraid I can't rise to anything

---

1 Douglas was billetted at the Thayers' house in Wickwar, see *KD* p.114.
2 Hardie was planning a sequel to *Augury*, but it didn't materialise. See *KD* p.118.

new at the moment.[3] I hope they'll be some use to you. As I am buying (or rather have bought but not yet insured) a very old but speedy car, I may get to Oxford during next term.

Yours

Keith

PS (later)

Of those I am sending I should particularly like you to include 'John Anderson' (which incidentally will appear much more effective in print, and with the stuff in inverted commas in italics, than it does in my writing). After that I like them myself in this order – 'The Garden'; 'A speech for an Actor'; 'A Ballet'; and I shall be rather distressed if you include 'Sandhurst', because though the sentiments are true they are not very original and the verse isn't very inspired after all.[4] Will you send any you don't want to Michael Meyer (Ch.Ch.) is case they're not too late to be of use to him.[5] (Send them fairly soon, as I imagine they'll need forwarding.)

K

180. *To Jean Turner*   Private Hands

n.d.   C Sqn [Letterhead] 2nd Derbyshire Yeomanry
                                     White Horse Inn/Wickwar/Glos.

Dear Jean,

I hardly even think you deserve to be thanked for such a letter – my goodness, who said I was trying to kill you. Yet you are conceited enough to assume it, and then to tick me off for writing to see what happened to you? Well you needn't worry Madam, whether it's in character or not I shan't write next time you fail to answer. Pray write to me exactly when and how it suits you. Satisfied? And may I add that this attempt (I suppose) to squash my conceit is getting a little too much in character for *you*: the only

3 So often responding to notice of his work, Douglas might have been encouraged by Hardie's request to try something new: on the end cover of a book in Mrs Thayer's possession he started what was to become 'Time Eating' (*CP* p.71); see *KD* p.120. Within weeks he had four new poems to send to T.S. Eliot (see *KD* p.118).

4 For 'Sandhurst' (uncollected) see 'The Critic' Letter 160; the other poems enclosed, with variant texts are in *CP*: 'John Anderson' p.56, 'The Garden' (as 'Absence') p.49. 'A speech for an Actor' (as 'Leukothea') p.55, 'A Ballet' p.52.

5 Meyer was preparing *Eight Oxford Poets*, which was published in 1941.

interesting paragraph was yours at the end, the comparison of subjects, and that wasn't particularly inspired.

Would you like to stop work for a weekend some time if I can get to town: if you have any ideas of what you'd like to do?

They brought another down last night almost on top of us. It started as a little whine miles up and got louder and louder. When it was at its loudest they threw out all their bombs somewhere just the other side of the village. We have just returned from a week in Bristol during which not a bomb fell. But last night the whole sky was lit up with A.A. fire, planes, bomb explosions, and a fire which seemed to stretch all over Bristol.

Keith

181. *To Jean Turner*   Private Hands

n.d. [April 1941]   C Sqn [Letterhead] 2nd Derbyshire Yeomanry
                     Officers Mess, White Horse/Wickwar/Glos.

Dear Jean,

Were you in London and if so are you all right? If you get this please answer fairly soon.

I was over in Oxford about a week ago (Easter Monday actually) but I was pretty sure you were in London and I tried the Appletons first, who were in. After that I took out to tea the younger Agarwala who is not so bad as I thought and was looking fairly normal for once. They also had a peculiar Latvian playwright somehow attached to the household. In fact their life seems to be continuing in an undisturbed and generally arty-crafty way.

I shall stop this and I'll write you a proper letter when I hear from you that you remain unblitzed.

Love

Keith

182. *To Jean Turner*   Private Hands

n.d.   [Letterhead] 2nd Derbyshire Yeomanry

Jean dear,

I'm awfully glad you escaped. My car has (of course) bust, so I can't come over to Oxford. But do come down here for a weekend if you can. I am feeling slightly more cheerful, as there seems to be a

polo pony to ride, and I have ridden it two or three times and begun teaching it to jump, which it has never done before and finds rather terrifying. The Sadlers Wells people have been performing in Bath with considerable success – I went twice, and saw *The Prospect Before Us* which I've never seen before, and is v. good: also *Façade* with the new decor which isn't nearly so good. No time for more at the moment.
Love
Keith

183. *To Jean Turner*   Private Hands

n.d.   C Sqn [Letterhead] 2nd Derbyshire Yeomanry/ Wickwar

Dear Jean,
I suppose you can't come this weekend can you: I shan't mind if you don't, except that you'll have further to go next time. We are going on a gunnery course in South Wales for a week and from there straight to Horley or some such place in Surrey. It's possible we may move again from there almost at once. We go on manoeuvres on Monday, arrive back on Friday, go away to Linney Head on Saturday and straight from there to Surrey. However I suppose you could come there. I shall be awfully disappointed if you don't come fairly soon though (if you don't, I expect you won't at all). It would be best of all if I could get a weekend off. Actually it wouldn't be hard to get from Saturday after duty till Sunday night if I stayed in the area.
    Incidentally if you careless talk[1] about this there will almost certainly be an invasion and a successful invasion.
Love
Keith

184. *To Jean Turner*   Private Hands

n.d.   C Sqn [Letterhead] 2nd Derbyshire Yeomanry
                                Castlemartin, Pembroke, S. Wales.

Dear Jean,
How is Oxford? If I can get leave I shall come there for a week but

---

1 'Careless talk costs lives', a poster of the time.

can you find out where if anywhere I could sleep? I am due for 7 days off but that doesn't mean much. We are in a most pleasant but isolated bit of the country in South Wales, Linney Head for a week firing various gunnery practices. I am firing point officer on one range and have to see that everyone shoots and no one gets shot: [sketch: armoured cars, soldier resting beside the road:] The sea is in the background, and convoys come past occasionally.

The drawing is a rough view of surroundings but doesn't include the sunlight and sea air. Last night being full moonlight there was a fairly heavy raid on Pembroke, and several bombs unpleasantly near us, as it sounded.

We had a lovely drive down, my first visit to Wales, starting from Wickwar at 5.15 a.m. and having breakfast in Brecon. Then lunch on the way and here for dinner. The Officers Mess is in a rather wrecked farm with holes in the floor and 'natural' sanitation. Thank God the roof's o.k.

Excuse this writing I'm balancing the paper on grass and its very windy *and* the pen isn't too good. Bunny Agarwala came over to Wotton the night before we left, and I took her out for a drive and another officer and the girl friend she's staying with. She is very 16 years old but quite fun.

I must stop it's too much effort to hold all this down. Write soon.
Love
Keith

185. *To Jean Turner*   Private Hands

n.d.   C Sqn [Letterhead] 2nd Derbyshire Yeomanry
                                          Castlemartin/Pembroke/S. Wales

Dear Jean,
We are in South Wales on a very desolate sea coast firing guns for a week: after that I may get leave and I'll try to come to Oxford if there's any chance of getting anywhere to sleep. How are you progressing towards Schools? I hope you'll manage to come for a weekend to wherever I am after this. Apparently it's still to be Wickwar for a bit. I am getting quite good with medium and heavy machine guns and tomorrow an aeroplane is going to tow a target for us.

This evening we're going out to dinner in Tenby and I hope I'll find time to post this (and remember) I'd like to hear from you. I

177

can't compete with this bloody pen any more.
Love
Keith

186. *To Jean Turner*   Private Hands

n.d.   [Letterhead] 2nd Derbyshire Yeomanry/Wickwar/Glos.

Dear Jean,
Thank you for your note, and invitation: I think I wrote you from
Linney: I'm now back in Wickwar, only to find I must do a course
at Karrier Motors, Birmingham, for a week. If it wouldn't be too
much trouble, will you hang on to the ticket another week? I am
applying for leave, but shan't hear for a day or two, as I'm in
Birmingham. To make it as quick as possible, I'll ask the chap who's
trying to wangle leave for me, if he will telegraph you when he
telegraphs me. If our projected move (now postponed) takes place,
it will stop my leave till after that week. If it doesn't, or if it does,
you *must* come for a weekend sometime, pudding or no pudding.
I wish you'd believe it will pep me up no end if you do take that
much trouble, and greatly disappoint me if you don't. Linney was
great fun, on the whole.
    Look out for a book pub. Routledge & Kegan Paul in about 2
months, another bloody anthology of Oxford ravings.[1] I hope
Natasha really is unpleasant because she'll certainly cut *me* dead next
time she sees me.
Love
Keith

187. *To Jean Turner*   Private Hands

n.d.   C Sqn [Letterhead] 2nd Derbyshire Yeomanry
                                    White Horse Inn/Wickwar

Dear Jean and Denise,
I spared you the afternoon performance as you seemed rather filled
up with things to do, and went to enquire about trains. I met
someone I knew from the Slade at the station and talked for some

---

1   *Eight Oxford Poets.*

time, returning in time for tea with Bunny whom I took to the Cowley Baths. There of course she was taken ill and had to be brought home in great agony and a cloudburst. In the evening I had supper with Mother and then packed.

The real piece of merry news is that we don't move till Tuesday (the swine) so I could easily have come to the dance. I'm going to one at the Assembly Rooms in Bath with Maitland-Magill-Crichton and other ornaments of the *Tatler*.[1] Obviously I can't afford to keep up their pace so I shall probably go and comb my hair in the gentlemen's lavatory for most of the evening. I was asked to a tennis party as well but unfortunately after I'd fixed the dance. I had a pleasant ride this afternoon and a huge tea with cucumber sandwiches and cakes, and I'm repeating that tomorrow, having been reluctantly compelled to leave some cakes on the table. We go somewhere between Horley and Dorking – I'll send you an address when I know it.

Love

Keith

Don't let Flan get sent down.

188. *To Jean Turner*   Private Hands

Friday [n.d.]   [Letterhead] 2nd Derbyshire Yeomanry

Dear Jean,

I'm sorry I didn't see more of you in Oxford, but you saw how it was. I hope you thought a little better of the minx from Birmingham when you met her.[1]

I am not off to India:[2] in fact I may not be off to anywhere for a week or two. But my ultimate destination, still well ahead of the Regiment, is the Middle East. So with any luck I'll be in action within two or anyway 3 months. Then I think the simplest thing would be to get conveniently incapacitated, come home, and ignore the war, in Oxford. Diana and I are engaged, but I hold out no hope

1   Fellow officers.

1   Diana, a sixteen-year-old girl to whom KD had become engaged before leaving for the Middle East; see *KD* p.123.

2   In May Douglas had successfully applied for a September course for joining the Indian Army. The course was cancelled.

for the engagement, from either end. It is simply for these reasons, that we really would like to get married, and are in love, and that being engaged gives a very slender extra chance to both of us, to exercise a certain amount of self control and wait. But it's a long time, and she's very anxious to get married and start having babies straight away. Meanwhile I am for the wars, when the various officials and the convoy system meet at a point. I think on the whole the feeling of uncertainty is pleasant. I leave behind the requisite sweetheart, Mother, friends etc., to mourn my loss, and enemies etc. to be glad of it. Perhaps some of them will still hold these official positions when I come back. Meanwhile, if it won't bore you too much, write an occasional note to Mother, and perhaps take her out a little, and I'll be very grateful and you'll feel virtuous – anyway I think you like her don't you?

Goodbye for the moment anyway. I shall probably be writing a sort of circular letter to Edmund, if anything gets through, and he'll distribute news of me if anyone is faintly interested. See and don't get invaded while I'm gone.
Love
Keith

189. *To Marie J. Douglas*   BL 59833 f.28

Friday [n.d]   Hartswood Manor

Dear Mother,
A message from Division arrived while I was away saying the position is altered and we are to go straight to the Middle East. Blast them. Meanwhile unless I telegraph you otherwise my address may be for some weeks (2nd Derbyshire Yeomanry), Officers Mess, 55th Training Regiment R.A.C., Farnborough, which I should think for the moment will reach me sooner than anything about Army P.O. 1000. Could you telegraph me there if patrols appear?

They wouldn't mind if you came and stayed in Farnborough (or with Mary Steedman at Camberley).
Love
Keith

Six

1941−1942

n.d., [PM London 17 July 1941]   Draft Serial RW7KY/F
[on envelope] On Active Service   c/o APO 1000

Dear Mother,

Too much port, said by Sir Reggie[1] to be the best of all wines, caused me acute discomfort during the night and has given me quite a head today. They hadn't even cooled it so it wasn't very enjoyable to drink. Still Sir Reggie wouldn't have admitted it to be port at all in that state. I've hardly recovered now and have eaten nothing. However I and all my goods are still together and I have a fairly comfortable berth with a window onto the boat deck and an electric fan. I share it with one chap (Michael Hutton) who is underneath, you'll be glad to hear.

My car is only 15 miles from here, I'm sorry I couldn't go and have a look at it again. I'm afraid this mayn't reach you for some time, but in any case I must stop because it probably won't go at all if I don't. I hope you can decypher it all and don't miss anything.
Love
Keith

191. *To Edmund Blunden*   Texas

n.d. [?August 1941]   Draft Serial RW7KY/F
               RAC c/o APO 1000

Dear Edmund,

The wonders of the ocean are a little diffident but present themselves now and then; and the sun and moon have certainly been doing strange things.[1] I have at last begun a novel but it bores me, however I'm plugging away.[2] Unfortunately I can't manage verse as well so that is stagnant. There is very little in the line of duty and not much excitement. People are pretty boring and identical. I share this cabin with a love sick young man who uses me for a sort of confessor of which I get heartily sick. I pull his leg without compunction but it

---

1   Sir Reginald Spence; see biographies of recipients of letters.

---

1   The 'fantastic moon in the Atlantic' was to appear in 'Negative Information'
   (*CP* p.81) a couple of months later.
2   Nothing of it survives.

will stretch to any length apparently without his noticing. Myself, I narrowly missed being married before I left, and am very relieved still to be independent. Though I should like to think I was stinging the Pay Office for a marriage allowance.

At the moment I'm over sunburnt and very sore. But I suppose it'll pass. I force myself to do some P.T. every afternoon and so counteract to a certain extent the four huge and excellently-cooked meals a day. We get most of our entertainment (a few of us) from watching the rest. Many of my former mentors at the Equitation School provide more than most. The cryptic quality of that sentence, which I must admit reads like one of Torquemada's, is a sop to whatever Base censor may peruse this. For the moment I censor it myself, but all letters, particularly to Oxford, that home of strange foreigners, are liable to reopening.

There are occasional concerts, of the sing-song-music-hall variety, but none touch great heights, although we have on board a professional accordionist, a very good performer on the banjo, and the composer of the once celebrated Penny Serenade; (or one of the composers of it – these songs seem to be written by more and more people's collaboration, the simpler and more banal they are.)

I trust you and others to maintain the atmosphere of Oxford and the finances of Merton in a state fit for heroes to return to. If I still escape marriage I shall be back in the flesh, or disembodied, to compete with Duns Scotus.[3] I don't suppose we should clash much – I never could work in the library for long – and should probably spend all my time on the river, in the Ashmolean, and browsing round Blackwells, or L.M.H.

There's no news as yet for you to pass on, except that of course I'm bored, healthy, and only kept from pining away by a rumour that there are women on one of the other boats. If they're there, I wonder if the Samuel Goldwyn moonlight has the same effect on them.

Love to Sylva, and all my friends (if any).

Keith

3 Medieval philosopher and theologian, who is supposed to haunt Merton College library.

n.d. [PM Oxford 6 Sept. 1941]   Draft Serial RW7KY/F
[on envelope:] On Active Service   c/o APO 1000

Dear Jean,

We are beginning to look like heroes already – considerably thinner and pleasantly tanned. The voyage is by no means over, and already has been interesting and at times mildly exciting. The first spectacle was provided by porpoises, and very soon after that flying fish, at first singly and then in shoals, began to leap out practically from under the ship. They are quite small, about 7 inches long and 14 across the wings, or less, and reflect the sun brilliantly when they fly. So far no sharks, no whales. At the moment we are at a sort of halfway house port, confined to the ship, with very little to do except buy unripe fruit and vegetables at exorbitant prices from natives who wear very scanty and ragged but colourful clothing and sing snatches of the Lambeth Walk as a sort of reckless chant.

Last night I was inveigled into the Chief Officer's cabin and had to listen to his reminiscences of 31 years at sea, some of which were quite interesting, for about 3 hours. The time was taken up by a mechanical consumption of whisky and soda. When I rose somewhat carefully to depart I had consumed 16. I suppose any mosquito which tried to bite me last night must have staggered back wondering what hit it. Actually it was so hot that even 16 whiskys and sodas had almost no effect on me and haven't even given me a head this morning. In fact if only I could bring myself to like whisky and soda I might have had quite a good evening. I have written thousands of letters on the way but whether any of them will ever reach anyone God knows. Among others I wrote to Edmund, so if you get this, ask him if his arrived. I shall be even more interested to see if any more get back.

It seems to be about lunch time – we are still being given meals calculated to keep out the December snows, and we sit and stream as we eat them. However it's probably very slimming – in fact it certainly is. Even some of the officers who looked as though they had to wear brassieres when they came on board, are now comparatively tolerable to look upon. It's amazing how much less revolting tanned fatness is than dead white neverbeenundressed English skin. Myself, I am quite bony.

Well, bugles, gongs etc announce lunch. Probably any base

censor who gets this will find it quite a treasonable letter – as I've dared to reveal that we're on a ship, and hot – both of which everyone knew before we began.
Love to you and Denise
Keith

193. *To Marie J. Douglas* (fragment)   BL 56355 ff.126–7
(4 pages; copy in Marie J. Douglas's hand)

n.d.   RW7KY/F RAC c/o APO 1000

My dear Mother,
What a long time since I had any communication with you except in imagination. It's been for the most part an interesting period and if only we could have exchanged at least a letter a week I could have sent you all sorts of interesting descriptions – but keeping a diary or making a sort of diary letter – while I admit it's an excellent idea – is something I could never do. Actually I can't remember what I told you about last. Did I describe Chica, a monkey bought out of a Sierra Leone humboat [*sic*]? Probably I mentioned her. We had to present Chica to the crew because the Military wouldn't have her on board. She had all the usual attractive – and unattractive – simian traits. She was affectionate and had an amusing little face; most of the affection of course cupboard love. When a mango was brought into the cabin she would stand up and hold out her hands, making a sort of impatient clicking noise. She liked apples too. But as a monkey, so to speak, she was rather a failure. She would not swing on the trapeze we put up for her but fell off it most ungracefully whenever she was put there. And when she made a mess in someone's seaboots we were glad she hadn't stayed in the cabin. She was fondest of a cockney member of the crew who always addressed her as 'well yer ugly barstard' with more success than any of the other sailors' endearments had. The crew of that ship were a mixed lot and included a sort of vagrant commercial artist, who really was good at his job, though not capable of anything particularly sublime – He was an interesting chap and apparently well-educated. At one time he had been in the Palestine Police in peace time.

South Africa was one long and very expensive holiday. There is plenty of hospitality for the troops and for anyone who is content to return for that 10 days ashore to a homely comfortable family life.

For the rest, girls are booked up like taxis for several days ahead, and having set out to go to a dance the first night, we came back at 10.30 without having had a single dance. The social and entertainment life of Durban is something like what one has seen in American society films. We connected on the second day with a retired colonel in a seaside village called Isipengo Beach. There we used to repair whenever possible; we hired a 27 h.p. Studebaker for 21/- p.d. between 3 of us and flashed backwards and forwards in it to the bright spots of Durban, the Hotel Edward, the Stardust, The Athlone, the Roadhouse, the Doll House, the Blue Lagoon. At these places we danced or sat in the car in the moonlight while Indian waiters brought relays of toasted egg and bacon sandwiches. In the day time we bathed at Isipengo beach or in the seawater baths on the front at Durban, or at Tiger Rocks, where the surf pulls you out into deep water unless you keep about 6 ft. from the beach, and sharks swim hopefully up and down in the calm water outside.

I went to the Durban Gold Cup meeting, but it was a great disappointment after Cheltenham. By their dress the crowd might be at a flower show. In any case South African taste in dress is appalling and runs chiefly to pink. There were no tic-tac men no bookies shouting – everyone placed their bets in stolid Dutch silence. Even towards the finish of the race scarcely everyone cheered. All you heard was Afrikaans and South African English with continually the peculiar exclamation 'Ach, sis man' – Afrikaner women call each other man or rather 'men' as they pronounce it. The S.A. accent more like South American with a touch of English *nouveau riche*. It sounds more like someone imitating an accent than a natural way of speech! 'Our Daivid, ah think yuh bett' pork you' caw they'. They never pronounce the plural of women any different from the singular 'Look at therse woman owr' they'.' They can't say there or hair or where. It is always they' and hay' and w'ay'. One gets used to it in time.

I've asked one of the girls we took out to write to you because her letters should reach you quicker than mine. I believe she can't spell particularly, but she is quite well meaning. I enclose some photos which the censors may permit to reach you.[1] If not ask Mic [?] if he's received any.

We are now on rather a luxury boat, with the additional

---

1 These have been lost.

complication of 200 women passengers who are causing a certain amount of trouble and strife.[2] One of them has become engaged to John M.[3] who had the bomb-like Rover at Farnboro'. He's a nice lad and she seems to be rather superior to the rest of them. She was married two years ago but her husband was shot down. The other girls have been very unpleasant about her getting off so soon, and rather a strained atmosphere prevails. Some of the other girls are pleasant enough. The Officers' Sun Deck at night would present an amusing appearance if suddenly flood-lit.

The last lap is as unlike being at war as any of the others. Action must still come as a hell of a jolt. Particularly after the peacetime atmosphere of Durban, which is an almost unnecessary mass of lights, and where we sat in the cinema with 2lb boxes of chocolates.

Cigarettes on this ship are 3d for 10. In South Africa there is more fruit than they can get rid of. One night we went up to Durban University to look down on the whole town, lit up. It was a lovely moonlight night (almost every night was the same) and there are hundreds of crickets which cheep regularly as you hear in American films. Sometimes we used to drive up the south coast in the late evening and just swing the car down on to the sands. There is no shingle. Beauty spots are Hill Crest and the Valley of 1000 Hills, where the floor of the valley is a set of little humps and hollows said to have been made by an angry giant, stamping to kill pigmies. The town is full of a hotch potch of races. In the non-European quarter are several sorts of negro, including of course a few Zulus, though most dislike the town and stay away, and between the common nigs and the white population is a sort of half way population of Indians and Chinese.

There appears to be quite as many Indians as natives. They have their own settlements, where the women dress in bright and, I think, very beautiful saris. The native women carry their children on their backs and as they grow older and have more children their breasts grow longer and longer until they can throw them over their shoulder to feed the child on their back. Almost every native or

2 One of the women passengers was Mary Benson (the South African novelist), to whom Douglas sent a batch of his poems once arrived in the Middle East: 'Villanelle: Bells in the town…', 'Pas de Trois', 'Russians', 'The God' and 'The God Speaks'(Parts I and IV of 'A God is Buried'), 'The Prisoner', 'Time Eating', 'Song: Dotards do not think', 'The Marvel' (*Brotherton*).

3 John Masefield, nephew of the poet.

Indian woman we saw was either pregnant or nursing, sometimes both. I think there is much to be said for birth control.

This ship was never designed for going through really tropic waters. The heat in the cabin is incredible. There are no portholes and the apparatus for pumping air is quite inadequate. There is also a fan but it can't cope with this heat. The tropics have had an appalling effect on my beard. The hair has nearly doubled itself. You can imagine my face looks almost as if it had been painted blue.

The war sounds to be in a more hopeful stage at last, but I think this lot have a hot time ahead of them before the pendulum swings over. I wonder how long it will take us to get out when Peace is declared?

I have written to John Hall and sent 2 more poems[4] to add to the [fragment ends]

194. *To Marie J. Douglas*   BL56355 f.128

(Airgraph) 26 August 1941   Middle East RAC
                                                            Base Depot

So far I have had 2 postcards, but I gather more is coming. I don't know how large it's necessary to write but perhaps if I can get some black ink I shall be able to make letters smaller. I'm sending back some stuff for T. S. E. in my next letter. At the moment I'm hanging about but it won't be for long. We had a pleasant and interesting voyage out, with 10 days riotous holidaymaking in S. Africa. I think people down there are writing (or have written) to you and Diana. Cables up to now have not been worth sending as they take longer than letters. If you have closed my account with the National Provincial I want you to open it again and arrange with Glyn Mills to go on paying into it. That is what I have arranged this end as curiously enough it's the easiest way to get the most money. In S. A. I cashed a £10 cheque and put a note to say if it bounced, to bounce it on you, as if you closed my a/c you must have had my 60 days pay, kit allowance, etc. I wonder if you know where Rita[1] is – if so let me know. Life here appears to be appallingly expensive,

4 No record of these remains.

1 An aunt.

but I must have some reserves of pay to draw on if only I can fix
with a bank to cash cheques. I must have an account at Nat. Prov.
Oxford though. I wonder if you will be able to read this. Let me
know, anyway. Love to you.
Keith

195. *To T. S. Eliot*   · BL 60587 f.1

n.d. [October 1941]   APO 1000 Cairo

Dear Mr Eliot,
If you are interested, here is the only poem I've produced since
sailing from England.[1] Life is likely to be very active from now, and
I think you'd better have this while I've time to send it.
I hope it reaches you.
Keith Douglas

196. *To Edmund Blunden*   Texas

n.d. [PM 10 October 1941]   [Palestine]

[At top:] NO, I haven't written any more poems.
Dear Edmund,
Excuse the Calligraphy – I'm writing in bed in the 23rd Scottish
(very Scottish) General Hospital somewhere (and having been
brought here in the dark and a stupor I don't know myself where)
in Palestine. In Cairo (than which I never expect to find a more
unsavoury habitat of more unsavoury people) I picked up some bug
out of a swimming bath, which with the casual aid of the RAMC
deafened me, gave me a temperature and provided more agony than
I have ever had in my life. I was posted to a Regiment[1] shortly
afterwards and not wishing to be left behind I set out with the others
eating Vegenin tablets in much the same way as people used to think
Americans chewed gum. By the time when, in the early hours of
the morning, we arrived at the particular stationless spot in the

---

1   No poem survives with the letter. It was 'Negative Information'; see Letter 197,
    for the text of the poem.

---

1   The Nottinghamshire Sherwood Rangers Yeomanry. The history of the
    regiment in the war can be found in T.M. Lindsay, *Sherwood Rangers* (1952).

wilderness where the Regiment lives, I had run out of dope, and was therefore staggering like a drunken man and at my wits end. I spent the rest of the day with millions of flies and tons of sand, on a camp bed and in the evening set out in an ambulance for what the M.O. said would be a 2 hr drive to this hospital. How anyone unconscious stays in an army ambulance God knows. I hung on and after 3 hours by my watch, when we had stopped about 10 times I asked the driver if he had any idea where he was. After making him repeat his answers several times I found he didn't know, and it was only by sheer luck it turned out that we were already in the hospital grounds. Here I still am after, I think, about 3 weeks. I have read 32 books, 32 being all I could get, among them the works of such master writers as Ruby M. Ayres (*My love Came back*)[2] – this book took about ¼ of an hour to read as I was able to read a paragraph at a time, instead of, as with Charles Morgan, a word at a time. I have consumed also many detective stories, but by rather unfair systems of deduction (I.P. by comparison with other detective stories) I usually know who dun it. However among all this I found *The Fountain* (C. Morgan) *A Passage to India* (which I'm afraid I hadn't read) *Now East, Now West*, S. Ertz, *Les Silences du Colonel Bramble*,[3] *Corduroy* (A. Bell), all of which I enjoyed a lot, but most of all *The Fountain*, and all of which I praise almost without qualification except of type. *Corduroy* is rather untidy. I've found some interesting 'period pieces' – *Stella Maris* by W. J. Lock with beautiful, really well-done wash illustrations – why can't we have them now – I suppose they're too expensive – and a wonderful Hodder & Stoughton paper-covered adventure called *Jim goes North*,[4] about a gold-rush in Alaska, with a villain who really knows his job and is moreover called Jasper, and a sweet, innocent heroine. In the *Frozen North* men are not only men but Nature's Gentlemen as well. I enjoyed it a lot.

In Cairo I was forced to speak French for hours to various beautiful Eastern damsels – but it wasn't worth the effort – they are too mercenary, their parents are not at all accommodating, and I am too poor. I left Cairo with 5 piastres.

2 No novel of hers has that title: perhaps it was a slip for her *My Old Love Came*?
3 By André Maurois: about the British army in the First World War.
4 George Goodchild, *Jim goes North: being the further adventures of 'Colorado Jim'* (1926).

You may be interested to hear that my companion and comrade in arms (since he has been posted to the same regt.) ever since I left England is one John Masefield, a nephew of the illustrious person of that name. He is most un-literary, but an amusing chap – he spent 3 years in the Rhodesian police as a trooper, and returned to England, having his 'A' licence, under the impression that the Royal Air Force might be interested in someone who was fit and had about 100 hours flying experience. But they were very dilatory and he arrived, via the RASC, in the Tank Corps: I see I've come to the end. My address is NOTTS. YEO. M.E.F.

Love to Sylva and Claire.

Keith D.

197. *To Edmund Blunden*   Texas

n.d. [PM 17 October 1941]   Notts SR Yeo MEF

Dear Edmund,

I've been in hospital with a bug in my ear and now, gradually recovering, have produced a poem, which I send you. I think I sent another of these sans poem off into the blue with your name on it, last week. So in case it arrives, and because there can't be much more ink in this pen, I'll not write much now.

Keith

I've sent a copy of this to TSE, as he apparently wrote to my mother asking to see what I sent home.

Write me an Airgraph[1] if you've time. It'll get here in a month. Let Jon [*sic*] Hall have any poems he wants but please demand them back when he's finished.

Negative Information

As lines, the unrelated symbols of
nothing you know, discovered in the clouds
idly made on paper or by the feet of crowds
on sand, keep whatever meaning they have,

---

1 Airgraph: a form of economical air mail used during the war in which a letter was written onto a special form which was then photographed. The reel of film was flown to Britain, developed and cut up, each piece of filmed letter being delivered to its addressee.

and you believe they write, for some
intelligence, messages of a sort;
these curious indentations on my thought
with every week, with each hour, come.

Perhaps you remember the fantastic moon
in the Atlantic – we descried the prisoner laden
with the thornbush & lantern -
the phosphorescence, the ship singing a sea-tune.

How we lost our circumstances that night
and, like spirits attendant on the ship
now at the mast, now on the waves, might almost dip
and soar, as lightly as our entranced sight.

Against that, the girls who met us at one place
were not whores, but women old & young at once
whom accidents had turned to pretty stones,
to images alight with deceptive grace.

And in general, the account of many deaths -
whose portents, which should have undone the sky,
had never come – is now received casually.
You & I are careless of these millions of wraiths,

For as often as not, we meet
in dreams of our own dishevelled ghosts;
and opposite, the modest hosts
of our ambition stare them out.

To this, there's no sum I can find -
the hungry omens of calamity
mixed with good signs, & all received with levity
or indifference by the amazed mind.

16.10.41

198.* *To John Hall*   BL 53773 f.43

(Airgraph) 16 October 1941   Notts Yeomanry MEF

Dear John,
If it's any good to you here's a brand new poem, with no strings.

You'll probably need a magnifying glass.
'Negative Information' [see Letter 197 for text (with slight variants)]

198. *To John Hall*   BL 53773 f.43

n.d. [PM 17 October 1941]   Notts SR Yeo MEF

Dear John,

I have sent two airgraphs which attempt to explain the situation of
my poems at the moment.[1] I am helpless and if you weren't in too
much of a hurry to wait for this letter, the best I can do is to try to
remember which poems I'd like to go in and tell you to select for
yourself with those in mind.[2] My 2 airgraphs were in reply to a cable
from my mother, sent as from you. Finally she copied out your letter
on an airgraph and sent that. Well, then – I should like one or both
poems called 'Soissons' to go in. 'Villanelle of Spring Bells', 'Time
Eating', 'The Marvel', 'Kristin', 'Poor Mary', 'Stars', 'Canoe',
possibly 'Extension to Francis Thompson', under a less pretentious
title. 'Shadows', 'Burial of a God', a 'Song' beginning, or having a
verse beginning 'Dotards do not think'. 'Russians', the 'Poem' I sent
you by airgraph and which I will write out again if there's room, and
a song which I'll try and put in with this if I remember it.[3] If you or
the publishers take violent exception to any of these and prepare [*sic*]
any of the others to be had from Blunden (or my mother may have
one or two) select for yourself. Of the 2 Soissons poems one appeared
in *The Cherwell*, the other has never appeared anywhere. 'Villanelle
of Spring Bells' was in *Augury*, 'Time Eating' has never been
published as far as I know (all these unpublished Michael Meyer may
have published since I left in *The Cherwell* or grabbed for 8 *Oxford
Poets*). 'The Marvel' is unpublished, 'Kristin' was in *Bolero*, 'Poor
Mary' in *Fords and Bridges* of your editorship, 'Stars' in *Augury*,
'Canoe' in *The Cherwell*, 'Francis Thompson' in *Cherwell*, 'Shadows'
in *Cherwell*. 'Burial of a God' part 1 in *Kingdom Come*, the rest
unpublished, 'Dotards do not think', unpublished, 'Russians' in

---

1 Hall wrote to Mrs Douglas, 30 October 1941, that the airgraphs had not arrived
   (BL 56356 f.21). Letter 198★ may be one of them.
2 Hall was planning a three-poet collection – Douglas, Hall and Alan Rook – for
   John Lehmann; see *KD* p.131.
3 The poems were copied at the end of the letter.

Kingdom Come, and the 2 from the Middle East unpublished. You might include 'Haydn – Clock Symphony' (*Kingdom Come*). Now, as to commitments. Michael Meyer has asked me for poems for a book called *8 Oxford Poets*, to be published by KEGAN PAUL, I believe, and with a foreword by John Lehmann (or so he said). I gave him a free hand with my stuff, as I couldn't do anything about it at the time. Sidney Keyes of *The Cherwell* will know about this book (so perhaps will John Lehmann), and what it involves, or whether it has died. If anything, supposing your project really and certainly materialized, I would rather drop K.P. and Michael Meyer than you and Alan and the Hogarth Press. But I would rather, of course, contribute to both. Certainly I would rather you had better poems of mine than K.P. if you quarrel over any. All this is somewhat unofficial and not to be flung in the face of the progenitor of *8 Oxford Poets*. For your biographical note My full name is Keith Castellain Douglas, my ancestry Scottish and pre-revolution French, I was born in January (24th) 1920 and educated at Christ's Hospital (shades of Blunden, Coleridge, Lamb, Leigh Hunt etc.) and of course Merton Coll. Oxon. where apart from Groups and Editorship of *Cherwell* I have no distinctions, but a year to go. I am interested in clothes, drawing and painting (my own and other people's), horses, [three quarters of a line cancelled] (that takes too long) music, ballet, stage design.★ Recreations, tap-dancing, rugger, water-polo, competitive swimming. That should be more than enough. On the other side I'll try and put poems. Is this Michael Swan of whom you speak an ex-schoolfellow of mine with a glass eye? If he is, he dislikes me intensely, or did. But perhaps it's someone else, even someone I should have heard of. By the way you understand I'm not able to copy an MSS out so please try and return them.
★Present work – 2nd Lieut. Royal Armoured Corps.
[unsigned]

Do I wander away too far

Do I wander away too far,
from the hot coast of your love
whose southern virtues warmed me?
how long, how long can I be safe
for the poisionous sea and a cruel star
the one by day and one at night have charmed me

and are you stricken with a fear
that I must be a seastruck lad
or that the devil armed me
with a compass in my head
for the poisonous sea and a cruel star
the one by day and one at night have charmed me

I see all night the hissing fire
when star and sea communicate
and they have alarmed me
with their interest and hate
for the poisonous sea and a cruel star
the one by day and one at night have charmed me.

All day on a flat calm sea we steer
but though the false sea fawn and curl
for weeks it has not calmed me.
Let them bind me to the rail
for the poisonous sea and a cruel star
the one by day and one at night have charmed me.

Yes I am a lost soul my dear
and I have jilted myself and you
soon when the sea's embalmed me
I'll fade into the deceitful blue
for the poisonous sea and a cruel star
the one by day and one at night have charmed me.

[Beside the fourth stanza Douglas writes:] I am in 2 minds whether
or not to include this verse.
'Negative Information' [see text in Letter 197; beside fourth stanza
Douglas writes:] N.B. This is different from the other copy I sent
you.[4]
'Palestine 16.10.41'.

199. *To Jean Turner* Private Hands

n.d. [PM 17 October 1941]

Dear Jean,
I've just got a letter from you posted God knows when and mostly

---

4 The 'other copy' is Letter 198*. The text in this letter has variants in
  punctuation.

about the radiogram – I don't know the chap who had it, nor do I know how to spell his name. He was an Egyptian called something like Shahbit (Simon) and shared with John Taylor (Abu's brother) but I expect it's resolved itself now, probably by John keeping the radiogram. Anyway it's very old and will probably crack up soon. I wonder if you are now a leading light of the B.B.C. If you are get a job announcing in the African service and you can say goodnight to me when you read the 6 o'clock news (it reaches us at 9.0). I wish I hadn't come to you last on my list of letters because there are lots of things I wanted to say to you but I'm so exhausted now my brain won't think and my hand won't write anything but sheer woffle [*sic*]. For instance I was going to tell you all about a rather Charles Morganatic idea for a novel,[1] the hero of which will be a slightly adapted and more normal Hamo Sassoon. I wanted to explain the characters and the plot in detail, so as to clarify my own ideas. The scene (of course) is Oxford. I know nothing about anything else – though of course there are vacations. But beyond these impressive or rather very unimpressive bones I can't get – for one thing my hand is in such a hurry to get to the end of the letter that it won't let me think, or won't wait for me while I think anyway. I feel an awful fraud in this hospital because I'm only here with bugs in my ears out of a swimming bath in Cairo, and everyone else is bandaged and riddled with bullets from Greece and Abyssinnia and Syria, all with a hundred gruesome tales to tell. But they are quite nice to me. I've been here a month with terrific agonies and stone deaf most of the time. They don't know how it happened or what it is. I don't either really. Thank God it's nearly over. The other letters I've written you should reach you soon. I forget if I wrote from Cairo. What a bloody town – I like what I can see of Palestine though, from the hospital windows. I've been up for a day or two but haven't got used to walking again as yet. And today I tried to run 20 yards and nearly passed out. In about a week I hope I'll join my new regiment, which is also my address: P/170611 2/Lt K.C.Douglas, Notts Yeomanry, MEF.
Love
Keith
Write me an airgraph. Yes, I *am* still engaged to D[iana] as far as I know. Congratulations on your DEGREE! Love to Denise.

---

1   No trace of this remains.

200. *To Brenda Jones*   BL (newly acquired)

n.d.   Notts SR Yeo MEF

Dear Brenda,
Excuse pencil – I never have a pen and anyway I'm in hospital in
the wilds of Palestine so let that be an excuse. Not with heroically
acquired wounds but plain (excruciating) earache – it's died down
now, but under the impressive title of OTITIS it kept me deaf,
dopey and dead to the world for a month. I'm still slightly deaf, but
up and in rather a limited way about. As soon as I leave here I join
what should be my regiment for the rest of the war (the Derby Yeo
having been left languishing in England) and I shall then be a
Sherwood Ranger (see address above). This is a more recently
unhorsed regiment and retains 8 officer's chargers for the officers to
ride in their spare time.[1] So I shall be quite happy.

    How is your journalistic career: hurry up and come out to Cairo
as a war correspondent – it's a pleasant town for them 'as money,
speaks French, and ignores guides. But for most of us, its bloody. I
loathed it, and anyway I caught my earache there in an insanitary
(though *apparently* clean) swimming bath at the Heliopolis Sporting
Club. The most pleasant thing about Cairo I found the open air
cinemas. But nothing up here compares with the beauties, natural
and female of South Africa. I've never enjoyed myself so much, or
for so long on end as I did there. It cost £26 (all the pay I'd saved
on the voyage) for 10 days, but it was worth it. I hope your father
and mother are well. Love
Keith

201. *To Edmund Blunden*   Texas

n.d. [26 October 1941]   Notts SR Yeo MEF

Dear Edmund,
Here are 2 more poems, probably I think the last for some time, as
my convalescent period which has consisted of doing nothing but
sunbathe and bathe in the Mediterranean, is now over. I return to
duty and the Notts. YEO. m.e.f. the day after tomorrow. I gather

1 See *KD* pp.135–6.

from rumours that duty even then is not over heavy and I may still get an occasional bathe. I've not yet paid my respects to Jerusalem which I suppose I ought to do before I leave this country. Those who have, however, seem little impressed. I have been for some very long walks along the shore and on although it's Palestinian winter it's hot enough in the day time – I consumed 4 ginger beers within two minutes of my return from my walk yesterday. I stick to ginger beer because the only available beer is Australian. The Mess is almost too luxurious and certainly too expensive. However in a day or two I shall once more live among sand, lizards, flies and mosquitoes, not forgetting the feverbringing diminutive sandfly. I have not had sandfly fever yet so I must have one or two 'goes' of it before I become immune I suppose. I hope to year from you sometime. The Post Office, possibly even the lodge, will supply you with one of these or an Airgraph form.
Love to Sylva
Keith

Adams

Walking alone beside the beach
where the Mediterranean turns in sleep
under the cliffs' demiarch,

walking thinking slowly I see
a dead bird & a live bird
the dead eyeless, but with a bright eye

the live bird discovered me
stepping from a black rock into the air:
leave the dead bird to lie. Watch him fly

electric, brilliant blue
beneath he is orange, like flame –
colours I can't believe are so;

as legendary flowers bloom
incendiary in tint, a focal point
like Adams in a room.

Adams is like a bird
alert (high on his pinnacle of air
he does not hear you, someone said);

in appearance he is bird-eyed,
the bones of his face are
like the hollow bones of a bird.

And he stood by the elegant wall
between two pictures hanging there
certain of homage from us all

as through the mind this minute
he draws the universe
and, like our admiration, dresses in it

towering like the cliffs of this coast
with his stilletto wing
and orange on his breast:

he sucked up, utterly drained
the colour of my sea,
the yellow of this tidal ground,

swallowing my thought
swallows all those dark fish there
that a rock hides from sunlight.

Till Rest, cries my mind to Adams' ghost;
only go elsewhere, let me alone
creep into the dead bird, cease to exist.

Nathanya 1941

The 2 Virtues

Love me, and though you next experiment
with Arabian books, or search the exact centre
and the limit of love's continent
with an orator, a dancer, or a sailor
there's none so fierce as I nor so inconstant.
I've the two virtues of a lover
hot as the Indies, mutable as weather.

Hot, since of his own heat must
the lover touch you to a flame
firing the heart and its imprisoning dust
like saints, to be in heaven when they burn
reciprocating heat; alight remain
until the flames die out above
the dying salamander, love.

Then being true to love, I'll be inconstant;
not to be so, would cheat you of the last
and most of love, sorrow's violent
and rich effect. In that lagoon the lost,
the drowned heart is wonderfully recast
and made into a marvel by the sea,
that stone, that jewel tranquillity.

Sarafand 1941
Sorry about all these alterations – I copied from the wrong version.
Hope it's intelligible.

202. *To Marie J. Douglas*   BL f.56355 f.129

(Airgraph) 26 October 1941   Notts SRYeo MEF

By the way I shall be quite near where Uncle Gordon died. I don't
know when you'll get this as P.O. have run out of stamps.

Dear Mother,
I escape from the final (convalescent) clutches of the RAMC the
day after tomorrow, to return to, or rather to begin duty at the above
address. The last few days I have been basking by and bathing in the
Mediterranean, and am once again, in spite of three or four weeks
indoors, noticeably sunburnt, and covered with salt and sand most
of the time. I usually walk several miles along the sands (with
intervals of rock, they stretch indefinitely), and finally bathe (sans
costume) with some four miles of shore to myself. There is a sort
of sea-kingfisher here, brilliant blue on the back, and orange
underneath, with a long black beak.[1] They appear by themselves

---

1 See 'Adams', Letter 201, and 'The Sea Bird' *CP* p.86.

always and sit very upright on the rocks with the long beak. There are also very large white gulls with S-shaped necks and very long legs which I imagine are cormorants. I hope there's some mail waiting at the Regiment. And I suppose already it's time to wish you (and *of course* the Duncanson ménage) a Happy Christmas.
Love
Keith

203. *To Jean Turner*   Private Hands

n.d. [PM Oxford 20 November 1941]

Dear Jean,
I'm going to try the experiment of writing along this way, and although I'm starting at the top, I don't know whether I'll get as far as the bottom – I'm waiting for a hot bath, and Palestine or no Palestine, shivering. I spent the day bathing and sunbathing, but now it's cold. This is the only effect of winter, at any rate in its first stages here, that it becomes devilish cold in evenings and mornings. Did I write last that I was in hospital (of course the order you get letters mayn't be the right one). Anyway, today is my last in a Convalescent Depot. It's an easy life – plenty to eat and nothing to do but sunbathe and bathe in the incredibly blue, clear, warm Mediterranean. But nothing to do gets tedious, and in any case I don't like to be away from the Regiment because I'm dropping behind the others who joined with me. My particular companion at the moment is (luckily, from my point of view) slowly recovering from pneumonia and sandfly fever, so we shall start about equal. His name is John Masefield which is not quite such a coincidence as John Masefield is his uncle. He himself is not in the least poetic and at the age of 28 has been a Daimler Works mechanic and a Rhodesian Motorcycle Police trooper. Between these two jaunts he was left a fortune which he spent in 2 years, it not being a very large fortune in any case. At this point I have my bath. Now – although any change in calligraphy is a very subtle one, let it denote the lapse of time for since I had my bath, I have also had a very good dinner (and a whisky and ginger-ale which drink will be my ruin if I can ever afford as many as I want) – and I have seen quite a good film called 3 *Loves Has Nancy* – but J. Gaynor, though she acts well is an unattractive sight and sounds terrible.

Well I have been walking beside the sea waves and have rather unoriginally been inspired, presumably by the waves etc, to produce 3 rather unoriginal poems.[1] There are millions of mosquitoes in this room, thirsting for blood – unlike the one which I slapped on my arm this morning. That one burst, covering me with the blood of my fellow-officers. By a very vague association of sounds (see 'There are mosquitoes...') I am reminded of a soldier who is supposed to have written home – 'I can't say where I am, but there are Pharaohs at the bottom of my Garden.' I wish it were true. Most of them couldn't possibly spell Pharaoh (can I?) and they begin every paragraph [inserted: 'I should have said every sentence as each sentence has a para to itself'] with Well dear or Well Pal according to sex. There are two alternatives for The opening – the original finds you as it leaves me gambit, usually omitting 'in the pink', and for more intimate letters, i.e. to wives, mothers a rather surprising Darling Mum once again I take great pleasure in writing... the ends of their letters are a galaxy of Xs which is very awkward for a conscientious censor, Xs being usable as a code for conveying censorable information. Orders are to erase all Xs. It was left to my university education to evolve the idea (still my own copyright) of adding several more Xs. This is quicker and less trouble generally than crossing out even a few, and justice is done, for the wicked have their code spoilt and for the good, their well-intentioned messages are emphasised.

I can't think why this is such a facetious letter. I can only hope it arrives when you're feeling fairly tolerant. I wonder if you ever got the radiogram. Do you know I wish Denise were a friend of mine (à propos of radiogram) but I suppose if she wanted to be she would be. Actually I don't think she ever will be unless we meet entirely by accident somewhere where neither of us ever expected to be. It's a pity because I like her a lot since my 21st and her efforts to entertain Mother, which amply succeeded. Don't pass this bouquet on (not intact, anyway). The bit about Mother doesn't mean I didn't realise what a lot (and far more than Denise) you did. But then you *are* a friend of mine and she isn't. Truly I hope I'll be able to do something to pay you back. Write soon.
Lots of love

---

1 'The Hand', *CP* p.83; 'The Sea Bird', *CP* p.86 and 'Adams', *CP* pp.84-5; see also, Letter 201.

Keith
I meant to tell you about an attempt (his, not mine) at fraternisation
with an Arab. But alas no room and I'll forget next time.

204. *To J.C.Hall*   BL 60585 f.13

(Airgraph) 30 November 1941   Notts SR Yeo MEF

Dear John Hall,
Here is another poem if it's any use to you. If not will you send it
straight along to Edmund Blunden please?
  Use first line as a title

>   These grasses, ancient enemies
>   waiting at the edge of towns,
>   conceal a movement of live stones,
>   the lizards with hooded eyes
>   of hostile miraculous age.
>
>   It is not snow on the green spurs
>   of hilltops, only towns of white
>   whose trees are populous with fruit;
>   with girls whose velvet beauty is
>   handed down to them, gentle ornaments.
>
>   Somewhere in the hard land
>   and vicious scrub, or fertile place
>   of women and productive trees
>   you think you see the devil stand
>   fronting a creature of good intention
>
>   or fair apples wher ethe snake plays –
>   don't you? Sweet leaves but poisonous,
>   or a mantrap in a gay house
>   a murderer with a lover's face
>   seem to you the signs of this country?
>
>   But devil and angel do not fight,
>   they are the classic Gemini
>   for whom it's vital to agree
>   whose interdependent state
>   this two-faced country reflects. Curiously

though foreigners we surely shall
prove this background's complement
the kindly visitors who meant
so well all winter but at last fell
unaccountably to killing in the spring.

I hope this is legible.
Best wishes
Keith Douglas

205. *To Jean Turner*   Private Hands

n.d. [PM Kensington 4 December 1941]

Jean dear,[1]

Thank you very much for a letter of phenomenal and gratifying length. I am bored stiff, being now isolated in sand to all intents and purposes – although we live practically in a village full of most delectable cafés (of the continental type), where the troops are allowed to disport themselves, our kindly and (you can bet) beloved Colonel has forbidden officers to go there.[2] The man could perhaps be forgiven for being an unimaginative fool in matters of that sort, if he were any use on the military side. But any of the 2nd Lieutenants knows four times as much as any Major in the regiment, twice as much as a sergeant, twice as much as a trooper, and 10 times (at a moderate estimate) as much as the colonel. In spite of living in unnecessary isolation, under canvas, with the most primitive sanitation, inefficient cooking and no proper light anywhere, I am charged almost exactly twice as much as when I lived in civilian billets in England and lived in a pub, and 3 times as much as in the palatial Training Regiment mess in Farnborough. Mess bills in Egypt were as high, but at least we got something in return. I don't know what I'd do if I drank or smoked a quarter as much as the others – but I shall drink and smoke if the third indulgence isn't provided soon. Haifa and Tel Aviv, and for that matter, our village, are well supplied with girls, whose appearance here is ordinary but who would make the occupants gasp of any room they entered in

---

1 Jean was in the WRNS by this time.
2 Colonel Kellett, 'Piccadilly Jim' in *Alamein* (see *KD* p.137).

England. There are people who keep saying you can't beat English girls – but for sheer beauty, no English face or figure can compare with almost any Arab child, any Egyptian or Syrian girl (provided she hasn't run to fat and sallowness, as some do). Talking of Syria, I took my troop for a tour through Syria in a 2 ton lorry last weekend.[3] It was much enjoyed by all. We didn't see many signs of the Syrian campaign – a few shrapnel splashes, burnt out vehicles, and blown bridges, round which we had to make detours. The mountain views are better than any description could be. We came up the coast road (if you have a map) through Haifa, over the Libanese border up to Beyrouth, through 'the village that men still call Tyre' where I was delighted to observe some old ships like swans asleep, though perhaps not quite so colourful as Flecker's. Beyrouth was disappointing – an early blackout and the fact that everything closes early as a precaution against Australian orgies, made sightseeing difficult. We climbed out of Beyrouth and camped the first night sleeping round the lorry on the first hilltop we came to, or rather in a little dip beside it. In the morning my troop sergeant and I went up the hill to some Arab huts and asked for eggs. The woman spoke a sort of Arabic French, but couldn't understand our efforts at ordinary French. Her house consisted of 2 rooms, one of which filled with chickens, dirty bedding, thumb sucking children etc, was open. At the door of the other she knocked, and a figure in pyjamas emerged. This was a Syrian French schoolmaster who appeared to have gone native. However he said these were the only lodgings he could get. He was the perfect host in spite of his attire and a certain amount of beard, and with a grand gesture of hospitality made us free of his bedroom, while the woman set off with £3 (about 6/-, Syrian pounds are a bit deceptive) to buy us eggs. We drank coffee and smoked Arab cigarettes, until after about an hour, when the woman returned, we rejoined the troop, minus our 3 quid, and + 30 eggs. The rest of the troop having given us up had had breakfast from bully and tea and we sent them up to wash in our Syrian friends' water. Meanwhile we ate some eggs. That day we climbed almost all day to Zable, a little village where we shopped, buying potatoes and Turkish delight. From Zable we went to Rayak, hoping to get through to the 2000 year old ruins at

3 Two overlapping poems emerged from the trip, 'These grasses ancient enemies' and 'Syria'; both are included in later letters.

Baalbek, but a bridge was blown and we couldn't get through. So we came back to Zable and took the main road to Damascus, which began to descend in a breathtaking spiral. We were getting a bit behindhand, so I took over from the driver, and got the lorry into Damascus about ½ an hour before dark, by dint of driving which left everyone, including myself, rather shaky. On the way we passed the burnt out remains of someone who had been less lucky and gone straight over the edge. (Burnt out remains of a lorry, not a person). Damascus also wasn't very thrilling, and we camped outside on a very cold windswept plain. Then we set out for Tiberias and the Sea of Galilee. On the way we came up with a very slow Arab-driven lorry loaded with potatoes, sacks and sacks of them, After some debate we brought the lorry close behind them, two troopers jumped off ours and onto the back of their lorry, and threw two sacks of potatoes onto the road. This was as far as we got efficiently, and while they were getting back to our lorry, Arabs working on the road warned the Arab driver, who stopped and leapt out. By this time one sack was hidden under greatcoats in our lorry. We generously pressed the other sack upon him, swung off the road and passed his lorry and escaped. Just after this, we crossed into Palestine and began spiralling down again to the Sea of Galilee, 600 ft below sea level, and very warm even in winter. It's a lovely sight and lovely to bathe in, being fresh water and very clean, though with about 1 fish per square foot. We had lunch there and hurried on home, arriving at 5.30 after more furious driving on my part. Still being censor-conscious, I have (I hope), omitted to mention anything of military importance, since presumably the enemy know that Syria and Palestine exist and are in our hands. I haven't mentioned where we began from so of course you don't know where I am.

Syria is well worth a journey of a few thousand miles. And the Sea of Galilee, and Nazareth, are not as tourist conscious as you'd expect – I don't think this is a relapse because of wartime – because in wartime everything is more rather than less commercialised.

I tried playing rugger in dust instead of mud yesterday – it wasn't very pleasant. Saliva immediately connects with the dust and forms a singularly unattractive greyish paste in the mouth.

I was very glad indeed to get your letter Jean, and more so because apart from Mother scarcely anyone has written to me. I know from her letters that it's possible for letters to get through. But Diana has only written twice and I am inclined to cross her off (which to tell the truth I am glad to do with such a clear conscience). As to her sending me *The Statesman*, I shouldn't think she ever heard of it – her intelligence is sufficient, but her upbringing and education are pretty narrow and limited. She is a very kindly placid sort of girl but I never meant to get engaged to her, and only did so as a shock absorber to reproachful tears. Edmund B has written 3 or 4 lines on a card, a German Jewess in Gloucestershire whom I met twice has written twice, and 2 girls in South Africa have written several times and sent parcels.[4] Thank you very much in advance for the books. I do hope they'll come, (Merry Christmas) I wish I could afford to send you another present (I sent a sort of brooch from Cairo). No letters from Pennock, D. Lockie, Harvey etc.

Much love

Keith

All this of course is legible Τοῖς Πολλοῖς (or perhaps it would be safer not to try a Greek dative after all these years), but I still have a little to say. I sent Jon [*sic*] Hall some poems, and heard again via Mother from T. S. Eliot who wishes me (dear unimaginative man) to give more attention to ineffective adjectives.[5] Of course I'd like to hear from Denise, B. Sze, Pennock, D. Harvey, Natasha, (by the way I see Natalie has got married, did you know her – her name was Jimenez, of the Slade). Keep an eye on my poems if you can and see if they appear in anything. Also has *8 Oxford Poets* appeared?[6]

KCD

206. *To Marie J. Douglas* (fragment)   BL 56355 f.130

n.d. [December 1941]

I should be glad to hear if it arrives and if so whether there is about £10 to pay on it.

Before I forget – will please ask Aunt Rita if she knows anyone in Haifa for me to go and call on? I can get there at weekends occasionally, also Tel Aviv, but preferably Haifa, and preferably people with daughters, naturally. Please let me know any addresses

---

4 None of these female correspondents has been traced.
5 Eliot's letter was of 24 January 1941 (*Miscellany* p.76). Eliot also made marginal comments (BL 53773; see *KD* pp.138–9).
6 It did not appear till 1942.

as soon as possible as we're getting fed to the teeth with having to go and spend the earth in nightclubs instead of being asked to dinner as we were in South Africa. Also, does she know anyone in Cairo, in case I go back there some time?

I had a very pleasant weekend trip to Syria, with my troop in a 2-ton lorry, though you would have shuddered to see my driving, hurrying to get to Damascus before dark, down spiral mountain roads with a sheer drop on one side. I got there alright and without taking as many risks as I appeared to, but the troop looked a bit green. The other drivers are nuts, Syrians and Australians, are undoubtedly the world's worst, and *will not* get out off the crown of the road.

We went to Beyrot, Zable, Damascus and on the way home had lunch at Tiberias and bathed in the sea of Galilee, lovely fresh water 600 ft below sea-level. I'm thinking of going on weekend leave to Tiberias some time − it's getting perishing cold here and the rains will be on soon. On our way up to Beyrot we came through the old Phoenician trading ports of Tyre and Sidon and between Tiberias and home our road went through Nazareth, which, it being Sunday was crowded with convent schoolgirls going for walks in crocodile. My hair is beginning to come out in handfuls − I hope I shan't return to you bald. I am riding 2 or 3 evenings a week, also playing rugger, soccer and hockey. Rugger in dust isn't much fun, but it keeps me from getting *too* fat. I'm pretty fat as it is, since actual Regtl. work doesn't give much bodily exercise. The push in the Western desert seems to be doing well − if they don't look out they won't leave anything for us to do. I should look silly if I came home without ever Going into action.

Well, Merry Christmas although this won't get there in time. We are (as last year) getting no Xmas leave. Whatever you do don't forget to ask Rita for names and addresses in HAIFA.
Love
Keith

207. *To Jean Turner*   Private Hands

(Airgraph as Christmas Card), n.d.   Notts SR Yeo M.E.F.

[Sketch of Mary with baby Jesus at her exposed breast, behind her a rifle with bayonet, a machine-gun and a bomb, also some stencil-

type lettering. Bordering the sketch:] A CHRISTMAS
GREETING 1941 Keith

208. *To Marie J. Douglas*   BL 56355 f.131

(Airgraph) 16 February 1942

ASK MR BROWN IF HE KNOWS ERIC DE LA RUE OF MY
REGIMENT

Happy Birthday (it *is* March?)

Dear Mother,

I've received a great many letters, airgraphs, and air mail postcards
from you. Diana's letters are also beginning to come through. You
don't seem to have received all mine. For a month – January – I
was busy, in various sorts of trouble, and without writing facilities.
I had the misfortune to kill an Arab who ran out from behind a lorry
into a truck I was driving. The thing seems to be cleared up now.
My latest trouble is an attempt to seize me away, by Division, as a
Camouflage Staff Officer. In spite of the possibility of extra pips, I
don't want to go, and my fate at the moment depends on whether
the Colonel can make them change their minds. He is going to try
tomorrow. My pay troubles (thank you and Glyn Mills for letters
and statements) are cleared up. The girl I met in Cairo in January –
Renée Mani, whose family were so kind to me, has written to you.
She says when you get the letter you will say *Hélas, quand cessera
Keith de faire des rencontres*. But I thought you'd like to hear from her.
When I left them, I wrote a bread and butter letter in very bad
French to old Madame Mani, who was apparently, Renée says, so
touched that she wept. I have never had to kiss so many people at
once as when I left [?] them, Mother and five sisters, all on both
cheeks. Here is headline news in case I've written too small:
DIANA'S LETTERS ARRIVING: I MAY BE LEAVING REGT
FOR STAFF: ADDRESSES CAME BUT I WAS HOPING FOR
JEWISH ONES – SHOULD HAVE KNOWN BETTER – fancy
living in a country for years and only knowing English people! PAY
PAID ME OUT HERE NOW. LETTERS SENT YOU BY
RENÉE MANI.

Love

Keith

n.d. [February 1942][1]

My dear Margaret,

Thank you so much for your decorative airgraph. The information given you was in substance correct – e.g. that we are in an isolated and sandy spot, but we still have 7 of the noble animals, and I get a ride most evenings, though we frequently encounter the other animal on our way, much to the horse's terror. Actually I have just returned from a month's course near Cairo and am now an expert camoufleur – though (of course) no one is in the least interested in my qualifications, or in having anything camouflaged. While there I managed to get in to Cairo on most of the evenings and all the weekends and met some very pleasant people. In particular I spent a great deal of time with a family of French Egyptian Jews. They took me among other places to a Jewish Wedding which was a fantastic sort of musical comedy but had impressive moments, and the singing was lovely. I went dancing a good deal, and ate an immense amount, particularly of strawberries and cream which oddly enough are plentiful in Cairo, and very cheap. A less attractive occasion was that on which an Arab called Sayèd Abdul (whose name is engraved forever on my memory because of the number of reports I've since had to make about him) ran out from behind a parked lorry into a truck I was driving. I swerved as far as possible but it wasn't far enough and I hit him with our mudguard. This flung him to the road and when I got back he was lying with blood coming out of his mouth like a fountain. His left foot was broken clean off except for a bit of flesh on one side and, luckily, the artery. He stank. The warm weather is just beginning again in the promised land, and I'm going for a ride this afternoon by myself as everyone else seems to have something to do. There are one or two jumps about and some of our 7 horses are rather special.

I have of course left your letter in my tent so this will have to hang about until I can sort it out of the mass of papers I seem to have collected, before I can address this and post it.

As *8 Oxford Poets* of which I am one has sold out the 1st edition in 3 weeks, Mother is to receive the princely sum of 30/- on my behalf. It must be a very bad book (Denise says it is) to have sold

---

1   Dated by Margaret Stanley-Wrench. Her reply survives: BL 56356 f.31.

out so quickly. I had nothing to do with the compiling of it, because I was in the mill at the time, and Michael Meyer chose which of my poems to include. I gather Jon [*sic*] Hall is trying to foist onto John Lehmann a book of his, mine, and Alan Rook's poetry.[2]
Love and good luck, please write again soon.
Keith

210. *To Marie J. Douglas*   BL 56355 f.132

n.d.

My dear Mother,
I am sorry there will have been such a gap in letters by the time this arrives – that is largely due to my encounter with another member of the Douglas family, one Major Sholto Douglas, Royal Scots. I duly went to a God forsaken spot near Cairo for a month's camouflage course, and got there by driving 400 miles across the Sinai desert. On the way we had a tire-burst [*sic*], luckily only about 6 miles from the Egyptian frontier post. It happened in the evening about 6.0, an hour before dark. We had no spare inner tube, and the burst was so complete as to split the outer tube and chew up the inner tube so much it wasn't recognisable as a tire [*sic*]. I cadged a lift for most of my party on an Australian YMCA lorry going to Cairo and stayed the night with my driver on the truck. In the morning I hitch-hiked to the frontier post, cadged an inner tube from a convoy passing through, hitch-hiked back and we set off. We arrived about midnight at the camp, and I found myself allotted a completely bare hut room of brick and plaster with very detachable whitewash. I blew up my li-lo, crawled into my blankets and went to sleep. In the morning I was woken by a very dirty Egyptian servant. He appeared to understand nothing: the breakfast provided was literally filthy, and everything was mahfish (Arabic for nothing doing or there isn't any). A notice in the mess stated that we were to pay 18 piastres (about 4/6) but that suggestions for improvement would be welcomed. After 3 days of it I and one Frank Stoakes (of Merton) wrote about 3 pages of vitriolic but constructive suggestions. We used the truck I had brought to take us the 26 miles

2 See Letter 198; this was to be a longish process which was to end with *Selected Poems* (1943) with poems by Douglas, Hall and Norman Nicholson.

to Cairo each evening, but one morning about midday I was driving in to collect some I.A. pay for Frank, when an Arab ran out from behind a stationary lorry. He ran right across me, so without braking fully I swung in towards his starting point to give him more room. Unfortunately he had seen the truck too late and tried to run back. I hit him with one mudguard and broke his left foot more or less clean off under one wheel. He had burst some small artery in his stomach and vomited blood all over everyone but we got him off to hospital within five minutes and made out an accident report. Unfortunately this had to go before Major Douglas, who threatened to have me court-martialled for using a W.D. vehicle for personal use. I replied (later having given him time to cool off) that the truck was under my charge, and that I had authorised the journey, which constituted it a matter of duty, whatever he thought. This he had to admit, and instead, rather than give in, he said some officers had told him I'd been a leading light in complaining about the mess. To this I replied in polite but meaning phrases that I still thought the messing filthy and that I should be glad to know who the officers were and to have their accusations made to me in his (Major Douglas') office. However, he wouldn't tell me their names so gave in and instead announced his intention of taking over the truck which although he wasn't entitled to, I couldn't stop him doing. However, I'll continue the tale in my next.
Love
Keith

211. *To Marie J. Douglas*   BL 56355 f.133

[On front] No.2 OPEN 2ND

Dear Mother,
I think my last letter left you at the point where Major Douglas, unable to Courtmartial me, had confiscated the truck under my charge. Well, not long after that, I was made Orderly Officer without the customary day's notice, and that evening I had tickets to go to a concert in Cairo by the Palestine Orchestra. The tickets were 75 piastres (15/-) each, and although I hadn't paid for them, it seemed a bit hard to have to waste even someone else's money. There was no chance to telephone, so I got someone else to do Orderly Officer for me. This was quite in order, and I went along

to the orderly room and said I'd got someone else, and what was I to do? They replied that all I need do was give them my deputy's name and room number. This I did, and departed to my rendezvous in Cairo. But my deputy 'thought it would be all right' if he didn't mount the guard. He knew the Orderly Sergeant would be there and do it for him. But not only the Orderly Sergeant, but also Major Douglas was present at Guard mounting, purely by chance, and I believe the only time during the whole month. He sent for the Orderly Officer in terrific wrath. My deputy appeared and said I had never told him he had to mount the Guard. This was a lie, in any case. But it was no excuse, since if he accepted the responsibility, it was his job to find out its extent. However, the use of my name as a red rag diverted the bull's attention, and I was sent for the next morning. After being kept waiting ¾ of an hour, I was told the Commandant did not wish to see me, but that he had awarded me a week's Orderly Officer (equivalent of a week's C.B. for a trooper) and was writing a report about me to Middle East. The adjutant read me the report, which mentioned the truck and the accident, very carefully but not very truthfully worded, and continued to say that I had no sense of discipline and had no right to be an officer. The adjutant added in a whisper (the Commandant's office being next door) that he didn't think the letter would be sent, but was intended to put the wind up me. So I waited, doing Orderly Officer, for 2 days and then counter-attacked by applying for weekend leave, inventing 2 more fabulously expensive concert tickets and a fiancée in Cairo. At the same time I put in a most formal report beginning Sir, I have the honour to submit the following, with reference to etc. etc. saying that it was not my fault if my deputy failed, when I had provided him and informed orderly room, and even if I was technically responsible for his actions during my absence, giving me 7 days Orderly Officer and writing a report to M.E. would do no one any good. Furthermore, I added, perhaps he (Major Douglas) was not aware of the fact that my truck, when he had (illegally, I pointed out) taken it over, had made its first journey under his authorization, at exactly the same time of day to collect pay for exactly the same officer. Since he had threatened to courtmartial me for authorizing such a journey, this would sound a little odd, if I had to report it to my Colonel. My Colonel, moreover, did not like to hear of his officers being harshly punished without even being interviewed and asked for an explanation of their actions, and would not be

particularly pleased with Major Douglas for taking over a Sherwood Rangers truck and using it for his own purposes. In any case was it fair to keep me in camp when my fiancée, who lived in Cairo and could not see me at any other time of the year, was thus being more punished than I? And if, as he had twice told me, I had failed the course, not through lack of knowledge of the subject, but for not finding a proper deputy orderly officer, and for complaining about a filthy mess in a book specifically provided for complaints, he had better send me back to my regiment straight away, but must be prepared to explain why to my Colonel, who (I mentioned casually) was an M.P. The desired result was obtained. I was immediately taken off Orderly Officer, and as I had already squared the Transport Corporal, there was no need to take back custody of the truck. I used it as before. A THIRD LETTER OF GENERAL NEWS follows.[1]
Love
Keith

212. *To Marie J. Douglas*   BL 56355 f.135

n.d. [PM Staines 28 March 1942]

Dear Mother,
I hope you've got some more letters from me by now. There are one or two things you still seem to be in doubt of. I left off the novel when I came off the boat.[1] Masefield was never wounded and has been with the regiment ever since he came out of hospital after his pneumonia. My pay difficulties are more or less cleared up at the moment, and I've arranged for pay to be paid me direct out here. *If* there is any money in Nat. Prov. for use, keep it and use it – I have enough now – about £15 a month and allowances. At the moment I am in a hopeless situation and don't quite know how to get out of it. I have been arbitrarily made a Camouflage Staff Officer. This doesn't mean any promotion, although I believe I get extra pay. It's not even anything to do with the result of my course and it's happened just when I particularly wanted to stay with the Regiment. As with everything in the Army, I arrived here to find no one knew what I was supposed to do, there is no office for me

1 Not located.
_____
1 No trace of the novel remains, but see Letter 199.

and the car and driver I'm supposed to have don't exist. I've been here 3 days and seem to be completely ignored. What I want is an interview with the General to tell him I don't want the job. My Colonel saw him before I came here, and he was alleged to have said he'd see me as soon as I arrived, but it seems to have slipped his memory. So I have had nothing to do for 3 days but write letters, and it looks as though this may continue indefinitely. If nothing happens in another two days I shall ask for an interview, and if I can't get away I shall threaten to resign my commission. This usually has the desired effect as they are short of officers and don't want to lose any. But if I have to resign it I'll do that sooner than sit here drawing extra pay for doing nothing when I could be with the Regiment.

I wonder if you've had a letter from Renée yet. By the way, in case I forget, my address is now C Mess. H.Q. 10th Armoured Division, M.E.F., though I hope it will change again soon.

This place is very similar to the last I was in, and there is nothing whatever to do with all the spare time I've got. I have seen G.S.O.'s [General Staff Officers] 1 and 2, a Colonel and a Major, who obviously have no idea what I'm here for, but are determined not to let me get away, their line being 'It says in black and white that you ought to be here, *and* you've done a camouflage course, so *obviously* you've got to stay'. This is the intelligent principle which is of course responsible for our armies' notable successes and the extreme elasticity of its organisation. I hope I'll have better news next time.

Love
Keith

213. *To Edmund Blunden*   Texas

1 March 1942   HQ10 Armd Div MEF

Dear Edmund,
Thank you very much for your letter – you really must get hold of an airgraph form so that it takes a few months less to get here. I am incapable of being decently content I'm afraid. I was fed up with sitting in camp doing nothing. Now I am 10 times fedder up with being an elegant little staff officer with quite a lot to do, and no chance of getting back to the regiment. Mon Général is one Clarke,

who says you were his Intelligence Officer in the last show – 'Marvellous feller, always bringin' me reports in astonishin'ly neat handwritin', astonishin'ly neat. And then he'd dish in a bit of astonishin'ly good poetry, too. Well, you'd better write and tell him I'm still tickin' over, what? Good.'[1] I am getting a certain amount of flying and going down to Cairo by plane tomorrow – my job is Camouflage, and the only comfort is that one day I may be sent up to the front line to observe, and I think if I do go General Clarke will find it an astonishin' long time before they find where the feller's got to – puttin' in a bit of fightin' on the sly, what? At the moment I am just getting used to living in a house and having a bath every night. I have a room distempered in light blue and unfurnished except for a wash stand sans basin and a very battered dresser (and my camp bed and basin). The dresser is somewhat brightened by a few Penguin covers, and I soon evolved a method of mural design by pencil and nail-file, which produces three tones, black pencil, blue wall about the colour of that [the letter paper], and white plaster where I scratch with the nail-file. So I have covered the walls with ballet dancers. Eventually I bought some paint and did a large group portraying *Der Tod und das Mädchen*, to my own choreography and without costumes except for death's cloak. Colours being black, blue and white, with a red backcloth behind painted like red clouds, and the words décor, choreography, mime set at angles round the design in this sort of lettering [written in open-face], only somewhat neater and better-proportioned. I've had several letters from Jean Turner whom I think you know. She is now a Wren and likes it, except for the stiff collars. Stella Joan App. also writes occasionally – I hear Betty App. caught impetigo from her scrawny husband's embraces.

I've heard no more of Eliot but I daresay I shall be able to catch up with him afterwards: I certainly seem to be in for cellophane preservation while the others do the dirty work and get all the experience I wanted.

I had an accident last time I was in Cairo and killed an Arab – he did the usual chicken-crossing-the road stunt, at the double, from behind a stationary vehicle. I was exonerated but somewhat shaken. It is curious how doll-like a broken up body looks, in spite of blood.

---

1 Blunden's letter has not survived, but for his extensive reply about Clarke and other matters see *Miscellany* pp.89–90.

A pity it's not so odourless as a doll.

I've been disappointed in attempts to meet anyone interesting in Palestine. The Jews resemble rabbits exactly except in gracefulness and pleasant appearance. The girls are lovely until they marry, which they seem to do about 16, and from then on are dirty, slovenly, smelly, sullen, and permanently (it appears) in the last and most ungainly stages of pregnancy. The men seldom wash or shave and are usually out of condition and wear sort of prismatic spectacles. They are also sullen unless behind a counter, a bar, or a tray. And yet there must be many of the brilliant refugees hidden among these morons. Perhaps I'll find them yet.

Love to Sylva.

Keith

214 *To Marie J. Douglas*   BL 59833 f.29

Telegram [PM 2 March 1942]

All my love my address is HQ 10th Armoured Division Middle East
Douglas

215. *To Jean Turner*   Private Hands

n.d. [PM ?2 March 1942]

Dear Jean,

I've just had another letter from you – it looks kind of old. I wonder when is the last you had from me? You are enjoying yourself, aren't you. Why don't you manage to get sent to M.E. or don't they have such things here – there seem to be most kinds of Mädchen in Uniform. I am a Cam. staff officer: I don't want to be but I can't escape yet. I have begun flying but my tummy isn't much used to it yet. Tomorrow I'm going to Cairo and shall see a few friends. In Palestine I know no civilians. I am fairly flush at the moment so I shall have a good time and dance as much as possible with Renée, Judith, Fortunée, Rosette, Evelyn, but mostly with Renée. Why should the nicest of them have such a suburban name. She's the plainest too, and when she's tired she looks awful. But we get on and she can put up with me when I'm in a bad temper, which I don't think the others could. Tomorrow I shall arrive off the plane as sick as can be and have to kiss all of them and Maman too, on both cheeks; my God.

Palestine is about at its best now, the fields being covered with a sort of buttercup and brilliant scarlet anemones. The Arab women and children are very decoratively dressed in patterns of black and red and other colours. Also there are Yemenites a sort of cross between Jew and Arab, who wear a cross between European and Arab dress. I.e. the women have striped trousers appearing from under their skirts down to their ankles. I live in a room now in a Jewish country town, and have (incredible) a bath every day. I get about a great deal in the course of my duties and thank goodness have plenty of reasons for visiting Haifa, which is my favourite M.E. town. It would be so nice if you could come out here now because it would be such fun to shew someone round. As it is, there's no one who doesn't know enough to show *me* round instead. I had a letter from Betty Sze, who seems to be degenerating into an unintelligent gusher. I wrote and said so to her, but I doubt if she'll take it much to heart. Also a letter from Blunden, who doesn't seem to be conscious of the existence of airgraphs or the possibility of sending a postcard by air mail. The G.O.C. of this Div. was Blunden's C.O. during the last war. By the way in case I forget to put it in, my address is H.Q. 10 ARMD: DIV: MEF. You put my regiment in brackets, if you like. I am duty officer for the weekend and this is the 12th letter I've written so you must excuse me if my mind wanders occasionally. You may feel insulted to come so late on the list if you like, but you had better console yourself with the fact that even after 12 letters I can write 3 sides of an air mail lettercard to you in writing less than half the size even of letters to Diana (who is being a good deal too devoted for my conscience – I suppose I *shall* marry her in the end). I do wish someone would teach her how to dress before I come back.

She could look marvellous but usually appears rather fly-blown, until one looks at her eyes. She's about the most childish person in outlook I've ever met. I suppose I ought to say childlike because its more charming than aggravating. I think its an awful pity for her she picked me. No one *ought* to pick me, not exclusively.

The ant season seems to have begun again but thank God not the flies – yet. I expect I shall find them in Egypt when I get there.

My room here is distempered light blue and I have covered it with murals of ballet-dancers, but you wouldn't be interested. I hear

you've pinched my copy of *8 Ox. Po.* Well hurry up, there's nothing that gives conceited people a kick like seeing their work in print. From what I hear the poetry in it is lousy though I understand one of mine appealed to some dried up female don. That's about the mark of the whole book I should think, if it really sold out in 3 weeks. I bet *Augury* was a lot better and Basil B. would probably be glad to give copies of that away now. Incidentally you might, if you have an account at Blackwells, send me a copy of *Augury* because I think Renée would like to see it and if not I should be quite glad to cast an eye over it again, not so much for its literary merits as because re-reading it would transport me back to Oxford again and recall the tremendous thrill of seeing it actually *out* for the first time. It was good, as a whole, although it contained some sludge. Some people liked it, but I fear not many. Blackwell was rather pleased when all the London copies of it got burnt. Well, write again – I know you will, but soon.
Love
Keith

216. *To Marie J. Douglas*   56355 f.134

n.d. [PM Staines 28 March 1942]   HQ. 10 Armd Div MEF

Dear Mother,
Thank you for 2 more airgraphs – as you will probably know by now from other letters and from Diana and from a telegram, I am a camouflage Staff Officer. I am not very pleased to be given a cushy job without having done anything to deserve it and in spite of every effort to avoid it, but anyway I'm trying to fix to be sent up the desert on my own and hope to attach myself rather unofficially to a fighting unit and see what I want to. I am going to Cairo again soon and hope to see Renée again and also call on Fidèle, though I try to avoid English people for two or three reasons such as (a) They frequent all the most expensive and uninteresting places (b) Once abroad, they become more insular and unintelligent than ever (c) One can meet quite enough of them in England while there are interesting people here whom I'd never have met otherwise. I suppose it was too much to expect Auntie Rita to have the energy or originality to break out of the magic circle. I'm surprised she didn't add Lady McMichael to the list. Spinneys I haven't searched

out. They are the International stores of Palestine. He was a Sergeant-Major who stayed here after the last war and made good. They might be very well in with a lot of Jews but hardly of the intellectual kind.

The Jews en masse are horrible and I can sympathise with anyone who feels an urge to exterminate them. They are like rabbits but not so pretty. Every other rabbit characteristic, promiscuous breeding, dirtiness, lousiness, cowardice, they have in abundance. They are filthy sullen slovenly swine, and I can't be more accurate than that. We should have done much better to put our money on the Arabs who apart from having a slightly villainous inclination and being very dirty and uncivilised, are very pleasant amiable people. If the Jews are educated they only learn how to profit from people. But the Arabs work without being so keen on returns, and are very eager to learn. They are sending travelling cinemas round to Arab villages where they have never seen snow, or tanks or the sea or big guns firing or football, or hundreds of other things which appear on news films. They have an educated Arab commentator who explains things simply as the film is shewn. The women have to sit behind the screen but enjoy it none the less.

City Arabs have been spoilt by English habits of tipping and overpaying and regard all the English as fools who ought to be swindled (which they are).

I live in a square white Jewish house with a couple of balconies. My room is distempered light blue and I've painted, drawn or scratched ballet-dancers all round the walls. Some are scratched away to white plaster with a nail-file and filled in with pencil. One is black silhouettes with white lines scraped on them and a red pattern behind and two are watercolours with scratched highlights. The army are giving me a £25 camera in due course so I might get photos of them when I learn to work it.[1] By the way, at the regiment I used to pinch these lettercards ad lib but the issue is one, or one airgraph per week so I *may* have to keep to it here.
Love
Keith

1 Prints of Douglas's photographs are in both the Brotherton Library and BL 53775A.

n.d. [PM Staines 27 March 1942]

Dear Mother,

Thank you for another 2 airgraphs: I don't know how it managed to be six weeks. But you will have heard a certain amount of explanation by now, and I've sent you a couple of cables since then. I am now leading a luxurious life and don't seem to have much hope of escaping to something more active. Meanwhile I'm taking advantage of it, as seems only sensible. I've been and met the local Air Force and can fly (on duty) more or less whenever I like. I get very sick in an hour (though not, so far, actually), so heaven knows what will happen when I get into the plane on Monday to fly to Cairo. I am hoping to get a few unofficial lessons later on. I fly mostly in trainers, so I have a set of controls moving about in front of me as the pilot moves them in his cockpit. Conversation through the voice tube is rather difficult and I was very surprised the first time I put a hand out-side the windscreen; although 120 mph is pretty slow for nowadays, it raises a bit of a wind. I'm going to try and visit Fidèle Castellain[1] when I get to Cairo, though I shall spend most of my time with the Manis. Did I tell you they know a Mrs Castellain who lives in London. At first I thought it must be Aunt Anne, and couldn't understand when they said how pleasant and good-looking she is. But it appears she is French, and a widow who has taken her maiden name, so she is a real home-made Castellain. I wonder if anyone on our side knows her? She had a Syrian husband.

I have had a very nice letter from my squadron leader saying he won't rest till he gets me back to the regiment, but I'm afraid he's in for a pretty restless time.[2] The Colonel evidently intended to get rid of me for one reason or another, because he (The Colonel) told me he would see the General and arrange for my return and when I left shook hands with me and said he had seen the General and fixed everything and I should soon be back. When I interviewed the General I found the Colonel hadn't said anything at all to him. Meanwhile I shall try to escape to the front line somewhere, by myself which has provisionally been granted without any definite

---

1 Castellain was Mrs Douglas's maiden name.
2 The letter survives: BL 56356 f.198.

when or where. Then make sure that when I come back I have some claim to a cushy job.

John M. is with the regiment so I doubt if I'll see him again. I hear Owen Bodycombe and the others are on their way here, though David Crichton was very ill and got re-graded into a cushy war-house job.[3] Rather lucky for him as he'd just got married. I'm afraid there's little chance of *their* asking for me back, as I volunteered to leave them.

One of the few advantages of being here is the chance to hear very good music occasionally. I haven't met anyone of interest here, except the Manis in Egypt, of whom I wrote to you, and at least one of whom (Renée) has also written to you.

I had a letter from Betty Sze – poor girl, she's getting worse and worse and becoming quite society – she said she thought Diana 'a very striking girl but *very* experienced-looking', and having given a very journalistic description of a sunrise in the Suez Canal ends 'I can just *hear* you thinking what a fool I am'. If I didn't know her I would think so too, but it might be better if she were a fool.

Love

Keith

218. *To Jean Turner*   Private Hands

n.d.

Jean dear,

Thank you a lot for a couple of letters and 2 parcels of books – one of which incidentally seems to enclose a note not intelligible to me and probably not intended for me. I have just had a hectic month in Cairo, and escaped another engagement by the skin of my teeth. She was a French Jewess (and in fact still is, and is following me to Palestine in due course). She is very charming (of course) but I don't think I want as one Stoakes of Merton, now out here, put it, 'a lot of little Solomon Douglases'. Philip Schapiro of Merton, and John Waller, are out here – I've met neither, but saw John Waller's name in an article on 'Poets in the Army' in a local rag, *Parade*.[1] Philip

---

3 Douglas's friends from the 2nd Derbyshire Yeomanry.

---

1 *Parade* was an illustrated weekly for the forces in the Middle East.

lives in a huge hotel in Cairo and does nothing, except for an occasional visit to the Egyptian parliament, with his patronising arm round the neck of some wog minister. Do you remember Kenneth Brooks of Merton who wrote the music for Blunden's famous appearance in Dryden's *Secular Masque*.[2]

It's a lovely day but nothing to do and no one to do it with until Renée comes here. Isn't it typical of all English and my blasted Aunt in particular that after living off and on in Haifa for 10 years she can't give me the address of any one not English to call on. When the place is stiff with fantastic refugee genii and all kinds of amazing people.

I am going to stop now and go out for a solitary ride. I shall possibly call on my only acquaintance in Pal; a Jewish-Lithuanian cop called Mosshe Yting.[3] But all [he] ever does is tell me stories of his amazing, not to say incredible, heroism during the trouble, in which he went about braining tens and twenties of Arabs with a wheelbarrow. He speaks a sort of cockney German. (E.g. Heite instead of Heute).

Love
Keith

219. *To Jean Turner*   Private Hands

18 March 1942   HQ 10 Armd Div MEF
[PM Kensington 14 April 1942]

Dear Jean,
Thank you for 3 consecutive airgraphs. It's very sweet of you to write to Mother and she enjoys getting your letters and is most grateful to you. I think I have written you since I became a camouflage officer – indeed I've had a great deal of time for writing letters, and little else to do. I suppose one day someone will turn up who wants to know something about camouflage but at the moment there is nothing. I have been flitting about between here and Cairo, where I had a French-Egyptian-Jewish girl friend. She now wishes to cross out the girl and remain mine sincerely, which means that she will probably have to become a procuress. I have just had a most

2   As 'Chronos', at Merton in December 1939.
3   Not traced.

sententious letter from her extolling the beauties of platonic friendship, somewhat pompously. She's very sweet but 27 years, sundry almost incredible misfortunes and an attempted suicide have left their mark. What a family: of five sisters and 3 brothers, one brother died, another sister had a brick dropped on her head which finished her career, (she was a ballet dancer), and two have had fiancés killed in air smashes. The atmosphere of gloom is not so noticeable as you might expect, and they are all most generous and amicable, but naturally subject, individually to fits of utter depression which make my own efforts in that direction look very amateur. I think this letter will not be written with my customary ease of language and inspiration because 1. I am perched on the edge of a sofa 2. leaning on a too small rickety table, and 3. this air letter card having been folded in four for some time refuses to lie flat. In addition there is no news, except a little which is highly censorable and not very interesting anyway. I've been bored for so long I feel as though I could never be very interested in anything again. Meanwhile it sounds as if people at home are being almost restricted to death – I shall expect everyone to look as if they had been holding their breath for years when I come back. Meanwhile I'm afraid we eat and drink the best, more or less unrationed, if rather expensive. Cream, chocolate and cheese are consumed in disgusting quantities and I am of course as fat as usual. But not, I'm afraid, as beautiful. I made the mistake of travelling on the same bus as some Jewish workmen and picked up a bug which bit me 8 times and gave me blood poisoning for about 3 months. To this living in camp, sleeping in army blankets and shaving in cold water added impetigo. All these things are now healed (They were about at their worst on Christmas day, when my face was more or less falling to bits). The result is a series of indelible red splodges on my chin which look like the results of kissing someone with too much make up, and I have red scars all over my arms and legs. We have just returned from a visit to the Jordan valley where I camped out for one night by the Dead Sea and received 51 bites from mosquitoes in spite of keeping my head under the blankets. I didn't sleep a wink all night. You know what a noise one mosquito can make. There were literally thousands there: when it got light there were about 3 per square foot over an area of 20 acres. I killed a great many but it was rather like the first stages of the battle of Britain, and the havoc they left behind was also reminiscent. Four or five people had their eyes closed and I had bites on the soles of my feet which made it uncomfortable to stand while other bites made it equally painful to sit down.

It's a good thing Palestine is such a delightful country, (if not delightfully populated) because I imagine the Jews and Arabs, more particularly the Arabs, will keep many of us out here when the official war is over.

I was shewn over a Jewish communal settlement the other day – rather impressive and a paradise for children who live together away from their parents, grouped according to age. They go to visit their parents for about 2 hours at weekends and all day on Saturdays. The parents work like stink. No one has any money of his or her own. But they all seem pretty happy, particularly the kids.

Love to you

Keith

Hurry up and send Ye Oxford Poets

220. *To Jean Turner*   Private Hands

n.d. [PM Egypt 22 March 1942; PM Kensington 12 June 1942]

Dear Jean,

Thanks for another letter – I'm charmed to think of you as a Wren – or was until I saw a picture of the new Wren hat which looks like something out of a 19th [C] family group and ought to have HMS Benbow written on the front and a present from Margate inside it. I am living in idleness, boredom and extreme poverty. I see a good deal of Cairo now and then where I stay with rather an Oxonian collection of people, David Hicks, once of Worcester and the fiancé of Betty Sze's (Mrs Betty Carey's, by the way) best friend, also Bernard Spencer a minor poet who once edited things with Spender – but to do him justice, has forgotten it, and a gentleman of most effeminate appearance who rather surprisingly fought in the International Brigade as a machine gunner. Among his booty is Nieves, a very hot (in every sense) Spanish wife. Hamo Sassoon has arrived out here but I haven't met him yet. I believe various publications containing something of mine are appearing or rumoured. I still haven't seen a sign of *8 Ox. Po.* yet. Meanwhile I'm writing in a thing called *Citadel* (unpaid, of course)[1] financed

1 *Citadel* was a largely literary monthly; Douglas's first contribution appeared in July 1942 (see Letter 224).

by the Anglo-Egyptian union, at which Hicks (who edits it) is a sort of schoolmaster. I am the only subaltern in this emporium – the exception to prove the rule that no one does any work at a Div. H.Q. and everyone gets paid three times too much. I lecture all morning and paint things all afternoon, while the others snore through the heat of the day, and then do office work in the evening. For this, after some mathematical gymnastics by the Pay Corps, who have decided to reclaim something or other, I get £4 a month pay. No one else gets less than £35, as far as I know. I am getting so exasperated that I picked up and hurled to the ground army typewriters, one, with dire results. I now have to make up a lot of excuses and reports to explain this unmilitary behaviour. Renée, incidentally, is succeeded by Olga (Latvian, Palestine Area), Fortunée, Reman, Marcelle, Pilar, (Cairo area, Iraqui, Turk, Turk, Spanish).[2] So the situation is well in hand.
Love
Keith

---

221 *To Marie J Douglas*   BL 59833 f.35

n.d. [in tiny writing on cut out paper 2" × 1"]

I am having tea by the Pyramids with an RAF chap who's going back to England on Sunday (tomorrow) so I bought these. The round one is for you and butterfly for Diana if she would like it. Keep whichever you like, though. I can't stay out of the conversation any longer
Love
Keith

---

222. *To John Waller*   Graham

23 April [1942]   HQ 10 Armd Div MEF

Dear John,
I don't know if you are resident in Cairo but assume from your alleged connection with the Victory Club that you are or were in

---

2 A Marcelle appears in 'Cairo Jag' but she is 'Parisienne' and may be a composite person from several Douglas knew.

that neighbourhood. I have to come to Cairo occasionally (at least once a week) and should quite like to meet you for dinner somewhere if possible.

I am sorry you allowed yourself to take part in producing such a shocker as *Orientations*. It is worse than anything in that line I've ever seen which is saying something. It should have been edited by Geoffrey Grigson.[1]

I am a Camouflage King at the moment, but hope to escape it as I prefer being an ordinary regimental officer. I haven't written anything for some time.

Yours
Keith Douglas
I see *Parade* awarded you an honorary hockey blue in rather a clumsy sentence. What drivel some of their 'Poetry' letters were.[2]

223. *To Olga Meiersons*   BL 56355 ff.174-6 and 53773 f.7 and f.11

n.d.

Dear Olga,
As heaven knows when I shall be able to write a letter so undisturbed again, I may as well send you this at once even though it's only a day since I saw you. Sitting by a telephone gives me plenty of time for correspondence.

Yesterday evening (for which, thank you many times) would have been ideal as a prelude to a week of meetings. We enjoyed our conversation and were finding out a lot about each other. It's a pity you weren't tipsy, but one can't crowd everything into one evening.

If we meet again (and I shall try very hard to arrange that we do), expect nothing of me except that I shall interest you. If you are ever bored with me, it will be because I am bored with you, and I don't think I shall ever be bored with you. I shall never ask you to do anything for me that I wouldn't do for you.

I'll write to you whenever I have anything particular to say – but I never write letters regularly – I'm sure you don't either. I am sentimental, as you say all Englishmen are, and therefore although

1   The editor of *New Verse*, he published Douglas in 1937. Letters from Grigson to Douglas are in BL 56356.
2   John Waller's poem 'Photograph Album' was in the 17 January 1942 issue of *Parade*.

I'm disillusioned, I'm not cynical. Most of all I am never cynical about making love. If I tell you between two kisses that I love you more than anyone in the world – you can believe me. But not for long – love comes in waves, it can't be kept burning at the same pitch for years, or it just burns you up altogether. But friendship can: I have few enough friends to be able to count them. To most of them I don't write more than once a year, and they write back to me less often than that. But I know that if I walk round a corner one day, anywhere in the world, and meet one of them, we shall begin exactly where we left off at our last meeting.

If I can get back to see you I'll let you know as long beforehand as I can and I hope you'll keep as many evenings as possible free. If I come to see *you*, I shall be quite single-minded about it, and shall make all my arrangements for those few days centre round you – you will be the focal point of my world for that time and I hope you'll live up to it and spend as much time as possible with me. I hope I shall come for 3 or 4 days. During that time, let's go to your cellar again, let's bathe, and one evening dress up as finely as we can and go to a dance.

When I was in England, I once wrote to a girl and asked her to spend my leave with me. She accepted and somewhat to my embarrassment appeared complete with suitcase and asked when we were going to sleep? She was so angry when I said I had only meant, spend the daytime part of my leave with me, that she has never spoken or written to me since. So be warned, if I ask you to spend some leave with me, I shall mean, be prepared to come out and have a good time, but *not*, as the Americans say, to give me Your All – you can have your sleep.

By the way, is your rather beautiful ring an engagement ring? From your conversation, I imagine not, in spite of its adorning the third finger of your left hand.

Just because I've got to stay in today is as lovely as a day could be. I should like to be riding, or bathing, or driving about the country in a fast car – all these in company with someone young, feminine, beautiful, intelligent, (in that order). Oh, I shall come back all right, even if it has to be after the war.

You said you like poetry, so I am going to enclose a poem or two – if I can find any, with this. My poems aren't written in thumping dactylic metres like your friend Thomas Hood's, so perhaps you'll not like them. I don't make use of alliteration much either – it's your Germanic instincts which demand such things go. My verse is not particularly regular, but it has a certain amount of meaning, and rhythm as well, though subtler than Hood's, I like to think. You shall see: don't feel bound to give an opinion of the poems. They are, as they say in the army, 'Forwarded for your information' and you're not expected to comment on them. This is a situation I did not mean to allow. I have begun a new page just when I haven't much more to say.

You will probably see that the whole of this letter is about *me*, and deduce from that, that I'm conceited. But at this stage I can hardly write about you (I hope you'll write about yourself), and there isn't much news to give you. I could of course write a general essay on camels or Palestinian politics or Lebensraum, but I think it's more important to tell you things about myself and save you the trouble of finding them out for yourself – there's plenty more to find out anyway. I hope your letter will be all about *you*.

Also I hope you aren't entirely made of india-rubber. I have a rubber outside myself, but the inside is of more sensitive and fragile material, so be careful. This really is the end for the moment.
Keith
[on reverse]

This is the evening of the same day – after an afternoon of answering telephones I felt I owed it to myself to get slightly drunk – I don't do this often but occasionally, on impulse, and if I decide to get *un peu gris*, it doesn't take many drinks to make me so. Then, I have been reading a book called *Valse des Fleurs*, about Imperial Russia of the 19th century.[1] Whenever I read such fantastic descriptions it reminds me that England will never be my home country. I must make my life extend across at least half the world, to be happy. I love people, and I think my only real ambition apart from those ambitions connected with making my living, is to meet more and more people, each different and more fascinating than the last, and to love them all, and to be loved by them. You understand that I never say things like this unless I am drunk, but [breaks off here. 'Turn your back on Monte Nero' (*CP* p.42 as Part I of 'A God is Buried') follows, with the note by Douglas:] In Gorizia, in N. Italy, there was a great deal of bloody fighting over the bridges of the Isonzo river, in the last war. In ancient days the Romans built

1   By Sacheverell Sitwell, 1941.

230

villas here and put up statues. The idea of this poem is that where the young sapling trees are growing to replace the trees destroyed by shell fire in 1914–18, an ancient Roman stone statue of a god is buried. The golden oriole is an Italian (and European) bird with a voice like a flute.

['A baron of the sea, the great tropic/ swordfish', (*CP* p.73 as 'The Marvel' but here without stanzas 5–7 and with other slight variants) with the note by Douglas:] This poem is written around the fact that if you take a swordfish's eye out, you can use it as a magnifying glass to burn things by magnifying the sun's rays until they catch fire.

['How silly that soldier is, pointing his gun at the wood' (*CP* p.37 as 'Russians' with slight variants) follows, with a note by Douglas:] During the Russian campaign against Finland, a Russian regiment was reported to have been discovered frozen to death, the soldiers still holding their rifles ready to fire.

224. *To Olga Meiersons*   BL 59833 ff.30–1

n.d. [June 1942]   10th Armd Div MEF

My dear Olga,
I was on the point of sending a telegram, so I am quite pleased to have your letter. As ever you are so serious and monitory. Thank you also for the photographs – I tore one up immediately, in which you looked like a rabbit in a silly symphony.[1] No one saw it. The other two, which I think are good, I kept; I think the 'bang' of curls on your forehead gives you the appearance of a rather 'odd' lady novelist, or else a retired prostitute, but it may be something to do with the lighting. Anyway, that photograph has a worldly, cynical and tragic quality. The other is most like you, but technically a bad photograph. Who took them? All that may sound very carping and critical, but I was very glad to have them. The large one of you which you gave me to take away with me adorns my tent, where it has been mistaken, (owing to lack of hair) for the portrait of a young man. But don't dare think anyone would mistake *you* for a young man.
    You want to know if I believe in anything and imply that you

1 Surviving photographs of Olga are in the Brotherton Library.

believe in nothing. Well, I do believe in something, and I have come to the conclusion that the particulars of my creed shouldn't be examined too often. If you have something valuable, keep it in a safe place and look at it only occasionally, to see if it is all right. If you keep taking it out to play with it you'll break it or lose it sooner or later.

I have a useful headquarters in Cairo now, having met an Oxford acquaintance, David Hicks who is a sort of schoolmaster in the Civil Service (British) out here.[2] He lives with an ex-member of the International Brigade, (a journalist called Keith Scott-Watson, with a charming Spanish wife – booty, I suppose), and a moderately well-known poet and one-time colleague of Stephen Spender, Bernard Spencer. I can go and sleep there whenever I'm in Cairo, so no more hotel bills.

The question of the Turkish Delight still is not solved What can I do, not to hurt or insult her? She is intelligent and would be a delightful acquaintance and a good friend but she expects me to sleep with her, even if I only visit her for an afternoon. And I think she is in love with me, she doesn't seem to make a habit of sleeping with people. Myself, I need to sleep with someone sometimes, but I hate the idea of 'using' her, because she's really too good a person to be used, and ignored the rest of the time, and anyway I feel pretty low if I sleep with someone I'm not in love with. I wish the most natural desires and functions weren't rendered almost monstrous by the ridiculous arrangements of society. When you think what it is like to be really happy, and how little is necessary to make us happy, it's quite absurd to see how seldom anyone is happy.

But we shouldn't be so serious and introspective in our letters. I have managed to write home again. The general futility of this existence got me down the other day and I smashed an army typewriter by picking it up and hurling it on the ground. It will never type again, but it had so many fiddling little things wrong with it like jumping up or down a line or letters sticking and the bell not ringing that it suddenly exasperated me. I shall probably get more fits of this. It is necessary continually to accept as a fact that all men and Englishmen of the bureaucratic type in particular are naturally and chronically and invariably stupid. If I forgot this principle for long I should go crazy. My *God* they are idiots, all of

2 See *KD* pp.147–8.

them, and the seniorer the stupider, civilian or army.

You say, only letters written by their intimates reveal the lives of great men. That's what I mean – what I left unsaid was that the intimates of great men are, more often than not, insignificant people, since there aren't enough great men in any generation to go round each other. I didn't mean fan letters.

I'll look what photographs I've got but I am definitely *NOT* photogenic, and I don't think you'll find any of them either pleasant or even recognisable.

David Hicks, earlier mentioned in this letter, edits a sort of Anglo-Egyptian (with emphasis, particularly lingual, an Anglo) literary review called *Citadel*, which I am writing poems and '*réportage*' for. My first efforts appear in July number.[3] Incidentally although I don't think it sells outside Cairo, it would probably sell much better in Palestine. At the moment, like most of those magazines, it runs at a fair loss, paid for by the Anglo-Egyptian Union.

I shall stop and write to Mother and others in England – where by the way another book of poems by 3 people, ~~myself~~, sorry, John Hall, Norman Nicholson, myself, is about to appear.[4]

Much love, and longing to see you again.

Keith

225 *To Marie J. Douglas*   BL 60585 f.15

(First of two Airgraphs) 13 August [1942]

Submit to Editor Poetry for Fabers the following,[1] and in addition look among poems you already have for a sonnet containing verse 'like all, this storm will blunder along the hills.'[2] also another poem about a garden of which at the moment I can only recall a line 'and even Cupid on his ornamental stone'[3]: and a poem called Soissons,

3 'Syria' (for text see Letter 227a) and 'Death of a Horse', a story (see Appendix).
4 In May Hall had found a new publisher for *Selected Poems*, Norman Nicholson replacing Alan Rook as the third of the poets to be included.

1 The context for this letter might be a letter from Tambimuttu to Douglas's mother, 27 July 1942, saying he had been trying to contact him to publish his poems in *Poetry (London)*, of which he was editor, 'and two anthologies that I collect for Messrs Faber and Faber' (BL 56356 f.38).
2 'Sonnet: Curtaining this country', *CP* (as 'A Storm') p.14.
3 'Absence', *CP* p.49.

not the one in *Eight Oxford Poets* but another of which one verse ends 'the devils pilloried on that holy wall/ Must smile to see our faith broke to the wide.'[4] Please select any others you like which have not appeared outside *The Cherwell*, and send them. If it's an anthology actually you could take what you like. As Blackwell did not pay anything for *Augury* he has no right to anything in it, and we could use any of those such as 'Stars'. You might submit *'Pas de Trois'*, the one about ballet dancers. Here are some more.

'Song: Do I venture away too far' [follows][5]

I hope you can read this – it seems to be about all I can get on this. I think you or Blunden have a copy of it anyway. I am going over to another airgraph.

Love
Keith

226 *To Marie J. Douglas*   BL 60585 f.14

[Second of two Airgraphs] [13 August 1942]

'The Marvel' [follows][1]

You should have these already. But I want to make sure they go.
Keith

227. *To Marie J. Douglas*   BL 56355 f.138

(Airgraph) 18 August 1942   HQ 10 Armd Div MEF

Dear Mother,

Thank you for several airgraphs which have been waiting for me at Div. I had your telegram just as I was departing for the desert so could not answer it at once and after that I was unable to get any forms or letter cards as I was not with a formation or in barracks, so I got Milena[1] to get a civilian airgraph form and send you the only

---

4   'Soissons 1940', *CP* p.48; the other poem is 'Soissons' *CP* p.47.
5   The poem, as 'Do I wander away to far', is in Letter 198 (with variants).

---

1   The poem was written a year earlier, at Linney Head, Wales; see *CP* p.73.

---

1   See next letter. For Milena see biographical list and *KD* pp.151–4.

poem I had ready at the time. I am glad to hear of the various contracts hovering in the offing although I am afraid it's not likely that I shall have any more new poems to send you for some time. But here is one new one.

Devils[2]

My mind's silence is not that of a wood,
warm and full of the sun's patience
who glances through the foliage waiting
perhaps for the entry of a god:
silence I welcomed when I could.

But this seeming silence is
the fastening of a soundproof trap
whose idiot crew must not escape.
Within all day they make their noise,
all night against my sleep their cries.

Outside the usual crowd of devils
are flying in the sky, walking running
on the ground, invisibly spinning
through the black air alive with evils
and turning, diving in the wind's channels.

Inside this deceptive wall
the devils of the mind can't hear
the devils talking in the air
who think my mind void. That's all:
there'll be a devils' alliance if it fall.

I think I am going back to my original regiment which is a few miles from where I am now.[3] But at the moment I am wanted by that and the Colonel of the Sherwood Rangers so it rests with the General to decide. Anyway it seems that I'm rid of camouflage at last, and not before I was heartily sick of the whole subject. But I mustn't count my chickens too soon. I missed being bombed and shelled by one day and went back with some trucks to be mended. I was kept hanging about a long time and as I owed a mess bill in

2 The text in *CP* (p.92) differs from this.
3 The 2nd Derbyshire Yeomanry, who had arrivved in the Middle East.

the barracks in Alex I put up with Milena's people who were very kind to me and washed and mended all my clothes for me. I will write again as soon as I can get another form.
Love
Keith.

227a *Milena Gutierrez-Pegna to Marie J. Douglas*   BL 60585 f.16

(airgraph) 9 September [1942]   452 Ave. Fouad 1er/Alexandria

Dear Mrs Douglas,
Keith asked me to send you this poem for Faber and Faber, as he can't get any military airgraph forms at present. He has already sent a copy to Edmund Blunden.

> *Syria*[1]
>
> These grasses, ancient enemies
> waiting at the edge of towns
> conceal a movement of live stones,
> the lizards, with hooded eyes
> of hostile miraculous age.
>
> It is not snow on the green space
> of hilltops, only towns of white
> whose trees are populous with fruit
> and girls whose velvet beauty is
> handed down to them, gentle ornaments.
>
> Here I am a stranger clothed
> in the separative glass cloak
> of strangeness. The dark eyes, the bright-mouthed
> smiles glance on the glass and break
> falling like fine strange insects.
>
> But from the grass and the inexorable lizard,
> the dart of hatred for all strangers finds
> in this armour, proof only against friends,
> breach after breach, and like the gnat is busy
> wounding the skin, leaving poison there.

1   *CP* p.89, with slight variants. The copy to Blunden has not been located.

I hope you will be able to read this. Perhaps I should have used block letters [the airgraph is typed]. I am writing another Airgraph in my ordinary handwriting, to introduce myself to you. Keith is very well but a little busy at the moment, I think he is trying to change his job, or something. He has not had time to write anything lately except he says an air letter card which he sent you about a week ago.
[unsigned][2]

228. *To Marie J. Douglas*   BL 56355 f.139

20 September [1942]

Dear Mother,
It appears to be arranged at last that I am to leave this ridiculous job and return to the SRY [Sherwood Rangers Yeomanry]. I discovered that Kellett had actually asked for me several times but the people here had told me he had not so as to make me think I had no chance of going and to prevent me from annoying them with applications for transfer. I am jolly glad anyway.

John Masefield was killed pushing back the recent German attempt to advance, so I suppose we shall never know whether he was bats or not. I have recently written you lots of letters, airgraphs, lettercards etc., as I have at last managed to get time to write at the same time as I had something to write on. Milena has written to you too. This is just to send on two more poems, which please present to Tambimuttu if you think it's worthwhile by this time. I didn't know him but heard a certain amount about him from Michael Meyer. Here they are:

> *Egypt*[1]
>
> Aniseed has a sinful taste:
> at your elbow a woman's voice
> like I imagine the voice of ghosts,
> demanding food. She has no grace

---

2   The continuing airgraph 'in my own handwriting' is missing.

---

1   Typed down to line 14 then at page foot: 'next 2 lines part of this verse, of course'.

but, diseased and blind of an eye
and heavy with habitual dolour
listlessly finds you and I
and the table, are the same colour.

The music, the harsh talk, the fine
clash of the drinkseller's tray
are the same to her as her own whine,
she knows no variety.

And in fifteen years of living
found nothing different from death
but the difference of moving
and the nuisance of breath.

A disguise of ordure can't hide
her beauty, succumbing in a cloud
of disease, disease, apathy. My God,
the king of this country must be proud.

[down centre of page, between the two poems]: another fallacy you
seem to have got into your head is that Mila and I are going to travel
everywhere without you. We thought of taking you to Spain for a
bit.

Christodoulos

Christodoulos moves, and shakes
his seven chins. He is that freak
a successful alchemist, and makes
God knows how much a week.

Out of Christodoulos' attic,
full of smoke and smells, emerge
soldiers like ants; with ants' erratic
gestures seek the pavement's verge;

weak as wounded, leaning in a knot
shout in the streets for an enemy—
and dross of Christodoulos' pot
or wastage from his alchemy.

They flow elsewhere; by swarthy portals
entering the crucibles of others
and the lesser sages' mortars:
but Christodoulos is the father

of all, he's the orignal wise one
from whose experiments they told
how War can be the famous stone
for turning rubbish into gold.

I wrote to Tambimuttu but didn't enclose any poems because I
didn't know whether the address POETRY, London, would reach
him, and typing out poems is such a nuisance that I didn't want to
do it perhaps for nothing.

I have just found one more photograph of Milena which I shall
send you I think, because it'll only get lost out here if I don't.[2]

Thank you for 15 *Poets*[3] and some very opportune socks which
the mess sergeant has just sent over. Your choice of reading for me
seems inspired and is probably the only thing which will make me
still capable of thinking and having some literary taste at the end of
this.

What by the way gave you the idea that all your letters are boring
– I shew some of them to Milena and she says she already knows
quite a lot about you and a lot more about me from them, and your
account of Mr Miles' beloved, (who sounds as I should have
imagined her – I am inclined to think that it was only the character
and good sense of the original Dolly which prevented her from
being selected) greatly amused Norman Ilett, who said it was well
up to your usual high standard of description. He was sent on an
unusually stupid expedition the other day which most of the people
on it knew to be asking for what they were about to, (and did),
receive.[4] He said goodbye fully expecting not to return, and even
gave me three pounds as an advance legacy. But he was back in two
days demanding the three pounds, which having been entrusted to
me were of course, spent. Mila has some good photographs of all
three of us and his senior officer Alec Foster.[5] I met rather a nice

2 Perhaps that reproduced in *KD* p.151 and now in the Brotherton Library.
3 Oxford, May 1941 reprint (now in the Brotherton Library).
4 Ilett, Sub-Lt RNVR, took part in the Tobruk raid; see *KD* p.153.
5 Now in the Brotherton Library.

chap who used to be in Eastbourne College, Keith Roll, who knew
uncle Claude. He also returned I think, although minus his boat.
Must stop, I'll let you know as soon as I really have moved to the
regt. Love Keith
HQ address will find me anyway

229. *To Jean Turner* Private Hands

n.d. [September/October 1942][1]

Dear Jean,
I don't know if this will appeal to you. It's so beautifully made, rather
than well shaped.[2] And the man who sells it me, with an expressive
Eastern gesture tells me his father made it years ago.
I'm off to the desert at last.
Love
Keith

230. *To Olga Meiersons* BL 59833 ff.32–3

7 October [1942] HQ 10 Armd Div MEF

My dear Olga,
Thank you for your letter, which has at last reached me. I don't
know why they have mixed up my correspondence lately, but all
sorts of letters, even offficial ones have gone all over the place after
me. Never mind, you've discovered me again.
      I am afraid I'm not much worth finding, though. I think I told
you about the Chinese girl I once nearly (or as I thought then,
nearly) married. I don't know if I made it clear that all my life since
then had been a kind of recovery from that episode. I had recovered
anyway, as far as one ever does. Now I have done exactly the same
thing over again. I met in Alexandria a Spanish-Italian girl, I just
saw her walk past on the beach, and went mad about her, without
any will to love her. Well, the incredible happened, for a bit. I
introduced myself, took her out, and she seemed to fall as much in

---

1 With its reference to being 'off to the desert at last' this letter could be from a
   little later, perhaps the end of October 1942.
2 Possibly a silver wire brooch shaped like a butterfly (in Jean's possession).

love with me as I was with her, in the same mad sort of way. But the story went on more incredibly still: after she had agreed to marry me, but I knew with doubts in her mind, (about what I could not make out, except that she seemed afraid we could not get on together by temperament) I went to the desert. It happened that my best friend had come to Alex, and I had introduced him to Milena. I have known him 8 years, and we were always together at school and at Oxford. Well, you see what is going to happen. But it sounds too theatrical for real life. I came back by accident, having broken down with a lorry outside Alex. I towed it in, in the dark, and went to her house for the night. She was out with Norman. That seemed pretty natural. And I sat down to wait. They came in soon afterwards, and immediately a sort of strain settled on the room. Everything everyone said was forced out. Milena went up to find some blankets for me and I went after her and asked her what was the matter. She told me, partly, but not about Norman – she hadn't even told Norman. That is the worst night I've ever spent, bar one. I'm still feeling somehow how a man might feel who has to walk miles and miles home with a bad wound, dragging his feet, trying to hold himself so as not to feel the wound too much. It has opened the old wound as well. A week before, she was, or seemed, happy with me – now it is absolutely, irrevocably over, and she is as beautiful as ever, and I think, happy, if only I'll leave her alone.

If you think that makes me no use to you, just write once, and say so. I'm not much use to anyone at present [three and a half lines line cut out] just now I am on 2 days leave in Cairo staying with David Hicks, who knows you, so I suppose you know him. He was in Palestine recently and I think brought you a note from me. He says, by the way, he will send you some copies of *Citadel*.

He is in as bad a state as I am, so I'm not sure if the visit has done us good or not. We talked a long time last night. Naturally, for me, this alters nothing in the way I feel about you: ours is an understanding, and I think we love each other. One can't stop loving. But there are these women in the world who send me mad. I suppose I shall meet others, and if none of them will marry me, I shall never marry. Perhaps it is better than marriage to have friends like you. Please Olga, never think that anything that happens to me would alter that. Even if I had married a woman I was mad about,

I should keep my friendships, and if it broke my marriage and ruined my greatest happiness, I would still keep them – I can't help myself. But I [three lines cut out] that I don't wan [half a line cut out] don't think I shall get to Palestine for years, literally; but probably I shall sooner or later, or you will leave it. I don't like, almost I hate and fear, many Jews – yet I feel more and more that in the end it will be a Jewess I marry. Probably from constantly suffering real and fancied injustice, I have acquired something a of a Jewish mentality myself.

Nothing can be done for the moment – I must sweat it out. You could help me a good deal, if you will: so long as you don't feel I'm coming back to you as a sort of second best – I'm not, you are where you always were. I shan't write you intelligent or intellectual letters – indeed I try as far as I can not to think at all. This is quite enough disjointed waffling. I shall say goodbye for now and hope they don't prevent this outburst reaching you. I suppose you want to know what Milena looks like – can I have this photo back please?
Love
Keith
Sorry about these [ink smudges in the margin]

231. *To Brenda Jones*   BL (newly acquired)
n.d.

Dear Brenda,
It's a long time since I wrote to you or heard from you – warnings and exhortations about Christmas mail have reminded me of one or two gaps like this. The best I can do is to write the requisite letters, though when they'll be posted lord knows – we seem to be out of touch with postmen just now, although there must be one within a mile or two with a lorryfull of English stamps to put on these things and possibly even some mail from England.

What news? Mine is not hopeful nor interesting, much. As usual I have just had a narrow escape from marriage, this time to a bee-utiful Spanish-Italian person called Milena Gutierrez-Pegna who I believe now expects to be Milena Ilett. Do you remember Norman Ilett, of Mid. B, now Sub-Lt RNVR? I introduced him, and he cut me out. I must say he looks very nice in his white uniform – he was always a bit brown and out here has become a sort of golden chocolate – if such a colour exists, and of course is incredibly lean and full of heroic tales.[1]

Myself, I never do anything heroic. I have been mucked about somthink terrible by almost everyone, civil and military. Just now I live rather behind everything with the rations which is nourishing but boring. Luckily I have a very good batman, one Ward who was at one time 2nd huntsman or some such thing to the Crawley and Horsham. Charles Gregson – if you knew him, son of the redoubtable Mrs M.F.H. Gregson has got the M.C. for some sort of heroism in an armoured car.

I am still writing vaguely, sometimes for a periodical in Cairo, run by an old Oxford friend of mine in the Civil Service, and, so my Mother tells me, I am a contributor to a magazine in England called POETRY, and to various books such as *Poems from the Forces 2, Modern Reading No. 6, 8 Oxford Poets*, and various volumes with similarly boring titles.

Even if you are now turning out bomb releases or smoke candles, 20 to the minute, I hope you've not got rid of the horses – I shall want a ride again one day. Love to your father and mother and love to you.

Keith

[on verso] My address as before

232. *To Brenda Jones*   BL (newly acquired)

(Christmas Card) 18 October 1942   HQ Armd Div MEF
Directive/XMA/(Greet.)/42.
W.E.F. 2359 hrs.24.12.42

[Sketch: 3 flying military men, one floating down, one playing a lute, one with a halo playing a fanfare trumpet. Text: 'Certified Official…', 'MOST SECRET', 'Hosanna, Grade I', 'Halleluja, strength Nin[…]']
A MERRY repeat MERRY XMAS stop A HAPPY NEW YEAR message ends.
From Keith
K. C. Douglas Lt. P/170611

---

1 See *KD* p.158. Ilett was refused permission to marry Milena by the Royal Naval authorities.

233. *To Jean Turner*   Private Hands

18 October 1942 (airgraph)   HQ 10 Armd Div MEF

[Christmas Card sketch: winged officer blowing trumpet, other
officers flying and diving with typed words around it:] 'w.e.f. 2359
hrs., 24.12.42…' 'URGENT' 'CONFIDENTIAL…most secret' 'a
MERRY repeat MERRY CHRISTMAS and a HAPPY NEW
YEAR' 'Certified Offficial' 'OFFICER ONLY' 'KCDouglas Lt
P/170611'

234. *To J.C. Hall*   Hall

n.d. [PM Egypt 29 October 1942]   Cairo

   The Knife

   Can I explain this to you? Your eyes
   are entrances the mouths of caves
   I issue from wonderful interiors
   upon a blessed sea and a fine day
   from inside these caves I look and dream.

   Your hair explicable as a waterfall
   in some black liquid cooled by legend
   fell across my thought in a moment
   became a garment I am naked without
   lines drawn across through morning and evening.

   And in your body each minute I died
   moving your thigh could disinter me
   from a grave in a distant city:
   your breasts deserted by cloth, clothed in twilight
   filled me with tears, sweet cups of flesh.

   Yes, to touch two fingers made us worlds
   stars, waters, promontories, chaos,
   swooning in elements without form or time
   come down through long seas among sea marvels
   embracing like survivors on our islands.

This I think happened to us together
though now no shadow of it flickers in your hands
your eyes look down the banal streets
if I talk to you I might be a bird
with a message, a dead man, a photograph.

For M. G-P[1]

The Offensive

I
Tonight's a moonlit cup
and holds the liquid time
that will run out in flame
in poison we shall sup.

The moon's at home in a passion
of foreboding. Her lord
the martial sun, abroad
this month will see Time fashion

the action we begin
and Time will cage again
the devils we let run
whether we lose or win:

in the month's dregs will
a month hence, some descry
the too late prophecy
of what the month lets fall.

This overture of quiet
is a minute to think on
the quiet like a curtain
when the piece is complete.

So in conjecture stands
my starlit body; the mind
mobile as a fox sneaks round
the sleepers waiting for their wounds.

---

1 Milena Gutierrez-Pegna; see above.

This overture of quiet
is a minute to think on
the quiet like a curtain
when the piece is complete.

II
The stars dead heroes in the sky
may well approve the way you die
nor will the sun
revile those who survive because
for the dying and promising there was
these evils remain:

when you are dead and the harm done
the orators and clerks go on
the rulers of interims and wars
effete and stable as stars.

The stars in their fragile house
are the heavenly symbols of a class
dead in their seats;
the officious sun goes round
organising life, and what he's planned
Time comes and eats.

The sun goes round and the stars go round
the nature of eternity is circular
and man must spend a life to find
all our successes and failures are similar.

If you don't want any of these, please send them on to my mother,
c/o National Provincial Bank Ltd. Staines, Middx., or any better
address you know.
Keith Douglas

235. *To Marie J. Douglas*   BL 60585 ff.17–18

18 October [1942]

'The Knife' [text in previous letter][1]

1   With slight variants.

'The Offensive I and II' [text in previous letter]
No news to add to these at present, that would be passed, although
I have a good deal to say about the way I have been treated recently
by the people in charge of me, who whatever I do firmly refuse to
allow me to be of use to anyone. I hope to pillory them in a book
one day, although they're so typical and uninteresting that I doubt
of anyone would read it.

I sent copies of these to John Hall care of you as I can't remember
his address.

Keith

236 *To Marie J. Douglas*   BL 59833 f.34

(Airgraph as Christmas card)   HQ 10 Armd Div MEF
21 October 1942

[Sketch of officer as angel blowing trumpet; words around it]
XMAS/Greet/Cds/42
with effect from 2359 hrs. 24.12.42
PRIORITY Hallellujah PRIORITY
MOST SECRET
Hosanna strength fife say again HOSANNA strength ninah off
MERRY repeat MERRY XMAS stop AND HAPPY NEW
YEAR
Distribution List Z
For MARRY read MERRY
Keith

237. *To David Hicks*   BL 53773 f.47

[?] October 1942

       Milena[1]

       I listen to the desert wind
       that will not blow her from my mind,
       the stars will not put down a hand,
       the moon's ignorant of my wound

---

1 In *CP* p.96 with title from first line, and variants.

moving negligently across
by clouds and cruel tracts of space
as in my brain by nights and days
moves the reflection of her face.

Skims like a bird my sleepless eye
the sands, who at this hour deny
what violent heat they have by day,
as she denies her former way.

All the elements agree
with her, to have no sympathy
for my tactless misery,
are wonderful and hard as she.

O turn in the dark bed again
and give to him what once was mine
and I'll turn as you turn
and kiss my swarthy mistress pain.

KEITH DOUGLAS
Wadi Natrun Oct.42[2]
Dear David,
I haven't time to write – this is the finished version and *I* think it's
not as bad as *you* would expect. Please print it if you can, and soon
– because it will all help my getting accustomed to the situation.

2 At Wadi Natrun Douglas joined the Sherwood Rangers after their first tank
   battle. Surrounded by the preparations for the El Alamein offensive, he himself
   was to stay out of the fighting, with the Headquarters group.

Seven

1942–1943

n.d. [PM ?4 November 1942; PM Kensington 8 December 1942]

Jean darling,

As far as any worry is ever justified, which is no distance at all, those expressed in your letter may be justified. To which cryptic sentence may be added that I am back, and thank heaven for it, with the regiment, and life is pretty mobile and interesting. I have a camera and a permit to use it, being a camouflage king. You spoke of one of my first letters to you as 'painfully censor-conscious' so must this be, so I had better add what I usually find in letters I censor – I am well and plenty of grub, well dear, roll on when the blinkin war will end an I will see you all again well dear I must close now XXX but I won't close, before telling you, in case I didn't, that I almost got married to one Milena Gutierrez Peña in Alex but she withdrew at the eleventh hour and preferred, in two heartrending scenes, Sub-Lt Norman Ilett RNVR late of Christ's Hospital and BNC[1] – you may remember him. Mother will have photos of the wench. *Should* you ever find yourself in Alexandria ask for news of me from her or her father – Gutierrez-Pegna, 452 Ave Fouad 1er, Rouchdy Pacha, Alex., or from N.L. Ilett, Sub Lt RNVR HMS Mosquito Alex. If you land yourself in Cairo, which is less likely, David Hicks, Anglo Egyptian Institute, 3 Sikket El Mahgrabi, Cairo, or Renée Mani, 139 (Victory House or Setton's Buildings) 3rd Floor, Emad el Dine St., Cairo, may know my whereabouts. Palestine – Olga Meiersons, Kedem Bookshop, Jona Hanavi St., Tel Aviv. South Africa, Valerie Butler, P.O.Bothas Hill, (The White House) Near Durban, Natal. Love and Christmas and kisses etc.

Keith

239. *To Marie J. Douglas*   BL 56355 f.140

n.d. [PM Staines 10 December 1942]

Dear Mother,

I hope you can read this: anything you read in the papers around

---

1   Brasenose College Oxford.

the end of Oct, the date of this letter, may concern me.[1] I am extremely well and have managed to collect a large amount of clothes, chiefly socks and pullovers from Army issue. We get some American stuff which is far superior to British. I have an American 'comforts for the troops' pullover, which is very posh. As you will know by now, the Milena business is off, she has decided to marry Norman Ilett who concurs. Did I tell you John Masefield was killed? I suspect Hamo Sassoon was put in the bag at Tobruk with the rest of his regiment; unless he did not rejoin in time.[2]

As you have probably gathered I'm back with the regiment, which has done and is doing very well indeed. I am still supposed to be with Div HQ, but they forgot about me, and I trotted off when no one was looking, they haven't noticed yet, although they told me they couldn't spare me to return to the regt![3] A chance we might be home soon I believe at last.

K   address straight to the regiment

240. *To Olga Meiersons*   BL 56355 ff.177–8

n.d. [?December 1942]

My dear Olga,

Thank you for your sweet letter, and for the returned photos – no, I never imagined for a moment you would keep them: it was just old English politesse, I didn't like to say you *must* return them. I have had a busy time since I saw you last – the regiment has been filmed and the C.C. of our Brigade has broadcast. Churchill, it appears has mentioned us (naming no names) in a speech. The first few days, my first in any kind of action, were undeniably sticky, and the Germans undoubtedly fought as long and as well as they could. But when they broke they broke properly, and the pursuit was very like hunting in England, except that instead of killing the fox when we found him, we gave him a tin of bully beef and searched him for souvenirs.

My worst day was spent in a tank full of someone else's blood

---

1 The battle of El Alamein started on 23 October 1942. Douglas's experiences from this point are recorded in his narrative *Alamein*.
2 He was not taken prisoner. See Letter 259.
3 Douglas drove to the battle of El Alamein against orders and within twenty-four hours he was in action in a tank; see *Alamein*.

from the day before. The flies were incredible. As far as credit goes, don't pay too much attention to the eulogies of gallant airmen, or even of the tank chaps. The gunners deserve the greater part of the praise. As Churchill more or less said.

If I can get a leave long enough, I shall come to Palestine. If I should fail to get there, please never stop writing to me, and I am determined in any case to revisit Palestine in peacetime – I hope the Arabs will behave themselves. If you write to me when I am in England, write to me c/o Merton College Oxford, and if you get no reply (I think you will though because they always know where I am), send a letter to Christ's Hospital Club, 26 Great Tower St. London, or to Christ's Hospital, West Horsham, though if you send it to Horsham, put Mid. B 1934–8, after my name. Don't worry, I'm not all that religious, Christ's Hospital is a school.

Anyway I shall see you again one day. Perhaps you'll come to England. I shall certainly be off again, I can't stop in among more or less undiluted English people for long, much as I like a few of them. As long as we keep writing, and blame the postal authorities, and not each other, when we get no reply, we'll be all right.

I spent a whole day broken down by the roadside talking to the crew of a German tank who had given themselves up. One of them had been in Paris and was armed with the usual postcards. My German was more adequate than I thought, although pretty lousy on the whole. One of them had a pretty thick local accent of some kind which puzzled me – I am stone deaf anyway after 2 weeks of gunfire and my ears will go on singing for months yet.

I have acquired a camera, some excellent clothes, a new camp bed and air mattress, and an Italian automatic. I had 3 Luger pistols but gave 2 away and then lost the 3rd, much to my chagrin. I've also picked up some German novels here and there – a detective story *Die Zeugin Auger fehlt, Also sprach Zarathustra*[1] von Friedrich Nietzsche, whom I regret to say I've read none of, except quotations, a sea story which I seem to have lost and *Das fressende Haus* by someone called Siegfried von Vegesack.

I've also found millions of letters all very uninteresting. Look I must stop, I'm supposed to be on a job. Write again soon.
Love
Keith

---

1 In possession of Desmond Graham.

n.d. [On front] FREE CHRISTMAS MAIL [December 1942]

Dear Mother,

This is our usual free Christmas issue one – I hope it gets there, without a stamp, and remains legible, as I haven't a pen. As I shan't date it I can say it's written within a few miles of the enemy, who we hope won't be there much longer. You'd think they'd have the intelligence to go home and call it a day, and I suppose they will have by the time you get this. You needn't be worried by anything in my present situation – it will be long past history when this gets to you, and if you've had no swifter communication from the usual authorities, you can be sure I'm OK, or at least was not affected by this lot. I have been trying cooking with flour and margarine, making sort of jam puffs, today, and of course in spite of all precautions have sat in the jam, and temporarily spoilt my new German trousers: but the puffs were a great success. The country here is slightly reminiscent of Ashdown forest in certain places, and we have come across sheep straying across a main road, somewhere on our way, and heather here and there. It is very cold before and after sundown, with a bitter wind, but reaches a fair heat at midday; I begin and end the day in 2 pullovers, shirt, trousers, tie, battledress top, silk scarf, and British warm; sometimes with a leather waistcoat thrown in. By midday I am down to shirt and trousers and, perhaps, stripped to the waist. I am quite fat again now, as we've done little but eat for some time. By the way, I'm surprised you let them sell you that brooch as this regiment's. Anyway you know the kind you want now – you should be able to get it from the right part of the country. If I am back in Cairo or Alex some time I'll see what I can find. I did buy one for Renée Mani once. I haven't heard from anyone except Olga Meiersons (Tel Aviv – Latvian) for weeks. Not even Milena, who promised to write when I last saw her. I suppose she's writing to Norman. Will you thank Diana for her wire and say I'll write when I've paper and time and a chance to get the letter back. A merry Christmas and I'm sorry I'm not in a position to send you any presents.
Love
Keith

n.d. [PM Staines 26 Februruary 1943]

Dear Mother,

Thank you very much for the 3 books, which have just arrived – most opportunely, 5 days before Christmas. We are somewhat in the wilderness, but luckily a party scouting for water found an unfortunate lamb wandering, who will be the 'A' Squadron Officers' Christmas dinner. We are hoping a mobile canteen will show up before the day, as we're out of whisky. During the last few days I've had time to experiment with the ration issue, and we find quite palatable porridge can be made from smashed oatmeal biscuits. From these we also make cakes, with Palestinian tinned jam – a bit rugged but very good: a handful or two of flour is issued occasionally and becomes the outside of bully, jam, or treacle fritters, with a bit over to thicken the Mackonochie gravy. Altogether we feed well. We have had a good deal of ersatz coffee one way and another – it is, to me, indistinguishable from the real stuff, and much more economical. I think I told you the Axis armies have been living pretty well. We have used up our loot now, but we had a sort of German ovaltine, Italian tinned cherries, German and French brandy and wines, and casks of Chianti. The Italians strew behind them as they retreat those decorative bottles in straw jackets. I had a narrow escape when I saw 5 bottles full of wine nestling in a basket in an Italian infantry position. Luckily before I could stop the tank, the driver ran over it, and the mine, or whatever was under it, went up in smoke and blew the track off the tank. We, being inside, were O.K. Some of the booby traps are quite cunning, particularly as they don't necessarily go off the first time anyone touches them. The dirtiest are bombs tied to British, German and Italian dead. I think the idea is an Italian one. On the whole the Germans behave a hell of a lot better than the Italians. All the men of this regiment who were at one time or another prisoners, were well treated by Germans. Italians ill treat their prisoners: yet Italian prisoners are very cringing and offer cigarettes watches etc to whoever takes them. Germans do maintain a sort of dignity. I was talking to a Panzer crew who had been in Paris. They knew all the places where Betty and I used to go and eat, around Montparnasse, and said it's not true that the Champs Elysée's fountains have been removed.

By the way, has anyone sent me a copy of *Modern Reading No* 3,

for which presumably the £10 was payment? I wonder if John Hall has got any other poems of mine published?[1]
Love
Keith

243. *To Margaret Stanley-Wrench*   BL 57977 f10 and f.11

(2 Airgraphs) 8 January 1943   Notts SR Yeo MEF

Dear Margaret,
Thank you for innumerable airgraphs, all most welcome. Mail is a true luxury to us now, only less valuable than sleep, which is, as ever, the most satisfying thing of all. I wish I could counter your green pictures of England, but I have not a naturalist's eye or memory. There are indeed flowers of various indeterminate sorts and colours even on these bits of desert, mostly they are mauve and yellow. Occasional and quite veritable daisies and dandelions. Birds come and go, wagtails, geese, quail, and a curious sand coloured lark. I have an idea it's somewhere round here St Paul made one of his journeys.[1] Mother sent me something called *Modern Reading* containing a poem of yours (one you sent me), and advertising you as a contributor to *Kingdom Come*. Over to sheet 2

John Waller still ornaments some base occupation at Cairo – he's had a pretty comfortable war, I imagine. So have I, at times, but I've made up for it since, and salved rather a guilty conscience.

I think I wrote to you describing our Christmas. Thank you for your little horses, which arrived quite clearly and most seasonably. I sent you a fanciful design on the same paper, of winged generals blowing horns among the clouds and announcing a Merry Christmas w.e.f.2359 hrs 24.12.42. If it never reached you, try Jean, or my Mother, or ask Mother to find a copy from David Roberts or Blunden. You do know my Mother don't you? If not write to her. You soon will – Jean does.
Love
Keith

---

1 John Hall hadn't liked Douglas's more recent poems, sending 'Egypt' and 'Christodoulos' on to Tambimuttu (see Hall letters BL 56356 f.41 and 60587 f.64).

1 St Paul's conversion was to figure in Douglas's poem 'Desert Flowers' (see below) a few months later.

244. *To Marie J. Douglas*   BL 53773 f.48

(Airgraph) 10 January 1943

Poem 'The stars are dead men in the sky'[1]
I don't know if you have this. John Hall hasn't as far as I know.
Love
Keith

245. *To Marie J. Douglas*   BL 56355 f.143

n.d. [PM Staines 1 March 1943]

Dear Mother,
There seems to be very little mail getting through from me to you
– in fact you have not received one or two things which I know
have been in posts which definitely arrived in England. For instance
I drew a Christmas card for you and one for my batman which were
sent by the same post and were drawn the same. He has had a letter,
a month ago now, acknowledging receipt of the one he sent. Yet
nothing has arrived from you or Jean or Diana to say you have had
these. My batman was at Div. with me so his letters have to follow
him round through the same number of addresses as mine do. Yet
your books arrived for Christmas most seasonably and on the dot.
So I don't know where it is all going. I've not received *Poetry
(London)* or a copy of *Modern Reading No 3* with my poems in,
although *Modern Reading No 5* has come. Nothing from Blunden
for months. It incenses me that he should have his room stacked
with review copies of books which he doesn't want, by the hundred,
and here are we starved for books, and it never occurs to him to
send any. In fact I've even asked him twice, but he doesn't do
anything about it. You might see if you can chivvy him into it.
     At the moment we are more or less keeping up with the BBC
and the newspapers, which probably provide you with a map
showing our position somewhere on it. Our chief needs are tobacco
– which Valerie Butler sends me from South Africa, and books of
which we can never get enough. Penguins are best because we
haven't much room for baggage. Valerie sends chocolate too, but
even from South Africa it arrives pretty jaded. I've just had a letter

1 'The Offensive II' (see Letter 234) variants in this version include a fifth stanza.

from you enclosing a picture of Christine and Gary having been married. He does look a twit, but so does she in the photograph. A note from Mila has just come to say she is officially engaged to Norman and hopes to get married very soon. I sent her £3 for a wedding present – I owe it to Norman anyway, so it wasn't as generous as it sounds.[1] I suppose you'll meet her eventually, I wonder what you'll think of her.

We found a German illustrated paper with an account of the Dieppe raid in it, more vivid than convincing. I translated it and read it out to the squadron, together with one or two other items. The advertisements suggest there is not much to be bought in Germany: except medals, uniforms and cures for rheumatism. There were two pages of Deaths. Must stop.
Love
Keith

246 *To Olga Meiersons* (fragment)   BL 56357 f.7

n.d. [January 1943]

'Lines written before the Alamein Offensive' [See Letter 234 for the text of this poem, with slight variants, in *CP* as 'The Offensive I'] I'm too tired to go on, we were woken at three this morning to get us off-loaded from the Hospital train.[1]
Goodnight Olga darling, write soon.
Love
Keith
P.S. If I can't get to Palestine I want you to buy me a doll in Jerusalem, at the shop next to the King David. In fact could you do that anyway and smuggle it over to Cairo I wonder – I should hate to have to pay customs on the parcel.

---

1   See Letter 230.

---

1   Douglas had been wounded at Wadi Zem Zem on 15 January. The whole action and events following his being wounded are narrated in *Alamein*.

26 January 1943   No1 General Hospital MEF[1]

Dear Mother,

I have now arrived, after a most uncomfortable journey of nearly 2000 miles in various forms of transport, where I shall stay put for a week or two. I think there are fewer bits in me than I originally imagined, though there may be something in my left thigh and in my right calf and there's definitely something in my right foot because although I can walk on it and wiggle the toes it is numb, as if it had gone to sleep. Anyway I shall know in a day or two as I was X-rayed yesterday, and you can be sure that by the time you get this whatever it was will have been taken out, and I shall be almost out of here, if not quite. Anyway I've had a very small amount of pain and am quite undisfigured. My temperature is a bit subnormal, but the lowest I can see on my chart is 97, and yesterday evening it was 98, which it probably will be again this evening. We are fed at all hours of the day with most delectable food, and it seems incredible that in 10 days I could come to this from living entirely on tinned stuff and half a gallon if water a day for all purposes, with fresh meat about once a month, oranges about as frequent, and an occasional small amount of oatmeal or flour. Not that we didn't live extremely well on these rations, when we had time to cook. Service biscuits, particularly oatmeal ones, can be powdered with a hammer and mixed with a little water and sugar and condensed milk make very reasonable and realistic porridge, which is filling and hot. Out of biscuits and jam most professional looking cakes were made in petrol-tin ovens, and when flour was available every kind of cake, dumpling, jam roll and pancake was evolved from it. We captured from the enemy a sort of paper strips, which, like Japanese water flowers expanded in water and boiled up into very good sliced cabbage, carrots, swedes etc, with plenty of flavour and goodness left in. At other times I've got hold of scrumptious tinned cherries and some very pleasant Macedonian cigarettes, of which we had several crates in the regiment at one time. I had all my clothes cut off, but am hoping my batman hasn't lost my other kit, and won't before I can get back. All I retain at present is the large leg-pocket

---

1 At El Ballah. For Douglas's time there see John Stubbs, 'A Soldier's Story', *PN Review* No. 47, 1985.

of my battledress, luckily containing my pay book, identity card, and money. I believe the enemy have most of my shirts and *New Writing*:[2] anyway they haven't got me and some of the clothing was captured German so I've had some free wear from it anyway. I was sorry the doctor cut my leather waistcoat off me so clumsily. What with the blood and the cuts and tears I didn't think it would be worth keeping. But it's a great loss.
Love
Keith
Write to this address and the regt. alternately and I'll be sure of getting some.

248. *To Marie J. Douglas*   BL 56355 f.145

(Airgraph) 1 February [1943]   No1 General Hospital MEF

Dear Mother,
I have written you 2 lettercards since I was wounded, and censor permitting you should soon receive them. If you don't, but do get this, which I am making as uninteresting and non-committal as possible, let me know. I am very well but can't walk yet: a piece of stuff has been prised out of my foot and I'm waiting for it to heal, which it should do in a week or so. I hope to be out of here in at most 3 weeks – till then see if you can reach me with a lettercard or airgraph. I have written you a great deal before I was hit, but as I had nothing from you you probably had little of mine.
Keith

249 *To Jean Turner*   Private Hands

(airgraph) 1 February [19]43   No1 General Hospital MEF

Dear Jean,
I shall have to invent a new calligraphy to suit this horrible nib. Thank you for an airgraph I had a day or two before I was hit. I am likely to be here a week or two so try writing here by some tolerably speedy postal channel. None of my letters seems to have arrived

---

2 *Penguin New Writing*: a book-sized literary magagazine which was extremely popular during the war.

anywhere for months, so I suppose some censor has taken a dislike to me. I am nearly well again but for my foot which had to be opened up and de-peppered. You might drop a line to Margaret Stanley-Wrench if you know her address and say I've had her letters and written to her several times. I've heard nothing of Blunden for a long time now, do you know anything of him? I never get answers from anyone now, very soon I really intend to give up writing.
Keith

250. *To Olga Meiersons*   BL 56357 f.8 and BL 53773 f.57
    (2 fragments)

n.d.

I was discussing Rupert Brooke with someone the other day, who has a book which a very sentimental hospital sister has lent him.[1] I wrote a poem to slip into the book when he gives it back (unsigned, of course) which I hope will shock her sentimentality a bit. [a downward arrow points to the poem]

> *Gallantry*[2]
>
> The Colonel in a casual voice
> spoke into the microphone a joke
> which through a hundred earphones broke
> upon the ears of a doomed race,
>
> into the ears of the poor boy, the fool
> whose perfectly mannered flesh fell
> in opening the door for a shell –
> they had taught him how at school.
>
> Conrad luckily survived the winter
> he wrote a letter to welcome
> the auspicious spring, only his silken
> intentions severed with single splinter.

1 See Letter 247 n. 1.
2 The text has variants from *CP*.

261

Was George fond of little boys?
We alway suspected it,
but who can say now? George is split,
we never mention our surmise.

It was a brave thing the Colonel said
but the whole sky turned too hot
and the three heroes never heard what
it was, gone deaf with steel and lead.

But the bullets cried with laughter
the shells were overcome with mirth,
plunging their heads in steel and earth
(the air commented in a whisper.)

Here is another poem, which I thought of sending to *Esquire*, as it's
not particularly clever.[3] If you do see *Times Literary Supplement*, look
in it, I've just had a poem called 'Devils' in it – my mother got 3
guineas for it.[4]

Cairo Jag[5]

Shall get drunk or cut myself a piece of cake,
a pasty Syrian with a few words of English
or the Turk who says she is a princess; she dances
by apparent levitation? Or Marcelle, Parisienne,
always preoccupied with her dull dead lover –
she has all the photogrphs and his letters
tied in a bundle and stamped *Décedé* –
all this happens in a stink of jasmine.

But there are the streeets dedicated to sleep,
stenches and smells; the sour cries
do not disturb their application to slumber
all day, scattered on the pavent like rags
afflicted with fatalism and hashish. The women
offering their children dry paper breasts

---

3 Sections I and II of 'Cairo Jag' were published as a single poem in *Personal
   Landscape* (Cairo), vol II no. 2 (?Summer 1944).
4 *TLS*, 23 January 1943.
5 The text has variants from *CP* pp.102 and 153–4.

brown and twisted, elongated like the skull,
Holbein's signature. But this stained white town
is something in accordance with mundane convention;
Marcelle drops her Gallicisms and tragic airs
suddenly shrieks in Arabic about the fare
with the cabman; links herself so
with the somnambulist and legless beggars.
It is all one, all as you have heard.

[beside the title 'Cairo Jag':] You may recognise some of the people
[at the foot a note to 'Holbein's signature':] Can you tell me, is
Holbein's signature a skull or some other bone? What does Holbein mean? There is a picture of some king granting a charter to
explorers with a long bone in the foreground which you have to
squint at foreshortened.[6]

II
But by a day's travelling you reach a new world
the vegetation is of iron,
dead tanks, gunbarrels split like celery
the metal brambles with no flowers or berries:
and there are all sorts of manure – you can imgine
the dead themselves, their boots, clothes and possessions
clinging to the ground. A man with no head
has a packet of chocolate and a souvenir of Tripoli.

III
There are new ethics here and fresh virtues.
We have our wise men and lawgivers
artists – for we discovered new arts:
I think some have new religions, and
there are socialites, the smart set, rulers
and little rulers. In all this dry land
the beautiful trees of metal
the noble dead whom we honour as companions
with every indignity, the music is loud or soft
as variable and unexpected as the swing bands
as the classical orchestra of Sculz in Cairo.

6   Hans Holbein, 'The Ambassadors' in the National Gallery, London.

IV
You do not gradually appreciate such qualities
but your mind will extend new hands. In a moment
will fall down like St. Paul in a blinding light
the soul suffers a miraculous change
you become a rue inheritor of this altered planet.

I know, I see these men return
wandering like lost sounds in our dirty streets.

No paper for the other poem, I'll show it you when I come.
Love
Keith

250a. *To Marie J. Douglas*   BL 59833 f.44
        from Under Secretary of State for War[1]

(Telegram) 3 February 1943

REGRET TO INFORM YOU OF REPORT RECEIVED FROM MIDDLE
EAST THAT LT K.C.DOUGLAS DERBYSHIRE YEOMANRY ATTACHED
TO THE NOTTINGHAMSHIRE YEOMANRY ROYAL ARMOURED
CORPS WAS WOUNDED IN ACTION ON 15TH JANUARY 1943
LETTER FOLLOWS SHORTLY UNDERSECRETARY OF STATE FOR WAR

251. *To Marie J. Douglas*   BL 56355 f.146

(Airgraph) 3 February 1943   No 1 General Hospital MEF

Dear Mother,
This is very feeble ink and a horrible nib so I shall have to write
fairly large: it doesn't matter – there's no news, except that I am
getting positively obese with staying in bed and eating so much. I
can walk now, and so long as I stay on my toes, without limping. I
can't yet put my right heel on the ground, but I don't think it will
be long – the M.O. is quite happy about it. There's no reason in
fact to detail my symptoms so lugubriously – it sounds like a W.I.
conversation – but it takes up space and really there's no other news
except what you read in the papers, which seems quite good. I wrote

1 A telegram from Mrs Douglas telling Jean Turner survives (Private Hands).

a lot of letters as soon as I got in here, but have elicited no replies
so far. Nothing from you or Diana for a long time. I shan't be here
more than another month at most so look at the date of this to see
where to address.

Keith

[Alongside] How do you like your new job?[1]

252. *To Sir Reginald Spence*   BL 56355 f.183

(Airgraph) 3 February 1943   No 1 General Hospital MEF

Dear Sir Reggie,
I'm afraid it's a fairish time since I wrote to you or anyone else –
I've been kept pretty mobile and busy since I escaped from my
camouflage job by running away when no one was looking. Now
I have filled myself with pieces of steel and have a bit of leisure while
I get well. Actually I'm about healed now but for a foot which had
to be opened up and is keeping me in bed. Excuse this scratchy
writing – it's that sort of nib. I hope to rejoin the regiment quite
soon. I was pretty sick about this packet as I fell not far from the
winning post, and by the unimpressive act of tripping a tripwire
attached to a booby trap. Don't write to this hospital, address to the
regt.

Keith

253. *To Marie J. Douglas*   BL 56355 f.147

(Airgraph) 7 February 1943   Notts SR Yeo MEF

Dear Mother,
I am up, and can walk quite well already – all healed except my foot
which had to be probed. As soon as this heals I'll be as new, except
for (I think) a permanently numb big toe, so I shall be able to tread
on drawing pins. Everything, including the toe, moves in all
directions, quite as efficiently as ever. So I hope to emerge soon. A
letter here now takes a fortnight to go 100 miles, so I have no great
hopes of this reaching you in record time. Hardly anything reached
me when I was with the regiment, and my own letters even to an

---

1   As housekeeper to Col. and Mrs Baber; see biographies.

officer in hospital in Alexandria never arrived so it seems hardly worth bothering about mail: it's a waste of time to write it. However, we might be home soon. Keep an eye out for any useful jobs, and keep touch if poss. with John H., Blunden, T S Eliot, Tambimuttu etc.

Love

Keith

[Alongside] How goes new job?

---

254. *To Jean Turner*   Private Hands

(airgraph) 24 February [19]43   Notts SR Yeo MEF

Dear Jean,

I heard from another member of your organisation saying she was for North Africa some way back, I suppose you wouldn't be? Anwyay, I am still a long way from there now, and can't put a shoe on yet, because of a bulbous dressing on my foot, although I can walk perfectly well, and indeed dance, if there was ever anyone to dance with. There are one or two of the proverbial pretty nurses here, but they are a good deal too busy to succumb to the charms of their patients – even if an atmosphere of ether and sticking plaster were conducive to romance. The only available entertainment is, 3 times weekly, a very dim – figuratively and literally – film. I am, of course in a shocking state of repression. You no doubt will be quite the other way. Do you know where/how Denise se trouve these days?

Love

K

---

255. *To Marie J. Douglas*   BL 56355 f.148

(Airgraph) 25 February 1943

Dear Mother,

I hear you have had the substance of Edmund's letter – good.[1] I had written to you a week before that, and also by the same post. The

---

1 No letter from Blunden to Douglas survives between March 1942 and May 1943, though other letters show some were sent. A letter from Douglas to Blunden of 31 January 1943 was also lost. See *Miscellany* pp.114–15.

first letter was from a casualty clearing station, and I had to give it to a very stupid padre, who probably either forgot or lost it. Anyway I expect you've had some by now. The same padre had promised to come back and get a message from me to send by NLT telegram, but he didn't, and by the time I got here I thought a letter would do as well. I am up and walking quite all right again, but there are still two places to heal. This is very boring, but although I could get out for the day I want to keep my money. The last leave I had was when I went to Oxford with Diana. All the time I was in Alex I was on duty bar evenings and one or two afternoons.
Love
Keith
[At top] What is Christine's address?

256. *To Marie J. Douglas*   BL 56355 f.149

4 March 1943 [PM Staines 15 March 1943]

Dear Mother,
These don't seem to be arriving any too quickly, and all mail here is in a hell of a state. I do seem to find myself under some unpleasant senior officers. The officer in charge of the surgical division of this hospital is the only unpopular doctor in the hospital. He looks like a rather intelligent aborigine – and does in fact hail from Australia. He refuses to give me even a week's leave because he says – and no one can deny it – that I'm a junior officer. Junior Officers who have the good fortune to be medical and not surgical cases can get leave for the asking. Any RAMC private can have a week's leave every 3 months. Officers in the New Zealand hospital get leave automatically without asking. At the moment the C.O. of the hospital, the captain in charge of my case, and the sister who normally does the dressings, are all on a fortnight's leave. Yet officers who come back from the desert and who have been in action continuously for 3 months, are not allowed leave if they're junior – i.e. captains, or below. Whether this is so in other hospitals I don't know, but if anyone asks for dates and facts, you know when I came in here, the hospital is the 1st General Hospital and the Colonel is Lieut-Col C. M. Marsden RAMC, Regular Army (of course). The O.C. Hospital will not go against any decision of the officer in charge of a particular Division, so there is no appeal. Col. Marsden knows

I have business to attend to – arranging about kit left in Cairo and Alex, which I shall not have the chance of attending to again – and that will mean losing the kit, and he also knows that I've had no leave for over 18 months. Another Lieut. who asked him for leave and was refused, had had none since 1940. Yet anyone living in safety in a base area gets leave regularly. Naturally we don't ask for leave regularly when we're in action – but to be refused it after we've been wounded and are in a base area, and when we're entitled to leave and have business to attend to seems to me quite monstrous. If this is the way they reward the gallant blah blah 8th Army, I hope they'll publish it and take credit for it. It's on a par with invaliding Sergeant Hannah V.C. out of the RAF on a measly pension for himself, wife and child, because the government are too stingy to pay for his consumption treatment, though they admit the disease was aggravated by his service. The news of that infuriated the fighting members of all 3 services out here. You might mention the leave question to *Picture Post* or some such paper: and although it has been pointed out, it's worth mentioning again that it is the Government's practice – see General Orders – to reward officers who are wounded in action fighting for the country by taking away their rank and pay. An acting paid captain or major (or any higher rank) who is severely enough wounded in action to be in hospital for 21 days, loses his acting rank and pay. Although I believe a staff officer does not. One reason given for the no sick leave rule is that officers going on sick leave get drunk etc, and have relapses. This might be true in the case of medical cases, but cannot be true in surgical cases since all surgical cases are discharged as fit or unfit for duty, and if fit for duty, as I shall be, they must be fit for leave. Col. Marsden doesn't make this excuse but says its 'up to our units to give us leave.' This is ridiculous: my unit is nearly 2000 miles away, as he knows, and cannot be communicated with by ordinary people in under 20 days.

The reason given for the demotion of wounded officers is that after 21 days another officer is appointed to their acting rank in their unit, and so they must (Q.E.D.) lose a rank since someone else has gained one.

If you are interested in seeing what a hell of a mess the whole thing is, get hold of a book called *War in the Sun* by a journalist called Hodson.[1] What he says in it I can vouch for as accurate. There

1 James Lansdale Hodson (1942).

is also a pseudo funny book called *Oriental Spotlight* by Rameses which in fact is scarcely exaggerated at all, and gives a very accurate picture of Egyptian life just before the war.[2] The bit about the British army of course is superceded by Hodson's remarks, but the rest stands. The illustrations are accurate and not exaggerated at all.

If only people would do something to improve things when facts are published by Hodson, Douglas Reed[3] etc, instead of regarding them as subversive propaganda, we might get somewhere. Incidentally, while we praise Russia for using captured German equipment, any of our troops who try to do so have it forcibly taken away from them, and it is taken to salvage dumps where good material is allowed to rust and grow useless. Needless to say, the Germans made use of what they had from us. There's nothing we can do about it – if the censor permits you to have this information, maybe you can get hold of some MP or other in England, though of what MPs I've met my opinion is not high.

K

257. *To Marie J. Douglas*   BL 56355 f.150

n.d. [11 March 1943]

Dear Mother,

A few airgraphs are beginning to drift through from you, written not later than 16 February – it's now March 11th, which isn't very good, although I don't see what excuse they can have now, mail ought to be better instead of worse than ever. I don't know how long mine are taking, but they certainly aren't arriving in the order I sent them. I'm now in a convalescent depot with very incompetent doctors and orderlies and no nurses. They have been putting sulphonamide dressings on a perfectly clean open wound, which are meant to draw out pus and so simply draw out blood and keep the wound open and very painful (for the first time). So I'm tearing the dressings off as soon as I come away and putting on dry ones. Vaseline would be better, and I'm going to buy some next time I go to Ismailia. We are beside the Suez Canal and have a YWCA at

---

2 A copy Douglas or his mother owned is now in the Brotherton Library.
3 Douglas Reed's *All Our To-Morrows* (1942) concerned English politics, chiefly after 1940.

our gates, where I went to a dance the other night. Dancing unfortunately isn't a thing in which Hospital Sisters excel. I had one or two pleasant dances with Palestinian ATS girls, who do know how to dance. But as we were in a party with various sisters, we had to stick to them. The Colonel at the hospital who refused me and others leave, has now changed his mind, I hear, and gave the batch after us a fortnight, which is pretty scandalous, I think. I am getting a week from here and hope to get more from the Base Depot, so that I can arrange for my tin box to be sent home if I can't come back to Cairo to collect it. I am claiming for lost kit but I don't know how much I'll get. I'm glad you like Mrs B.[1] but don't work too hard – I like the idea of a flat as headquarters – preferably in Oxford or London. I had another letter from Hamo who is thinking of staying out here after the war.[2] He is learning written and spoken Arabic and tried to join the Arab Legion but refused to change his name, so they wouldn't take him, although they accepted him apart from that.

I shall be a mass of scars when I come home, though not very big ones. When I was in Palestine I had a sort of impetigo, or desert sores on my face which has left little red marks. There are 5 desert sore scars on my right hand and 3 on my left, and heaven knows how many on my legs. A scar under my arm, 3 on my back, one on the inside of my right foot, and inside right calf, and a big one and a little one at the back of my left thigh. Also a scar from shingles over my right eye. But the general effect isn't very noticeable. The only one that will show more than a fleabite is the hole in my thigh, which is really an operation scar, the original hole was very small. The one inside my foot is a long straight cut but being inside won't show. There is still a ball bearing in my right calf, but it hardly left a mark going in, and doesn't hurt or impede me at all, although I can feel a lump there if I press it. Being round it won't do any harm. A boy of 20 in the next bed to me was hit by a burst of aeroplane cannon fire and had 3 or 4 inches of his thigh bone blown away entirely, as well as bullets in stomach and hands. After 14 weeks in

1 Mrs Baber, for whom Mrs Douglas now worked.
2 Hamo Sassoon did, working in Syria and Iraq; later he was in Africa.

bed he's getting up in a walking splint and will eventually be quite O.K. bar scars.

Love
Keith
Tell Diana I sent her love and am writing. Hope her foot is well again.

258. *To Brenda Jones*   BL (newly acquired)

n.d. [PM Horsham 25 March 1943]

Dear Brenda,

Thank you for your letter – you are become quite witty, aren't you? I'm sorry to hear you're a cowgirl, although I feared as much – I hope you preserve a certain amount of glamour in your few off moments (from your shady reference to affaires, I imagine you do). As I think I wrote and told you, I am recovering from various wounds received in a misguided attempt to See Tripoli First – I missed it by 100 miles, not very much in 1600. The Germans captured some of my kit in their headlong retreat – but I don't think it gave them much satisfaction, as my pack only contained a very cheap set of shaving things and a few captured German socks, trousers and shirts, not much of a thrill for whoever discovered it. I was rummaging in the remains of my tank for some cigarettes to give to some wounded in a nearby hole, and emerged from the driver's seat to see a German Mk III tank about 100 yds away, obligingly scanning the middle distance with field glasses. So I ran like hell, and gave the cigarettes to some equally deserving chaps in a hole about a mile away, where I eventually arrived very puffed, carrying a man with no legs, to speak of, round my neck. I was very thankful when eventually I stepped on a mine, as I already had a number of uncomfortable minor ailments a splinter in my foot, various desert sores (equivalent to boils, more or less) shingles (which I'm told is a nervous disease, but which took the form of an immense blister on my forehead and a headache), and one eye more or less blacked out, also my moustache (a recent acquisition), and my eyebrows and eyelashes burnt off by the shell that hit my tank.[1] By that evening I was reclining in an ambulance and a comfortable

1 All this is described in *Alamein* Chap. XVIII.

stupor induced by large quantities of morphia and brandy. Actually, my discomforts are only just beginning. I had a very lazy and pleasant time in hospital, and of course got very fat, and have now been sent to a convalescent camp, which is supposed to make us fit for duty again. I arrived feeling fine but was reduced to limping painfully about after half an hour, because they put on what I can only describe as an incendiary dressing over an open wound. I tore it off and put on a dry one of my own, so as to go to a YWCA dance – the only entertainment for miles. Here I danced with various repressed and toothy hospital sisters and a Palestinian AT with a glassy stare, either a moron or a drug addict. I narrowly escaped with my honour from a more than usually r and t sister, and came away with my tongue hanging out.

I went shopping in Ismailia the other day, and spent £8 on practically nothing – namely lunch, some powder, a shirt and tie, shorts and a pair of suede boots with crepe soles which cost £3 85 piastres, (about 4 English pounds). And they creak.

My ex girlfriend has added insult to injury by inviting me to her wedding to Mr Ilett,[2] late of mid B. I shall go because it'll save me staying in a hotel in Alexandria and I can spend all the time with my Greek girl friend, who speaks no English, so that we converse entirely in execrable French. She is more voluble than I am, and therefore makes more mistakes. Her letters are made worse by appalling spelling mistakes. However, thank God she writes at all – if I depended on letters from England I'd have some long spells without any. Much love to you and love to family.
Keith

259. *To Marie J. Douglas*   BL 56355 f.151

27 March 1943   No 1 General Hospital MEF

Dear Mother,
No photographs to send you but I thought you might be interested to read this account of the regiment published in *Gen*, a Middle East magazine. It spells all the names wrong as most articles of the sort do, but gives a reasonable account of our history up till the letters I wrote you from Mersa Matruh last November.

2   It never took place. See above; and Letter 261.

They are trying to refuse me leave here although I've had none for 19 months, but I'll probably get some from base depot. Anyway I'm determined to have some. I think the Letter Card will never reach you, as I think the Padre at the CCS [Casualty Clearing Station] must have lost it. Though I wrote to you and Diana on Jan.25th. The postal services are absolutely appalling. A letter takes 10 days to get to Cairo from here, and even a telegram 3 or 4.

I had your 2nd wire today: I'm glad Diana had mine – I hope I'll be somewhere about to send you one for yours. I expect to be out of here in 10 days or so but the last stages of healing seem so much longer and slower than the 1st. I shall stop this as you'll have had all today's news on airgraphs before this arrives. I've had a lot of mail lately from Titsa, Olga, Milena, Mary, Fortnée, Hasida, David Hicks, John Fox,[1] Norman Ilett, Joe Arsenault, Hamo (who is in Tripoli) and Peter Speakman, all in Cairo, Alex, or Palestine (except for Hamo).

Love

Keith

From England I've had letters of some antiquity from Diana, Yourself, Jean, Margaret Robinson, David Roberts and family, Ray Pennock (who says Robin Chadburn (Bexhill) disabled and out of army from m/c accident) Morvethe [?] Kingsmill, and Imry Petters.[2]

260. *To Olga Meiersons*   BL 56355 f.179

2 April 1943   2 Convalescent Depot

My Dear Olga,

Thank you for another letter. I don't know if I can afford 25 PT [piastres] for bed and breakfast. Naturally I will if I can: I don't think it's any good writing any more about it. It's evident you're in as bad a state as I am; neither of us can suffer fools gladly, and we are both hemmed in by them. Further, I have the misfortune to have had to depend on first a villain and then an aged idiot to get my leave at all. I am formally requesting it today. Leave in Palestine is not allowed without giving 14 days notice, which I can't do. So we shall

---

1 John Bethel Fox (Raoul in *Alamein*) was Douglas's closest friend in the regiment (see *KD* p.137); Joe Arsenault, a friend from Christ's Hospital, was in the Middle East and they had met (see *KD* pp.151–2); Peter Speakman has not been traced.
2 Morvethe[?] Kingsmill and Imry Petters have not been traced.

see what we shall see. I suppose the war will eventually end, but the trouble is that all these idiots live on when one would have thought there was a golden opportunity to liquidate them.

As you see, I am as bitter and sickened as you are, not by the war, but by the bloody fools who are surviving it in every country of the world. When we meet it'll be good for us both if we do more kissing than talking.[1]
Much love from
your conceited friend
Keith
James M'Gregor is looking forward to meeting your girl[?] friend. He is a little more intelligent than I had thought. K.
[At head of letter] I'm having ultra violet ray treatment and healing at last.

261. *To Marie J. Douglas*   BL 56355 f.152

(Airgraph) 27 April 1943   Notts SR Yeo MEF

Dear Mother,
Thank you for some more letters. I see you haven't received any since I left hospital. I went on a week's leave with Olga Meiersens in Palestine and after that spent a week with Milena (not yet married owing to Authorities changing their minds on the appointed day). Olga may be writing to you: she writes that she has begun a letter but hasn't sent it yet. I don't know if she will give you much idea what she is like. She tries to seem very cynical but is in reality quite the reverse. She has always been very sweet to me, although I never have any money and always have to spend all hers and give her a cheque later. She is Latvian and is quite alone in Palestine, all her family and relations having disappeared in Russia: she can get no news of them. In appearance she is like Christine would look if she had black hair and eyes. Just now she is thinner than ever because of rationing in Palestine. She is 27. I met her when I was first at Div. HQ. I expect to go back to the regiment any day. Re captaincies,

1 From this meeting Douglas wrote 'Tel Aviv', *CP* p.113: 'Do not laugh because I made a poem/ it is to use what then we could not handle – / words of which we know the explosive/ or poisonous tendency when we are too close.'

there are only a certain number in any unit. I could have got one by taking a staff job.

K

262. *To Olga Meiersons*   BL 56355 ff.180–1

16 May 1943   [verso of letterhead of Carroll Snider] Notts YEO

Dear Olga,

I shall write large as this is a soft pencil and I have no pen. Don't worry – although I'm back with the regiment all is well. My silence is due to extreme busyness about the most pacific tasks, such as obtaining wine, sheepstealing, etc. Everyone is most happy that the campaign is over and the amount of prisoners and captured material beggars description. The country people here are very nice to us. Beer and other good things begin to reach us, and it seems we are in for a good time, as far as it can be organised. I am hoping to ride again, as there are plenty of horses, mostly with high Mexican-type saddles. Thousands of mosquitoes and fleas about unfortunately.

That *was* a bloody photograph – it made you look like a gorgon – I tore it up. I wish I could take some of you: even my drawing wasn't that bad.[1]

I found a wine factory and bought 52 gallons yesterday – considerable noise last night. Good red wine is about 20 mils a litre – or vin rosé.

Must stop for now.

Love

Keith

I'm glad you wrote to Mother – I haven't myself for some weeks, but can't get any Air Letter Cards now. K

263. *To Marie J. Douglas*   BL 56355 f.153

(Airgraph) 23 May 1943

Dear Mother,

I have just had the first up to date letter from you for some time, although quite a lot of old ones have caught me up. By the way I'm

---

1 Lost. One of Milena remains in reproduction, *KD* p.160.

sorry about the A on this machine but there is nothing I can do about it. It also has a habit, as you see, of slipping and running away with itself at the end of each line. I have certainly written to you several times since the 4th March, so perhaps the letters will arrive in due course. And I'm glad you got Robert Stainton's car go [sic]. Keep his address, as he might be a good chap to know after the war, being a headmaster of sorts. I think I said in the accompanying note that the brooch was a present to you from Olga Meiersons, whose address is c/o Kedem bookshop, 46 Jona Hanavi St. Tel Aviv. She has written to you as well I think. You should also be having a letter in due course from Madame Barbara of Sousse, the address is Hopital Civile, Sousse.[1] Her husband works at the hospital and I've had dinner there a few times. She has definitely sent off a letter to you. She speaks no English, so if you write to her remember to write in French. By the way if you still don't have Mila's address its M. Gutierrez Pegna, 452 Avenue Fouad 1er, Rouchdy Pacha, Alexandria. I missed all the fighting in this country and have simply been occupied in driving all over Tunisia buying wine for the officers and men – it costs about sixpence a bottle and some of it is very good, notably the 1941 vin rosé. I shall be interested to see Stephen's reviews – it sounds rather as if his wife told him what I thought of him and he is having his own back.[2] Never mind, I shall probably be writing reviews of him one day, if not recollections and an obituary. Mme Barbara's son [?] is an up and coming poet and has won a medal of the French Literary Society of Tunisia. The Derby Yeo you read of are the First Line, not the ones I was with. In one of your letters you asked about Parkhouse and Denys Wrey. Denys is some sort of Town Major in Tripoli I believe and Parkhouse a staff officer. David Crichton is employed shepherding War Correspondents. In case you haven't had my other letters by the way I ought to mention that Flash Kellett and his successor as Colonel of this regiment were both killed by shellfire during the Tunisian battles – you may have seen it in the paper.[3] And you might be amused to know that Stanley Christopherson, my squadron leader, tells me he recommended me for an MC after I was wounded but Flash thought not, or anyway he didn't forward the

---

1 It survives; BL 56356 ff.234–5.
2 Stephen Spender, 'The Maturity of the Poet', *New Statesman* 17 April 1943.
3 See *Alamein* pp.143–4 and 'Aristocrats' (Letter 278).

recommendation. This is not particularly mortifying except that I think it's a pretty ribbon. They are thrown about a good deal and with obvious exceptions usually have the appearance of consolation prizes or being drawn out of a hat. I have met people in Geoffrey's regiment but so far not Geoffrey himself.[4] It seems to be true that he is a staff king of some sort. All staff kings are captains, but for those who remain with regiments there are only a certain amount of vacancies and until these are created by departures or casualties one simply has to remain a lieut. It is not an automatic promotion like 2/Lt to full Lieut. People quite often get posted elsewhere as he has done to get promotion. You needn't worry about having made a fuss about the hospital leave question because it wasn't that chap's fault that I got leave, I wangled that by being posted away. The point is it shouldn't have been necessary to wangle it. On to another airgraph. K

264. *To Marie J. Douglas*   BL 56355 f.154

(Airgraph) 23 May 1943   Notts SR Yeo MEF

Dear Mother,
I think I have managed to improve the position of the letter A this time although the spacing still seems to be all to hell and it's not yet typing properly or black enough. I'm afraid the other one which really has all the news on it, will not be legible. I mentioned in it that two people have written to you, a Madame BARBARA from SOUSSE and Olga Meiersons of whom you have heard before, from Tel Aviv. We are now in a pleasant spot and although it has been very cold it is making up for it now and we bathe every day. I had dinner with the Barbaras in Sousse the other night and we are trying to lay on a dance for the troops with the local maidens here. I have been pretty well all over Tunisia which I think is a lovely country and would be nice to live in after the war. I now speak French pretty fluently if not very correctly, and could certainly learn to speak it well if I stayed here. I have had one or two letters from Diana. She writes like someone in the *Daily Mirror*, it is certainly high time she was reintroduced to someone who talks English, and the sooner she is taken out of England altogether, the better.

4   Not clear who this is, but see Letter 272.

However she still seems perfectly content. She never mentioned her foot in a single letter to me. I went to Tunis the other day but got there a day or two early before any of the shops were open again. Now they say it is all organised again and one can buy most things, though probably at exorbitant prices. I have to go there again soon on a wine buying expedition. The number of prisoners taken is quite incredible and there are streams of them on the roads. The day they capitulated we were driving back from bathing and were passed by a convoy of them driving themselves in their own transport. It is supposed to be the biggest victory over the Germans since Napoleon beat the Prussians at Jena. I went up and had a look at the last positions they had vacated in the hope of finding some loot but found nothing but very dead bodies and refuse of every kind. I brought nothing back except about fifty fleas. I actually caught and killed thirty two the day after, and you can imagine how many bites I had. I counted up to two hundred and didn't bother to go on although there were some I didn't count. It's amazing how they all come to me; some people who went came back without being bitten at all. Insect powder seems quite ineffective against them. I have had meals and spent nights with various families all over Tunisia, some still quite comfortable with furniture, wireless and Frigidaire, others without even a door left to their houses. I provided my own rations as a rule, except when eating with the French Army who seem to have very good fresh rations and barrels of wine. Everyone is very glad to give us what hospitality they can, very pro British and particularly partial to Eighth Army. Towns are not much good as all the food in them is usually reserved for Americans, who eat like horses and pay far more than we can afford. Eggs in American occupied areas are sixpence each, elsewhere about sixpence a dozen, or from Arabs a dozen for a packet of cigarettes and two hens thrown in for an old blanket. I don't think I'm likely to see Cairo, or England again for some time. I don't know what I'll do about the stuff I had to leave in Cairo. But I intend to come out here again anyway. I should like to marry and live in Tunisia. Still not received *Selected Poems*, though I had 2 books, thanks. You wrote *Selected Poems* on the outside of the parcel but didn't put them in.
Keith

265. To Marie J. Douglas   BL 56355 f.155

28 May 1943 [PM Staines 15 June 1943]   Notts SR Yeo MEF

Dear Mother,

In case you haven't had airgraphs – although you're more likely to get them than to get these – I'll give you my news since returning. As you'll see, I've had very little mail from you, and don't know how soon mine will be despatched to you. I arrived to find the regiment sitting idle, with shells from the German long-range stuff bursting a few miles away. I had flown up in a day and arrived in a back area where dances are already being organised for the back-end troops. All these back-end people now sport the 8 Army badge and are regarded universally as heroes – the fighting troops do not wear it; not the ones who did the fighting anyway: having seen the people who do wear it, we are not particularly anxious to. The papers here always included a good many pictures of so-called Desert Rats, who are invariably dirty and half-naked, although actually they are the back-end people who have a chance to keep clean and don't bother to. The fighting troops, even on half a pint of water, kept themselves smart, and the Highland Div in particular who fought some of the bloodiest actions, were always as though on parade: I never even saw a dead one who hadn't got his stockings properly pulled up and clean red hackles. When I first arrived I was sent back some hundreds of miles through Sousse and Sfax and Gabes to Gafsa, to buy wine. I tried at the French military wine control, who only gave me 2 litres, but threw in a hell of a lunch in which we all ate lots of raw onions and drank far more wine than they would allow us to buy. I took photos of all of them, and my driver, who knew no difference between wine and beer, didn't wake up till long after dark. We went back with 2 fighting French[1] and 2 civilians on the truck, and slept beside the road. They all helped except one who did not care for the food we prepared or the blankets we gave him, so I left him in the middle of the road miles from anywhere to find himself something better. We dropped the soldiers at Sfax after they had helped to buy two sheep which we tied up with belts in the back of the truck. The remaining civilian, who is a boy of about 18, took me home with him when we got to Sousse, and his mother provided us all with supper (mostly

1 Forces de Gaulle had brought together to fight the Germans.

by making us concoctions of our own rations, as she had no food over), and iced our wine. We also drank most of their only bottle of vermouth. I slept on an immense oriental divan between clean sheets and the drivers slept on the truck with the sheep, which proved a necessary precaution, as they (the sheep) nearly escaped in the night. The truck is a large one so they weren't forced into very close proximity. Anyway they were quite happy after a good dinner and listening to the wireless. The good lady took your address and has I believe written to you. Her name is Mme Barbara, Hôpital Regional, Sousse.[2] Almost immediately on my return I was sent out again to First Army to get some of their canteen food and rations as 8 Army was getting nothing and 1st Army living like kings. I stayed the first night with a Free French regiment and the news came during dinner that Tunis and Bizerte had fallen.[3] The result was that five of us finished 6 bottles of wine, a bottle of cognac, and three bottles of whisky. The Captain, Coy Commander, went down with a wump on the floor and was still drunk when I left the next morning, and a Lieutenant was sick in the tent in the middle of a sentence. I made myself sick outside afterwards, as I had to be fit for duty early the next morning. This created a very good impression as I had drunk as much as anyone and still remained on my feet and coherent (in French, too, as no-one spoke any English). The Captain enquired vaguely on waking next morning '*Où est notre cher vieux camarade d'la Huitième Armée*', and complained that I hadn't lasted the evening. But he was assured I had outlasted him and moreover it was added in my favour that, '*Le lieutenant est gentleman – il est allé dehors pour dégueuler.*' I spent the next night near *le Kef*, and just arrived back for the last few days of the battle. The Germans opposite us were the last to surrender, and came in in processions of immense length, driving their own vehicles. After this it was assumed that the many promises made to 8th Army that they should go home or rest would be honoured. We were soon disabused and offered as a consolation prize 4 whole days of leave, some in the Tripoli area, where there is nothing whatever to do, and some in a leave camp here, where the men are inspected and disciplined as much as ever. You can imagine what effect this has had. I hope someone will ask a question or two in Parliament, although of

2 She did; see Letter 263.
3 See Douglas's account in *Alamein* pp.145–52; see also *KD* p.197.

course they'll get no satisfactory answer. Everyone is quite resigned to not going home and wouldn't have complained of that at all, but that they were repeatedly promised they should go home. This I presume was a carrot – quite unneeded – to get the donkey to come from Alamein to Tunis. That is understandable if not very laudable, but why they are now subjecting us to an intensive course of what is known in the army as buggering about I don't know. It is done to young recruits to bring them up to the mark – a continual arrangement of nuisance parades and routine for routine's sake – but to do this to seasoned troops who have fought in a way which at the most conservative estimate must be called efficient, and was even at times deserving of some of the press adjectives – to chivvy such people up and down like this is an outstanding piece of impertinence and will probably have results. I have been made entertainments king and have almost succeeded in arranging a regimental dance although it seems to be the aim of all area authorities to prevent any troops in their area from enjoying their leisure. We had a small party of 6 officers and 2 French nurses, 2 English nurses, Mme Barbara and family. The English nurses sat like puddings the whole evening, and looked like puddings, and talked about as brightly as puddings. The French girls were very full of go and made us ashamed of the English ones. I daresay the poor things were tired, but the French nurses have just as much work and they seem to be able to look nice and be entertaining after it. Must stop.

Love K

266. *To The Editor, Poetry (London)*   BL 60587 f.4

1 June 1943   Notts SR Yeo MEF

Dear Tambimuttu

I have just received a letter from a secretary of yours whose name is illegible:[1] she includes a memo of one Schooling whom I connect with rancid butter, as possibly he can explain; and a request for poems. I am sending you some. There are more, if I hear that you have received these and want more. I think you had better write and ask Mr Edmund Blunden if any of these have been used by the

1   The letter, probably from Betty Jesse, is lost.

Times Lit. Supp.[2] Copies were sent him some time ago: please send him the ones you don't want, anyway, in case he never received them.

I may have written some more by the time I next hear from you, but, *enfin* Tunisia, like Grishkin, is nice, and it is amazing what you can get for a tin of bully beef from a hungry civilian population. I am hoping to use some as rent and move in on a family, in which case I shall be busy. Anyway, there must be some leave, somewhere. Such things must be after a famous victoree.
Yours
Keith Douglas

267. *To The Editor, Poetry (London)*

(First of two airgraphs) 1 June 1943

BL 53773 f.50

Lt KC Douglas
Notts SR Yeo MEF

Landscape with Figures[1]

I
Perched on a great fall of air
a pilot or angel looking down
on some eccentric chart, a plain
dotted with useless furniture,
discerns dying on the sand vehicles
squashed dead or still entire, stunned
like beetles: scattered wing-cases and
legs, heads, appear when the dust settles.

But you who like Thomas come
to poke fingers in the wounds
find monuments annd metal posies.
On each disordered tomb
the steel is torn into fronds
by the lunatic explosive.

2 Copies sent to Blunden have not survived. The *TLS* published 'The Regimental Trumpeter Sounding in the Desert' (*CP* p.103 as 'The Trumpet') 26 June 1943; 'Devils' had appeared there 23 January 1943.

1 The text of this and the following poem have variants from *CP* pp.109–10.

268. *To The Editor, Poetry (London)*　　　　　BL 53773 ff.51

(Second of two airgraphs) 1 June 1943　　　　Lt KC Douglas
　　　　　　　　　　　　　　　　　　　　Notts SR Yeo MEF

Landscape with Figures

2

On scrub and sand the dead men wriggle
in their dowdy clothes. They are mimes
who express silence and futile aims
enacting this prone and motionless struggle
at a queer angle to the scenery,
crawling on the boards of the stage like walls,
deaf to the one who opens his mouth and calls
silently. The décor is a horrible tracery
of iron. The eye and mouth of each figure
bear the cosmetic blood and the hectic
colours death has the only list of.
A yard more and my little finger
could trace the macquillage of these stoney actors:
I am the figure writhing on the backcloth

Wadi Zem Zem 16.1.43

269. *To The Editor, Poetry (London)*　　　　　BL 53773 f.54

(Airgraph) 1 June 1943　　　　Lt KC Douglas Notts SR Yeo MEF

'Gallantry' [text with variants in Letter 250]
El Ballah General Hospital 1943

270. *To The Editor Poetry (London)*　　　　　BL 53773 f.55

(Airgraph) 1 June 1943　　　　Lt KC Douglas Notts SR Yeo MEF

Words

Words are my instruments but not my servants;
by the white pillar of a prince I lie in wait
for them. In what the hour or the minute invents,
in a web formally meshed or inchoate,

these fritillaries are come upon, trapped:
hot-coloured, or the cold scarabs a thousand years
old, found in cerements and unwrapped.
The catch and the ways of catching are diverse.
For instance this stooping man, the bones of whose face are
like the hollow birds' bones, is a trap for words.
And the pockmarked house bleached by the glare
whose insides war has dried out like gourds
attracts words. There are those who capture them
in hundreds, keep them prisoners in black
bottles, release them at exercise and clap them back.
But I keep words only a breath of time
turning in the lightest of cages – uncover
and let them go: sometimes they escape for ever.

El Ballah 1943

271. *To The Editor Poetry (London)*   BL 53773 f.56

(Airgraphs) 1 June 1943   Lt KC Douglas Notts SR Yeo MEF

   Desert Flowers

   Livng in a wide landscape are the flowers –
   Rosenberg I only repeat what you were saying –
   the shell and the hawk every hour
   are slaying men and jerboas, slaying

   the mind: but the body can fill
   the hungry flowers and the dogs who cry words
   at nights, the most hostile things of all.
   But that is not new. Each time the night discards

   draperies on the eyes and leaves the mind awake
   I look each side of the door of sleep
   for the little coin it will take
   to buy the secret I shall not keep.

   I see men as trees suffering
   or confound the detail and the horizon.
   Lay the coin on my tongue and I will sing
   of what the others never set eyes on.

284

272. *To Marie J. Douglas*   BL 56355 ff.156–7

(Two Airgraphs) 9 June 1943   P170611 Capt. K.C. DOUGLAS
                                           Notts SR Yeo MEF

Dear Mother,
When I last heard from you, you had nothing still since March 4th,
although Diana has had some more recent. I've heard twice from
her and once from you since her operation. I hope the new form
of address will please you, although it will be a long time before I
get the pay through. I have not met Geoffrey, but did bump into
Geoffrey Wagner, who was at Edgeborough and Oxford with me,
and whom you may recall as coming to tea with us at Boarshead
once or twice. I also went to tea with him and his mother at
Crowborough. He introduced me to Richard Lewellyn Lloyd, the
author of *How Green Was My Valley*, and I gave them a lift in my
truck. Geoff is a life-long friend of Jon [*sic*] Hall's and also writes for
Tambimuttu – who, it appears is Senegalese[1] and a complete shit.
He had been hoping to meet Keith Douglas, the poet, but had not
realised he already knew him. So it is a collection of coincidences.
I have been organizing entertainments for the officers and men, and
we have had an officers' cocktail party in a civilian house at one
place, and an all ranks dance with a civilian band at another. There
was a good deal of trouble about the band. I hired an orchestra which
split under two rival leaders, just after I had hired it. One half
consisted of the good musicians, whom I wished to hire: the other
of the original secretary of the orchestra, under whose name the
original orchestra had operated, with some very bad musicians who
had never been in any orchestra before. I hired the good ones and
tried to put the bad ones off, which was dfficult as I had hired them
under the secretary's name. An hour before the dance the secretary
and his father arrived with numerous cousins etc. and made a
tremedous noise until we hired them to save further ructions. My
French is now so fluent that I have been mistaken for a Frenchman
3 times by French people, although they always find out in the end
because my grammar is lousy. My accent must be reasonable though,
probably inherited from you. The country here is marvellous, we
bathe morning noon and night in deep blue translucent sea, I am
browner than ever in my life and hope to spend my leave at

---

1   Tambimuttu was in fact from Ceylon (thus Singhalese), now Sri Lanka.

Monaster, a peace time resort where even now I can go to a dance
every night. I shall be living with a French family.
Love
Keith

273. *To Mr Hill*[1]   BL 60585 f.30

n.d. [?June 1943]

'Moonlight Wadi Natrun' ['The Offensive I', text (with slight
variants) in Letter 234]
Keith Douglas
Captain, Sherwood Rangers (Notts) Yeomanry
Acknowledgement if published to Editor *Citadel*
Dear Mr Hill,
The exact conditions of your competition escape me at the moment:
and the record of them has been lost. So I do not know if you
demand as many as possible, or only single poems. If only single,
you'll have to take the one you prefer and forget I sent you the
other. It is more or less by chance and not by design that the gerboa
appears in one of these poems and the fox in the other.[2]
KC Douglas
I am afraid the typewriter has not weathered the campaign very well.

274. *To J. C. Hall*   Hall

(Airgraph) 10 June 1943   Notts SR Yeo MEF
[date stamp 12 June 1943]

Dear John,
I am having a hell of a good time in Tunisia, which is the best
country I've struck yet, particularly as one gets towards Algeria. My
French is ungrammatical but fluent and is a great help. I bathe 3 or
4 times a day in more or less Bermudan waters (I wish I had a glass
boat), and we have very amiable dances and parties now and then.
You have been making cutting remarks about my poems for so long
I ought to retaliate but I haven't seen any of yours for a long time,

---

1 The addressee is not known. As this is an original and not a copy, the letter was
   presumably never sent.
2 'Desert Flowers' (*CP* p.108): it is not with the letter.

except here and there. The nastiest and truest thing I can say is that you are getting too involved and precious, chiefly because you now find yourself in a backwater and have nothing to write about that is relevant. The same applied to me in pre-Alamein days and I reacted differently but if anything produced worse. With regard to your criticisms of my stuff, I think you are beginning to condemn all that is not your own favourite brand, and are particularly anti réportage and extrospective (if the word exists) poetry – which seems to me the sort that has to be written just now, even if it is not attractive. Mother sent me some copies of female psycho-analyst reviews of my work which made me retch;[1] and described that shit Spender's efforts. I gave two officers a lift the other day and they turned out to be an old school fellow of mine and a friend of yours, Geoff Wagner, and Richard Green Valley Llewellyn Lloyd.[2] I've not seen our book yet. Write again soon.
Keith

275. To J. C. Hall   Hall

26 June [1943]   Notts SR Yeo MEF

Dear John,
This is such a bloody pen that I shall write in pencil after all. I have at last received a copy of *Selected Poems* and of *PL*,[1] and – by the hand of Geoff. Wagner, Sheila Shannon's review in *The Spectator*. First of all, *Selected Poems*. It is a handsome little pamphlet, though it would have a longer life in a paper cover than in that ridiculous cardboard, the back of which comes off after a few hours. I like the type and the presentation of the poems. On the selection, Norman Nicholson appears the best of us – which perhaps he is, being the eldest. I think a few more biographical details might have been given in front. I don't think you were fair to yourself, but you know best what is best of yours. I particularly like 'Walking to Westminster' and 'Journey to London' and 'Earthbound'. I would say 'Elegy on a Hill', but it puzzled me a bit, though the feeling of it is impressive, that is to say the feeling it gives and the feeling I suppose you had

---

1 Sheila Shannon, *The Spectator*, 30 April 1943.
2 See Letter 272.

---

1 *Poetry (London)* No. 8, see below.

when you wrote it. I think you need a little more cynicism, or should I say indifference to emotion once felt, in your poetic make-up. I am getting at the same thing as the Shannon bitch (bitch for what she said about me). You are too much affected. I don't want that you should lose the sensitiveness, or even some of it. But that you should be deeply affected, and yet not show it so much – a little more of the traditional English man – however much you deplore him – would make your poetry stronger and more impressive. I think the selection you have made of me is surprisingly near what I'd have made myself. I am glad you put in 'Caravan', although I don't think 'Famous Men' *and* 'Images' were *both* necessary. I wish the dates of all these poems could have been put on them, as it would have made it easier for reviewers not to talk cock about them. By the way, although you discovered a piece of gammy syntax in 'The Marvel', and corrected it, someone has made nonsense of a verse of the 'Villanelle', (which was correctly printed in *Augury*), and complete nonsense, by changing one word, of 'The Prisoner' (this has also, as I should expect, been done by Tambimuttu). The verse in 'The Villanelle' reads, in your printing: 'Birds feel the enchantment of his wing (whose wing?)/ and in ten fine notes dispel 20 cares'. I wrote 'Bird feels the enchantment of his (bird's) wing and … dispels …'. I am sorry if the omission of the definite article misled you. The point of 'The Prisoner' is that the 'ambitious cruel bone' is the prisoner, who wishes to escape the bright flesh and emerge into fulfilment as a skeleton. 'There was the urge (to break the bright flesh and emerge) OF the ambitious cruel bone.' There is no question of escaping from the bone. I know it's unavoidable at such a distance, but it's annoying. Finally, if you happen to know S. Shannon, point out that the meaningless phrase she cites is used with intent and the words carefully chosen. I shall write to her myself, not so much to correct her as to make her acquaintance and correct her in future. I am also writing to Tambi to say I am *Not* in the Tank Corps (which is a formation which doesn't exist).[2]
Cheerio
Keith.
I should be very interested to see any other copies of *Poetry London*.

2 Publishing 'The Prisoner' in *Poetry (London)* No. 8, Nov.-Dec.1942, Tambimuttu had put in the biographical note that Keith Douglas 'is out East serving with the Tank Corps'. This was an improvement on the note in the previous issue, No. 7: there, Douglas 'is out East serving in the RAF'.

(Airgraph) 26 June 1943   Notts SR Yeo MEF
[date stamp 29 June 1943]

Dear John,
I have written you a long lettercard all about *Selected Poems*, which
I have at last received and which I liked. Thank you very much for
all you have done towards keeping me in print in England. I'm sorry
Sheila Shannon didn't agree with you that it was worth it. Anyway
she gave you and Norman a write-up.

   Did you ever receive the poems I wrote in hospital? I am not
likely to produce anything but virtual repetitions of these, until the
war is cleared up now, because I doubt if I shall be confronted with
any new horrors or any worse pain, short of being burnt up, which
I am not likely to survive. With which cheerful thought my space
is exhausted.
Keith

277. *To Brenda Jones*   BL (newly acquired)

8 July 1943   Notts SR Yeo MEF

Dear Brenda,
How are you? I hope you are still remaining unmarried; far too
many of my friends are married, and practically all of them are
engaged. I am pretty fed up with the spot I've landed in after the
campaign. 8th Army have not so far been rewarded very lavishly for
their efforts. We were kindly given 5 days leave some time back
after about 6 months fighting: but we all live in hopes. Not that I
want to come back to England, except to see people. I just want to
travel somewhere new, as I've got a bit used to Africa. I shall come
back to Cairo after the war I think; there is a lot to be got out of
Egypt and Palestine which one doesn't have time for in the army.

   I missed all the Tunisian fighting luckily, by being wounded at
Zem Zem. When I got back there was nothing to do but buy
lashings of wine and have dances with the local Tunisian French
beauties – and they are beauties, even though the most beautiful
usually turn out to be semi-Arab or Jewish. My French, though very
incorrect, is now fluent and adaptable to most situations.

   I am now trying to organise a Brigade Concert Party in which it seems I have to act, tap dance, sing into a microphone, and imitate various film stars. It is immensely hot and flies are so bad I haven't much enthusiasm for it.

I am still writing poems occasionally and my latest ones have been reviewed in *The Spectator* and various other magazines. They were published in a Bale and Staples *Modern Reading Series*.

How are you and your horses, bulls, pigs, carrots etc? I hope in spite of being in the Land Army that you have contrived to escape having legs like treestumps which seem to be the regulation issue for WLA: and that you are still pretty and well-dressed and have the sense to realise how good looking you really are. I don't think you did, when you were younger: you used to be a bit scruffy. I ought to send you one of the remarkable brassieres they wear in Palestine – they all go about resting their chins on them – uplift carried to a ridiculous degree, but better than the usual Englishwoman's custom of using her bosom as a belt. I am rather bored just now as most of my old friends have been killed or left the regiment, and there's only one entertaining person about – an officer who has just joined us, and luckily brought a gramophone and some ballet music, also Tchaikovsky's 5th (and *Swan Lake* among the ballet). I have pinned up photographs of French, Spanish, Jewish and Greek girl friends, but so far lack any English ones. Won't you send me a photograph, please? I think I've known you long enough, and I think of you more often than I write to you, honestly. Besides I won't pin you up. You shall live in a box which held chocolates as recently as last week. Cheerio to your Ma and Pa.

Love to you.

Keith

[at side:] Sorry this is such a mess. I write in a sandstorm with no table.

278. *To M. J. Tambimuttu*   BL 60585 f.19

(Airgraph) 11 July 1943   Notts SR Yeo MEF

Dear Tambimuttu –

> *Aristocrats*
>
> The noble horse with courage in his eye
> clean in the bone, looks up at a shellburst:
> away fly the images of the shires
> but he puts the pipe back in his mouth.

Peter was unfortunately killed by an 88;
it took his leg away, he died in the ambulance.
I saw him crawling on the sand; he said
It's most unfair, they've shot my foot off.

How can I live among this gentle
obsolescent breed of heroes, and not weep?
Unicorns, almost,
for they are fading into two legends
in which their stupidity and chivalry
are celebrated. Each, fool and hero, will be an immortal.

These plains were their cricket pitch
and in the mountains the tremendous drop fences
brought down some of the runners. Here then
under the stones and earth they dispose themselves,
I think with their famous unconcern.
It is not gunfire I hear, but a hunting horn.

Dear Tambimuttu – here's another poem if it's any good to you.
Thank you very much for your letter,[1] which I am answering on
another airgraph. [Douglas then writes out again lines 1–2 and line
14 for clarity]
Keith

279. *To M. J. Tambimuttu*   BL 60587 f.7

(Airgraph) n.d. [11 July 1943]   Notts SR Yeo MEF

Dear Tambimuttu,
Thank you for your letter, and for publishing my poems – I had
given up all idea of writing in the Army until your efforts and John
Hall's nerved me to try again. I'll go on sending you poems as they
come – I send you one, 'Aristocrats', with this. But sometimes there
are very long gaps. I would very much like to publish a selection of
my poems in book form: but I would like it to be in my own
selection, and so if you want me to do that would you let me know
how many poems you'd want, and let me have a list of titles of all
my poems which you or my mother or Edmund Blunden have in

---

1 Probably Tambimuttu's airgraph, BL 56356 f.56.

England. I would certainly include plenty of M.E. poems and would like to write 3 or 4 pages of introduction. If you want any articles on poetry I could send you one or two – for instance one on the lack of Owens, Sassoons etc in this war.[1]
Yours
Keith Douglas

280. *To M. J. Tambimuttu*   BL 53773 f.61
[Letterhead: Governo Generale Della Libia/Comando Superiore Forze Armate Della Libia/Quartiere Generale. Inscribed by KD at the top:]
W IL DUCE/W IL RE/RITORNEREMO/VINCEREMO DUCE.

11 July 1943   Notts SR Yeo MEF

Dear Tambimuttu,
Thank you for your airgraph, and suggestion that I should make a selection to appear in book form. This I should be glad to do. I've written you an airgraph in reply to that, but as they say overseas mail is quicker than airgraphs now I'm writing a letter. If I make a selection someone would have to send me a list of titles of poems which you or my mother or Edmund Blunden have now, because I can't really remember all that exist – I had completely forgotten writing the last poem in John Hall's selection of my stuff.[1] As to including a lot of ME stuff, there isn't as yet a very great deal to include; because I like to write in comfort or not at all and the nearest to comfort available most of the time is not near enough. A few flies are enough to destroy my inspiration, if they keep on the job the way Egyptian, Tripolitanian and Tunisian flies do. What I have written has been written in hospitals, Con. depots, Base depots etc – emotion recollected in tranquillity – and as I'm now living in a hole in the sand with a piece of canvas over it, in the inadequate shade of a palm tree, I don't expect to be very creative. I am angling for the job of Brigade Entertainment Officer while we are sitting around, which would enable me to live in a house, with my own room and a vehicle at my disposal. If I get the job I'll send you bags of literature, in all forms and on all subjects. On the back of this I

1 'Poets in This War': see Appendix.
_____
1 'Negative Information'.

have rewritten a poem I sent you by airgraph in case the airgraph is illegible.
Yrs.
Keith D
[on verso] 'Aristocrats' [Text in Letter 278]

281. *To Brenda Jones*   BL (newly acquired)

(Airgraph) 4 August 1943   P170611 Capt. Douglas K.C.
[PM 5 August 1943]

Dear Brenda,
I think you owe me a letter – but as I have an airgraph over you shall have an extra one, although there are others with a better claim. I am back in Palestine for a week or two. I hitchhiked 2000 miles in a bomber to get here – God bless the USAAF. I am working hard all the week but hope to get a weekend in Tel Aviv, although the air there is almost too expensive to breathe these days. I was introduced to a girl there last week who has offered me a room next week-end. I know what she means but as she hasn't said it in so many words I still hope for a night's rest. I have to accept the offer in any case as I can't afford a hotel room, and I shall get a free breakfast from her: also she has some nice gramophone records. So you see what evil ways I get into when you don't write.
Love
Keith
I have written to Liz BRODIE.[1] Does she still exist?

282. *To Marie J. Douglas*   BL 56355 f.158

(Airgraph) 4 August 1943   Notts SR Yeo MEF

Dear Mother,
It's some time since I heard from you, though I gather you had the news of my promotion. I don't quite see what is happening to my letters – even Diana hasn't had any recent ones although she seems to get more than you do. Do you think your bank fail to forward them? I am in Palestine on a course at the moment – I hitchhiked

---

1   From the farm in Southwater; see *KD* p.50. The letter is lost.

2000 miles in 3 days by lorry, truck, bomber and train. I saw Milena and Titsa[1] in Alex on my way, and spent last week-end with Olga. David Hicks has been sent to Teheran, permanently, I fear. I think I may go and see the British Council in Jerusalem to find out if they would take me as a lecturer after the war. I should like a job here or in Egypt or Tunisia – not Tripolitania as I don't much like Italians. You might enquire your end and also about courses in Costume design, Décor and Interior decoration. I like the idea of your being lent a house.

Love

Keith

283. *To J. C. Hall [fragment]*   Hall[1]

10 August 1943

... Incidentally you say I fail as a poet, when you mean I fail as a lyricist. Only someone who is out of touch, by which I mean first hand touch, with what has happened outside England – and from a cultural point of view I wish it had affected English life more – could make that criticism. I am surprised you should still expect me to produce musical verse. A lyric form and a lyric approach will do even less good than a journalese approach to the subjects we have to discuss now. I don't know if you have come across the word Bullshit – it is an army word and signifies humbug and unnecessary detail. It symbolizes what I think must be got rid of – the mass of irrelevancies, of 'attitudes', 'approaches', propaganda, ivory towers, etc., that stands between us and our problems and what we have to do about them.

To write on the themes which have been concerning me lately in lyrical and abstract forms, would be immense bullshitting. In my early poems I wrote lyrically, as an innocent, because I was an innocent: I have (not surprisingly) fallen from that particular grace since then. I had begun to change during my second year at Oxford. T. S. Eliot wrote to me when I first joined the army, that I appeared

---

1   Titsa is described in *Alamein* p.77.

---

1   Only one of this series of airgraphs making a single letter survives: the text of paragraph two down to 'view the world' is from that airgraph in Hall's possession; for the rest the source is *CP* pp.134-5, reprinting earlier editions.

to have finished with one form of writing and to be progressing towards another, which he did not think I had mastered. I knew this to be true, without his saying it. Well, I am still changing: I don't disagree with you if you say I am awkward and not used to the new paces yet. But my object (and I don't give a damn about my duty as a poet) is to write true things, significant things in words each of which works for its place in a line. My rhythms, which you find enervated, are carefully chosen to enable the poems to be *read* as significant speech: I see no reason to be either musical or sonorous about things at present. When I do, I shall be so again, and glad to. I suppose I reflect the cynicism and the careful absence of expectation (it is not quite the same as apathy) with which I view the world. As many others to whom I have spoken, not only civilians and British soldiers, but German and Italians, are in the same state of mind, it is a true reflection. I never tried to write about war (that is battles and things, not London can Take it),[2] with the exception of a satiric picture of some soldiers frozen to death,[3] until I had experienced it. Now I will write of it, and perhaps one day cynic and lyric will meet and make me a balanced style. Certainly you will never see the long metrical similes and galleries of images again.

Your talk of regrouping sounds to me – if you will excuse me for exhibiting a one-track mind – like the military excuse of a defeated general. There is never much need to regroup. Let your impulses drive you forward; never lose contact with life or you will lose the impulses as well. Meanwhile if you must regroup, do it by re-reading your old stuff.

Of course, you will never take my advice nor I yours. But in these tirades a few ideas do scrape through the defences on either side. Perhaps all this may make it easier for you to understand why I am writing the way I am and why I shall never go back to the old forms. You may even begin to see some virtue in it. To be sentimental or emotional now is dangerous to oneself and to others. To trust anyone or to admit any hope of a better world is criminally foolish, as foolish as it is to stop working for it. It sounds silly to say work without hope, but it can be done; it's only a form of insurance; it doesn't mean work hopelessly.

[Keith]

2 A catch phrase of the time, referring to the city's ability to weather the Blitz.
3 'Russians' *CP* p.37.

(Airgraph) 12 August [1943]   Notts SR Yeo MEF

The Sniper[1]

Under the parabola of a ball
a child, turning into a man,
I looked into the air too long.
The ball fell in my hand. It sang
in the closed fist: Open, Open.
Behold a gift, designed to kill.

In my dial of glass appears
the soldier who is going to die.
He smiles, and moves about in ways
his mother knows, habits of his;
the wires touch his face. I cry
NOW. Death, like a familiar, hears

and look, has made a man of dust,
from a live man. This sorcery
I do: being damned, I am amused
to see the centre of love diffused;
the waves of love travel into vacancy;
how easy it is to be a ghost.

The weightless mosquito touches
her tiny shadow on the stone
and with how like, how infinite
a lightness, man and shadow meet.
They fuse. A shadow is a man
When the mosquito death approaches.

Is 'The Sniper' any good to you? Incidentally NOW in verse 3 is
meant to be in capitals. Have just written you a letter.
Best wishes
Keith

1   *CP* p.119, 'How to Kill', with variants, esp. l.18 'How easy it is to make a ghost'.

285. *To J. C. Hall*   BL 53773 f.81

(Airgraph) 12 August 1943

'The Sniper' [see Letter 284 for text with slight variants]
Blunden has this, but probably won't use it. Don't lose *The Knife*.
K.

286. *To Edmund Blunden*   Texas

3 September 1943   [Letterhead] Middle East RAC Base Depot

Dear Edmund,
No news since I last wrote to send you the photographs. I don't
think you have seen this poem – or at least, not the revised version.[1]
I am afraid it may be a bit grisly for *TLS*: but on the other hand not
'clever' enough for Tambimuttu and his clan. What I am aiming at
is a series of pretty simple pictures. The first of this kind was
'Christodoulos'[2] – I don't know if you had it. Mother has a copy if
you didn't see it.
    I am sitting at Base Depot before rejoining the unit, having just
had a course in sunny Palestine, interspersed with some pleasant
week-ends among the modern architecture and other modern
amenities of Tel Aviv. One who fought on the German side at
Cambrai is of opinion that the German Army of this war will crack
very suddenly.
    I wish I believed him.
Yrs
Keith

287. *To Marie J. Douglas*   BL 56355 ff.159–161

n.d.   [Letterhead] Middle East RAC Base Depot

Dear Mother,
I seem to be hanging about here for some time, as for once the
mountain is coming to Mahomet. I enjoyed my course in Palestine,

---

1 No poem survives with the letter, but it was probably 'Vergissmeinnicht' (*CP*
   p.118).
2 See Letter 228.

as you've probably heard in other letters, and finished by staying with a family called Hofstein[1] (from Hamburg so it's a good thing they intend to stay in Palestine after the war.) Mrs Hofstein was just as kind as Milena's mother, and mended and ironed my things for me as well as putting me up and feeding me out of the family rations. I gave her your address and asked her to write to you. She will probably write in French as she speaks it better than English. Her daughter Eve has given me a book I wanted very much, the poems of Rainer Maria Rilke, in German and printed very beautifully at Leipzig. Eve is very sweet but has a (not unnaturally) jealous fiancé, a policeman, late of Berlin. She wants to get rid of him and her parents don't want her to marry him, but having got engaged she hasn't the guts to start all the unpleasantness that would result from breaking it off. This I can understand from experience. The policeman is a very nice chap but he'll drive Eve, who is vaguely intellectual and about twice as intelligent, to distraction.

I am enclosing some photographs of Olga, which I took while I was in Tel Aviv.[2] She is at the moment remarkably happy. When I first went there she was feeling very fed up and saying she hadn't enough money to eat and if she died no one would give a damn etc. etc. Luckily she was due for a holiday and while she was away from Haifa she introduced me by correspondence to a girl called Vera Nova who works as secretary to a firm of dental mechanics. She didn't know Vera very well herself, but I thought she (Vera) seemed extraordinarily nice, so I explained Olga's state of mind to her and by the time Olga came back, Vera had got her a dental mech. job, where she has the same pay, and a rise in 3 months, and about ½ the working hours. That has made a tremendous difference to her, because what she really needed was some spare time. While she was in Haifa she met a man she had thought was dead, and he proposed to her, and she really likes him, so she thinks she will probably marry him after the war, and altogether feels the world is pretty good. She certainly deserves it.

Vera Nova, who is also from Germany, offered to give up her room and sleep with friends so that I should have somewhere to sleep for the week-end – this the first time she ever met me. I can't help thinking there are very few people who would do that in

1   See *KD* pp.222–3.
2   Photographs of Olga survive in the Brotherton Library.

England even for someone English.

It is a bit of a change after all that hospitality to come back to Egypt, where no one will do anything for anyone else except at an exorbitant price. The Gutierrez-Pegnas are more or less unique. Indeed Titsa Hoffman (the Greek girl with lovely teeth whose photo I sent you) asked a friend of hers, who teaches her music, and lives in Rouchdy Pacha, if he knew the Pegnas. He made a sour face and she asked why. 'Oh, they have people coming and going at their house all day, soldiers and officers and all kinds, and the daughter goes out up till all hours.' All except the Arabs are glad enough for us to keep the Germans out of Egypt, but it isn't even 'thank you Mr Atkins when the band begins to play'[3] here. And after the war you will see, Egypt won't even allow British people to have jobs in Egypt. The whole country is a sink and the king is the biggest shit of the lot. He is the biggest landowner and exploits more fellahin working all day for next to nothing and living in mud huts, than any of his great fat oily subjects. He also keeps storerooms in which he amasses such things as potatoes, prior to 'arranging' a shortage of these commodities, so that he can sell them at four or five times the proper price. He refused to allow Palestinian oranges to be brought through Egypt for the troops in the desert, although Palestine had offered unlimited oranges free, because he wanted to (and did, as the British Government did nothing about it) make us buy Egyptian oranges. The result was we had about one orange in six months instead of at least one a day. It wasn't a question of transport, because we got revolting dried fruit instead, and the space taken up by that could have been filled with fresh oranges.

I had the satisfaction of smashing a taxi the other day – taxidrivers are some of the worst thieves. This one knew he was the only taxi in the neighbourhood and as it was late demanded twice the fare. As Titsa and I knew the fare, we refused to pay it, so he got out and opened the bonnet and said 'Very sorry. Taxi broken'. It obviously wasn't, so Titsa and I said 'Where?' and pushed him out of the way to look at the engine. I yanked all the distributor leads out and mixed them up and split the vulcanite top of the distributor. Then we said: 'Yes, you're quite right. It's broken. Goodnight' and went off and took a tram before he realised what we'd done.

---

3   From Kipling's poem 'Tommy', the lines became a catch phrase in the war.

I must stop as I am going to the dentist – it's some time since I had my teeth looked at and I'm sure something must need doing.
Love
Keith

288 *To Marie J. Douglas*   BL 59833 f.40
    (fragment, copy in Marie J. Douglas's hand)[1]

n.d. [?September 1943]

you seem to imagine that after the war I shall be buzzing about the world without you. Well, get that idea out of your head. Whoever is in my life and whether I marry or not I shall always want you. I don't know how you manage to be like you are when I think of the atmosphere in which you grew up and Granny and Grandpapa and the people who surrounded you. But the fact remains I have never met anyone like you for quick fair and complete understanding and summing up of things, even the ones with which you completely disagree. You always seemed to know beforehand the difficult things I wanted to tell you (nothing is difficult now) and you have many times been the anchor which prevented me going off the deep end. Things which loomed impossibly large and difficult to face somehow shrunk to normal proportions when I mentioned them to you.

You know there is nothing and no one in my life I would not want you to know. All the bad with the good. And somehow all my friends who know you seem to like you – even the most incredibly unlikely ones… I am planning to take you to Spain after the war (I'd like to recognize what part of your nature and mine comes from there, though I think I know already) and Mme Barbara has invited us to stay with her in Sousse. My friends in Palestine and Alexandria also want to meet you. You would not feel lonely if you came out with me when I get a job on the British Council…

1 Presumably Mrs Douglas has copied the piece from a letter. Quotation marks close it but do not start it. Mrs Douglas has put 'KCD /42' at the foot whereas the reference to Mme Barbara indicates 1943. This error suggests the copy was made some years after that date.

289. *To Milena Gutierrez-Pegna*   Graham

29 September [1943]   Notts SR Yeo MEF

My dear Milena,

I don't know if you received my first letter, written a week or two ago when everything was up in the air. Anyway, it now appears I am to remain in this neighbourhood indefinitely with very little to do. I am trying to land a journalist/army job here, but so far have only trodden on the tail of it.

I have spent a great deal of money hanging about here and have nothing at all to show for it, except a new watch, which is quite unreliable. I had a struggle with a dentist who has completely wrecked the inside of my mouth trying to pull out 2 wisdom teeth – he got them out in the end, in several pieces. I have also had blood poisoning, desert sores, etc., and one way and another haven't much enjoyed myself.

I've met innumerable women, all of whom were too stupid to take out more than once, and about 50% of whom failed even to keep their first date with me. There remains a Spanish girl called Pilar Romeo, whose portrait I am going to do if I have time. She is a difficult subject because all her attraction lies in her expression when she speaks. She has lovely hands and reasonably nice eyes and hair; but seems much affected by the semi darkness in which her family always seem to live.

I spent an evening two or three days ago with a Greek family (real Greek Greeks) who sang us Greek folk songs and played Greek dances. The wife lived in England for a long time and all of it in Sussex in all the towns where I lived. She was in the same district of the same town in 1934 as I was.

A girl whom I met at Hick's old flat said 'I didn't like Egypt when I first came out here; but when you've been in the country for a bit it grows on you'. Everyone said 'How long have you been here?' and the answer was 10 days – we told her to wait a bit longer and it would grow on her so much she'll have to scrape it off.

Cairo seems very crowded – more even than usual, and just as filthy, and disheartening. You may find me darkening your door in Alex again some weekend soon. As I am not going to war for a bit I might bring Masha[1] to stay with you, and if she likes you you can

---

1   A doll Douglas had taken into action as a good-luck charm.

keep her. Poor dear, she has hurt her face, but a bit of paint will put her straight. Love to your mother and father and much love to you.
Keith

290. *To John Waller*   Graham

20 September 1943   [Letterhead] Middle East RAC Base Depot

Dear John,

I have a message asking me to ring you up, and a letter which has followed me to Palestine and back. Thank you very much for the letter and your offer in it. I should like to talk about the offer, if it's still open; and if not at all events we ought to meet some time. I have just written to one Petch, of the British Council to sound them about post-war jobs, as they seem to be expanding madly.

As you see I am a Captain – by the skin of my teeth. If there seems to be any chance of going into action again I should probably want to go – not that I like action that much, but I don't see why my friends should get blown up while I drop out. On the other hand, if we're going to hang about, I shall be wanting a job, and if I am already out of it when the regiment departs I shall just try to get back. And if I don't get back I shan't worry, much. A conscience is a nuisance. I find most of the people in the regiment extremely stupid and boring. I hate fighting: but if I stay behind I feel much worse. I have already been blown up once, but it didn't ½ larn me, unfortunately.

I shall try and ring you up, but the phone here is a bad one, and I am bad on phones, so if you don't hear from me until this I'll attempt to meet you next Sunday, which must be about the 26th I think, in the Bar *au petit Coin de France* at 6.30. I'll wait till 6.45.
Yours Keith

291. *To John Waller*   Graham

Friday [n.d.]

Dear John,[1]
I still don't know if I'll make it on Saturday [two words illegible]
anyway can you (if it's not too late) send me the particulars by Phil
Shaw who brings this, for this article re Kiev.[2] If not, I'll think of
some[thing?]. And after two days of this camp I have no hesitation
in saying please go right ahead to get me an interview re the PR
East Africa job.
Keith
Give Phil a drink?

292. *To M. J. Tambimuttu*   BL 53773 f.85

(Airgraph) 3 October [1943]   Notts SR Yeo MEF

   Behaviour of fish in an Egyptian teagarden[1]

   As a white stone draws down the fish
   she on the seafloor of the afternoon
   draws down men's glances and their cruel wish
   for love. Slyly, her red lip on the spoon

   slips-in a morsel of ice-cream; her hands
   white as a shell, submarine
   fronds, sinking with spread fingers, lean
   along the table, carmined at the ends.

1 Waller comments on a photocopy (Graham): 'This might be the last letter I
   received. He was in a base camp, which he always hated. From here, I think
   his regiment was posted back to England and the Second Front. But he wouldn't
   have [known] about this.'
2 Not traced.
─────────────
1 *CP* p.121, with variants.

A cotton magnate, an important fish
with great eyepouches and a golden mouth
through the frail reefs of furniture swims out
and idling, suspended, stays to watch.

A crustacean, an old man clamped to his chair
sits near her, and may coldly see
her charms through fissures where the eyes should be;
or else his teeth are parted in a stare.

Now a young man, a lean dark mackerel
lies in the offing; as through water looks
through currents of sound. The flat-eyed flatfish sucks
on a straw, staring from its repose, laxly.

And gallants in shoals swim up and lag,
circling and passing near the white attraction;
sometimes pausing, opening a conversation;
fish pause so to nibble or tug.

But now the ice-cream is finished, is
paid for. The fish swim off on business
and she sits alone at the table, a white stone,
useless except to a collector, a rich man.

Dear Tambimuttu,
I hope you can read this: I've repeated doubtful words in block
letters.
KCD

293. *To M. J. Tambimuttu*   BL 60585 f.20

(Airgraph) 5 October 1943   Notts SR Yeo MEF

> *This is the Dream*

> The shadows of leaves falling like minutes.
> Seascapes. Discoveries of sea creatures
> and voices, out of the extreme distance, reach us
> like conjured sounds.   Faces that are spirits

cruise across the backward glance of the brain.
In the bowl of the mind is pot-pourri.
Such shapes and hues become a lurid
décor to The Adventures.   These are a cycle. When

I play dancer's choreographer's critic's role
I see myself dance happiness and pain
(each as illusory as rain)
in silence. Silence.   Break it with the small

tinkle;   apathetic buzz buzz
pirouetting into a crescendo, BANG.   Until
as each scene closes hush the stage is still,
everything is where it was.

The finale if it should come is

the moment my love and I meet
our hands move out across a room of strangers
certain they hold the rose of love.

[in margin] Spacing and punctuation are intentional with the exception of <u>seascapes</u> in line 2 [a space had been typed after the initial 's'.]
Keith Douglas

294. *To M. J. Tambimuttu*   BL 60585 f.21

(Airgraph) 5 October 1943 [dated at top 15 September 43]

'Behaviour of fish in an Egyptian teagarden' [See Letter 292 for text[1]]
Please let me know if you receive this but can't read it.
K.

1   The text there has variants.

5 October 1943 [dated at top October 43]   Notts SR Yeo MEF

Enfidaville

In the church fallen like dancers
lie the Virgin and St. Thérèse
on little pillows of dust.
The detonations of the last few days
tore down the ornamental plasters
shivered the hands of Christ.

The men and women who moved like candles
in and out of the houses and the streets
are all gone. The white houses are bare
black cages. No one is left to greet
the ghosts tugging at doorhandles
opening doors that are not there.

Now the daylight coming in from the fields
like a labourer, tired and sad,
is peering about among the wreckage, goes
past some corners as though with averted head
not looking at the sorrow this town holds,
seeing no one move behind the windows.

But already they are coming back; to search
like ants, among their debris, finding in it
a bed or a piano and carrying it out.
Who would not love them at this minute?
I seem again to meet
the blues eyes of the images in the church.

If this differs from the handwritten version sent,[1] please print this
version.
Keith Douglas

---

1   Possibly BL 53773 f.64. It has slight variants.

[October 1943]   [Letterhead] Governo Generale della Libia

Dear Edmund,

I was very greatly glad to get a full length letter from you. I expect the war will no longer be getting you down so much as the peace. Poor old Beveridge;[1] he will be no match for all these profit seeking reactionary shits, I am afraid. I could, in common with most members of all three services, go on about that for several pages; but the result would only reach you as a mass of excisions.

I am now able to get into Cairo occasionally although I still live in primitive conditions. I see a good deal of various poets whose names may have reached you – Bernard Spencer, Terence Tiller, Robin Fedden and occasionally Larry Durrell. In the opposite camp lie (and lie and lie) John Waller whose face is folding up on him, and that dirty, inky little wretch G.S. Fraser who looks anything but New Apocalyptic. I think he grows watercress in his ears, which are always full of rich Nile mud.

At the moment this whole côterie of bards – less Waller and Fraser who are not interested in such things – is quite overturned by the entry into it of a seventeen year old ex silk stocking maker, called Penny, who has told lies to the Army and is thought by the ATS to be of age. She has evidently been a prodigious reader and can join in our literary discussions with zest although she makes some pretty startling remarks at times. Her views on sex are revolutionary and all too frequently aired. Her conduct however has nothing to do with them. But of course none of this could have produced the explosion without the most dangerous element, her beauty. In four days she had us all off our feed, alternately sighing and glaring jealously at one another: and has now departed for Palestine, much in the manner of ZULEIKA DOBSON taking the train to Cambridge.[2] Unfortunately for us all she is coming back. Of which I suppose more news in my next.

As it is fast getting too dark to see the keyboard, and as I can't type without seeing it I shall go on, (and as there is no news anyway),

---

1   William Henry Beveridge, economist, whose *Report on Social Insurance…* (1942) laid the foundations of the Welfare State in Britain.
2   Max Beerbohm: *Zuleika Dobson: an Oxford love story* (1912).

to type out three poems, which I have sent on airgraphs to Tambimuttu, who will probably find them illegible.
[Poems follow]
'This is the Dream' [see Letter 294 for text (with variants)]
'Enfidaville' [see Letter 288 for text]

I don't expect you to like 'This Is the Dream' much, and I'm not sure that I do myself, but it seemed just good enough not to scrap, and certainly nothing more can be done with it. The one I enjoyed writing most was of course the behaviour of fish.

Have you come across the poems of Louis Aragon? And what do you think of them. Cyril Connolly goes off the deep end much too easily about anyone he thinks he has discovered but all the same I think 'there is something there'.

> Mon patri est comme une barque
> Qu'abandonnerent ses haleurs
> Et je ressemble à ce monarque
>
> Plus malheureux que le malheur
> Qui restait roi de ses douleurs.

I wish I could be as neat as that

> Mon amour j'étais dans tes bras
> Au dehors quelqu'un murmura
> Une vieille chanson de France
> Mon mal enfin s'est reconnu
> Et son refrain comme un pied nu
> Troubla l'eau verte du silence.

Everyone chooses that one apparently, but I like it too. Probably if I knew enough about French literature I should know it had all been done by someone else before. If so I'm glad of my ignorance. Love to Sylva.
à bientôt
Keith (Fish over the page)
'Behaviour of Fish in an Egyptian Teagarden' [see Letter 292]

5 November 1943   Notts SR Yeo MEF

Dear Olga,

I can't remember what number Adam Hacohen [?], so I've sent you a letter to c/o Vera Nova, and I shall send this to Kedem[1] with please forward on it, so I hope you'll get one or other of them. I suppose it will be a long time before I see you again, and perhaps you'll be married: anyway keep on writing to me. See if you can get hold of a copy of *Personal Landscape* – 'Renaissance Bookshop', Rue Fouad, Cairo has them, and sends them somewhere in Jerusalem – you'll find poems of mine in it now and then though I don't write for *Citadel* any longer.[2] If you don't get married, you know you can always come to England after the war, and I'll find somewhere for you to live, even if you're broke, and see that you are amused. I've said much the same to Vera Nova, so you can come together if you can get on that well: actually I'd probably be gladder to see you by yourself, but probably neither of you'll come. I shall very likely be out here again after the war, working for the British Council – in Greece or Palestine if I can make it. I've been to see the Great men here and they seem tolerably favourable.

I sent you my poem about the behaviour of the fish in an Egyptian tea garden – did you get it? If not – and as you haven't replied, I begin to think you didn't have it – in case not, anyway, here it is again. (PTO) I've no news, anyhow, though I shall (I hope) have some the next time I write.

[Poem] 'Behaviour of Fish in an Egyptian Tea Garden' [see Letter 292]
Like it?
Love
Keith

---

1   The bookshop where Olga had worked.
2   The British Council supported literary magazine that David Hicks had edited.

Eight

1944

298. *To Marie J. Douglas* [1]   BL 59833 f.39

(Telegram) [PM [?]Dec. 1943]

HOPE ARRIVE LEAVE SOON STOP GET THINGS OUT MAY ARRANGE
YOU STAY CORNWALL STOP—KEITH

299. *To M.J. Tambimuttu*   BL 60587 ff.17–20

Sunday 2 [January 1944]   Feock, Cornwall [1]

Dear Tambi,

I had a shot at finding you when I was in town on the 31st, but
failed to find even the Diary, [2] which I wanted to take away – I hope
you aren't losing it or showing it to anyone at all official. I have
collected nearly 80 poems, and discovered the negatives of some of
the photographs, though not as yet of the dead men. [3]

I have been thinking over the idea of a book containing prose,
verse, photographs and drawings, and I think the best arrangement
would be to produce a fairly small volume, called something like
Landscape with figures, or Figures on a battlefield, with an oddish
jacket. [Annotated sketch of a cover showing a face follows, with
comments on lettering and insertion of a photograph where one eye
should be] The whole mise en page would have to be better arranged
but I could do that.

Inside the book 10 prose pieces taken from the diary, dealing with
actual scenes, and cutting out, for the moment, the bits of character
study etc., which would cut out a lot of my difficulties: the idea
being entirely to give a vivid picture, more than an account. 10
photographs, which need not necessarily be selected from mine –
although at least some of mine would do (I can get the dead men
negatives). 10 poems, all to do with the battlefields between Alamein
and Tunisia, possibly one or two letters from the battlefield to my
mother or anyone else, and 10 drawings. There might be a sort of
'leave section' of the book clearing out of the battlefield back to

---

1 Having embarked from the Middle East on 17 November, Douglas arrived at
   Chippenham Park camp, Cambridgeshire, on 12 December (see *KD* p.229).

---

1 The home of Douglas's fellow officer Jack Holman.
2 *Alamein* was delivered to Tambimittu written in a page-a-day diary, BL 53774.
3 Surviving photographs are in the Brotherton Library.

Cairo, which could include 'Behaviour of Fish in an Egyptian Teagarden', and an excellent photograph of the teagarden which I happen to have,[4] and a description of being wounded, in hospital, and on leave.[5]

This may sound very disjointed, but I think my careful arrangement could be more of a unity than simply poems and a straightforward account. If it seemed too much you could cut out the drawings.

It would need some sort of a preface, which I could write. That's all at the moment. If you cared to produce the big mass of poems in an ordinary verse volume you could still do that. If so I want to write a sort of essay at the beginning. The poems divide into School and Oxford, Army at home and in Palestine, and poems about Cairo and the battlefield. The styles of these 3 groups are so different that they would have to be separated and a little written about each Division in the preface.

I shall be in town two days about the 6th and 7th or 7th and 8th, and should like to see you if possible (let's say the 7th) as it may be my last chance for some time. Also, I want the book (Diary) back when I go back to the regiment, on the 8th or 9th. So if you can't see me, please give the Diary to Betty Jesse[6] and I'll ask for her and get it (also your comments, if you don't see me). I'll ring up as soon as I get to town and try to make a definite appointment with you. I am writing this from Porthgwidden, Feock, Cornwall. My address at the Regiment, is

Capt. K. C. Douglas
Notts SR Yeo
Chippenham Park. North Camp
Ely
Cambs

(in case I didn't give it you before.)

When I next come I'll leave the whole bulk of poems for you and you can see if you like them. Please don't lose them if you can

4 In the Brotherton; reproduced *KD* p.227.
5 The 'Diary' was probably completed up to what became Chapter XVII of *Alamein*. By March Douglas was to write three more chapters covering the Zem Zem action, his being wounded and being brought back to hospital. Finally, Douglas added the section Zem Zem, which starts with him at Enfidaville, back with the regiment, and includes flashbacks of his leave. See Letter 308.
6 Tambimuttu's assistant at *Poetry (London)*.

help it, because although I have copies of most of them they are scattered and will be hard to get at.

Hoping to see you
Keith Douglas

300. To M.J. Tambimuttu   BL 60587 ff.21–2

30 January 1944   Chippenham N. Camp/Ely/Cambs

Dear Tambi,

I believe I am getting leave for 12 days from Monday Feby 14th. This is certainly my last leave for 3 months, possibly for a great deal longer (or for good, I suppose). It may be permissible for me to get away from Saturday to Sunday at another time – but I doubt if that'll be much good for catching you. So I shall come straight up to London on Monday and stay if necessary till Wednesday, in order to see you.

I hope by that time you'll have read over the typed version of the diary and decided what you like and dislike in it, and if you want it at all.[1] I shall bring with me the following drawings, from which I suggest we select 10.[2]

1. Tanks advancing up a sand track (watercolour).
2. Composition based on a Pietà, of casualty being taken out of a tank (watercolour).
3. as 2 above. (Pen drawing).
4. Face of a man burning to death (watercolour, with explanatory notes in ink).
5. Sketch of bodies and junk, with notes of ideas for a poem (pencil).
6. Shapes of derelicts (watercolour).
7. Tanks under HE fire.
8. Derelicts (watercolour).
9. Broken trees and buildings (watercolour).
10. Tank crews cooking (pen drawing).
11. Crusader tanks moving up into battle (watercolour).

1 Presumably the typescript made from the 'Diary', sent to the printer and now lost. A fragment of a typescript draft Douglas made around September 1943 survives (BL 60586) and has been reprinted: *Miscellany* pp.98–114.
2 A number of the drawings were to appear in the 1946 *Alamein*; the originals are in BL 53775.

12. Men hit by anti-personnel mine (pen drawing).
13. Derelict lorry and anti-tank guns (watercolour).
14. Cairo street scene (caricatures) pen and wash.
15. Explosion of a booby trap (pen drawing).
16. Self-portrait in a steel shaving mirror (pencil).

Whatever these may seem to you to lack, as pictures, they give an accurate idea of the appearance of things, with one exception. In the case of the man burning to death I have had to retain all the features, to give the chap some expression, although of course they're expressionless, as their faces swell up like pumpkins. But I've got the effect I wanted, of pain. Or I think I have.

I may also bring you a poem or two more – and if you're interested in short stories about the Middle East I have four so far written and may have more when I come.[3] But I don't expect you want short stories. I shall have some more of the diary – but it's all very similar.

As to the title of the book, I think it should be something more individual than Journey into Battle, which sounds like a war-correspondent's account. Here are some more suggestions although there's bags of time yet.

1. Another Part of the Battlefield
2. The Iron Trees (this sounds as if its aping Sidney Keyes, though).[4]
3. A Man in Armour, or, Men in Armour.
4. The New Country.
5. The Iron Country.
6. Anatomy of Battle or Anatomy of a Battle.

I like 1, 6, and 5, in that order (I've been writing them down as I thought of them.) I'll do a design for a jacket if you decide on a title.[5]

Send me a date and time, please.
Keith Douglas
PS I suppose it's with your knowledge and consent that the BBC are proposing to broadcast 'Enfidaville'?[6]

3 The two which survive are printed in the Appendix.
4 Sidney Keyes, *The Iron Laurel*, 1942.
5 See Letters 308 and 309.
6 The BBC has no surviving record of this.

301. *To Jean Turner*   Private Hands

n.d.   Notts SR Yeo./Chippenham N.Camp/Ely/Cambs

Dear Jean,
Thank you for your note – I'm sorry I couldn't get in touch with
you on leave, but I'll be getting some more. At the moment it's no
good writing you a letter as I feel so savage about this filthy country
and the way it is run that I couldn't say anything entertaining or
amusing. I now live in a tin hut and a sea of mud (which freezes
every few days) and no laundry arrangements or showers, with about
½ as much food as civilians are eating. I'll try and ring you up but
I have to walk 2 miles to a village to do it.
Love
Keith
PS I'm getting 11 days leave sometime in the next 12 weeks – we
might spend some of it together in town: or Oxford (Appletons wd.
put us up there).

302. *To Jean Turner*   Private Hands

n.d. [early February 1944]   Chippenham N. Camp/Ely/Cambs

Dear Jean,
I'm sorry about my last unpleasant note, but really I was about as
fed up as I could be. Look, I'm going on leave for 12 days about the
14th and hope to be in Oxford from 16th on. I'd love to see you.
Or I'll be in town 14th–16th. If you can do anything about it, (or
if you want me to come to Bletchley,[1] which I'll do if necessary –
though I hope it wont be) write me details c/o Joan Appleton,
Charter Club, Oxford with DO NOT FORWARD on it, or if it's
about London, wire to above address – I'll be back from wet
Scotland (where I am now) on Sunday evening. By the way, I hope
you got that note to Bletchley (I wrote the address from memory
as I'd lost what I wrote down from your father's dictation).
     I'm longing to see you again – the unenthusiasm about Bletchley
is about Bletchley, not you – and of course I'll come there if you

---

1   Where Jean was stationed.

really can't escape, but Oxford would be pleasanter, wouldn't it?[2] I
said write c/o Joan App. because she runs the club and will keep
the letter. I hope I'm staying with the Apps although they haven't
answered my letters asking if I may. Betty App. has had a baby and
stinks of nappies.
Love
Keith

303. *To Bette Jesse*   BL 59835 f.1
Saturday n.d. [February 1944]   Chippenham Pk.

Dear Betty,
I have begun writing letters at once, like one does after getting back
to school. I hope you're feeling less depressed now – you didn't
enjoy your ride much, did you? I'm not so stiff as I thought I should
be. You wouldn't believe me if I told you how much difference
you made to my leave by coming out dancing – (so I *won't* tell you,
and we'll assume it made no difference at all).[1]

I'm sorry I rather bitched up the evening towards the end. Things
got twisted up when you suddenly said: 'It must be nice to have a
mother who wants you all the time'. I couldn't believe you would
make such a Little Nell remark without some reason, and the reason,
the only one I could think of seemed to be that you wanted to tell
me a story. I wanted to hear it (and I wanted to tell you my own,
I suppose) because that is what turns an acquaintance into a friendship. When I was very small I climbed up some scaffolding once,
and a workman underneath told me to jump off and said he would
catch me. After he said it 3 times I jumped and he did catch me. On
Thursday night I repeated this performance, only you stepped out
from underneath and grinned like a cat while you watched me
'working it out', as though anyone has to work it out when he's
dived onto his neck. Then you lectured me like a Mother Superior
while I was down and couldn't kick. No wonder I spilt your beer.

2   Jean notes on the letter 'Keith didn't seem to realise that by this time we were
    all… not allowed to leave our station. I remember a rather abortive phone call
    from Keith to my WRNS quarters at WALTON Bucks.'

1   Betty had arranged a ride for them in Hyde Park on the last day of Douglas's
    leave; see *KD* p.232.

Of course it doesn't matter but I think you decided I was a bit dotty; so that's the explanation. I could provide a plot for Dickens myself (possibly in collaboration with Freud, now that they're both in limbo) so you see you kind of set me off. Never mind, skip it; I'll behave quite properly and cattily again next time – I don't know (nor care) if you've commented on my erratic behaviour to Tambi or your husband or anyone; but anyway this letter is for you and the nearest waste paper basket. The *Bête Noire* style will begin again in our next issue.[2]

Thanks for fixing the ride – Guy is going to fix a free one if he can, next time. And don't forget to expedite the diary if possible (I mean its acceptance, censoring and ultimate appearance). Now, (and all your fault), I have to think of and write a poem called *Bête Noire*![3] I'll hold you to your promise to come out again on telegraphic notice.
Keith
PS My batman is quite a young Jeeves, he was waiting on the doorstep, with a fire going, my chocolate ration laid out, hot water and a change of clothes – the 4 most important things in the right order.
[envelope, f.2, has sketch of devil with note] suggestion for B. Noire on Squander Bug[4] lines

304. *To Bette Jesse*   BL 59835 f.3

n.d.   [Letterhead] Notts SR Yeo

Dear Betty,
Thank you for a letter I was rather pleased to get. I'm delighted to hear my behaviour was excellent in many ways, why didn't you make it completely the curate's egg and say excellent in parts? I can't think how you could have said it more politely anyway – so thank you.

You're a strange person if you don't want any sympathy – possibly you mean pity. Personally I can always do with any amount of sympathy, although I don't often get it, ask for it, or feel it for anyone else. (Sometimes I do all 3).

---

2 From a remark of Betty's about his being her *bête noire*; see *KD* p.233.
3 Douglas did, or at least attempted to do, so; see *CP* pp.126–7, and see Letter 304.
4 A figure used in a publicity campaign to prevent waste.

The Diary has come back from the Colonel.[1] He says (or words to this effect), 'Keith, I have read and enjoyed the ms. Now I am not quite sure what is expected of me. I assume I don't have anything to do with the security angle, which seems O.K. From the Regimental angle, it seems a pity to go for Black Michael[2] to such a tune, if in the final form he is to be easily identifiable. Some of your remarks about Flash[3] will raise a storm, but I suppose it's a free country and you can write what you like within the limits of the law.' I should have copied it out, because on examination, it's a masterpiece. For me to have said directly to the Colonel what I've said in the diary would let me in for a Court Martial. As it's confidential there's nothing like that involved. As it is, he can't afford to let the stuff about Michael pass, but he can't defend Michael (since that admits he needs defence) and he is not going to give away his own opinion of Michael or of Flash. All that is implicit in the letter, and it's very well done. A chap who can write that sort of letter is someone whose orders I don't mind obeying. All the same, I hope it shook him.

I'm sorry there are no results. But I suppose you'll get someone to read it sometime: after all, I suppose they do read everything that's submitted sooner or later.[4] Anyway it's sweet of you to try. If you finally come to the conclusion that it's no *use* trying, please send it back, and I'll scrap it.

Meanwhile please write sometimes; I shall try and get up to town for a thirty six hours now and then – it will be on a Saturday. My relationship with you has a lot of unknowns and I hope I never quite get the equation to come out, because it's fascinating and I need something to keep me from becoming mud. Last night I went to a dance in Cambridge with five Chinamen.[5]

Keith

PS I'm sending up an excuse (to be used as a preface) for not writing a poem called *Bête Noire*.[6] Also some drawings.

---

1 Col. Spence: Douglas had shown him the 'Diary' to clear it for publication.
2 'Sweeney Todd' in *Alamein*.
3 'Piccadilly Jim' in *Alamein*.
4 This could refer to a check on the legalities of publication; see Letter 309. A legal report on the ms survives, dated '5–6–44', the day before Douglas embarked for Normandy, BL 53773 ff.160–2.
5 Olive Sandall in a letter to Graham recalled this occasion.
6 Published in *CP* pp.129–30.

PPS Sensitive is not the word you want either. I'm afraid you mean raw, only it doesn't sound so nice. K.

305. *To Bette Jesse*   BL 59835 f.4

n.d.

Dear Betty,
Do you remember Johnny[1] in the Diary? The curious half-French person who put everybody's backs up – except women's? Well, he's come back – to see *me*. And he's pleased to see me, too: not just ordinary polite pleased, but like a puppy who's been left alone in a house. This amazes me, but it's nice, I suppose. Why should I write and tell *you*, when I've already written you one letter which no one has posted, and anyway, as you say, we don't know each other? The only thing to do is not to post it, or to pretend I'm not going to post it for a day or two (and then tear it up or post it). Really I feel quite happy and I didn't realise what a rare sensation this is. Nothing worries you, you say, so you wouldn't know what my state of mind has been like. Anyway I'm being terrifically unemotional with Johnny – I have to be or he'd fall on my neck.
    I do know why I'm writing to you, as a matter of fact: because this evening is a little like the day I got your letter saying you'd got a horse and you were coming dancing. Gosh, this is drivel, isn't it. Betty I hope this isn't a mirage, this little golden age, even if it's only for a week or two. Please forgive this outburst, if I'm weak enough to send it to you.
Keith

306. *To Bette Jesse*   BL 59835 f.5

Saturday 10 [March]   [Letterhead] Notts SR Yeo

Dear Betty,
Thank you for your letter, for the information in it, for being sweet to me and sweet to Tambi on my behalf. If I may say it without committing a breach of security (*my* security) it has seemed a long time between the letters, although I know you wrote as soon as

---

1   John Bethell-Fox, who is 'Raoul' in *Alamein*.

you'd any reason to. I find it hard not to write to you sometimes, though I certainly shan't allow myself to do it too often: and I enjoy getting your letters more than most things (that's not saying much, *au moment*).

About Tambi, is it any good my saying will he either make up his mind or send it back because someone else wants it? I am writing a letter to this effect and I'll put it in this one. If you think it's a good thing, give it him. If not, tear it up. Needless to say I don't want it (the book) back and no one else wants it, though I dare say I could persuade Faber's, who view me with a kindly eye (Uncle Eliot's) or Gollancz. Incidentally, we have *another* new Colonel.[1] Our last was too good for us and has gone, militarily speaking, to a Better Place. The new new Colonel is not going to be privileged to read the diary – once is enough.

Well, what *have* I been doing? Not much wine, one very indifferent woman and no song. 2 court martials, very boring ones (I was NOT the accused) and 119 men to look after. A long-lost friend materialised, and I wrote you a daffy letter. I am going to send it you (another enclosure):[2] to do this is letting down my shield a bit, but if you can understand it, it might do some good. If you don't understand it I'm mistaken in you. I didn't dance even once with the Chinamen, though at a later dance I had one loopy foxtrot with a Chinese-girl (national costume complete). Otherwise all I've done is go to a party with some incredibly stupid young students (can it be that I behaved like that only four years ago?). *Lilliput* is going to pay me 6 guineas for a description of a horse being dissected – that's much too little, isn't it?[3] All the students except 3 were Jewish – the women lustful and sweaty, which is a combination that makes me retch.

The one indifferent wench referred to turned out to be a girl guide or something and doesn't hold with deodorants, so she's out, and my opinion of the London School of Economics has struck a new low. That sounds almost like Walter Winchell, doesn't it.

The part of your letter about me and the very small piece, no more than a hint, about yourself, reminds me of the letters I get from a Latvian-Jewish girl in Palestine who thinks she knows all about me, and herself, and life – presumably because the first two

1 Col. J. D'A. Anderson.
2 The previous letter, 305.
3 'Death of A Horse', July 1944 (reprinted in the Appendix).

have made the same sort of mess of the third. Not that I want to discourage you from writing what are the most interesting bits in your letters, or even to suggest I've heard it before. Anyway Olga writes the most interesting letters I get (or got, before yours, which are beginning to compete with them). Hell, I shouldn't have said compete. For compete read anything you would rather read.

I won't comment on your complicated life because I don't know anything about it till you tell me (which I don't expect you to). Would it be too complicated for you to come out with me on Saturday evening a week from tomorrow, if you can get to town? If you want to go to a show or anything you'll have to book the seats. But the order of things is 1) Write back and tell me if you can make it 2) I'll telegraph that I've got permission and time 3) Book the seats and keep your fingers crossed till 4) we meet. If I can manage that day, it'll be the last, I fear, because awful things happen after that, nameless and unnecessary, but not, at first, perilous.[4] Later on of course, I shall have to engage someone to pray hard: I don't suppose you'd be any better at that than I am.

This afternoon I've been ordered to go and be jabbed for typhus, and I'm in the throes of a large calibre (writing to you I suppose I ought to spell it caliber: you and your favor) cold. This morning I had to give 3 'personal interviews' and listen to hard-luck stories. One chap has stolen someone's National Savings book and wants me to save him the consequences. The second is a bastard trying to trace his mother who has turned 'respectful', as her brother's letter says, and the 3rd wants leave to go and keep his name out of a smutty divorce case in which as far as I can see, it ought to figure pretty large.

Well, I hope I'll see you, Betty.
Keith

307. *To M.J. Tambimuttu*   BL 60587 f.27

[?10 March 1944]

Dear Tambi,
I don't know if you want the Diary to publish or not. But will you make up your mind by the 24th of March, and let me know by then,

---

4 Preparing for the invasion of Europe, they were to be in a sealed camp for security reasons, allowing no visitors or leave.

because if you don't want it or if I don't hear by that date I shall submit it to someone else *on* the 24th, who seems interested in it. I can't afford to wait because of military engagements which may be the end of me – so that date is final.

Yours
Keith

308. *To M.J. Tambimuttu*   BL 60587 ff.30–1

[March 1944]   [Letterhead] Nuffield House SW1[1]

Dear Tambi,

I've had the agreement from Betty.[2] I don't agree about the £10 for various reasons. I've signed my part of the 2nd agreement and Dorothy Sauter has signed yours, and you *have*, therefore agreed to publish two books. Now if you could use the majority of my poems in the War Diary, I wouldn't mind you amalgamating the two – although I still don't see why *I* should be punished, by a fine of £10, because *you* have changed your mind. Do you think it's fair, yourself? Secondly out of the 70–80 poems I've submitted to you for a book of poems (which you definitely asked me for) you *can* only use about 15 with the War Diary, so that the others don't get published at all. Now if I had not severed or allowed to drop, all connections with T. S. Eliot and with Fabers, I could probably have got those poems published by them. Now I don't suppose I'll get them published at all, unless you stand by your agreement. Of course I don't give a damn how *long* you take to publish the poems, within reason: publish the Diary first and the poems later (when they'll sell better, I think, as a result of people having read the diary).[3] Also I hear you like the *Bête Noire* cover drawing and so do I; and it seems a pity not to use it.[4]

To go back to the agreement – you are paying me only for my MS and you are using a lot of illustrations. That's OK. I submitted them with the MS, as part of it. But the fact remains that if you had

---

1   'Residential Club for Officers of HM and Allied Forces'.
2   A typescript agreement for *Bête Noire* is BL 56356 f.233; a printed contract for the 'War Diary' is BL 56356 ff.234–5.
3   The 'Diary' appeared as *Alamein* in 1946; *Bête Noire* was never to appear, being replaced by a *Collected Poems* in 1951.
4   BL 53775.

got anyone else to illustrate it you'd have had to pay him extra, above the advance royalties you're paying me. So it seems a bit hard to *deduct* £10, doesn't it?

Finally, merely from the point of view of £10 more, or less, as you know I owe my mother about £40 and she is quite broke, and so I must pay it. This doesn't leave me a lot over, and there are a lot of rather expensive things – e.g. a warm and waterproof coat, and a good sleeping bag, which I shall be needing for the next battle and which the British Government does not supply me with. So the £10 in itself makes quite a lot of difference.

So I suggest –

1. That deducting £10 is not very fair – Betty agrees with me, I believe.
2. That you don't deduct it.
3. That you publish the diary first and wait a bit and then
4. Publish *Bête Noire* – by which time I can let you have about 20 more poems – I already have 5 or 6.

After all – you have signed agreements to publish two separate MSS – and I think in the end you'll be glad if you do publish both.

Now – Page 3. Points about the Diary

1. I have completed it up to my arrival in hospital. This only makes it about 25 pp of type longer than it was, and does not include a description of my stay in hospital, or of the very small piece of the Tunisian campaign which I saw. I could go on, but it is a natural whole as it stands, and I think would be spoilt by a continuation.[5] I have some more drawings to go in it. (Pen ones).
2. *Title* – call it
   A Journal of some Desert Battles
   or A Journal of Desert Battles
   or A Journal of the battles from Alamein to Zem Zem
   with poems and drawings
   by
   Keith Douglas
3. I could write a last chapter, an account of the final surrender of the German armies in Tunisia – this would be another 10 to 15 pages, and ought to be inserted last, so that you have
   – one poem
   prologue

5 Douglas was to add a final few pages, 'Zem Zem', recounting his return to the regiment at Enfidaville and the final days of the campaign, in Tunisia.

- the main diary
epilogue
- the poems
- Description of the end in Tunisia
When I let you have the final MS will you
1. Let PL Solicitors look it over ref. libel.[6]
2. get it retyped and charge it to me out of the 2nd £30.
Sorry this is so long.
Yours
Keith
PS Militarily, things begin to move, for me, very soon now, so once you've got this MS I may be fairly busy.

309. *To Betty Jesse*   BL 60587 f.36 and 53773 f.49

26 [March 1944]   A Sqn Notts SR Yeo APO England

Dear Betty,

You seem to be receiving a lot of communications from me, none of them very interesting – although anyone in the office who recognizes my writing will be supposing I write you 'long marvellous letters' every day. Well, this one begins with business, too. I sent you a receipt for the £30. It doesn't look much like a receipt to me, and I had to pull the 2d stamp off a postcard: however my squadron clerk, who is something in the city in civvy street says it is OK. If you look carefully at the stamp you'll find the signature continues across it, although if you lift it up you'll find another signature underneath.

   Secondly, a few points about the Diary which have cropped up in my mind.

1. A censor may raise objections to the detailed description of wireless procedure during battle – giving away code names etc. It might be as well – since censors are not only ignorant but dimwitted *and* in a hell of a hurry – to mention that this procedure has been completely cancelled and is never used – and anyway the enemy knew all about it, because we captured an interception officer who explained all our own codes to us. The main point is that such a procedure no longer exists.

6 See Letter 304 n.4; PL: *Poetry (London)*.

2. *The Title* – I think we said
    A Journal of the Battles from
    Alamein to Zem Zem
    Would it make a more arresting title from the bookstall point
    of view to call it
    Alamein – Zem Zem
    A Journal of some desert battles
    with
    poems and drawings
    in that order. Whether any play could be made with the fact that
    the initials make it A – Z I don't know. As you probably saw,
    inside the cover I've called the beginning and the ending bits A
    and Z anyway to avoid the words Prologue and epilogue. You
    could probably get rid of the hyphen and imply it in the lay-out
    of the words e.g. [Sketch of what K.D. suggests] or something,
    like travelling labels (though not travelling label lettering, I hope).
    I am enclosing another poem which is relevant to the diary.
[Added upside-down at foot of this letter]
Will you look up SKELETAL in a dictionary (I haven't one) and
find out if it exists and means like a skeleton. If not, alter Skeletal
in 'Mersa' to skeleton. And please ensure Tambi has a copy of a
poem 'Cairo Jag' beginning 'Shall I get drunk or cut myself a piece
of cake' and that he uses it? Thanks.

        Mersa

        This blue halfcircle of sea
        moving transparently
        on sand as pale as salt
        was Cleopatra's hotel:

        here is a guesthouse built
        and broken utterly, since.
        An amorous modern prince
        lived in this scoured shell.

        Now from the skeletal town
        the cherry skinned soldiers stroll down
        to undress to idle on the white beach.
        Up there, the immensely long road goes by

to Tripoli: the wind and dust reach
the secrets of the whole
poor town whose masks would still
deceive a passer-by;

faces with sightless doors
for eyes, with cracks like tears
oozing at corners.A dead tank alone
leans where the gossips stood.

I see my feet like stones
underwater. The logical little fish
converge and nip the flesh
imagining I am one of the dead.

310. *To Edmund Blunden*   Texas

[March/April 1944]   Notts SR Yeo APO England

Dear Edmund,
I hoped I might hear an address from you after I got back, as I know
you've left Merton. I'm going to send this to Jean who seems to see
you from time to time. I'm afraid even now this is a short letter. As
you will see from my cryptic address I've been fattened up for more
slaughter and am simply waiting for it to start. Nicholson & Watson
have paid the £60 and 10% on any further sales for my diary of the
battles from Alamein to Zem Zem with poems and illustrations and
a measley £10 (+10%) for a book of poems called *Bête Noire* at the
moment, which, with my cover and illustrations, will probably
appear later. I am not much perturbed at the thought of never seeing
England again, because a country which can allow her army to be
used to the last gasp and paid like skivvies isn't worth fighting for.
For me, it is simply a case of fighting *against* the Nazi regime. After
that, unless there is a revolution in England, I hope to depart for
sunnier and less hypocritical climates.
I wish you good luck with your new ménage.[1]
Keith

1 Blunden was divorced and with his new wife, Claire.

Tuesday (I think) [n.d. PM 4 April 1944]   Chippenham –
        for the last time: but a letter here will follow me. I'll send
        you new address when I know it.

[At top sketch of horseman for cover of *Bête Noire*] The horse will
be along when I have a moment – Priority. K.

My dear Betty,

I hope I have time to write this without being interrupted, and
manage to say what I want to say. Sunday was a wonderful day.
These haywire occasions are what make people friends – and lovers,
sometimes. In a sense everything couldn't have gone wronger, but
in hundreds of other ways that was made up. If I never see you again,
it's not a bad time to remember as the last day of a short and peculiar
friendship, which has made me happier – and of course unhappier
– than I have been for a long time. But, before you start bawling
me out for being gloomy, I'll hasten to say I'm sure it's not the end,
although the flap is definitely on, now. (I see I've made some ink
smears somehow at the bottom of the page – sorry.)

I'm going to ask you in a letter – because so many things in
conversation embarrass you – if you will stay a whole week-end
with me, before the second (so-called) front opens – and if I get a
week-end, which isn't likely. This isn't because I want, as your
favourite phrase is 'to climb into bed with you'. As you must know,
of course, I am quite enough in love with you from a sex point of
view, to want that. But what I do want is not to have to fight against
the whole of London (or the clientèle of the Southern Railway) for
every moment I spend with you. It would be marvellous to be in a
room with you and shut the door on all the problems and perils of
both of us. You will probably feel that actually sleeping together
will only make for another complication, and I don't suppose you
want to sleep with me, anyway. But I hope you can see that it
needn't happen just because we shut ourselves up together. I'm
afraid this is very pompous, but I always get pompous when I'm
having a job to express myself (like an MP). Where this room would
be I'm not sure. The idea of a place like the Grosvenor probably
revolts you. It does me, as an idea. But it's the simplest because you
can walk in out of Victoria Station, which is to say, walking in as
one unknown person from the whole of England, and go up and
into my room without consulting or speaking to anyone, being

remarked by no one. Such complete anonymity – which is almost as good as solitude – would be difficult anywhere else. However, there are places out of town, I suppose.

That's a hell of a paragraph. If you can't agree with any of it, at least I know you'll understand it, and not feel it's an ordinary pass thinly wrapped up. And if you've nothing to say about it, don't refer to it in your next letter, and you needn't be afraid of this hurting my ridiculous feelings.

I have humbly to confess myself unable to deliver you a useful sermon on your cat's cradle of a life, even on paper.[1] A desire to help you which quite shakes me up, and a fair comprehension of what's happening, don't seem to be enough. I've discussed the R.C. business – as an abstract case – with two or three people who have more experience of Jesuits than I have, and they seem to think my remarks to you about what they'll do to Junior were a triumph of understatement. It's no good distressing you if you don't agree, but if you decide you do, it's possible I could do something about finding him somewhere pleasant to live which wouldn't be vastly expensive to you. It sounds pretentious to say I would try and help with money, when I'm notorious for being permanently broke and over borrowing; but once I'm in action I shan't want much money, and Mother has enough to live on, so that I could let you have some of my pay. Don't dismiss this idea at once, or be contemptuous of it, or amused at it – and don't think it would make the least difference to either of us, as friends, or change our situation at all. It's simply that I'm mad about being free and about other people being free, and if you decide to take your courage in both hands, I would do anything in the world – short of completely sabotaging myself, which wouldn't help either of us – to help you.

One other thing – as you see, references to being in love with you seem to creep in to conversation in letters of mine from time to time. Actually, I know no more certainly what's happening to me than you know what *will* happen to you. But you can be quite sure whatever it is, it isn't another problem for you; I am not dependent on you, you have absolutely no responsibility for me or need to worry about hurting *me* as little as possible, etc etc. You can skip me unless I happen to open up a way of escape for you. If so

1 Betty was on the way to a divorce.

330

use me as much as you like – you can be sure I'll use you just as much, if you do. What I asked at the beginning of this letter is something which means a hell of a lot to me, and so does everything else I have to do with you; I think about you a great deal, having an amorphous rather than complicated life otherwise. But it's all duty free as far as you're concerned: I'm an extra piece of furniture, if you like you can use it, but you can leave it behind in any of a hundred cloak rooms. You'll be glad to hear from now on it's just news, and you can read it when you like.

I've been on another long drive, to a small place on the coast where there is a tank range. In the evening we split up (7 officers) and 4, me included, went to see Charles Laughton in *The Man from Down Under* – lowest form of modern melodrama, about the worst film of the last five years. The other 3 went to a pub. When we came out of the flicks we hunted everywhere for the missing three for about an hour, and were at last going home, about 12.00, when we met John (the irresistible Frenchman), in the street. He said 'Frightfully sorry, we forgot the time. The others are playing billiards in a pub about 100 yards up across the crossroads'. I raised a tremendous display of authoritative wrath and said he, and they, could bloody well stay and play billiards for the rest of the night, and we'd send a truck for them at 5.0 in the morning. The rest of us then drove off, turned right at the crossroads, switched off the engine and lights and shoved the truck up an alley. We were then going to creep back and surprise them all as John was telling them the bad news. But unfortunately we couldn't find the bloody pub anywhere and didn't find it, until we had staggered round for an hour, having several encounters with canned black Yanks and knocking at every door where a chink of light showed. At last we rang a bell somewhere and a most presentable girl answered the door. We said: 'Have you got 3 Sherwood Rangers officers inside?' she replied: 'Yes. Are you Keith?' We went in and found the three of them drinking gin, in a horrible cold alcoholic rage. We hadn't meant them to be under the strain for an hour, but it had certainly shaken them. However, all was amicably settled at last and apart from losing the way and landing up with the front wheels of the truck in the sea, we got home without incident.

This is quite obviously too long. Never mind, read it in instalments – I should say, I hope you *have* read it in instalments. If all else fails, come out of town one Sunday and meet me at the

borders of the prohibited belt, and we'll really go for a walk.
Love
Keith
[In pencil at foot] Please expedite that £30, *si possible*.

312. *To Betty Jesse*   BL 56355 f.173

5 [April 1944; Postcard, 'Piétà: Ecole de Touraine']

Dear Betty.
Comparison of your letter of the 4th and my letter of the 4th is
rather amusing. I like yours better – probably if I'd been in a hurry
mine would have improved. I move at sparrowfart tomorrow – 4
o'clock (am). Let you know new address when *I* do.

You may receive some gold ear rings if my cheque doesn't
bounce. If you don't like them you know what you can do with
them. You'll have to alter them for unpierced ears anyway.

Here is the picture I asked you to look after: I did it in 1939,
(summer) in Paris, on a good day.[1] Perhaps it'll do for your wall till
I can do one.

Mother's address is Mrs Marie J. Douglas Little Fairlight East
Grinstead Sx. please send her £20 and me what's left after deducting
that and typing fees: if any. Had tea in Cambridge today with a
Frenchman in a red velvet képi
Keith
PS I think this card is about contemporary with the portrait.[2]
[along the side] Do you like this? I pulled it off my wall, as I'm
going.

313. *To Marie J. Douglas*   BL 56355 f.162

10 April 1944   'A' Sqn Notts SR Yeo APO England

Dear Mother,
Thanks for your telegram. I shall send off the tin box some time
soon. I've written Betty to send you £20 which you should have
soon; let me know if you don't get it, but Betty is pretty efficient,

---

1 A portrait of Yingcheng (now in possession of Desmond Graham).
2 That is, bought in Paris in 1939.

so I expect you will.

You'll have to send the sea-boots, if you can get them, to this address. I'm afraid I shan't be able to make any use of my membership of the United University club.

Will you look out a bush shirt and the American drill slacks and be prepared to send them when the weather gets hot, please? I'll remind Betty to send you proofs of the Diary when it's ready.

Is there a good bank in East-Grinstead to which I could transfer my a/c? I don't like leaving it with that man. Could you see a Barclays or NP manager there for me and decide which is a nice chap and let me know.

I hope you're feeling well again now. If not, don't bother about boots or anything else till you are.

In haste.

Much love

Keith

probably sending suitcase as well

314. *To Bette Jesse* BL 59835 ff.9–11

Monday [n.d. 10 April 1944]

[At top] You'll be getting a letter (drunk) with my address
Dear Betty,
I have been feeling very depressed waiting for your letter – which shows I am not so conceited – or at least that there are bounds to my conceit. Now it (in two parts) has arrived, I feel very much encouraged and for some reason much less frightened of the future. I can understand your not wanting to sneak about in and out of hotels. I don't myself. In any case I don't think London will see me again for some time: I don't think they'll let us far out of here. But I am going to find out how near here you are allowed to come from London, and I'll try and slip across the border and join you on a Sunday or on a Saturday, staying overnight. So, stand by for a telegram (to which you can reply although the reply may not reach me in time.) I am afraid all letters are going to take much longer. I shall try and send this illegally to speed it up. Then be prepared to escape out of London, and join me. It's a pity I'm not one of the troops who, if he were in the state of mind I am in, would cover pages with simple, hackneyed and sincere endearments. If we don't

meet, DON'T consider it an 'unfinished story'; go on writing to me and you know unless I'm killed or crippled I shall feel about you as I do now: so try not to be too impatient and rush off with someone else, my sweet. Not that being crippled will alter my feelings, but it might alter my chance of expressing them.

How nice of you to think of me when you saw a very *fat* and horrid male.

Spring is going like a symphonic accompaniment to one of Sam Goldwyn's hits – just too sugary and sentimental for words, sun and olde worlde cottages and lovers everywhere – and I, like any other dope in the film audience, am taken in (I hope you'll come and hold my hand and watch the show with me).[1] Will it happen? We must at least worry about it and get in a hell of a flap and then it *may*.

I am *so* overcome with spring that I sent 4 men under a lance-corporal to pick primroses to put in the rooms and huts – much raucous laughter from the remaining soldiery, and they (the 4 chosen) slunk away blushing.

Well, I'm happy, and it's your fault. I hope you'll get the earrings (which aren't wonderful, but all I could get that wasn't either prohibitive or repulsive).

Much love

Keith

PS I forgot to say, get this alleged actress to write to me if she wants to meet me – she won't meet me, or not for a very long time, but in action I want lots of letters – so she'll be doing *some* good in the world.

315. *To M.J. Tambimuttu*   BL 60587 f.39
                                          and 53773 ff.93,95 and 91

14 April 1944   Notts SR Yeo APO England

Dear Tambi,

Here are 2 new poems and another copy of the one I sent off yesterday, because I don't trust the Army Post Office an inch. If

---

1 Theatrical imagery, recurrent in Douglas's work, led to two more poems written at this time: 'Actors Waiting' (*CP* p.125) and 'On a Return from Egypt' (*CP* p.132) in Letter 315.

there are variations between the 2 versions of 'L'Autobus', use
whichever you prefer.
Yours
Keith

L'Autobus

The motorbus in the Rue Malika Nazli
motorbus of the School of the Incarnation
making bulldog grunts in its nose
turns out into the Saturday traffic whose
diverging streams embrace the white policeman.
The twenty-six young girls stare busily

conjecturing, twittering, out of eyes
black, grey, brown, violet, nocturnal blue
of a dozen countries. Their mothers' mothers were
perhaps Odysseus' bondwomen, the fair
women of the Troad, Tunisians, Syrians who
for centuries mingled with the swarthy coastwise

seamen, variegated women of the ports
and seabounded villages of many tongues
among the gulls' cries. Probably eyed ships
carried these children's ancestors on trade trips
among the wine-dark sea's white towns
famous for beauty and nefarious arts.

Now under the nun's eye they sit,
the neutralizing beam of holiness;
their touring eyes, ignorant of love or pain
to come, watch eagerly the intriguing game,
street counterplay of virtue and wickedness
in which their mothers were so versed, so adept.

Egyptian Sentry, Corniche, Alexandria

Sweat lines the statue of a face
he has; he looks at the sea
and does not smell its animal smell
does not suspect the heaven or hell
in the mind of a passer-by:
sees the moon shining on a place

in the sea, leans on the railing, rests
a hot hand on the eared rifle-muzzle,
nodding to the monotone of his song
his tarbush with its khaki cover on.
There is no pain, no pleasure, life's no puzzle
but a standing, a leaning, a sleep between the coasts

of birth and dying. From mother's shoulder
to crawling in the rich gutter, millionaire of smells,
standing, leaning at last with seizing limbs
into the gutter again, while the world swims
on stinks and noises past the filthy wall
and death lifts him to the bearer's shoulder.

The moons shines on the modern flats
where sentient lovers or rich couples
lie loving or sleeping after eating.
In the town the cafés and cabarets seating
gossipers, soldiers, drunkards, supple
women of the town, shut out the moon with slats.

Everywhere is a real or artificial race
of life, a struggle of everyone to be
master or mistress of some hour.
But of this no scent or sound reaches him there.
He leans and looks at the sea:
sweat lines the statue of a face.

On a Return from Egypt

To stand here in the wings of Europe
disheartened, I have come away
from the sick land where in the sun lay
the gentle sloe-eyed murderers
of themselves, exquisites under a curse;
here to exercise my depleted fury.

For the heart is a coal, growing colder
when jewelled cerulean seas change
into grey rocks, grey water-fringe,
sea and sky altering like a cloth
till colour and sheen are gone both:
cold is an opiate of the soldier.

And all my endeavours are unlucky explorers
come back, abandoning the expedition;
the specimens, the lilies of ambition
still spring in their climate, still unpicked:
but time, time is all I lacked
to find them, as the great collectors before me.

The next month, then, is a window
and with a crash I'll split the glass.
Behind it stands one I must kiss,
person of love or death
a person or a wraith,
I fear what I shall find.

316. *To Betty Jesse*   BL 59835 ff.12–14

n.d. [?24 April 1944]

Monday night
(very sleepy as well as canned)
Dearest Betty,
I am afraid this will be a little squiggly too. I got back at 3.30 a.m.,
and John went on by train and did his 4 mile walk. I did my 4 mile
walk, too; and slept a bit and then ran 2 miles at 07.30, pretty
energetically, to my surprise. Then I went on a TEWT – tactical
exercise without troops, i.e., wandering across country in a lot of
jeeps eating cheese sandwiches and maintaining military arguments.
Incidentally I was very unshaven because I left my razor and shaving
cream and flannel in a green bag either in the train or in your flat.
I also find I left my belt where I had dinner with John Fox before
coming to London and my khaki polo sweater on the train. The
lapse in the train was partly the too intense concentration on not
losing the silk handkerchief you gave me and partly to a truculent
civilian who said Graham Sutherland's[1] drawings were not so good
as his 4 year old daughter's, though similar. I told him to try and
retard the poor child's growth as she was obviously at her best age,
and might grow like Daddy if she was allowed to. John Fox and I
gave him a 2 hour lecture and ended by provoking him to recite 14

1 Sutherland had done the cover for *Poetry (London)*, as well as other illustrative
   work for the magazine.

lines of *Richard II*, quite well.

Well, you will be wondering why I am drunk again? Or aren't you interested. Anyway *I'm* not a *bit* interested; I went (by order) to a Brigade HQ cocktail party with the Colonel and some other stooges. I met a god awful land girl with some titled relations and a moustache, who writes short stories and poems so I drank about 4 gins and took her in the garden. After a bit I took her glasses off – to see if she looked better without them, but she didn't. I didn't want to be nasty so I said: 'You want to keep your face moving, then you'll be all right'. Thinking this over I didn't think it sounded so nice after all, so I tried to improve it by saying she had a nice dress anyway: but unfortunately about then I spilt a pint of gin down the front of her so I had to walk her round the garden to get her dry. She seemed to be incorrigibly wet (this is beginning to look like *your* writing – do you influence me so much, already?) so I left her wet and came away. Now I've had dinner but I am still frightfully canned.★ [At foot of page] ★It's so nice not caring what a person thinks so you can say exactly what you like to them. (This applies to the land girl, not to you, my sweet).

The Railway Military Movement authority shook John and me yesterday. We got there ¼ of an hour before the train was due to go and queued for some time. Suddenly 2 redcaps shut the gates to the platform with a clang and said No more allowed on the train. John began to have hysterics but we went on to the platform next door and climbed off the line into the wrong side of the train. And it wasn't a bit full. We got in a compartment where an amiable Yank was circulating a gin bottle. *And* we had the opportunity of delivering a joint lecture on the Nature of Poetry with special reference to D. Gascoigne, Milton, Verlaine and Louis Aragon, so it was an amusing voyage.

This next bit is the most important bit of the letter. I only hope being drunk will enable me to escape the various sorts of shyness that prevent me sounding sincere when I say nice things to you. But I want to say that I couldn't love you or anyone else more than I did at moments yesterday – not if I know you for years. You were so kind (in the sense that a girl is kind to her lover, not in the YMCA sense) and sweet (I am resuscitating old words that have been slaughtered but I am giving them back their virtue.)[2] and I blundered

---

1   This phrasing is echoed in 'To Kristin, Yingcheng...' (*CP* p.131), written around this time: 'Here I give back perforce/ the sweet wine to the grape...'

about and ended up annoying you with remarks about your face which were only prompted by a fear that you couldn't be as happy as you were making me. Dear Betty. Thank you for telling me your story: go on trusting me and perhaps I can do something to make you happier. I don't need anything to fight for now, but at least there is you to look at beyond the fighting, and I can get through any amount of fighting, however little I care for it, if I can think about you and have your letters. Never believe a single catty remark I make; you are a difficult person to address and I am as shy as you. I only hope you loved me yesterday as much as I loved you, whatever happens. My next letter will no doubt be saner, but there may be some things you are glad to read in this. DON'T say 'Thank you for your incredibly sentimental letter', because now I've said it for you, and anyway I should come to London leave or no leave and spit in your eye.

All my love
Keith
I wish I had kissed you goodbye properly – shyness again.
[ink sketch: three male figures contorted with shyness]

317. *To Marie J. Douglas* [fragment]   BL 56355 f.169

[?April 1944]

...Mrs Kellett[1] was down for the second time and this time demanded to be introduced to me: she is evidently anxious about the book. I told her I would ask you to send on your proofs (which you can keep, so ask her to return them). I don't know how long the proofs will be, as Betty has to find a printer to accept the job: she wants to get Faber's printer. I shall write Myrtle Kellett a letter for you to send with the proofs. She is more or less the last fence [On verso] If you haven't dyed it yet I'd like the other USA shirt, too.

1 The widow of Douglas's Colonel, 'Flash Kellett', from the El Alamein campaign.

318. *To Mrs Kellett*   BL 56355 f.184
      [Copy in Marie J. Douglas's hand]

14 May 1944

Dear Mrs Kellett,
I've asked my mother to enclose this apology (in the Greek sense, meaning more of a prologue than an excuse) when she sends you the Galley proofs of my Journal.

You, who know far more about the Regt. than I shall ever know, will soon make up your mind whether I have been fair or unfair. But in any case the account is a personal one, and based on my personal impressions at a time when my judgement, like anyone else's, was liable to be a bit warped anyway – so I don't think any intelligent person will attach much importance to what I say. Except as evidence of the mental state one gets into.

It would have been very much easier, mentally, to write nothing but eulogy; but I cannot believe there would be any value in it. I shall be very glad to hear what you think when you have read it.
Yours sincerely
Keith Douglas

319. *To Jocelyn Baber*   BL 56356

n.d.   Notts SR Yeo APO England

Dear Jocelyn,
I can't really keep up with Baber any longer because it's impossible to remember who it is I'm writing to when I address you so – you aren't any more like Mrs Baber to me than I feel like Captain Douglas (which thank God you never needed to call me). I have meant to write to you, or wanted to write to you quite often; but didn't for lack of interesting matter, and even now there's nothing to say, but I must write while a little time remains. We suspect the worst whenever anything arrives in an OHMS envelope – but of course it may be weeks – probably you know much more about it than I do.

This neighbourhood[1] is delightful and flowers and sunshine attend us all the time however oily and mechanical our duties are.

---

1 Sway, near the New Forest.

I get up (not from choice) and go for a swim at 7.30 every morning, though I can't say it seems to make me any fitter. All the women here are mortgaged up to the hilt, so to speak, or else beefy land girls – which is rather depressing. I'm not allowed a night in London any more, but I got there for an experimental day last Sunday travelling all night and arriving 0420, whereupon I went to sleep on a sofa (and subsequently in a bath at Nuffield House).[2] I left London 9.54 and arrived in my bedroom (I live in some style now, during the fattening process) at 03.30. Sleep at 03.30½. This was barely legal, as I didn't leave until after midnight on Saturday (i.e. on Sunday morning) and considered 03.30, on the other hand as Sunday night. Anyway, I said goodnight to the Colonel on Saturday night and good morning to him on Monday at breakfast, so he had no cause to complain.

I am having awful difficulty in selecting my wardrobe to suit coming events, but am gradually deciding on what the essentials will be. I've sent Mother miles of instructions about parcels etc. I think of giving her the run of my bank account in return for a constant stream of baby powder, eau de cologne, and razor blades. I *imagine* France will be cheaper even than Tunisia, and the same anywhere else I may find myself, so I'll need no money. Bully is currency in any ex-occupied country.

Well I had better stop before I commit some overwhelming breach of security – my mind is too full of odd things.

Much love to your family.

Keith

320. *To Jocelyn Baber*   Graham

28 [April 1944]

Dear Jocelyn,
Thank you a lot for your letter and the review of my book,[1] which was interesting, particularly the criticisms. To answer these – since I never go down without a fight:
(1) 2 identical descriptions of Sam. I've left these in, because, until

2 See Letter 308 n.1.

---

1 This does not survive. The gist of it, however, is clear from Douglas's response here.

you mentioned it, no one had carped at them, and although I had realised there was a certain amount of tautology, I didn't think the two descriptions were so identical as all that.

(2) The change of names was due to the fact that they sent the carbon copy of the first part of the book – I had meanwhile corrected the original typescript. The second part of the book I submitted with corrected names so the carbon copy was correct. Anyway, that one *is* taken care of.

(3) Night at Milena's.[2] You mind because it possibly seems to drag down the level of tragedy suggested by the charm round Norman's neck, and of a fine acceptance of this on my part – and that is I suppose because you sense a sort of crawling round behind Norman's back in my conduct, and a general atmosphere of dubious intrigue. You want 'selectivity' again – a suppression of something ugly, but true. (Personally I don't think of it as ugly but then I know why we embraced again.) This is all bound up with the question of allowing the sergeant in on it. Well, as you accuse yourself over this, let me only say you merit the accusation thoroughly. This bit I *have* altered, but not deleted. It is far too much intertwined with the whole story to cut out. There is no fusty scent, except what lingers from an incident which does not come into the story – but which led to the triangular situation – and for that fusty scent Norman is responsible, not I.

(4) Loot – dogmess, etc. I have discussed this with several people and the dogmess *definitely* stands. Loot is one of the most important things – and it is the thing that makes all that exhilaration in fighting. And believe it or not our utmost thought at the end of the battle was loot. By that you must not understand – as I believe you do – pillaging or corpse-robbing. But simply rummaging in the glorious brantub provided by any battlefield. One's requirements and desires in any case were pretty basic. In fact, it's a *picture* of a dogmess; so you can't cut the dogmess out – and I am afraid I refuse to cut it out to suit the connoisseur sensibilities of yourself, Lavender and Stella – or for Mother, whose objections are based on her incorrigible sentimentality which has already done her untold harm. (I'm not sure the instinct for selectivity isn't based on sentimentality,

2 In *Alamein*, Chap. XI.

anyhow.) Perhaps you will get to like it, like, *et ô, ces voix denfants, chantant dans la coupole*,[3] which so jarred on George Moore's ear at first, and finally became a favourite line of his. We'll see.

I'm thrilled by your account of the house in travail. I expect it will be magically transformed when I return to it. I'm sorry I missed the train on Sunday last – Mother must have been very disappointed. But really, it wasn't on, and by the time I was up and organised, I had missed the 10.30. I spent a good deal of the day with Betty Jesse, who intrigues me (luckily I intrigue her). I want you to meet her. I shall introduce you as the person I would have fallen heavily for if we (you and I) had both been 20 at the same time.

I am glad to hear John is keeping slim,[4] to make up for my own obesity, which is daily more aweful [*sic*]. I suppose coming events will deal with it. I hope a second book (and bags more loot) will emerge from these events.

Well, fair stands the wind for…?[5]

Love
Keith

---

3 Lines from Verlaine, quoted in 'The Fire Sermon' section of *The Waste Land*.
4 Col. John Baber, Jocelyn's husband.
5 Echoing (and defeating the censor with) Drayton's lines from 'To the Cambro-Britons. Agincourt': 'Fair stood the wind for France/ When we our sails advance,/ Nor now to prove our chance/ Longer will tarry.': the title *Fair Stood The Wind for France* was used by H.E. Bates for a new novel in 1944.

Appendix A

An Untitled Autobiographical Story
(*c.* 1932)

As a child he was a militarist, and like many of his warlike elders, built up heroic opinions upon little information, some scrappy war stories of his father. Most of the time he was down in the field, busy, with an absurdly purposeful look on his round face, about a tent made of an old sheet, and signposted with a board saying 'sergeants' mess'. He was quite at home there for hours, while he was four and five, telling himself stories as he ran about, and sometimes stopping a moment to contemplate the calf who shared that field, a normally quiet animal, but given to jumping five-barred gates. As you would expect, he played with lead soldiers, and toy artillery, and was most fond of the cavalry and the highlanders. Unlike the other troops who either marched sedately with sloped arms or sat bolt upright on their caracoling steeds, the highlanders were charging, their kilts flying at a swift angle out behind them and the plumes upon their heads also flying out, though often in the wrong direction for the broken heads were fixed back on with matches, and swivelled easily.

His father did not spend very much time with him, but would speak to him of war and boxing and shew the boy his great muscles, for here at least he could shew them off to unbounded admiration. He teased his son, and pinched and tormented him sometimes, but Keir liked his father better than his mother, who fondled him a deal too much and cried sometimes, even then Keir and Billy Cameron who lived near, were often about together in trees. They built a house once, in the big tree at the end of Billy's garden, but Billy fell out of it. So they were kept away from there and played in the garden itself. Captain Cameron entertained them with a service revolver and a bomb, but in the end they were left to themselves.

'My father,' said Billy, 'shot a German point blank. He saw him coming out of a pillbox and shot him before the German could shoot Daddy.' Keir was a little annoyed that Billy should tell this story, condensed though it had become, so often. But point blank was admittedly a good thing to say and in return he explained how his own father was shot by a Turk.

'*My* father wouldn't have let a measly old Turk shoot him,' said Billy and Keir's reposte was squashed. Yet he was very proud of his father and went home to his supper sadly down the road past Miss Drivers, and Colonel Transome, the old man who was so funny because he never wore a waistcoat, and Miss Peck and Mr Peck who made cider, and each of the other neighbours whom Keir pictured not by remembering their faces, but the colour of their front hedges and fences. He reached up and opened his own front door, which had a high knob. His father was inside, taking off his shoes, in a good temper. 'Hello, Old Bean,' he said 'been climbing trees?' Keir beamed. He loved to be called Old Bean. 'Hello dadda, Captain Cameron threw a bomb at me.' 'Oh, you didn't mind though did you? You're a tough guy.' 'Gee whiz I'm a tough guy, Daddy, tell me about Yukon Jake again.' Captain McDonald raised a chair in one hand and shook it. He recited ferociously

Yukon Jake
was as tough as a stake,
hardboiled as a picnic egg.
He combed his hair
with the leg of a chair
and drank his beer by the keg.

Keir repeated it furiously and with great pleasure. 'Now teach me to box' he said. He was not restrained from punching his father's amateur-champion broken nose by the entry of his grandfather, Mr Castellain, a courteous and courtly old gentleman who now spent his life playing patience. Mr C. received the bomb story less enthusiastically. He had once been in the volunteers, but had never fought anyone in his life. Harrow and Balliol and an addiction to natural history and good manners had made him a quiet spoken and kindly old man. Considerate and unselfish to his own class but almost unaware of the existence of any other.

The smell of his supper, which was a kind of broth prepared by his grandmother attracted Keir into the other room. 'Where's Mummy?' he asked Mrs Castellain. 'She went down to the village, dear, to do some shopping. Now go and wash your hands before you eat your supper. There's a good boy.' Probably that type of phrase annoys every child. It galled Keir, anyway, and he said pettishly 'Don't want to wash my hands. They're quite clean. I want my supper.' 'Now don't be rude to Granny. Go and wash.' 'I won't wash my hands—' Keir was beginning when his father came in and told him angrily to hurry up and go, and Keir went.

When he was coming downstairs he heard his mother come in through the front door. She looked pretty but tired out, and smiled at Keir who was a consolation to her for many things. 'I'm going to eat my supper Mummy.' 'All right dear, I'll come and watch you.'

Keir ate his supper, and talked a good deal, in spite of the reprimands of his grandmother, who still thought that little boys should be seen and not heard, and often said so. Outside the evening sunlight reminded Keir of fairies, for it did indeed endue the garden with a dreamlike quality. So he demanded a story from his grandfather, who was in the drawing room playing with cards.

'Very well, little man, I'll tell you a story in one minute, when I've finished this game of patience,' said his grandfather, in his curious calm voice which held no trace of foreign accent though its polite unruffled tones themselves must have come over the channel with his own grandfather, escaping the revolution by the aid of servants to whom he, luckily, had been kind.

Keir waited two minutes before he asked for his story again, and received the same answer, out of the corner of his grandfather's mouth, as the card game, for long the most exciting part of the old gentleman's life, drew to its most exciting moment and completion. The minutes continued to drag slowly by, and at last, Keir realised that he would soon be hauled storyless to bed. When he had asked once more and received the same unhurrying answer, he suddenly grew furious, and overturned the old gentleman's precious ricketty table.

Mr Castellain had never been so near anger in twenty years. But after Keir's simple explanation that he wanted his story, he said kindly, 'You're sorry you turned my table over, aren't you, little man?' And on Keir's admission of penitence (for he saw that would begin his story soonest) the story was begun.

In the morning Keir was woken by the sun and the birds and lay in bed listening to them and thinking to himself, until it occurred to him that people were about in the house and his mother's and father's beds were empty. He went and peered out, and saw through the bannisters a group of people standing in the hall, about his mother, who lay asleep on a stretcher or as it seemed to Keir a funny sort of bed. He realised almost at once that his mother was ill and ran downstairs on his bare feet asking what was the matter with her, as they took her away out of the front door. Someone he had never seen took him back to his bed with some unsatisfying explanation, and locked the door on him. He began immediately to scream and beat upon it, but they had all gone and he was alone, locked in. He became frantic, fell on the floor and shouted curses he had heard 'Curse damn bother darn bloody' in a string as long as he could put together, until he got up from the floor and hit his head on the door knob. It hurt and with some idea of punishing the door knob he hit his head on it five or six times more, very hard, and then subsided on the bed sobbing.

In a few minutes his grandfather came up and succeeded in calming him, explaining that his mother had an illness, called Sleepy Sickness, but she would be well soon, when she had gone to the Hospital and had a rest. With that, for the moment, Keir was content.

from An Unfinished Autobiographical Fragment with the Epigraph: 'O spires O streams …' (1937)

When he was four, his mother had been very ill. He never sensed anything wrong when she came back from hospital; and when his father, a hearty playmate whom he secretly feared and whole-heartedly admired, disappeared and Olwen too, he wept as much as his mother.

It was soon apparent that lack of a father meant lack of money, and after a curtailed prep-school career, Peter entered Christ's Hospital where, being somewhat old for his age, he had attained a certain seniority by his fifteenth year.

He was now, at the age of fourteen, tall (some five feet nine inches), and fair, with very white skin and large brown eyes, long-lashed. He sat now sprawled on a stone seat, whose white stone shone back the sun at him disconcertingly. Sunlight, the blue glare of sky and far off cricketing sounds mingled, coming gently to his notice through eyes half shut and dreamy ears, moving him to an indescribable feeling of melancholy and longing, which both compelled and denied analysis. He began stumbling in his mind after this ignis fatuus discontent, this definite and indescribable disquiet, and suddenly caught up with it: suddenly knew that it was a desire to share beauty, the pleasantness of this summer afternoon, with someone else, someone to understand not this only, but every tossed thought and ambition. This would be a girl evidently: he pictured her for many days after that.

Walking along Eastbourne front in the holidays, he looked carefully at the faces of the girls who passed him. Some, freckled and pleasant, attracted him instantly: any one of these might have been his sympathiser, and he turned heavily into the swimming baths, wishing that one of these faces belonged to an acquaintance. The pleasant artificial smell of the baths dispelled his gloom immediately. He changed quickly and climbed to the highest diving board. Here he stood rigid with muscles braced, yet trying to look as though each sinew stood thus in his body always. Two old women on the balcony regarded him with obvious admiration and whispered comments. Below him a hirsute out-of-condition young man leaned smoking against a pillar and shook ash into the bath. He was not interested in divers; his piggy eyes were turned with X-ray interest upon the charms of the baths attendant. Peter dived. He kept his body scrupulously straight, looking down upon the water as the air sang past him. Only a sideways wriggle in the air enabled him to avoid the underwater swimmer who broke surface suddenly beneath him, and he swam painfully to the rail smarting from flat impact with the water. The underwater swimmer followed him. She was small[…]

349

Appendix B

Poets in This War
(?May 1943)

I think it is true to say that of the poets who are now regarded as poets of the last war, the majority are writers whom the war inspired to their finest efforts, often to what may be regarded as their first efforts, and they are all soldiers.

The Great War was entered upon by us in a spirit of terrific conceit and was the culmination of a complacent period; so complacent that Kipling, although he was partly responsible for this mood, had some years before written a dignified and conditional warning 'Lest We Forget'.

The retreat from Mons, the aggregate of new horrors, the muddling generalship, the obsolescence of the gentleman in war demanded and obtained a new type of writing to comment on them (surprisingly perhaps to those who assess our national character). Rupert Brooke, who might have seemed our ready made herald and bard, appeared superannuated in a moment and wandered away fittingly, from a literary point of view, to die in a region of dead heroes. Instead, arose Owen, to the sound of wheels crunching the bones of a man scarcely dead; Sassoon's tank lumbered into the music hall in the middle of a patriotic song, Sorley and Isaac Rosenberg were hypnotized among all the dangers by men and larks singing. Such was the jolt given to the whole conception men had had of the world and of war, and so clear was the nature of the cataclysm, that it was natural enough not only that poets should be stirred, but that they should know how to express themselves.

During the period 'entre deux guerres' we were listening alternately to an emphasis of the horrible nature of modern war and to the vague remedies of social and political reformers. The nation's public character remained, in spite of all, as absurdly ignorant and reactionary as ever.

Those who wrote of war looked back to the last even when they spoke of the next, which was a bogy to frighten children and electors with: the poets who were still at the height of their fame before this war, who were accustomed to teach politics and even supposed themselves, and were supposed, versed in the horrors of the current struggles in Spain, were curiously unable to react to a war which began and continued in such a disconcerting way.

The long inaction on all fronts was not inspiring; everyone was too used to inaction. Dunkirk was over almost before most people had rubbed the sleep out of their eyes; inaction, as far as most soldiers were concerned, began again. This produced, as it was bound to, an amount of loitering, fed-up poetry, vaguely relatable to some of Turner's poems 1914–18.

So far I have not mentioned the name of a poet 'of the present war'. I might refuse to on the grounds that it is unnecessary: for I do not find even one who stands out as an individual. It seems there were no poets at Dunkirk; or if there were, they stayed there. Instead we have had poetic pioneers and land girls in the pages (respectively) of *New Writing* and *Country Life*. There have been desperately intelligent conscientious objectors, R.A.M.C. Orderlies, students. In the fourth year of this war we have not a single poet who seems likely to be an impressive commentator on it.

In England, Henry Treece is now the head of some sort of poetic school; of what kind I am not sure. John Hall, from the headquarters of the International Art Club in London, is writing very involved verses with an occasional oblique and clever reference to bombs or bullets. *Poetry (London)* is edited by one Tambimuttu; his uniform, if he has one, is probably exotic. John Lehmann is encouraging the occupants of British barrack rooms to work off their repressions in his pages. Of *Horizon* I know nothing up to date: what l do know answers the trend of these remarks. There are a number of very young men, sprung up among the horrors of War Time Oxford, some of whom, notably Sidney Keyes, are technically quite competent but have no experiences worth writing of.

John Heath Stubbs, who published some of the decade's worst printed verse in *Eight Oxford Poets*, their subjects are either escapist or as I believe evidence of lack of material, has written a long poem called 'Wounded Thamuz'. Their attitude to the war is that of the homosexual Guardsman returning from Dunkirk – 'Oh my dear! the noise! and the people!' They turn a delicate shoulder to it all. But no paper shortage stems the production of hundreds of slim volumes and earnestly compiled anthologies of wartime poetry, *Poems From the Forces*, &c. Above all there are a hundred shy little magazines, whose contributors are their most ardent supporters. Benevolent publishers, it seems, are constantly patting blushing young poets on the head (I am tempted to use blushing as Masefield does) and encouraging them to lisp in numbers.

The Middle East is the only theatre of war which is employing or has been employing large numbers of English soldiers for a long time, in active warfare; here the veterans of Greece and Crete have merged with the more recently experienced desert soldiers. Here too are magazines which rashly encourage embryo poets. *Gen* and *Orientations* and an occasional quarter page of *Parade* welcome their effusions: and receive them, from clerks and staff officers who have too little to do, and from the back end of the desert army. The poets who wrote so much and so well before the war, all over the world, find themselves silenced, or able to write on almost any subject but war. Why did all this happen? Why are there no poets like Owen and Sassoon who lived with the fighting troops and wrote of their experiences while they were enduring them?

The reasons are psychological, literary, military and strategic, diverse. There are such poets, but they do not write. They do not write because there is nothing new, from a soldier's point of view, about this war except its mobile character. There are two reasons: hell cannot be let loose twice: it was let loose in the Great War and it is the same old hell now. The hardships, pain and boredom; the behaviour of the living and the appearance of the dead, were so accurately described by the poets of the Great War that everyday on the battlefields of the western desert – and no doubt on the Russian battlefields as well – their poems are illustrated. Almost all that a modern poet on active service is inspired to write, would be tautological. And the mobility of modern warfare does not give the same opportunities for writing as the long routines of trench warfare. The poets behind the line are not war poets, in the sense of soldier poets, because they do not have the soldier's experience at first hand. English civilians have not endured any suffering comparable to that of other European civilians, and England has not been heavily bombed long enough for that alone to produce a body of 'war' poetry.

Nor can we produce a body of long range poetry inspired by shocking news items. The poet at home can only make valuable comments on social and political issues, which he may do more easily, both because he can see more clearly and because the censor will be more lenient with him, in retrospect.

Meanwhile the soldiers have not found anything new to say. Their experiences they will not forget easily, and it seems to me that the whole body of English war poetry of this war, civil and military, will be created after war is over.

Appendix C

Death of a Horse
(*Lilliput*, July 1944)

They stopped talking when the horse was led out. An orderly in a white coat led it out. One of its legs was broken, and the horse hobbled, almost hopped. Its expression was resigned and humble. It stood there, and they all stood there, looking at it with different thoughts in their minds. I expect, if you could have known what they were thinking, you could have told their characters.

Simon was thinking all the time: 'I wonder if it knows,' and after a time he thought: 'It does know, but it doesn't seem to mind.' Then the veterinary major came; he went into the shed and came out again with a clean white coat over his uniform, and a piece of chalk in one hand.

'You're lucky to see this,' he said. 'The last lot didn't have the chance.' He talked in a matter-of-fact way about an everyday occurrence. The horse stood there quietly, looking straight in front of it. As the vet moved to take hold of the headstall, it stumbled awkwardly, trying to shift to a more comfortable position.

'I draw a line from here to here,' said the vet. And he drew a line with the chalk, diagonally across the horse's forehead: from the base of the left ear, more or less towards the right eye. Then he drew another line, diagonally the other way. The horse stood still.

'You never want to go lower than this,' said the vet, pointing to where the lines cut. The orderly moved forward holding something, a sort of tube, which he put against the intersection of lines on the horse's forehead The horse still stared in front of it. Someone said: 'The old hammer type.' Simon stiffened. But he was ready to see the horse stagger, desperately trying to stand, and the death agony. The orderly's hand fell, he struck the tube and there was a small report.

The horse's knees gave way at once, so instantaneously that the eye could hardly mark its fall, and so silently that Simon might have been watching it through binoculars. It only stiffened and relaxed its legs once. The suddenness and silence of its death defeated his preparations to be unmoved.

'Now the jugular vein,' said the vet. He had a knife, and inserted it about half way down the horse's neck, so as not to spoil the skin, he said. The blood poured out exactly in the manner of water from a burst drain. The vet stood in blood, with blood running all round him, and blood jetting up over his hand. He held his hand in the incision and said casually: 'Take particular note of the colour.' It was almost black, very warm and thick.

At this point another man arrived, whose business it was to cut the horse up and take it away. First the vet was to explain the nature of the horse's insides. The man wore filthy sacking tied to him, covered with old blood. Simon noticed that the horse's face still had the same expression, though the eyes were already glazed; he felt that even now it was consciously assisting the demonstration.

The man took his knife, and drew a line with it along the exact centre of the underneath of the horse. His precision and the sharpness of his knife were uncomfortable to watch. The skin fell apart behind the knife, the vet talked on, and presently the horse lay stretched out into a diagram, to which the vet pointed as he spoke. The colours were brilliant, but not wholesome, and now a faint sweet sickly smell came from the horse. It occurred to Simon that the whole atmosphere was that of a ritual sacrifice; the vet, intoning what he had said so often before, the other man working in a scrupulous sequence, and the horse, the central figure of the ceremony, invested with the dignity due to a chosen victim. From this came the impression that the dead horse was taking a pride in its own dissection.

'The horse has a small stomach,' said the vet. 'Look!' And he flapped the stomach in front of him, like an apron. The stench was unbelievable. Simon began at last to feel sick; his hand searched frantically for his pipe, but it was not in his pocket. He looked firmly at the wreck of the horse, the crowd of spectators, some craning their necks for a better view. The horrible casualness of the vet's voice grew more and more apparent; the voice itself increased in volume; the faces merged and disintegrated, the wreck of the horse lay in a flurry of colours, the stench cemented them into one chaos. He knew it was useless. His one thought, as he felt himself falling, was that he had let the horse down.

Giuseppe

Giuseppe was a parachutist. That is, he was trained as a parachutist; he reamed to unpack and handle the weapons and equipment, he made the jumps. The whole of Folgore – 'the Division which will fall like mountain eagles with immaculate and beautiful heroism upon the enemy', Giuseppe's Colonel had said in his speech at the Foundation of Rome parade—the whole of Folgore had made the jumps. But they were betrayed by the Germans. The Germans (who could not think in terms of mountain eagles) had betrayed the destiny of Folgore. Folgore were sent to fight as ordinary infantry, and as ordinary infantry, singing their songs, leaping upon their parapets with bravado, and hurling their little red grenades into the very mouths of the British infantry, they had perished 'with immaculate and beautiful heroism.' Giuseppe had escaped.

He had found a motor cycle, and being luckily near the coast road, had caught up with the retreating army and attached himself to the Young Fascists, who had not yet seen action. Since then he had had many occupations and some changes of formation along the hundreds of miles of thirst and dejection – from Mersa to Tobruck, Tobruck to Benghazi and the green country, the trees filtering the sunlight gratefully, the white bungalows of the colonists. Passing through the plains strewn with blue flowers, to Sirte and Nufilia, Giuseppe was one of those who scrawled W IL DUCE and RITORNEREMO on the cracked white plaster of walls. But Tripoli had fallen, and still Giuseppe had gone back, back, with the Italians; dirty, covered with lice hating the Germans more than the English, tired of the war. He had become, in the end, viciously disposed towards everybody. And when, in the last fight for Tunisia, his formation were assigned to the defence of a great height in the Matmata hills, with the crowded walls of an Arab village built like a castle on its summit, Giuseppe was no more good as a soldier: jumpy, he was, sure of death, but not knowing when it would come.

Now he lay in a stone pit, blasted out of the mountain side by engineers. In the daytime it was not safe to move out of the pit; accordingly it stank and the walls moved with flies. The two others who shared the pit with him were trying to sleep, curled on the floor of it, sprawling among a mass of old magazines, letters, empty tins, broken Chianti bottles in their straw jackets. The empty cases of the Breda cartridges littered the floor round Giuseppe's feet: they had been fired in repelling the last attack. It was Giuseppe's turn on the gun. In the last attack they had thrown back the brown savages, New Zealanders, the officer had said when he visited the post afterwards. Maori, or some such name. Giuseppe and his comrades did not care, only that they had thrown them back. The shelling had seemed to split the mountain, and then here were these Maori, climbing like goats, hurling grenades into the posts, right on top of them with their flat noses and queer shouts. One of them had almost reached this post, halfway up the steep flank of the mountain. His body, stiff and dusty, with the blood congealed about the smashed eye, lay a yard or two down the slope, where it had caught on a toe of rock. Theoretically, Giuseppe thought, it was a good thing to have him there, to distract the flies a little from the men in the post. But here were the flies, still tearing away with their little telescopic suckers at the sores on his hand. Down the slope, he could hear a wounded man moaning, lying out in the full sun.

There were others further down, and scattered about among the fig-trees at the base of the mountain. Some dead. Some wounded. Earlier in his spell of duty, Giuseppe had seen a movement down there, and belted off a few rounds, without being able to see the result. Then the shelling had begun again. Now it was a lull.

Suddenly, with a pang of terror, he saw men moving down at the bottom of the slope, where the posts had been driven in, and their crews killed or captured. But he saw it was only the movement of two men, who had crawled up and were trying to drag away some of the wounded down a small wadi that ran to the edge of the fig-trees. They must have taken some risks to get *there*, he thought. Anyway, they've taken their last risk now. He sprayed bullets at them, not troubling to hold the bucking gun firmly, and saw them suddenly throw their arms and legs about like marionettes whose string is jerked too hard. Later he saw a few men running and dodging among the fig-trees. Evidently they had had enough. He fired at them too, but did not observe any hits. The afternoon dragged into evening and darkness.

An hour before dawn, after a cold night, and stiff with their cramped quarters, they were roused by an officer on rounds, and stood to, watching the sky lightening over the vast plain which their position commanded, on which the roads, the squares of fields, and the dark rough masses of trees stretched away for mile upon mile. The attack came half an hour or so afterwards. There was no

357

preliminary shelling. They heard the tanks somewhere at the foot of the hill, coming right up to the beginning of the slope. They must be mad, to attack a mountain with tanks. But the tanks withdrew, when they had smashed a way through the cactus hedges, and the infantry poured through the gaps. Giuseppe heard and recognised their war cries. In the dim light he could see them coming up through the posts below him. There was a continual rattle of small arms fire, punctuated by the boom of grenade explosions echoing in defiles and splits in the rock. Giuseppe's nerve gave way. He left his position and scrambled sideways in panic across the hill. Sometimes he fell and rolled almost down among the combatants, but he made his way, driven by a subconscious resolve to get to the side of the mountain away from the enemy, to the western slope; where, on a table of rock somewhat below the level he had left, were a few scattered Arab houses, to which a sort of track led up from the valley. Already they were fighting there. He saw two Italian soldiers come out to surrender in the increasing light, to be shot in the stomach before they could open their mouths or raise their hands, by a Maori with a tommy-gun. Giuseppe crawled, palpitating, under the wreck of a Spa lorry while he heard the terrifying noises of the fight dying away. Once a bullet smashed through the woodwork above him, and another whined away from a rock a yard or two off, but for the moment, he was safe. He crawled out a little way, after half-an-hour, to see if he could escape. There was no one alive in the area where he was.

Looking down he saw the immense side of the mountain sloping away to the fields and the outskirts of the shell-torn European town. Looking up, he saw the mountain tower against the rosy dawn sky. He heard a scream from somewhere high above him, a human scream approaching rapidly like the scream of a shell; and saw the body of a man fly out, black against the sky for a moment, making the motions of a swimmer, and screaming. The man fell with a short noise of impact on the hard ground, doubled up in an impossible position. Now the bodies of live men began to hurtle down, one after another. Most of them screamed. After a quarter of an hour, the falling of men stopped as a hailstorm stops, suddenly. In the early morning sunlight of a Tunisian winter day, Giuseppe saw the single figure of a Maori standing, high up, outlined against the sky. He was shouting down a message to the dead men. 'That's what you bastards get for machine gunning our wounded,' he yelled, in a voice cracked with fury and exhaustion. Giuseppe did not understand the English words.

The Little Red Mouth

The flashes of the six pounders and of the big tanks firing their seventy-fives impinged on the eternal glare of the sunlight, infinitesimal moments of brightness like the scratches which show when an old film is being projected. The boom floated across through the shimmery air, arriving late in my right ear. In my left ear George's voice said: 'King 3, bloody good shooting, you're making them sit up. Keep on chucking them. Off.' His words were a little distorted and uncomfortably loud; I took off the left ear-phone as well and let the whole apparatus dangle round my neck. From one of the dots on the horizon a long straight column of black smoke stood up, leaning a little to the left, expanding at the top. Grey smudges showed where the seventy-fives were falling short.

I picked up the jack-knife and carved another section of yellow cheese out of the tin on top of the wireless set. As I began to munch it, taking alternate bites at one of the biscuits I had laid out beside my field-glasses and Luger on the flat roof of the turret, I looked down into the gloom of the fighting chamber; at the faint gleam on the breech of the two pounder, the little staircase of cartridges climbing up to the feed slide of the machine-gun. The gunner was reading a Wild West magazine: the driver's back hunched forward, as he wrote a letter home on his knee; the operator, dozing. We hadn't moved for an hour; the enemy out of range of my obsolete gun, all the targets located – an hour of nothing to do. I thought: 'I'll have to restart the engine or the wireless will go dead. Spare dags need recharging anyway.' A quarter of an hour ago I had finished 'National Velvet.' There were no more Penguins left in the tank – only the *Oxford Book of French Verse*. I opened it at random and read:

> Sui-je, sui-je, suis-je belle?
> Il me semble, a mon avis
> que j'ai bon front et doulz viz
> et la bouche vermeillette:
> Dittes moy se je suis belle

and my eye fluttered down to the name, Eustache Deschamps 1340–1410. But it made me think of Sylvie, looking up out of the corner of her black eyes, under the long Syrian lashes, saying: 'Je suis jolie, hein? Dis-moi, j'ai un joli corps?' in the very tone of voice of the poem. Et la bouche vermeillette, (Oui, c'est du Max Factor. J'en ai trouvé deux boîtes, mais deux boîtes seulment a Rivoli. Et tu sais combien j'avais à payer?) Now, at half past twelve, Sylvie is probably on the beach at Stanley with that sub-lieutenant from Mosquito. 'Nuts 5,' said the earphones. I'm awake, I'm awake. 'Nuts 5, go forward on the left, see how near you can get to the ridge. Look out for 88s. Don't swan too much. Off.' I spoke into the white rubber end of the microphone and heard the driver grinding his gears. Through the glasses, with my mind still half-occupied in Alexandria, I had already seen the little dots, with the degree-scale of the binocular lens superimposed on them, growing smaller, receding – except three, from all of which smoke grew upwards into the dead still air.

Moving forward, oozing over the scrubby, undulating desert, my mind was still saying over, you know how a phrase can recur in your head for hours, till you forget how it came there: 'et la bouche vermeillette'. I wasn't thinking of it. I was thinking: 'Ought to go back for petrol soon. There may be a sniper in that derelict, like the one that got poor whatsisname, Sam's gunner, in the back of the neck yesterday. There may be snipers in these weapon pits.' I looked over the edge of the tank into as many weapon pits as possible. In one, away to the right, there seemed to be something more than the usual litter of packs, mess-tins, ammunition and letters. 'Driver, right. Steady' I said. 'Slow down. Halt.' I was looking down into the pit.

It was like a carefully posed waxwork. He lay propped against one end of the pit, with his neck stretched back, mouth open, dust on his tongue. Eyes open, dulled with dust; and the face, yellowish with dust, a doll's or an effigy's. He had a woollen cap on his head. The blood on his shirt was brown, hardened until the cloth was cardboard: he had opened his haversack and taken out towels to wrap round his legs against the flies. But the blood had soaked through the towels and the flies had defeated him. A crowd of flies covered him: there were black congregations of them wherever the patches of blood were, and they were crawling on his face in ones and twos. His left hand was raised, supported in the air apparently by rigor mortis, the fingers crooked as though taking hold. It was this seeming to be arrested in motion, which made the pose so vivid. The right hand clutched together a corner of the towel, as if he had seized it that moment, when a wave of pain washed over him. Pain, a climax or orgasm of pain, was expressed in his face and attitude as I would not have believed a motionless body and countenance could express it. It is not too much to say his position was a cry of pain.

I looked at him, trembling with horror, stunned into involuntary speech, saying over and over again, in an audible whisper: 'et la bouche vermeillette.'

Beni Yusef, 1943

Index

Agarwala, Bunny 156, 177, 178
airgraph 192
Algiers 84, 86, 99
Allen, Gracie 120
Anderson, J. D'A. Col. 322
Appleton, Betty 115, 139, 140, 217,
    318
Appleton, Bridget 135
Appleton family 115, 133, 134, 136,
    137, 175
Appleton, Joan 154, 217, 317, 318
Aragon, Louis 308, 338
Arsenault, Joe 273
Arthur, Jean 120
Austen, Jane, *Sense and Sensibility* 53
Ayres, Ruby M., *My Old Love Came*
    191

Baber, Jocelyn, 270
    biography xvi
    criticism of *Alamein to Zem Zem*
        341–3
    letters from KD 340–3
Baber, John, Col. 343
Bates, H. E., *Fair Stood the Wind for*
    France 343
Beaty, David 95, 109, 133
Beckett, Gigi 134–5
Beckett, Mr & Mrs, letter from KD
    123–4
Beckett, Toni viii, ix, 91, 97, 98–9,
    123–4, 154
    biography xvi
    letter from Betty Sze 81
    letters from KD 81–5, 86–90, 91–7,
        100–20, 124–33, 134–7, 138–42,
        143
Beerbohm, Max, *Zuleika Dobson* 307
Bell, A., *Corduroy* 191
Benson, Mary 188

Bethell-Fox, John 273, 321, 337, 338
Bevan, Brian 93
Beveridge, William 307
Blackwell, Basil 136, 138, 172, 220,
    234
Blunden, Claire 328
Blunden, Edmund x, 82, 98, 129, 141,
    152, 164, 180, 194, 204, 219,
    224, 234, 256, 257, 261, 266,
    281, 282, 291, 292
    biography xvi
    letters from KD 48–9, 52–3, 56–7,
        66–7, 72, 74–5, 142–3, 145,
        153–4, 159–60, 172, 183–4,
        190–3, 198–201, 216–18, 296,
        297, 307–8, 328
    letters to KD 142, 151
    Miscellany 217, 266, 315
    More than a Brother 66
    publishing advice to KD 142
Bodycombe, Owen 223
Boldero, John 158
British Council, KD's hopes for post
    with 294, 300, 302, 309
Brodie family 55
Brodie, Liz 293
Brooke, Rupert 261, 350
Brooks, Kenneth 224
Broster, D. K., *The Flight of the Heron*
    29
Brown, Rosemary 157
Buchanan, Margaret 157
Buck, A. H. 52, 66, 145
Butler, Valerie 251, 257

Cairo 197, 198, 211, 212–13
Carnet du Bal 81, 99
Castellain, Charles (KD's maternal
    grandfather)
    biography xvi

letters from KD 3, 5, 6
Castellain, Mrs Charles (KD's
    maternal grandmother)
    biography xvi
    letters from KD 3, 4, 6, 8
Castellain, Fidèle 222
Chadburn, Robin 157, 273
Cheltenham Ladies College 81, 88,
    135
Chesterton, G. K. 48
Christopherson, Stanley 276
Christ's Hospital 48, 101
Churchill, Winston 252, 253
Citadel magazine x, 226, 233, 241,
    286, 309
Coleridge, S. T., 'The Rime of the
    Ancient Mariner' 25–6
Connolly, Cyril 308
Cooper, Ray 130
Cranleigh School 13–14
Crichton, David 223, 276
Cunningham, George 54

Daladier, Édouard 67
Davies, John G. 158
Davies, Gwen Ffrangcon 99
de Gaulle, General 279
Design for Living 99
'Diana' (Coss, KD's fiancée) 207–8,
    219, 223, 227, 254, 257, 265,
    267, 271, 273, 277–8, 293
    engagement to KD 179, 197
Dobson, Meric 115, 157
Douglas, Keith
    Alamein to Zem Zem vii, xi, 205,
        271, 276, 280, 313, 314, 315,
        319, 320, 323, 324, 326–7, 342
    publishing arrangements 324–7
    reaction to criticism of 341–3
    army service
        2nd Derbyshire Yeomanry 162,
            235
        Cavalry Regiment 149
        enlists 74
        Scots Greys 144, 151
        Sherwood Rangers Yeomanry
            190, 235, 237, 248

    views on 163–4, 215–16
    artistic activity 50, 95, 217, 221,
        315–16
    book collection 54
    in Cairo 197, 198, 211, 212–13
    Christ's Hospital 37–57
        rifle incident 45–6, 47
    chronology xx–xxii
    cinema-going 99, 140, 331
    criticism of poetry, reaction to
        286–7, 294–5
    'Death of a Horse' (story) 233, 322
        text 354–5
    'Drunk' (story) 53
    engagement to 'Diana' (Coss) 179,
        197
    'Giuseppe' (story) 356–9
    literary influences 48–9, 52–3, 75
    Merton College, Oxford 66–75
    musical tastes 73, 290
    novel writing, references to 109,
        138, 172, 183, 197, 215
    poems
        'A Ballet' 174
        'A God is Buried' 188, 194, 230
        'A Speech for an Actor' *see*
            'Leukothea'
        'A Storm' 68, 233
        'Absence' 174, 233
        'Actors Waiting' 334
        'Adams' 199–200, 201, 203
        'Addison and I' *see* 'Stars'
        'Aristocrats' 276, 290–1, 293
        'Behaviour of Fish in an
            Egyptian Tea Garden'
            303–4, 305, 308, 309, 314
        'Bête Noire' 319, 320, 324, 325
        'Cairo Jag' 262–4, 327
        'Canoe' 71, 194
        'Caravan' 288
        'Christodoulos' 238–9, 256, 297
        'Dejection' 49
        'Desert Flowers' 256, 284, 286
        'Devils' 235, 282
        'Do not look up' 124
        'Egypt' 237–8, 256
        'Egyptian Sentry, Corniche,
            Alexandria' 335–6

'Enfidaville' 306, 307, 316
'Extension to Francis
    Thompson' 194
'Famous Men' 288
'Forgotten the red leaves' *see*
    'Pleasures'
'Gallantry' 261–2, 283
'Haydn-Clock Symphony' 112,
    124, 127, 194
'Haydn-Military Symphony'
    109, 112
'How to Kill' 296, 297
'I listen to the desert wind'
    247–8
'Images' 288
'Invaders' 84
'John Anderson' 174
'Kristin' 63, 194
'Landscape with Figures 1' 282
'Landscape with Figures 2' 283
'L'Autobus' 335
'Leukothea' 174
'Mersa' 327–8
'Mummers' 49
'Negative Information' 183,
    190, 192–3, 292
'On a Return from Egypt' xi,
    334, 336–7
'Pan in Sussex' 47
'Pas de Trois' 84, 124, 188, 234
'Pleasures' 63, 85, 124, 127
'Point of View' 68
'Poor Mary' 68, 194
'Russians' 188, 194, 231, 295
'Sanctuary' 124
'Sandhurst' 159, 174
'Shadows' 194
'Soissons' 194, 234
'Soissons 1940' 234
'Song: Do I venture away too
    far' 195–6, 234
'Song: Dotards do not think'
    188, 194
'Sonnet: Curtaining this
    country' *see* 'A Storm'
'Stars' 84, 112, 113, 124, 136,
    194, 234
'Stranger' 70, 71–2

'Syria' 206, 233, 236
'Tel Aviv' 274
'The Creator' 124
'The Critic' *see* 'Sandhurst'
'The Garden' *see* 'Absence'
'The Hand' 203
'The Knife' 244–5, 297
'The Marvel' 188, 194, 231,
    234, 288
'The Offensive 1' 245–6, 257,
    258, 286
'The Offensive 2' 246
'The Prisoner' 103, 156, 188,
    288
'The Sea Bird' 201, 203
'The Trumpet' 282
'The Two Virtues' 200–1
'These grasses, ancient enemies'
    204–5, 206
'This is the Dream' 304–5, 307,
    308
'Time Eating' 173, 188, 194
'To Kristin Yingcheng Olga
    Milena' 338
'To a Lady on the Death of Her
    First Love' 69
'Vergissmeinnicht' 297
'Villanelle of Spring Bells' 188,
    194, 288
'Waterloo' 28–9
'Words' 283–4
prep school 3–34
prose works 345–61
Sandhurst 150–3
in South Africa 186–9
stories, autobiographical 345–9
in Syria 206–7
The Cherwell, edits 52
'The Little Red Mouth' (story)
    359–61
in Tunisia 277–8
University College, Oxford 79–115
    finances 80, 85, 93
wounded at Wadi Zem Zem 258,
    264, 271, 289
Douglas, Keith Sholto, Capt. (KD's
    father)
    biography xvi–xvii

letters from KD 5, 7, 9, 12
Douglas, Marie J. (KD's mother) viii,
    291, 292, 330, 332, 341, 342,
    343
    biography xvii
    letter from Milena Gutierrez-Pegna
        236–7
    letter from Under Secretary of
        State for War 264
    letters from KD 5, 6, 8, 10, 11,
        12–20, 22–34, 37–44, 46–8,
        53–4, 67, 97–9, 137–8, 149–51,
        167–9, 173, 180, 183, 186–90,
        201–2, 208–9, 210, 212–16, 218,
        220–3, 227, 234–6, 237–40,
        246–7, 251–2, 254–6, 257–8,
        259–60, 264–5, 265–6, 266–71,
        272–3, 274–5, 275–81, 285–6,
        293–4, 297–300, 313, 332–3,
        339
Douglas, Phoebe (2nd wife of KD's
    father) 8, 9, 11, 12, 13, 14, 15,
    16, 19, 21
    biography xvii
    letter from KD 7
Douglas, Sholto, Major 212–15
Douglas, Walter 116, 141
Douglas, William, Dr (KD's paternal
    grandfather)
    biography xvii
    letter from KD 8
Dryden, John, *The Secular Mask* 95,
    224
Dudley, Denise 156
Duns Scotus 184
Durrell, Lawrence x, 307, 309

Eight Oxford Poets see Meyer, Michael
Eighth Army 279–81
El Alamein, battle 248, 252
Eliot, T. S. xvii, 142, 151, 152, 153,
    159, 165, 169, 171, 172, 173,
    189, 192, 208, 217, 322, 324
    advice to KD 164, 294–5
    letter from KD 190
    letter to KD 164
Elliot, Keith 130
Ertz, S., *Now East, Now West* 191

Evans, Edith 99

Façade 175–6
Fedden, Robin x, 307
Fisher, Madeleine 156, 157
Fiske, Kay 141, 158
Forster, E. M., *A Passage to India* 191
Foster, Alec 239
Four Feathers 99
Furneaux, Claudia 158

Gaynor, Janet 202
Gielgud, John 99
Goodchild, George, *Jim goes North* 191
Green, Roger Lancelyn 111
Gregson, Charles 243
Grey, Ruth Victoria 157
Grigson, Geoffrey 228
Gulliver 140
Gunston, Sir Derek & Lady 171
Gutierrez-Pegna, Milena viii, 234,
    236, 239, 241, 242, 245, 251,
    252, 254, 258, 272, 273, 274,
    275, 276, 294, 299
    biography xvii
    letter from KD 301–2
    letter to Marie Douglas 236–7

Hall, John C. x, xii, 189, 192, 208,
    212, 233, 247, 256, 257, 285,
    291, 292, 351
    biography xviii
    'Earthbound' 287
    'Elegy on a Hill' 287
    'Journey to London' 287
    letters from KD 193–6, 204–5,
        244–6, 286–9, 294–5, 297
    poetry, criticised by KD 287–8
    'Walking to Westminster' 287
Hammett, Dashiell, *The Thin Man* 171
Hannah, Sgt, V. C. 268
Hardie, Alec 90, 93, 100, 111, 114,
    115, 116, 117, 118, 119–20, 125,
    129, 130, 138, 141
    biography xviii
    letter from KD 173–4
Harrison, Rex 99
Harvey, Douglas 157, 208

Hatten, C. T. 74
Heath-Stubbs, John 259, 351
Heywood, Thomas, *Woman Killed
    with Kindness* 53
Hicks, David 226, 227, 232, 233, 241,
    252, 273, 294, 301, 309
    biography xviii
    letter from KD 247–8
Hilton, James
    And Now Goodbye 53
    Lost Horizon 53
Hodson, James Lansdale, *War in the
    Sun* 268, 269
Hoffman, Titsa 294, 299
Hofstein, Eve 298
Hofstein family 298
Holbein, Hans, *The Ambassadors* 263
Holman, Jack 313
Holtby, Winifred, *South Riding* 102
Hood, Thomas 229, 230
Housman, A.E. 71
Hugill, Nancy 157
Hunt, Leigh 48, 52
Hutton, Michael 183

Ilett, Norman 73, 74, 80, 86, 94, 101,
    104, 111, 113, 114, 124, 239,
    242, 251, 252, 254, 258, 272,
    273

Jacoby, Jocelyn 157
Jamaica Inn 85, 86, 99
Jefferies, Richard, *Amaryllis at the Fair*
    53
Jesse, Betty viii, xi, 281, 314, 324, 339,
    343
    biography xviii
    letters from KD 318–23, 326–8,
        329–32, 333–4, 337–9
    publishing arrangements for
        Alamein to Zem Zem 326–7
Jiminez, Natalie 157, 208
Jones, Capt. A. J., *The Second
    Derbyshire Yeomanry* 162
Jones, Brenda viii
    biography xviii
    letters from KD 198, 242–3, 271–2,
        289–90, 293

Kellet, Myrtle 339
    letter from KD 340
Kellett, 'Flash', Col. 205, 237, 276,
    320, 339
Keyes, Sidney 194, 351
    The Iron Laurel 316
Kingsmill, M. 273
Kipling, Rudyard 350
    Puck of Pook's Hill 26
    'Tommy' 299

Laughton, Charles 331
Lehmann, John 194, 212, 351
Levens, Robert & Daphne 94, 95, 126
Lewis, H. Langford 32
Lindsay, T. M., *Sherwood Rangers* 190
Litvin, Natasha 154, 157, 165, 171,
    178, 208
Lloyd, Richard Llewellyn, *How Green
    Was My Valley* 285, 287
Lock, W. J., *Stella Maris* 191
Lockie, David 156, 158, 208
London School of Economics 322

Macklin, W. R. 48–9, 52
Magee, Séan 170
Mani, Renée 210, 216, 218, 220, 223,
    224, 227, 251, 254
Marchant, Dr Stanley 40
Marlowe, Christopher, *Tamburlaine the
    Great* 52
Marsden, C. M., Lt Col. 267, 268
Martin, Yvonne 157
Masefield, John 188, 192, 202, 215,
    223, 237, 252, 352
Maurois, André, *Les Silences du Colonel
    Bramble* 191
Mayne, Jon 115, 121
Meiersons, Olga viii, 251, 254, 273,
    274, 276, 277, 298, 323
    biography xviii, 274
    letters from KD 228–33, 240–2,
        252–3, 258, 261–4, 273–4, 275,
        309
Meyer, Michael 157, 195, 237
    Eight Oxford Poets 174, 178, 194,
        208, 211–12, 219, 226, 234, 243
M'Gregor, James 274

Mitchell, Basil 132
Moore, George 343
Morgan, C., *The Fountain* 191
Morgan, Patsy Mulcahy 156
Moult, Thomas, letter from KD 85
Moung, Daphne Aye 96, 100, 116
Munich Crisis (1938) 55
Murdoch, Iris 158

Nashe, Thomas, *Lenten Stuffe* 52
Newstubb, Deirdre 155
Nicholl, Allardyce
    Masks, Mimes and Miracles 52
    The Development of the Theatre 52
Nicholson, Norman 212, 233, 287, 289
Nietzsche, Friedrich, *Also Sprach
    Zarathustra* 253
Nova, Vera 298, 309

Onyama, Charles 157
Owen, Wilfred 292, 350

Parade, magazine 223, 228, 352
Penguin New Writing, magazine 260
Pennock, Raymond 90, 93, 96, 109,
    111, 113, 114, 124, 130, 134,
    167, 208, 273
Petters, Irving 273
Pitt-Rivers, Julian 150
Poetry (London) 351

Rameses (pseud. of Claude
    Scudamore Jarvis) *Oriental
    Spotlight* 269
Reed, Douglas, *All Our To-Morrows*
    269
Richardson, Ralph 102
Rilke, Rainer Maria 298
Roberts, Hon. David ix, 48, 52, 55,
    145, 256, 273
Robinson, Margaret 273
Roll, Keith 240
Romeo, Pilar 301
Rook, Alan 212, 233
Rosenberg, Isaac 350
Rothkopf, Carol Z., *More than a
    Brother* 52, 66
Royal Scots Regiment 29

Rudd, Tony, *One Boy's War* 47
Rutherston, Albert 116

Saintsbury, G., *A Short History of
    English Literature* 67, 75
Salmon, Walter 140
Sam, Aileen 157
Sandall, Olive 320
Sapper, *The Dinner Club* 25
Sassoon, Hamo 62, 66, 67, 68, 74,
    111, 143, 150, 197, 226, 252,
    270, 273
Sassoon, Humphrey 158
Sassoon, Siegfried 292, 350
Sauter, Dorothy 324
Schapiro, Philip 223–4
Scott, Margaret 140
Scott-Watson, Keith 232
Shakespeare, William
    Midsummer Night's Dream 129
    Othello 93, 94
Shannon, Sheila 287, 288, 289
Sharp, Edward & Sons, toffee makers
    letter from KD 21
    letters to KD 22
Shaw, Phil 303
Sitwell, Sacheverell, *Valse des Fleurs*
    230
Snow White 93, 140
Sorley, Charles Hamilton 350
South Africa 186–9
South Riding 102
Speakman, Peter 273
Spence, Ian, Col. 320
Spence, Sir Reginald 47, 116, 130,
    183, 320
    biography xvii
    letter from KD 265
Spencer, Bernard x, 226, 232, 307
Spender, Stephen 154, 165, 226, 232,
    276, 287
Stainton, Robert 276
Stanley-Wrench, Margaret 261
    biography xviii–xix
    letters from KD 61–2, 63–4, 68, 79,
    133, 211–12, 256
Stevenson, William, *Gammer Gurton's
    Needle* 52

Sutherland, Graham 337
Swan, Michael 195
Sze, Betty viii, ix, 79, 80, 86, 88, 91,
    92, 96, 97, 100, 101, 104, 105,
    106–7, 117, 134, 137, 138, 139,
    152, 153, 208, 219, 223, 226,
    332
  biography xix
  letter to KD 90–1
  letter to Toni Beckett 81
  letters from KD 69–74, 120–3, 144

Tambimuttu, M. J. x, 233, 237, 239,
    256, 285, 288, 297, 321, 322,
    327, 351
  biography xix
  letters from KD 281–4, 290–3,
    303–6, 313–16, 323–5, 334–7
  publishing arrangments for *Alamein
    to Zem* 324–6
Taylor, Aleba Albert 113, 157
Taylor, John 197
The Importance of Being Earnest 82, 85,
    86, 99
The Man from Down Under 331
The Prospect Before Us 175
Thirkell, Lance 157
Thirty Nine Steps 130
Thomas, Margaret 157
Three Loves Has Nancy 202
Tiller, Terence 307
Time and the Conways 55
Towse, John xi
Treece, Henry 351
Tunisia 277–8
Turner, Jean 217, 256, 257, 273, 328
  biography xix

letters from KD 63–5, 67–8, 79–81,
    99–100, 151–3, 154–9, 160–3,
    165–6, 169–71, 173, 174–80,
    185–6, 196–7, 202–4, 205–8,
    209–10, 218–20, 223–7, 240,
    244, 251, 260–1, 266, 317–18
Turner, W. J. 351

Udall, Nicholas, *Ralph Roister Doister*
    52

Valero, Simha 156
Vegesack, Siegfried von, *Das Fressende
    Haus* 253

Wadi Zem Zem 258, 283, 289, 314
Wagner, Geoffrey 285, 287
Wallbrook, Anton 99
Waller, Sir John 130, 136, 223, 256,
    307
  biography xix
  letters from KD 63, 227–8, 302–3
  'Photograph Album' 228
Walwyn, Mrs Fulke 170
Webb, Barry 52
Winchell, Walter 322
Woodcock, Christine viii, 80, 88, 100,
    104, 118, 119, 154
  biography xix
  letters from KD 49–52, 54–6
World War I, poets 350
World War II, poets 351–3
Wrey, Denys 276
Wynyard, Diana 99

Young, Evelyn 157
Young, Michael 157
Yting, Mosshe 224